Monstrous Regiment

Monstrous Regiment

THE STORY OF THE WOMEN
OF THE FIRST WORLD WAR

David Mitchell

The Macmillan Company · New York

To my wife, Cecelia,

and to all those women who fought,

and fight, for The Cause.

CONTENTS

Preface xv

Trials of Strength

1 MISS NIGHTINGALE'S SURF 3
2 PARNELL IN PETTICOATS 11
3 "O MY SPLENDID ONES!" 29

The Recruiters

1 TWO NOVELISTS, A NURSE, AND A STUDENT 39
2 THE PANKHURSTS CHANGE FRONTS 45
3 PANKHURSTS VERSUS HUNS 50
4 PANKHURSTS VERSUS BOLSHEVIKS 64

Noblesse Oblige

1 PATRIOTISM IN HIGH PLACES 83
2 LADY MURIEL 90
3 LEILA, LADY PAGET 99
4 THE MOTHER OF THE BRITISH ARMY 107
5 THE VIEW FROM BERLIN 112

The Individualists

PART I: THE WESTERN FRONT

   1 A THIRST FOR ACTION *123*

   2 MAIRI CHISHOLM'S STORY, OR VALKYRIES
      IN KNICKERBOCKERS *128*

   3 SAPPER DOROTHY LAWRENCE *139*

   4 A DETERMINED MOTHER *145*

PART II: THREE FOR SERBIA

   1 FROM ODALISQUE TO WOMEN'S
      CONVOY CORPS *150*

   2 INCLINED WITH SOCRATES *153*

   3 THE CLERGYMAN'S WIFE *160*

   4 THE CLERGYMAN'S DAUGHTER *165*

Ministering Angels

   1 THE IMMACULATE DR. INGLIS *177*

   2 "THE DOCTORS IS LADIES" *187*

   3 THE VAD'S *196*

   4 TOMMY'S LITTLE MOTHERS *203*

The Servicewomen

   1 WOMEN POLICE *211*

   2 ARMY AUXILIARIES *221*

   3 THE STRANGE CASE OF THE HON. VIOLET
      DOUGLAS-PENNANT *229*

Women in Factories

1 THE MUNITIONETTES 247
2 MARY MACARTHUR 256

Our Sylvia

1 CATTLE TO THE SLAUGHTER 271
2 THE BATTLE OF THE EAST END 275
3 THE BATTLE OF THE EAST END (CONTINUED) 284
4 SYLVIA SEES RED 291

War and Peace

1 THE LADY IN THE BLACK MANTILLA 301
2 THE STATESWOMEN 312
3 THE HUN CODDLERS 323
4 DEFENDERS OF CONSCIENCE 331

The Countess

THE COUNTESS 349

Spoils of War

1 THE CANDIDATES 369
2 NANCY ASTOR'S CANNON 375

Index 391

ACKNOWLEDGMENTS

My special thanks are due to Jessie Kenney for much invaluable information about the suffragette movement and, in particular, for permission to make use of material from the diary that she kept while in Russia with Emmeline Pankhurst in 1917; to Vera Douie, Librarian of the Fawcett Society; to Rose Coombs and Victor Rigby of the Imperial War Museum's Reference Library; to Elsie Bowerman, MA, for information about the First World War industrial campaigns of the Women's Social and Political Union and about the origins and aims of the Women's Guild of Empire; to Mrs. Arthur Macmillan for information about the WSPU's industrial campaigns; to Elsie Bowerman and Yvonne Fitzroy for information about the Scottish Women's Hospital Units in Russia and Rumania, 1916–1917; to Stella Newsome, Honorary Secretary of the Suffragette Fellowship, for valuable guidance and contacts; to Mairi Chisholm of Chisholm, OStJ, MM, for detailed notes on her war work in Flanders; to the late Teresa Billington-Greig for information about Charlotte Despard; and to Olive Bartels, OBE, for information about her days as a suffragette and her work with Queen Mary's Army Auxiliary Corps.

I should like to thank Jessie Kenney, Mairi Chisholm of Chisholm, Mrs. Percy Horton, Oliver Marwick, Wilfrid Blunt, Geoffrey Dearmer, Alice Horam, OBE, Enid Bagnold, the Hon. Lady Salmond, Lady Rea, Dame Helen Gwynne-Vaughan, DBE, Michael McInerney, John Byrne, Mary Agnes Hamilton, Mary Sutherland, CBE, Mabel Lethbridge, OBE, Sir Harold Morris, QC, J. N. Buchanan, Dr. Letitia Fairfield, CBE, the late Commandant Mary Allen, and the late Teresa Billington-Greig, and others, who prefer to be nameless, for the trouble they took to read chapters and offer detailed comments. I am indebted to my wife for reading through the typescript, at various stages and in its entirety, with great patience and wisdom.

I am obliged to Violet Inglis for permission to make use of the manuscript dispatches and letters (at the Fawcett Library) of her aunt, Dr. Elsie Inglis; to Methuen & Co., Ltd., for permission to use material from *A Hospital Letter Writer in France,* by Lady Bradford, and from *Lady Muriel,* a biography by Wilfrid Blunt; to Lady Rea for permission to quote from the book by her sister, Lesley Smith, *Four Years Out of Life,* published by Philip Allan; to Mary Agnes Hamilton for permission to use material from her biography of Mary Macarthur, published by Leonard Parsons; to Mrs. W. B. Yeats and The Macmillan Company for permission to quote from W. B. Yeats's poem "On a Political Prisoner"; to George Newnes, Ltd., for permission to quote from *Back of the Front,* by Phyllis Campbell; to Vera Brittain for permission to quote from her book *Testament of Youth,* published by Victor Gollancz, Ltd.; to The Bodley Head, Ltd., for permission to quote from *Sapper Dorothy Lawrence,* by Dorothy Lawrence, and from *A Journey in Wartime,* by Lady Isabella St. John; to Constable & Co., Ltd., for permission to quote from *An English Wife in Berlin,* by Evelyn, Princess Blücher; to Geoffrey Dearmer for permission to quote from the book by his mother, Mabel Dearmer, *Letters from a Field Hospital in Serbia,* published by Macmillan & Co., Ltd.; to H. F. & G. Witherby, Ltd., for permission to quote from *The Autobiography of a Woman Soldier,* by Flora Sandes; to Victor Gollancz, Ltd., for permission to use material from *My Part in a Changing World,* by Emmeline Pethick-Lawrence, *I Have Been Young,* by Helena Swanwick, CH, and *A Threefold Cord,* by Maude Royden; to Hodder & Stoughton, Ltd., for permission to quote from *An English Woman Sergeant in the Serbian Army,* by Flora Sandes, and from *Women As Army Surgeons,* by Dr. Flora Murray; to Faber & Faber, Ltd., for permission to quote from *Bright Armour,* by Monica, Lady Salmond; to William Heinemann, Ltd., for permission to quote from *A Diary Without Dates,* by Enid Bagnold; to Longmans, Green & Co., Ltd., for permission to quote from *The Prison Letters of Countess Markievicz,* edited by Esther Roper, and from *The Suffragette Movement,* by Sylvia Pankhurst; to Oliver & Boyd, Ltd., for permission to use material from *Clifford Allen: The Open Conspirator,* by Arthur Marwick; to George Allen & Unwin, Ltd., for permission to quote from *Queen Mary,* a biography by James Pope-Hennessey, *The Making of Women: Oxford Essays in Feminism,* edited by Victor Gollancz, *Inside the Left,* by Fenner Brockway, *Conscription and Conscience,* by John Graham, and *My Ex-*

periences on Three Fronts, by Sister Martin-Nicholson; to The Macmillan Company for permission to quote from *Drums Under the Window,* by Sean O'Casey; to Commander Venn for permission to quote from the Emmeline Pankhurst letters to Dame Ethel Smyth that first appeared in *Female Pipings in Eden,* by Dame Ethel Smyth, published by Peter Davies, Ltd.; to Curtis Brown, Ltd., for permission to use material from *Pioneer Policewoman,* by Commandant Mary Allen; to Curtis Brown, Ltd., and the estate of the Baroness de la Grange for permission to quote from *An Open House in Flanders,* by Baroness Ernest de la Grange, published by John Murray; to John Murray for permission to quote from *My War Experiences on Two Continents,* by Sarah Macnaughtan; to Hutchinson & Co., Ltd., for permission to use material from *Miracles and Adventures,* by Mrs. St. Clair Stobart, *A Journal of Impressions in Belgium,* by May Sinclair, *The Home Front,* by Sylvia Pankhurst, and *Service with the Army,* by Dame Helen Gwynne-Vaughan; to the executors of the estate of the late Lord Beaverbrook for permission to quote from correspondence between Lloyd George and Bonar Law that first appeared in *Tempestuous Journey,* a biography of Lloyd George by Frank Owen, published by Hutchinson & Co., Ltd.; to Burns & Oates, Ltd., for permission to quote from *Soliloquies of a Subaltern;* and to Marshall, Morgan & Scott, Ltd., for permission to quote from *Pressing Problems of the Closing Age,* by Christabel Pankhurst.

In addition to the sources listed above and to those indicated in the text, I have found the following books of particular interest and value: *The Cause,* by Ray Strachey (G. Bell); *My Own Story,* by Emmeline Pankhurst (Eveleigh Nash); *Votes for Women,* by Roger Fulford (Faber & Faber, Ltd.); *The Strange Death of Liberal England,* by George Dangerfield (Constable & Co., Ltd.); *Unshackled: The Story of How Women Won the Vote,* by Dame Christabel Pankhurst (Hutchinson & Co., Ltd.); *The Life of Emmeline Pankhurst,* by Sylvia Pankhurst (Werner Laurie); *Memories of a Militant,* by Annie Kenney (Edward Arnold); *Lady into Woman,* by Vera Brittain (Dakers); *From a Victorian to a Modern,* by Dora Montefiore (E. Archer & Son); *Fate Has Been Kind,* by F. W. Pethick-Lawrence (Hutchinson & Co., Ltd.); *The Deluge:* a study of British society and the First World War, by Arthur Marwick (Bodley Head); *The Economic Effects of the War Upon Women and Children in Great Britain* (a Carnegie Endowment for Internation Peace study, 1918); *The Better Fight,* a biography of Dame Lilian Barker by Elizabeth Gore (Bles); *Women of the Empire in Wartime* (a symposium published in 1916); *Lloyd George's Munition Girls,* by Monica Cosens (Hutchinson); *Fortune Grass,* by Mabel Lethbridge, OBE (Bles); *Heavenly Adventurer,* a biography of Sir Sefton Brancker by Basil Collier (Secker and Warburg); *We Did Not Fight: 1914–1918* Experiences of War Resisters (Cobden-Sanderson); *Dr. Elsie Inglis,* by Lady Frances Balfour (Hodder & Stoughton); *Elsie Inglis,* by Eva McLaren (SPCK); *With The Scottish Nurses in Rumania,* by Yvonne Fitzroy (John Murray); *Flanders and Other Fields,* by the Baroness de T'Serclaes, MM, edited by David Mitchell (Harrap); *The Story of the Irish Citizen Army,* by Sean O'Casey (Maunsel & Co.); *Labour and Easter Week,* a selection from the writings of James Connolly, edited by Desmond Ryan with an introduction by William O'Brien (At the Sign of the Three Candles); *Joan Mary Fry,* by Ruth Fawell (Friends House); *Revolt on the Clyde,* by William Gallacher (Lawrence & Wishart); *My Life of Revolt,* by David Kirkwood (Harrap); *Modern Troubadours,* by Lena Ashwell (Gyldendal); *The Sword of Deborah,* an account of a visit to the WAAC in France in 1918, by F. Tennyson Jesse (Heinemann); *A Venture in Goodwill,* the story of the Women's International League, by Helen Ward (WIL); *the Official Report of the Women's International Congress at The Hague, 28 April to 1 May, 1915.*

David Mitchell

February, 1965

PREFACE

In Britain, some women had been in the thick of battle for nine years when war was declared in August, 1914. When Christabel Pankhurst and Annie Kenney were arrested and imprisoned in Manchester in 1905 after daring to heckle Sir Edward Grey, the Liberal leader, about votes for women, the struggle for emancipation entered a phase of sensational and effective militancy.

Under the leadership of Emmeline Pankhurst and her daughter Christabel, the tactics of the Women's Social and Political Union (WSPU) moved from heckling to window breaking to large-scale arson and the "storming" of Buckingham Palace. Generaled by Christabel after 1912 from a flat in Paris, the WSPU operated with military precision, superb discipline, and reckless courage. Other women's suffrage organizations, though they foreswore violence, were brought to a new pitch of urgency and efficiency by the example of the WSPU.

When war came, a remarkable and resourceful body of suffrage fighters stood ready for a new kind of action, and their leaders called on them to bring a new kind of pressure to bear on the Government and on public opinion. By doing their bit for the nation in time of crisis, they could prove beyond all question the justice of the claim to full citizenship.

An immense social revolution was spearheaded by the very women who had so recently been condemned as enemies of the established order, hooligans of the sex war. At the invitation of David Lloyd George, then Minister of Munitions, and in the teeth of trade-union hostility, Mrs. Pankhurst led a nationwide drive to recruit women for the munitions factories. Though it threatened a resumption of militancy after the war if women did not get the vote, the WSPU's concern now was for the efficient prosecution of the war. Never one to bargain or compromise with the enemy, Mrs. Pankhurst brushed aside talk of a negotiated peace as so much cowardly treason. The only kind of war she understood was total war.

The massive achievements of women doctors and nurses, of

women police and other service auxiliaries, of former domestic servants in factories and of the Queen herself, in her social welfare work, made emancipation inevitable. By 1915, the Prime Minister, Herbert Asquith, that cunning antifeminist, spurred by the sacrifice of Nurse Edith Cavell, admitted the value of women to the nation's war effort. "There are thousands of such women," he said, "but a year ago we did not know it."

In February, 1918, came the first installment of the vote for women, and in the General Election of 1918, sixteen women entered the lists as Parliamentary candidates. The tide was turning with a vengeance. The speeding of the women's revolution was one of the Great War's most important and resounding victories.

Trials of Strength

Miss Nightingale's Surf

"If Queen Elizabeth were alive today . . ." said Lloyd George at a Liberal Party rally in 1908, and, as he paused for effect, a cuckoo in the nest, a suffragette in the audience, took her chance. "She would be in Holloway!"

Uproar ensued. But then, for over half a century, ever since the struggle for equal rights for women began to boil in the depths and ruffle the surface of Victorian society, uproar had been ensuing. Right by right, skirmish by skirmish, women of the upper and middle classes had been winning back their self-confidence and self-respect, gaining the support of a few influential men, asserting their full humanity, building and flexing the muscles of the New Womanhood.

In 1852, Florence Nightingale, who spent much of her life in despair at the timidity and stupidity of her sex, summed up the frustrations of an educated woman in an essay entitled "Cassandra." The ideal woman of convention was not supposed to work: her freedom from serious activity was *the* symbol of status, of feminine success. "Give us back our suffering," cried Miss Nightingale, "suffering rather than indifferentism, for out of nothing comes nothing, but out of suffering may come the cure. Better have pain than paralysis. A hundred struggle and drown in the breakers. One discovers the new world. But rather, ten times rather, die in the surf, heralding the way to that new world, then stand idly on the shore."

The sentiments of popular handbooks on the Duties of the Fe-

male summed up the kind of thing that she loathed. A certain Mrs.
Ellis wrote in a chapter on "Behaviour to Husbands": "In the case
of a highly-gifted woman, nothing can be more injudicious than an
exhibition of the least disposition to presume upon such gifts. Let a
husband once be subjected to a feeling of jealousy of her importance, and her peace of mind and her free agency are alike destroyed for the rest of her life; or at any rate until she can convince
him afresh, by a long continuance of the most scrupulous conduct,
that the injury committed against him was purely accidental and
foreign alike to her feelings and inclinations."

The ideal of gentility poisoned many lives. Girls were shut up in
a vacuum of knitting and good works and polite conversation. Miss
Nightingale, writing from bitter experience, described how "the ac-
cumulation of nervous energy which has had nothing to do all day
makes women feel every night, when they go to bed, as if they were
going mad; and they are obliged to be long in bed in the morning to
let it evaporate. At last they suffer at once from disgust and incapacity: from loathing of conventional idleness and powerlessness to do
work when they have it."

When men and women met in the drawing room, they talked
only of trifles and remained fundamentally strangers to one another.
Yet the only acceptable escape for a woman was to marry one of
these strangers, and "the woman who has sold herself for an establishment, in what is she superior to those we may not name?" In any
case, marriage did not rescue a woman from aimlessness. A lady
must be ladylike. She must hold her skirts above the mire of reality,
displaying, as it were, a pair of pretty ankles in the process. She was
expected to divert people's attention, including her own, from the
boredom, the seaminess of life. This meant cultivating a wide range
of superficial interests. "A 'lady,'" wrote Miss Nightingale, "has too
many sketches on hand. She has a sketch of society, a sketch of her
children's education, sketches of her charities, sketches of her reading. Her whole life is sketchy. . . ."

"When," she wailed, "shall we see a life full of steady enthusiasm, walking straight to its aim, flying home against the wind with
the calmness and confidence of one who knows the laws of God and
can apply them?" She lived out her own answer; but such was her
resentment at the waste of human potential caused by the subjection

of women that she wrote: "The next Christ will perhaps be a female Christ." This feeling for salvation through martyrdom reappeared in the urgent ferocities of the suffragettes, the 1913 Derby Day death of Emily Wilding Davison (who had taken a first-class Oxford degree in English Literature, horsewhipped a clergyman in mistake for Lloyd George, and tried to commit suicide in Holloway prison because "the Cause has need of a tragedy") beneath the hooves of the King's racehorse.

Even enlightened male sympathy had strict limits. John Stuart Mill might demand an end to the morality of "chivalry" (based on submission) and the beginning of the morality of "justice" (based on equality), but John Ruskin restricted woman's sphere to "understanding and perhaps helping" the work of men. The Rev. Frederick Maurice, a founder with Charles Kingsley of Christian Socialism, was willing to open classes for governesses, even to agitate mildly about sweated female workers, but he drew the line when women set their sights on "the professions." Women's education was intended primarily as a safety value, not as a spur to ambition or achievement. "The more pains we take," he said in one of his Lectures to Ladies on Practical Subjects, "to call forth and employ the faculties which belong *characteristically* to each sex, the less it will be intruding upon the province which not the conventions of the world, but the will of God, has assigned to the other."

In some mysterious way, the sanctity of the home was assumed to depend upon women staying indoors and embroidering or making artificial flowers. Pioneer feminists had to defy or evade endless restrictions in order merely to move about and meet one another. They were not supposed to go anywhere, even for a walk, alone. When they went slumming with their medicines, their nourishing food, their blankets, and their prayer books, their fellow workers had to be members of their own sex, and even they could not be invited home unless they were of the right social standing and already known to the family. It took a world war to blast a really sizable hole in such barriers.

Infiltration was the strategy in the nineteenth centuy. When Elizabeth Blackwell came from America to set up in doctor's practice in London, the alarmed medical profession framed a new charter that excluded all holders of foreign degrees. This meant that somehow would-be women doctors had to get their training in Britain. But when Elizabeth Garrett (later Dr. Elizabeth Garrett Anderson), who entered the Middlesex Hospital as a nurse, wangled permission to attend students' lectures, her examination results were so good that the students demanded her removal. Her next move (1865) was to pass the examination of the Society of Apothecaries, whose charter did not exclude women. She opened a dispensary for women and children in London, and while working there she studied for the MD diploma of Paris University. Having gained this, she put her name on the British Medical Register—by virtue of her apothecary's license!

By the time Sophia Jex-Blake decided to take up medicine, the Society of Apothecaries had doctored *its* charter. When she was refused permission to attend lectures at Edinburgh University (chosen as the least hostile), she organized separate classes for women, guaranteeing to pay the lecturers. The authorities gave permission for the women to sit for the degree examination, but when one of them, a Miss Peachey, matriculated so well that she was entitled to a scholarship giving free access to the university laboratory, this was awarded to the man below her in the results.

A boisterous and frightening climax was reached when, in November, 1870, "ragging" students massed to prevent the women from entering Surgeons' Hall for a lecture. They shouted, they jostled, they threw mud and stood guard over the doors. When the women got in through a side entrance, a sheep was pushed, bleating, into the lecture room. Afterward, police had to escort them through excited crowds to their lodgings. They moved in an atmosphere similar to that surrounding Negro students in universities in the Deep South of America in recent times. Miss Peachey commented: "I began the study of medicine merely from personal motives; now I am also impelled by the desire to remove women from the care of such young ruffians."

After bitter legal battles, Edinburgh University won the right to withhold medical degrees from women students. Other universities followed suit, and British women went to study in Paris, Berne, Montpellier, Bologna, braving language difficulties, intense curiosity, even public obloquy, in their determination to qualify and practice in Britain—even if they were not on the official register. Meanwhile,

The Lancet continued to insist that "woman's sphere in medicine should certainly be limited to carrying out the desires and implicitly obeying the dictates" of male doctors.

Battered but dauntless, Miss Jex-Blake opened (in London) the first medical school for women students and tried to slip through yet another legal loophole, having discovered that a midwifery license entitled its holder to be placed on the register. When she and two others applied to sit for the examination, the entire Board of Examiners resigned to thwart her! But in 1875, Parliament passed a bill *enabling* universities to accept women students. Many still refused, but Dublin agreed to grant medical degrees to women. In 1877, after eight years of battle, Sophia Jex-Blake, who had already taken a degree in Switzerland, was reexamined in Dublin and finally entitled to put her name on the sacred register.

Similar maneuvers, though in a less frenziedly hostile atmosphere, were necessary to penetrate the senior universities of Oxford and Cambridge in the 1860's and 1870's. New girls' schools raised the standard and aims of education; and at Cambridge, Girton College (1869) and Newnham College (1871) were founded. Sympathetic dons agreed to lecture to girl students in their spare time and to mark their papers. There was no question of a formal degree being awarded, but in 1887 a Miss Ramsay of Girton got a first class in the Classical Tripos, though no man was placed higher than the second class. Sex discrimination led to absurd shifts. When class lists were published, a woman might be given as "equal to 10th Wrangler" or "between 8th and 9th Wrangler," and in 1890 Philippa Fawcett, Elizabeth Garrett Anderson's niece, was placed "above Senior Wrangler" in the Mathematics Tripos. To avoid the breath of scandal, social life was severely pruned: for a long time young ladies had to be chaperoned to lectures, and in Girton a public reception room about twelve feet square was provided for men visitors, who were allowed into the studies only if the door was left wide open and no one sat down. When undergraduates carried the effigy of a woman student through the streets of Cambridge and threatened to burn down the gates of Newnham, they were not disciplined—but the young ladies were "gated."

While the authorities of Newnham and Girton and, a little later, of the Oxford women's colleges of Somerville and Lady Margaret

Hall enforced conventlike discipline and the Slade School of Art in London forbade girl students to study from the nude, a remarkable young woman was preparing to force the question of sex out into the open. Josephine Butler had sheltered and nursed young prostitutes for some years before. After much soul-searching, she decided that she must fight the Contagious Diseases Acts. A system of licensing brothels and regulating prostitution, begun in 1864 on the Continental model, was rapidly applied to most military and naval centers. All the women living in certain areas were liable, on police accusation, to be declared "common prostitutes" and forced to undergo regular medical examination. Refusal meant imprisonment, agreement destroyed a woman's reputation. Despite protests from some doctors (men, they pointed out, were just as liable to spread venereal disease) and clergy and from Florence Nightingale, the system seemed likely to spread all over the land. This, it was argued, was the best way to protect the nation's health.

A campaign of public education by speech and pamphlet rallied support in all classes against the acts, though many people were horrified by the immorality of even broaching such a subject. A monster petition to Parliament was followed by a brilliant, suffragettelike intervention in the 1870 by-election at Colchester. The Government candidate, Sir Henry Storks (who not only had a disastrous name, but advocated police control for soldiers' wives as well as for prostitutes), was defeated on this one point. Colchester was a military center, and Mrs. Butler and her friends were refused lodgings, attacked by mobs, and went in danger of their lives, since the police made little attempt to protect them.

Her courage then and, a year later, in giving evidence before a hostile commission of peers, bishops, MP's, doctors, and naval and military "experts" brought her many supporters. She urged that the acts themselves were symptomatic of a rotten society. Legislation, she said, must deal equally with both sexes (men as well as women should be prosecuted for soliciting). But more important, a series of radical reforms was needed, among them the provision of industrial training and a wide range of jobs for women, as well as a giant housing program. Only so could the grinding poverty and the indecent crowding that bred disease and prostitution be tackled.

Mrs. Butler (who saw the operation of the acts suspended in

1883 and with the help of journalist W. T. Stead, fought the traffic in young girls) had given a severe shock to the moral doublethink in which women "fell" beyond redemption but men merely "sowed wild oats." She had also managed to focus attention on the economic facts and roots of life. Women were easily and ruthlessly exploited. There was little choice except the governess's hard pittance, the fearful seasonal sweating of the rag trade, the slavery of domestic service, the workhouse, or the streets. In industry, women were used as drudges, and men's trade unions were determined to keep it that way. There was a great surplus of women over men—it was estimated at a million in 1857—and some of them were glad to be shipped to the colonies to find husbands. This was a solution much, and facetiously, favored by the press.

By 1890, there were some fifty thousand nurses and nearly one hundred fifty thousand women teachers. Female employees multiplied in shops and offices. This "revolution" owed much to the fact that employers found women grateful for very small mercies and glad to get work at almost any price. Wages were all right as pocket money for a girl living in a middle-class home, but heartbreaking for a woman trying to support herself. A post office official calmly explained: "We get a better class of women for the same pay. They are more patient under routine, less liable to combine, and often leave on marriage when their pay would be increasing." Such docility did not commend them to male workers struggling hard to better their conditions, and it was assumed that if money and jobs were scarce, women must make the sacrifice and go without them. A deputation of schoolmasters demanded that their salaries should be increased by cutting those of women teachers. Birmingham's Education Authority was forced to stop employing women to teach small boys, on the pretext that it "encouraged immorality."

The first women's trade union—the Women's Protective and Provident League—was founded in 1875 by Emma Paterson, and it included dressmakers, upholsterers, bookbinders, artificial-flower makers, feather dressers, tobacco, jam, and pickle workers, shop assistants, and typists. It argued that the Ten Hour Act, since it applied to women but not to men, was a form of unfair discrimination, but the Trades Union Congress concluded that "it was their duty as men and husbands to use their utmost endeavours to bring about a condition of things in which the wives should be in their proper sphere at home, instead of being dragged out into competition of livelihood against the great and strong men of the world." Only gradually did men appreciate the urgency of helping women to organize industrially. When the Provident League became the Women's Trade Union League and widened its scope, it received one famous message that ran: "Please send an organiser to this union, as we have decided that if the women cannot be organised they must be exterminated." Women like Margaret MacDonald, Mary Macarthur, and Margaret Bondfield developed the work, and Mrs. Annie Besant, in her militantly feminist pretheosophical phase, led the girls of Bryant & May's East End match factory in a demonstration that showed the power of collective strike action to change conditions.

Even in domestic service, women's wages were lower than men's, for the same old reason that a man was assumed to have greater responsibilities. At a meeting in 1911, Maude Royden, a celebrated preacher and one of the most brilliant suffragist speakers of her day, claimed that there were more than five million women in England earning their living. About half were working in industry and earning an average weekly wage of about 7s. 6d. Home workers averaged 4s. 6d. a week, and the Government sweated them as viciously as private employers. Women worked for ten and a half hours a day making army or police uniforms in order to earn a shilling. They were paid 3¾ d. for basting and finishing police trousers, which represented four and a half hours' work. It was impossible, said Miss Royden, for a woman to keep "industrially efficient on such wages. She cannot keep her physical health, let alone the qualities of intelligence and mental vigour which make the valuable citizen." Mary Macarthur estimated 15s. as the minimum adequate weekly wage.

Small wonder, said Miss Royden, that desperate women often committed or attempted suicide. "Such facts alone have made thousands of woman suffragists. They will make suffragists of all men and women who consider what they mean in suffering—and in sin."

Yet there was a movement to curtail the work of women on all levels, even in nonprofessional jobs. Some men thought that there should be fewer barmaids and female acrobats and that married women should be barred from factories. What was left for women to do? The heaviest kind of laundry work, which would tax a man's strength, sorting refuse, gutting fish, picking fur. The work that women once did at home—brewing, baking, spinning, weaving, knitting, and dyeing, the manufacture of garments, soap, candles, medicines, and salves—was now done in factories. But men wanted to keep women out of factories, where the new machines could be tended just as well by women, especially if they were given the same education and training. The real danger, said Miss Royden, was not women who demanded equal wages, but those who accepted lower ones.

Men could be nurses, dressmakers, milliners, and cooks: the London County Council even provided a three-year course for male cooks, whereas the women's course lasted only six months and their wages were correspondingly lower. Of two thousand doctors responsible for the medical examination of girls for factory employment, not one was a woman. Only 18 out of 151 factory inspectors were women. Throughout the public services, the best-paid and most honorable posts were reserved for men.

These things, to add insult to injury, were decided in a Parliament elected by men and apparently dedicated to men's interests. Yet by 1909, there were more than two hundred thousand women in various trade unions, more than there were men when they got a wider vote in 1867. But unions without political power were mere toys. Lloyd George admitted that the prevailing inequality would be impossible if women had the vote. In Norway, where women were enfranchised in 1907, the wages of women in Government service were on a par with men's. The same thing had happened in New Zealand and South Australia.

2 §●

Parnell in Petticoats

Women had gotten as far as they possibly could, by personal daring and cunning, without getting the vote. The first women's suffrage group—the Ladies' Discussion Society—met in Kensington in 1865, when J. S. Mill was returned to Parliament, and it seemed that votes for women (at least for upper- and middle-class women) must be coming, so confident were they of the logic of their case and the ability of their new male champion. Many politicians in both parties had indicated support, but prejudice was very deep; and in the male-club atmosphere of Westminster, logic soon surrendered to tradition, especially when tradition was backed by the all-powerful Prime Minister, William Ewart Gladstone himself, who made it clear that male feminists would get no promotion.

Time after time, carefully worded petitions failed to make any impact. From behind the oriental-type grille that separated the Ladies' Gallery from the Commons, suffragists who had strained every twanging nerve to keep matters constitutional and on a "high" level heard Members of Parliament guffawing over jokes about pregnant Prime Ministers or trotting out the old nagging cant about God having ordained men to rule over women. MP's had no intention of "sacrificing their manhood" or upsetting "eternal decrees" because of a few overeducated women who were not in the least representative of their sex. As if to prove their point, three women—novelist Mrs. Humphry Ward, Mrs. Mandell Creighton (widow of the Bishop of London), and, most devastating, the radical Mrs. Sidney Webb —who had been prominent in support of the improvement of women's education came out against the suffrage. It was their belief that "the emancipatory process has now reached the limits fixed by the physical constitution of women."

Punch and other comic journals worked hard to manufacture the legend that "women who wanted women's rights also wanted women's charms." Antisuffragist MP's like Mr. Henry du Pré Labouchère "talked out" suffrage bills by holding forth interminably and facetiously on trivial subjects such as "The Lighting of Vehicles" or "The Danger of Verminous Persons." As a sop, the Liberal and Conservative Parties formed women's branches—the Primrose League and the Women's Liberal Association—the primary function of which was really "to help our husbands," as Mrs. Gladstone said. The Independent Labour Party, formed at the turn of the century, put women's suffrage in its program, and many women, including Mrs. Pankhurst herself, switched their support to Labour. But

ILP enthusiasm for The Cause soon cooled: Keir Hardie and George Lansbury might be keen, but for the rest, including Ramsay MacDonald (and Mrs. Pankhurst never forgave him for this), who had their full share of masculine prejudice, it was not practical politics, it could not expect priority, it would have to wait. They shared the view of the Conservative leader, A. J. Balfour, who, when asked in 1905 why his party had done nothing for women, replied: "Your cause just wasn't in the swim."

The "constitutional" suffragists in the National Union of Women's Suffrage Societies (NUWSS) were led by Mrs. Henry Fawcett, whose husband was a Liberal Cabinet Minister. Though nettled, they managed to keep their tempers. The NUWSS message was that since the political enfranchisement of women would liberate new energies for the good of society as a whole, men as well as women should join in bringing it about (the NUWSS newspaper was called *The Common Cause*). Hundreds of women traveled the country with this message. There was no war of the sexes: in unity lay strength. With their middle-class manners and clothes and their middle-class accents, they braved street-corner hecklers and lower-class missiles. Helena Swanwick, sister of the painter Richard Sickert and editor of *The Common Cause*, had taken a first class in Moral Sciences at Girton. She had always been delicate in health, yet she thought nothing of a year's work that included speaking at fifty-five public meetings all over England and Wales, at twenty-one public meetings in London, and at many private gatherings. In addition, she wrote books, articles, did her share of organizing, and took part in, and reported, International Suffrage Alliance congresses as far afield as Budapest. Ethel Snowden, the wife of Philip Snowden, one of the first Labour MP's and Chancellor of the Exchequer in the Ramsay MacDonald Administration of the 1920's, was even more energetic. She claimed to have addressed more than two hundred public meetings a year in as many different towns in twelve years of service with the NUWSS.

Mrs. Fawcett distrusted emotionalism. When asked to sign a petition that described her as "passionately desiring" women's suffrage, she demurred: "*Must* I be passionate? Oh, very well!" She was capable of joking about The Cause in a rather academic way ("The *Medea's* such a *good* suffrage play, my dear!"). But in the opinion of more and more women, antiemotionalism had had its day: it was time for a more drastic, less scrupulous approach that would brush aside diplomatic niceties, declare war on the recalcitrant sex, and focus public attention on The Cause by sheer sustained sensationalism.

The Salvation Army, founded in 1875, had shown, in a nonpolitical field, what men and women could achieve when working together under autocratic leadership. Its regulations stated that "the Army refuses to make any difference between men and women as to rank, authority and duties, but opens the highest positions to women as well as to men. The words 'woman' and 'her' are scarcely ever used in orders, 'man' 'he,' 'his' being always understood to mean a person of either sex. . . ." Within twelve years, the Salvation Army recruited fifty thousand members and, with its clear-cut message and soldierly organization, did far more than any suffragist speeches to break down antifeminist prejudice among the violently skeptical working classes.

The Cause also needed a simplified, fundamentalist gospel, an esprit de corps based on unquestioning obedience to a leader. There must be one objective—the vote—and, since men willed it that way, a woman's army willing to be ruthless to gain it. The Women's Social and Political Union, which took as its motto "Deeds Not Words," came into being in 1903 in Manchester. Emmeline Pankhurst, the widow of an eminent radical barrister who had helped to draft the first women's franchise bill in 1870 and whose political program had included the abolition of the monarchy, the disestablishment and disendowment of the Church of England, free and compulsory education, nationalization of the land, and a League of Nations, told some friends: "We must have an independent women's movement. Come to my house tomorrow and we will arrange it!"

Petite, impulsive, full of vitality, attractive, and fond of pretty clothes, Mrs. Pankhurst, the daughter of a Manchester cotton manufacturer, had explored the conventional outlets open to women in local government and found them wanting. She had served on the Education Board and as a Poor Law Guardian and had done relief work among the poor. After her husband's death (he had been twice her age when they married), she had been appointed Registrar of Births and Deaths in Manchester (a comparatively lucrative post that she had to resign because of her new activities) and continued to run a fancy-goods shop called Emerson's that aimed at being a kind of provincial Liberty's. The Pankhurst family had lived in London for some years, and during that time she had acted as hostess to leading lights of the struggling Socialist movement, including Bernard Shaw. She liked to do things well, but there were always financial anxieties, and she resented the pinching and scraping and the way her husband's open socialism damaged his earnings as a barrister.

Despite his wife's ambition, Dr. Pankhurst never got elected to Parliament, and the contests were an added expense. She had heard so much talk, some of it sparkling, and seen so few results. She was a frustrated but still very ambitious woman. Three daughters and a son were dependent upon her, and she provided for them. But she hated being tethered and longed to soar out of the commonplace and the provincial. She was determined to get something *done*. Her husband's intellectualism had gotten him nowhere in public life. She would trust to her instincts from now on. Her instincts told her that now was the time to declare total war—not only on all obvious antisuffragists, but on the great mass of the indifferent. Anyone who was not with her was, from henceforth, to be considered against her.

Her eldest and adored daughter, Christabel, replaced Dr. Pankhurst as Emmeline's political mentor. Like her father, she had had legal training. At Victoria University College, Manchester, she graduated at the top of the honors list of law students, an achievement all the more remarkable since (like her sisters, Sylvia and Adela) she had been expected to help in the shop and around the house. But academic brilliance by itself was not sufficient to gain entry to the legal profession. One also had to be a man. So Christabel had to seek another outlet for her talents. She began by taking an interest in the organization of women in the Lancashire textile industry, and she soon shared and then, with the encouragement of her mother, took over the leadership of the tiny WSPU. After listening to Christabel speak, Annie Kenney, an Oldham cotton-mill hand —later to become one of the WSPU's most tireless and effective members—joined and also recruited her three sisters. From the beginning, the WSPU had a working-class appeal that the NUWSS almost totally lacked.

There was something about Christabel—so young, so certain of her aims and her powers, so explicit about the failings of older suffragists—that attracted boundless admiration and loyalty or thoroughgoing aversion. Her youth, which irritated some, was to others a promise of new vitality for The Cause. Now only was she the daughter of parents whose passion for social justice was a byword in the North. She herself, after all her mother's sacrifices, after her years at Manchester Grammar School learning how to speak, look, and act like a lady, after reaching dizzy heights of scholarship, had been dragged down to earth by sheer male prejudice. Now, like a frustrated eagle, she prepared to take flight again, and such was the magnetism of her sense of destiny that it never seems to have occurred to that small band of disciples that she would not soon soar to new heights, and they with her. History, she convinced them, was on their side.

The General Election of 1905 was chosen as the moment to launch a campaign of militancy that lasted until the outbreak of the Great War. Christabel, though still a student (and frowned upon by the university authorities for dabbling in politics), had worked out its essentials. It was crystal clear to her that the promised backing of individual Members of Parliament, of whatever party, was not worth a snap of the fingers unless the Government of the day was prepared to pledge support of the suffrage. Since the Liberal Party was about to return to power, it followed that the Liberal Party must be harassed until it did give such a pledge and that Liberal politicians must be forced to declare themselves. Only so could the air be cleared of cant and of the wishful thinking so dear to the NUWSS. Her tactics closely resembled those used by Charles Parnell, the Irish nationalist leader, and Christabel was, in fact, soon nicknamed "Parnell in Petticoats."

Christabel herself took part in the first skirmish of the new campaign of realism. With Annie Kenney, she stood up at a great political meeting in the Free Trade Hall, Manchester, and dared to demand from Liberal leader Sir Edward Grey an unequivocal yes or no to the question: "Will your party give votes to women?" Thrown out of the hall by outraged stewards, she and Annie Kenney scuffled with the police outside and (as Christabel had planned) were imprisoned for creating a public disturbance. From that historic moment, thanks to a furore of headlines, the WSPU and votes for women became a national issue that no one could any longer ignore or escape. Seldom has a political tactician achieved such an immediate and resounding success.

Mrs. Pankhurst flung herself into the fray with a recklessness extraordinary in a woman of middle age and frail physique. During a by-election campaign in Devon her fiery oratory helped to defeat the Liberal candidate in what was regarded as a cast-iron Liberal constituency. It also helped to bring the campaign to a pitch of frantic violence. The windows of the Conservative Club were smashed, and a prominent Conservative supporter was found dead— murdered, many thought—in a millrace. She herself, regarded as an undercover Tory (the WSPU's persistent opposition to Liberal candidates bred rumors that it was subsidized by "Tory gold"), was beaten up by a group of Liberal workingmen—clay cutters—who knocked her into the mud of the lane where they had trapped her. Police rescued her from serious injury, but for long afterward she was in pain from a wrenched ankle and the aftereffects of a blow on the head. This did not put her out of action—only a few weeks later she was in London's Holloway Prison with Christabel. There she was solaced by the sound of suffragettes who marched around the prison walls singing and cheering. On her release she went straight to a big rally at the Royal Albert Hall. When she appeared on the platform a great shout went up from thousands of women, who stretched out their arms toward her in adoration. They piled wedding rings—those symbols of slavery—as well as money on the collection plates. "It was some time," wrote Mrs. Pankhurst, "before I could see for my tears, or speak for the emotion that shook me like a storm."

Liberal politicians, notably Asquith, Lloyd George, and Winston Churchill, were heckled and badgered by suffragettes wherever they went. Suffragette activity at by-elections sometimes brought about the defeat of the Liberal candidate. Churchill himself failed at Manchester, and Christabel's eloquence at the Peckham by-election of 1908 was such that the press admitted that the best speeches were made by the women. She became the idol of thousands of young women, and writer Max Beerbohm went into ecstasies over the "lively arabesques" of her platform gestures. When Christabel came out of prison, a fellow campaigner, Emmeline Pethick-Lawrence, rhapsodized in the WSPU's journal, *Votes for Women:* "Maiden warrior, we give you rapturous welcome. Go forth with the fiat of the future, strong in the gladness and youth of your dauntless spirit, to smite with your sword of destiny the forces of stupid and unreasoning prejudice and blind domination." But, though surrounded with adulation (she was presented with a silk standard embroidered with the dates of her imprisonments), and the focus of continual excitement, Christabel's brain stayed ice cool, her logic as immaculate as her flowing gowns. Some found her slightly aloof calm almost inhuman (and contrasted it unfavorably with her mother's emotional warmth). Others hinted that it was a sign of consuming personal ambition. Whatever the explanation, there was no doubt that this able and personable young woman had transformed the public image of The Cause and given it a brand-new urgency, modernity, and even sex appeal.

A series of spectacular mammoth meetings and street parades created the impression of a movement that had gaiety as well as weight and earnestness. Processions were organized, with hundreds of suffragettes in white "injured innocence" dresses, impressive militants like the Hon. Evelina Haverfield, daughter of Lord Abinger, on horseback, and Joans of Arc in armor. The careful scholarship of the NUWSS was almost as shocked as outright "anti's" by the showmanship of the WSPU.

The WSPU's first tentative maneuvers in London (where Annie Kenney arrived with £2 in her pocket and a determination to "rouse" the inhabitants) were given powerful help by Dora Montefiore, an experienced campaigner of international experience. Born into a large and well-to-do Conservative family near London (her father was Master of the Surrey Fox Hounds), she had begun her fight for women's rights in Sydney, Australia, where she lived with her husband. When he died, she returned to England to educate her children. In 1899, angered by the failure of orthodox suffragist methods, she outlined the tactic later adopted by Christabel Pankhurst. "How then," she wrote in a pamphlet topically entitled *Women Uitlanders,* "shall women bring pressure to bear to obtain equal rights with men? If nothing but war will meet the situation, then war must be declared by women at all Parliamentary elections by making woman suffrage a test question."

She followed this up by refusing to pay taxes to a Government in which she, as a woman, had no voice. In 1904 and 1905, bailiffs entered her house at Hammersmith, London, and took away some of her possessions, which were then sold at public auction to pay her "debts." Now, in consultation with Annie Kenney and Teresa Billington (then London Secretary of the WSPU), she planned a more spectacular resistance. In May, 1906, she barred her door to the bailiffs (but not to journalists), and the heavily publicized "Siege of Hammersmith" began. It lasted for six headline-grabbing weeks—the statutory period during which bailiffs were forbidden to force an entrance—and during that time, "Fort Montefiore," as her house was christened, was ringed with police and pressmen and curious crowds. A large red banner with white letters—WOMEN SHOULD VOTE FOR THE LAWS THEY OBEY AND THE TAXES THEY PAY—was erected in the front garden. Tradesmen and postmen dropped food and letters over the garden wall. Over the garden wall, too, large crowds, harangued daily by Mrs. Montefiore from an upper window (and by Annie Kenney, Teresa Billington, Sylvia Pankhurst, and other WSPU orators from the front steps), threw money to swell the Union's fighting fund.

The WSPU's next big boost came from Emmeline and Frederick Pethick-Lawrence, a devoted, wealthy, and well-connected Socialist couple who not only allowed the WSPU to use their Clement's Inn flat as its headquarters, but provided the financial and administrative skill that transformed the Pankhursts' provincial foray into a large-scale and extraordinarily efficient movement. Mrs. Pethick-Lawrence had a platform manner almost as effective as Mrs. Pankhurst's (who pleaded, hypnotically, "Come to uzz!" with a Lancashire burr and a revivalist ardor), and as Treasurer of the WSPU, she boosted its lagging finances and its support among the wealthy.

In 1909, the Hon. Mrs. Mona Taylor of Chipchase Castle wrote to Churchill: "I expect you will be troubled by the Suffragettes when in Newcastle. I have been a Liberal all my life until last summer, when I joined the WSPU and helped all I could to keep the Liberal out at the Newcastle by-election, in which we succeeded. I now give half my personal income to work against the Government. Why continue to oblige us to fight you?"

While old-style suffragists winced and Mrs. Swanwick fulminated in the columns of *The Common Cause,* suffragettes hurled themselves at the bloated fatuity of politicians who still burbled in the House of Commons: "What does one find when one gets into the company of women and talks politics? You are soon asked to stop talking silly politics, and yet that is the type of person to whom Hon. Members are invited to hand over the destinies of the country." They chained themselves to railings and even to a statue in the lobby of the Commons; they harangued MP's on the terrace of the House from a chartered river steamer; they hid under organs and concealed themselves all night on roofs in order to interrupt meetings. Thousands of extra police were drafted to protect Parliament from their "raids." They were arrested, and forthwith the courtrooms of Britain and newspapers all over the world rang with their self-justifications. Conducting her own defense, Christabel used her legal skill to cross-examine Lloyd George and Herbert Gladstone.

Mrs. Pankhurst revealed herself as one of the greatest orators of her time. "You know how unjust the marriage and divorce laws are, that the married woman has no due right of guardianship over her own children," she told one magistrate. "Great suffering is endured by women because of the state of the Law. Since my girlhood I have tried 'constitutional' methods. We have presented petitions and we have held meetings greater than men ever held for any reform. We have faced the violence of ignorant mobs, unprotected by the safeguards provided for Cabinet Ministers. We are determined to go on with that agitation, we are honour bound to do so until we win. Just as it was the duty of our forefathers to do it for you, it is our duty to make this world a better place for women. We believe that if we get the vote, it will mean changed conditions for our less fortunate sisters. We know how bad is the position of the women workers. Many women pass through this court who would not, I believe, come before you if they were able to live honestly and morally on their wages.

"We believe that your work would be lightened if we got the vote. I do not come here as an ordinary law-breaker. I would not be here if I had the same power to vote that even a wife-beater has, and the drunkard has. If you had power to send us to prison, not for six months but for six years or ten years or for the whole of our lives, the Government must not think that they can stop this agitation. We are here not because we are law-breakers. We are here in our efforts to become law-makers."

Convinced that a simple campaign with a single object—the vote —needed only one general, Mrs. Pankhurst had brushed off an early attempt, in 1907, to challenge the Pankhurst "dictatorship." Membership in the WSPU was, after all, voluntary: anyone could leave at any time if they wanted to—and if Mrs. Pankhurst herself was willing to serve under Christabel, why should others quibble? In this context, she thought, talk of "democracy" was nonsense. "It was as though," Christabel wrote later, "in the midst of battle, the Army had begun to vote upon who should command it and what the strategy should be."

Those who could not accept this logic broke away to form another militant organization—the Women's Freedom League—whose chairman was the venerable Charlotte Despard, the ex-Honorary Secretary of the WSPU. Though the Freedom League was strictly nonviolent in its tactics (a refusal to pay taxes was a distinctive ploy), relations with the WSPU remained friendly. A keen theosophist and Socialist, Mrs. Despard was more diffuse and visionary in her approach to the common objective. She was fond of quoting the poet Shelley's description of the New Woman in *Prometheus Unbound:*

> . . . frank, beautiful, and kind
> As the free heaven which rains fresh light and dew
> On the wide earth, past; gentle radiant forms,
> From custom's evil taint exempt and pure;
> Speaking the wisdom once they could not think,
> Looking emotions once they feared to feel,
> And changed to all which once they dared not be,
> Yet being now, made earth like heaven; nor pride,
> Nor jealousy, nor envy, nor ill shame,
> The bitterest of those drops of treasured gall,
> Spoilt the sweet taste of the nepenthe, love.

"It is this vision," wrote Mrs. Despard, "which makes one feel that life itself would be but a small price to pay for the joy of being one of the pioneers of a movement whose aim it is to prepare and reveal her."

It was to Mrs. Despard that the American poetess Ella Wheeler Wilcox, when she visited London in 1910, recited her "Battle Hymn

of the Women"—and gave her permission to use it as the Freedom
League's rallying cry:

> They are waking, they are waking
> In the East and in the West,
> They are throwing wide their windows to the sun;
> And they see the dawn is breaking
> And they quiver with unrest,
> For they know their work is waiting to be done.
>
> They are waking in the city,
> They are waking on the farm,
> They are waking in the boudoir and the mill;
> And their hearts are full of pity,
> So they sound the loud alarm
> For the sleepers who in darkness slumber still.
>
> In the guarded harem prison
> Where they smother under veils,
> And the echoes of the world are walled away,
> Though the sun has not yet risen,
> Yet the ancient darkness palls,
> And the sleepers in their slumbers dream of day.

The times frothed and bubbled with denunciations and manifestos, none more resounding and influential than *Woman and Labour*
—a book written by Olive Schreiner, the daughter of a German missionary in Africa and author of *The Story of an African Farm.* "We
demand," she wrote, "that in the strange new world that is coming
. . . where all things are assuming new shapes and relations, we also
shall have our share of honoured and socially useful toil. . . . We demand that in the factory, the warehouse and the field, wherever machinery has usurped our ancient labour-ground, that we also should
have our places as guiders, controllers and possessors. We demand
that high and complex training which shall fit us for instructing the
race which we bring into the world. We make this demand, not for
ourselves alone, but for the succour of the race."

Were men afraid to let women compete on equal terms? "Allow
us all to start from one point in the world of intellectual culture and
labour, with our ancient Mother Nature sitting as umpire, distributing the prizes and scratching from the lists the incompetent, is all we
demand. Throw the puppy into the water: if it swims, well, if it
sinks, well; but do not tie a rope round its throat and weight it with

a brick and then assert its incapacity to float." There might have to be adjustments, but: "For the present, we take all labour for our province! From the judge's seat to the legislator's chair; from the statesman's closet to the merchant's office; from the chemist's laboratory to the astronomer's tower, there is no post or form of toil for which it is not our intention to attempt to fit ourselves: there is no closed door we do not intend to force open; and there is no fruit in the garden of knowledge it is not our determination to eat."

Just to be alive and a member of the WSPU was exhilarating. "All," said Christabel, "belonged to the aristocracy of the suffragettes." She pitied those women who had not known such a "unifying" experience. One suffragette wrote that "the campaign was our Eton and Oxford, our regiment, our ship," and battling Annie Kenney was sure that "no companionship can ever surpass the companionship of the militants."

Ministers were mercilessly and ingeniously hounded. Three suffragettes followed Prime Minister Asquith to Clovelly in Devon when he went there for a weekend holiday and got so close to him in church that he fled through a side door at the end of the service. Later they buttonholed him on the golf links, a tactic that was repeated not long after at Lympne. Even during dinner at Lympne Castle, Asquith was not safe. A suffragette was hoisted level with the open window of the dining room and, leaning in, scolded: "We shall go on pestering you until we get the vote!"

A suffragette known as La Belle Maloney followed Churchill about and drowned his speeches by ringing a large muffin bell, and at Bristol Railway Station he was menaced by a woman with a dog whip, who cried: "Take that in the name of the insulted women of England!" After a speech at Queen's Hall in London, Lloyd George stepped into a waiting car, only to be given a severe shaking and lecture by a militant who had managed to slip in behind him and lock the door.

Women in elegant evening gowns (of which a special supply was kept in a wardrobe at WSPU headquarters) would suddenly seize Asquith by the lapels during society banquets and receptions and demand what he was doing there while hunger-striking suffragettes were being forcibly fed in prison. King George himself was startled when, as she dropped a Buckingham Palace curtsy, a debutante pleaded: "For God's sake, Your Majesty, put a stop to forcible feeding!" Yet in 1912, Asquith still maintained that there was "no clear proof that both the class [women] and the country want women to have votes." He even stated that the present agitation was "undemocratic," since it aimed to enfranchise only an upper-class fraction (some two million) of the country's women. The hypocrisy of this democratic pose infuriated Mrs. Pankhurst. The wedge of universal suffrage had to have a thin end. It was the suffragettes' job to hammer this home, and Asquith was determined to prevent them. That, to her, was the sum and truth of the matter.

Attacks on property began to figure prominently in a campaign that sought, by every means, to penetrate the armored torpor of British public opinion. Like everything else, window breaking was carefully organized. Cars were driven after dark to places where plenty of stones were available, and sacks were crammed with selected missiles. Picked "smashers" were issued hammers and inconspicuous black bags filled with stones. Oxford Street, Regent Street, the Strand, and the Haymarket were turned, in a matter of seconds, into splintering chaos when suffragettes who had been mingling with crowds of shoppers went into action.

Many militants did not agree with these new and violent tactics. They were never used by the Women's Freedom League, and some critics saw them as proof of a Pankhurst megalomania that threatened to cheapen the whole movement. Teresa Billington, one of the original members of the WSPU, was especially scathing. "The emancipation-in-a-hurry spirit has eaten up the spirit of emancipation," she wrote. "It has edged the working-class element out and ended in political chicanery, showmanship and snobbery." The game of provoking the Government and then complaining of punishment was, she thought, unworthy: "Such militancy is not revolution. It is the exploitation of revolution." In a drastic pounce, the Government arrested all the WSPU leaders—all except Christabel, who managed to escape to Paris. She was soon left in undisputed control of the new campaign. The Pethick-Lawrences, certain that such extremism would antagonize public opinion and throw away a hard-won moral advantage, but unable to persuade Christabel to draw back, left the WSPU.

The Pankhursts swept on unimpeded. In an impassioned address to loyalists after this new purge, Mrs. Pankhurst compared Government criticism of militancy to the behavior of "beasts of prey reproaching the gentler animals who turn in desperate resistance at the point of death." The suffragette army had a great mission, the greatest mission the world had ever known—"the freeing of one half of the human race, and through that freedom the saving of the other half." In a scene of rapturous, tumultuous excitement she declared: "I incite this meeting to rebellion!" Soon afterward, replying to the scandalized comments of church leaders, she claimed that in attacking the false gods of materialism the WSPU was performing a spiritual service to the community: "If we women are wrong in destroying private property in order that human values may be restored, then I say in all reverence that it was wrong for the Founder of Christianity to destroy private property, as He did when He lashed the money-changers out of the Temple and when He drove the Gadarene swine into the sea."

There was no arguing with a conviction of such monomaniac intensity. With the flesh wasting from her face, her blazing eyes set in dark bruises of exhaustion, Mrs. Pankhurst was the terrifying embodiment of the idea that hell has no fury like a woman scorned. Her opponents could not be expected to understand or respect the explosions of pride and frustration and ambition that shook and drove her. A typical reaction was that of the *Times,* which characterized the militants as "the hysterical, the neurotic, the idle and the habitual imbibers of excitement. Some of them are out with their hammers because of dreary, empty lives and over-excitable natures. They are regrettable by-products of our civilisation." The newspaper followed this up by publishing an extraordinary letter from Sir Almoth Wright, physician at St. Mary's Hospital. In his opinion, militancy was the result of mental illness. Nearly 50 per cent of women went slightly crazy in middle life and were therefore liable to become frenetic. "The mind of a woman," he warned, "is always threatened with danger from the reverberation of her physiological experiences. It is with such thoughts that the doctor lets his eyes rest on the militant suffragist. . . . One would not be far from the truth if one alleged that in public life there are no good women, only women who have lived under the influence of good men." There were, as he saw it, two kinds of militant. The sexually embittered,

"whose legislative programme is license for themselves or else restriction for the men," and the "incomplete, whose programme is to
convert the world into an epicene institution in which men and
women shall everywhere work side by side at the self-same tasks for
the self-same pay." Sir Almoth's reverberating conclusion was that
"even in animals—I say even, because in these at least one of the
sexes has periods of complete quiescence—male and female cannot
be safely worked side by side unless they are incomplete."

In 1913, too, suffrage and antisuffrage propaganda entered a new
medium. In New York, Mrs. Pankhurst starred in a film entitled
What 88 Million Women Want; while in England, cinematograph
audiences were amused, and suffragette sensibilities ruffled, by a
short slapstick comedy entitled *Milling the Militants.* In this, Mr.
Brown, a monumentally henpecked husband, is left to look after the
family while his domineering wife goes off to take part in yet another suffragette demonstration. He falls asleep and dreams that he
is Prime Minister, with full power to legislate for the suppression of
militant women. He sees his laws being put into effect—hard labor,
the stocks, compulsory wearing of trousers, and finally the ducking
stool. Gloating over this fantasy of revenge, he is rudely awakened
when Mrs. Brown empties a bucket of cold water over him and
scolds him for neglecting his domestic duties.

But the women were not content with dark thoughts. They put
their vengeance into ever more bizarre and sensational practice.
Paintings, including the Rokeby *Venus* by Velázquez, were slashed
in public art galleries, a mummy case damaged in the British Museum. Two railway stations, two churches, a grandstand at Hurst
Park Race Course, and the orchid house and a tea pavilion at Kew
Gardens were damaged or destroyed. On a single memorable night,
three castles in Scotland were burned down. Seaside piers, sports
pavilions, and haystacks were fired, and attempts were made to
blow up reservoirs. A small "bicycle bell" bomb splintered the Coro-
nation Chair in Westminster Abbey. The organ at the Albert Hall
was flooded, and stained-glass windows in fashionable St. George's
Church, Hanover Square, London, were shattered by an explosion.
Suffragette slogans ("No Votes, No Golf!") were cut or etched with
acid on golf greens, and at Balmoral, during the night, all the flags
on the King's own golf course were removed, and purple, white, and
green WSPU flags substituted, bearing such slogans as "Votes for

Women Means Peace for Ministers." This was done, said Mrs. Pankhurst, not in a spirit of wanton mischief, but to remind the dull, self-satisfied English public that it was no time to think of sport when the liberties of English women were being stolen from them. When newspapers appealed to the WSPU not to interfere with a game that helped weary politicians to relax and think clearly, the WSPU replied that it did not seem to have had any such effect on Asquith and Lloyd George—they still persisted in denying votes to women.

Not even the monarchy was safe from the rage of the militants. The King and Queen were hissed when their names were mentioned at WSPU meetings, and when they attended a matinée at Her Majesty's Theatre, they were startled when a suffragette, who had chained herself to a seat in the stalls, yelled up at the royal box, "You Russian Tsar!" In Dublin, Mary Leigh tossed a hatchet into an open carriage in which Asquith was riding. She followed this up by trying to set fire to the Theatre Royal, while another militant attempted to blow up a cinema. Both were sentenced to five years' penal servitude.

On trial for house burning, Miss Nina Boyle (a Freedom Leaguer) called out to the magistrate: "Good morning, Mr. Pecksniff, we shall meet again!" At Bow Street, the formidable Flora Drummond (known as "The General") boomed at prosecuting counsel: "Sit down, you jack-in-the-box. You've been earning your living easily enough by hounding down women." She then advanced on the bench, seized a whistle from a policeman who stood in her way, and flung it at the magistrate. The same magistrate, Sir Henry Curtis-Bennett, while walking near the edge of a cliff, was ambushed by two suffragettes (now popularly known as "outragettes") and wrestled perilously near to the edge. Other magistrates had hammers, shoes, tomatoes, and bundles of pamphlets hurled at them. Mrs. Pankhurst, on trial for instigating a plot to blow up Lloyd George's new house on Walton Heath golf course, near London, worked some telling counteraccusations into her closing speech at the Old Bailey. Shouting through protests, she alluded to the case of a judge of assize who had been found dead in a brothel, implying that it was scandalous that respectable women should be tried by such tainted creatures.

This was no isolated, cranky outburst. As Poor Law Guardian and as Registrar of Births and Deaths in Manchester, Mrs. Pank-

hurst had seen too many starving unmarried mothers, heard of too
many cases of incest and child rape, not to feel a smoldering hatred
for men's sexual irresponsibility. She had even been told, quite seriously, that men with venereal disease sometimes had intercourse
with very young girls because it was widely believed that this might
cure them. No sacrifice, it seemed, was too great to keep the bread-
winner in health. The knowledge of such twisted, fetid reasoning,
the thought of such incestuous promiscuity, sometimes heated Mrs.
Pankhurst to such a passion of indignation that she boiled over in
public. Dame Ethel Smyth, who, though a composer of some emi-
nence already battling prejudice in her own profession, gave up two
years of her life to the WSPU, remembered hearing "Em" (as she—
and she alone—called Mrs. Pankhurst) storm at the men in a large
audience in Glasgow. She lashed out at the city's bad record of sex
crimes against young children. "It was done," wrote Dame Ethel, "in
such a way that, though all the male heads I could see were bowed
in shame, you felt without a shadow of a doubt that every one of
those men would have died for her. . . . Then suddenly she
stopped, held out both arms, and, in a voice the deep pitying inflex-
ion of which I shall hear till my dying day, said: 'Men! Men! I know
what shame is in your hearts. It is enough. I will say no more!' "
After she had finished speaking, men, weeping with emotion and
repentance, jostled the platform to get near their denouncer.

Christabel gave a new and sensational impetus to this crusade
for decency in a series of articles published in *The Suffragette*
(which she edited from exile in Paris) in 1913. George Lansbury's
newly launched *Daily Herald* had already suggested the formation
of a "Guild of Honour" for mothers who would undertake not to
bear children until the vote was won. Christabel went further.
Fiercely, she attacked the sexual excesses and venereal disease prevalent among men. According to her statistics, the result of wide if
slanted reading, at least 75 per cent of men contracted gonorrhea at
one time or another, and 25 per cent got syphilis. She accused man
of being "not the Lord of Creation but the exterminator of the species." She urged women to think seriously of not marrying, since
many so-called women's ailments could be traced to their diseased
husbands, whose profligacy was also a prime cause of high infant
mortality.

The notorious Piccadilly Flat case, during which it was alleged that men prominent in public life had frequented a brothel stocked with whips and other instruments of perversion, was eagerly seized upon, and *The Suffragette* began regularly to feature newspaper reports of child assaults. Antisuffragists openly rejoiced that the "pathological basis" of suffragism had been made so plain, and even admirers of Christabel were dismayed. Rebecca West, then a young journalist on *The Clarion,* lamented: "There was a long and desperate struggle before it became possible for women to write candidly on such subjects. That this power should be used to express views that would be old-fashioned and uncharitable in the pastor of a Little Bethel is a matter for scalding tears."

The violence of the reactions alone justified Christabel's coup. She had meant to be controversial, and she had succeeded—to an unparalleled degree—in focusing attention on a subject that badly needed it. No doubt her articles provided useful political ammunition, but they also had real educational value. Helen Keller wrote to congratulate her. W. T. Stead, the journalist who had gone to prison to expose the evils of London's white-slave traffic, went down on his knees before her and burst into tears of gratitude for her intervention.

The articles may have frightened some people off and almost certainly had the effect of intensifying Government measures against the suffragettes, but they also brought a great volume of support for the WSPU from clergymen and churchgoers and from many women who had been impervious to other arguments.

A purity campaign, like the fight for the vote, cut across party barriers and class prejudices.

3 §**

"O My Splendid Ones!"

Through all the sound and the fury, a fiery core of hundreds of suffragettes kept steadily to their resolve to suffer any indignities, any hardships, to keep pressure on the Government. Denied trial by jury, imprisoned after perfunctory hearings in magistrates' courts, they hunger-struck not only to gain quick release but to demonstrate their contempt for a regime that denied them what they regarded as their human and constitutional rights. Mrs. Pankhurst summed up their attitude when, at her Old Bailey Trial in 1913, she told the judge: "I look upon myself as a prisoner of war. I am under no moral obligation to conform to or in any way accept the sentence imposed upon me." As early as 1908, the Government had authorized forcible feeding of suffragettes in prison. This was a frightful, traumatic experience. To be dragged by force, frog-marched to the feeding chair, bound in a sheet, and held down by wardresses while a tube was thrust up the nostrils by one doctor and food poured down by another was, as one victim put it, to be outraged in every part of one's nature and was calculated to drive prisoners insane—as happened in at least one case. One suffragette, herself a doctor, stated that the worst part of the whole experience was having to listen to the cries and screams of other prisoners as the forcible-feeding squad worked its way down the corridors, playing upon the cells as upon a great organ of pain.

Such methods often turned well-brought-up and conventionally inclined young women into anarchic, fanatical enemies of a society that could permit such brutality. They also shocked a public opinion by no means squeamish or naturally sympathetic to the "Screaming Sisterhood" of the newspaper headlines (the "mewing cats" of Lloyd George's phrase), put the Government in a very odious light, and mass-manufactured suffragette martyrs. Realizing this, Winston Churchill, when he became Home Secretary in 1910 (a year in which eighteen Liberal Parliamentary candidates were defeated partly as a result of WSPU intervention), decided on a new approach. The police, who had theretofore broken up suffragette demonstrations by making prompt and massive arrests, were instructed not to make any arrests except under extreme provocation, and magistrates were encouraged not to send suffragettes to prison. This way, the women might be deterred by the prospect of ugly, bruising street scrimmages and would be denied a chance of prison glory. Ever since his defeat at Manchester, when, severely heckled by Sylvia Pankhurst, he had bellowed that he would not be henpecked into giving votes to women, Churchill had been a determined opponent of the WSPU ("that fount of mendacity," as he once called it).

Churchill's deterrent was tried out on a large scale on Friday, November 18, 1910—soon to be known as "Black Friday." About 450 suffragettes marched on Parliament, then starting its autumn session, from nearby Caxton Hall and from the WSPU's headquarters in Holborn. Special detachments of police, on foot and mounted, had been drafted for the occasion. Excited spectators soon became involved on both sides. Police were jeered and jostled, women were punched, knocked down, dragged up, hurled about. Their faces were rubbed against railings, their bodies were trampled; one was said to have died after an assault in a side street. As in previous marches on Parliament, Caxton Hall served as a first-aid center and rallying point for the suffragette army. All afternoon, women went there to rest and to have their wounds bathed and bandaged and their torn clothing repaired before plunging back into the maelstrom. For six hours the struggle continued. Not until the evening was Parliament Square finally cleared of invaders.

It was a shabby, Pyrrhic victory. Churchill's tactics were discarded, but not the mentality that had prompted them. The Cat-and-Mouse Act of 1913 gave the Government power to release imprisoned suffragettes on "tickets of leave" (which were often openly raffled to raise funds) until they were physically fit enough to return to prison. This, added to forcible feeding, was an attempt to thwart the hunger-and-thirst-strike tactics by which the women sought to shorten their sentences. It was one of the shabbiest pieces of legislation ever to be pushed through Parliament—and one of the most ludicrous, for it gave the Women's Revolution a new dimension of dignity and martyrdom.

Sylvia Pankhurst, Emmeline's daughter (who between June, 1913, and June, 1914, survived ten successive hunger-and-thirst strikes), wrote from prison: "I am fighting, fighting, fighting. I have four, five and six wardresses every day, as well as the two doctors. I am fed by stomach tube twice a day. I resist all the time." A steel gag lacerated her mouth, and she once paced her cell for twenty-eight hours on end to weaken herself and gain release.

The aftereffects of such experiences could be cruel and lasting. When an ex-prisoner had her first food and drink, her pulses throbbed agonizingly, her skin flushed and broke out in eczema, her

bowels refused to work, sleep was impossible. "The extremities remain very red for some days and are often swollen and burning like
a great chilblain," wrote Sylvia, "heart and nervous symptoms often
persist for some time. It was usually the second day after my release,
in any case the day after the first meeting [timed to take place as
soon as prisoners were freed], that I had an absolute collapse. 24
hours of blinding headache and acute illness of the whole frame.
For five years afterwards I suffered substantially from the effects."
In July, 1914, Dr. Flora Murray, who devoted herself to the care of
Mrs. Pankhurst and other militant prisoners, reported that after
three days in Holloway, Mrs. Pankhurst had lost nearly fourteen
pounds, was suffering grievously from nausea and gastric disturbance, and had an irregular pulse. The carefully disseminated knowledge of such sufferings drove George Lansbury to shout at Asquith
in the Commons: "You will go down to history as the man who tortured innocent women. You ought to be driven from public life!"

The Women's Revolution grew more tumultuous. At the end of
May, 1914, Mrs. Pankhurst, surrounded by an Amazonian bodyguard twirling Indian clubs or armed with whips, led a deputation
to Buckingham Palace. Since the politicians would give no justice,
perhaps the sovereign might. A strong police cordon repulsed wave
after wave of women, and Mrs. Pankhurst herself was seized under
the arms by a burly policeman and yanked off her feet. She described the incident in a letter to Ethel Smyth. "Fortunately for me I
have 'young bones' or my ribs would all have been fractured. After
it I suffered from a form of nausea just like very bad sea-sick-
ness. . . . It was a gallant fight, a hundred against thousands.
Many of the prisoners were novices, militant for the first time, and
almost all adopted the hunger-and-thirst strike. Think what it means
for a first experience of prison to do the whole thing, and be ready
to do it again! O my splendid ones!"

Sylvia Pankhurst was busy rousing the cockneys of London's
East End. A May Day procession to Victoria Park, complete with
maypoles and children in festive dresses, was brutally broken up.
Women, reported Sylvia, were seized by the breasts and had their
arms twisted and their hair pulled. Though twenty of them had
been chained together (with Sylvia in the middle), the padlocks
were smashed open by blows from police truncheons.

But the pressure was telling. After years of prevarication, the Government showed signs of wavering. With another General Election in the offing and with the Labour Party resolved to make votes for women one of the main planks in its platform, Prime Minister Asquith agreed to receive a deputation of women from the East End, and Christabel wrote wistfully in *The Suffragette:* "The militants will rejoice when victory comes, and yet, mixed with their joy will be regret that the most glorious chapter in women's history is closed and the militant fight over—over, while so many have not yet known the exaltation, the rapture, of battle."

Then, suddenly, the Women's Revolution was confronted with the Great War. Together with the NUWSS and other suffrage groups, the WSPU called a truce and paused to work out its attitude toward this new and overwhelming catastrophe. Mrs. Pankhurst and Christabel were quick to adjust. Instinctively and deeply patriotic, they also knew that national emergencies have a way of bulldozing prejudices, hustling politicians, and providing unexpected opportunities.

The first need was to break off the old campaign with a formula of honor. Mrs. Fawcett told her followers: "Let us prove ourselves worthy of citizenship whether our claim is recognised or not." Mrs. Pankhurst exhorted her troops to put themselves unreservedly behind the war effort. They could—they deserved to—rest on their laurels and hold themselves in readiness for the fight that might still lie ahead after the Central Powers had been defeated. After all, she reasoned, "what would be the good of a vote without a country to vote in?"

Olive Schreiner had already pointed out that the increasing mechanization of war meant that women could easily become effective soldiers, that "the nation which is the first to employ women may be placed at a vast advantage over its fellows in time of war." The British Government did not seem to appreciate this; and since it was widely assumed that the fighting would be over by Christmas, it seemed unlikely that women would take much part in it.

But the war went on, and the barriers went down. Despite the hostility of male trade unionists, the number of women employed in industry in Britain increased by more than a million. About seven hundred thousand directly replaced men, and it was estimated that,

of these, some four hundred thousand were refugees from the rigors
and pittance wages of domestic service. Other women took over a
vast miscellany of jobs—digging graves, tilling the land, lighting
streetlamps, delivering mail, conducting buses, painting houses,
driving cars and hearses, toting baggage at railway stations. One
military hospital was wholly staffed and administered by women.
More than one hundred thousand of them joined the new Women's
Auxilary Corps, which worked with the Army, the Navy, and the Air
Force.

Directing this tremendous social revolution was a comparative
handful of women. Many were suffragettes or suffragists, trained
and toughened by years of agitation. Some entered the fray in a
spirit of ironic detachment. Those who were insatiable but theretofore frustrated individualists looked for adventure. For many of
them, the war was something of a paradox. It was the product of the
blundering of male politicians, of male thinking. It was, therefore, a
disgrace and might never have happened if women had been given
their fair share in policy making. But it *had* happened, and it was up
to women to make it a little more tolerable, a little tidier, a little
more efficient, than it might have been without their help.

A smaller, and immensely courageous, band of women dedicated
themselves to fighting the war mentality with all their strength.
They were determined to do something more than merely clean up
the mess men made. Among them were Sylvia Pankhurst, Mrs.
Swanwick, and Mrs. Despard (ironically enough, the sister of Field
Marshal Sir John French, Commander in Chief of the British Expeditionary Force). A number of women, including Catherine Marshall, once Parliamentary Secretary to the NUWSS, helped male
pacifists to organize their struggle against conscription.

But all this lay in an unimagined and unimaginable future. On
August 3, 1914, hundreds of suffragettes, the shock troops of the
women's war, were still shut up in prisons all over England, Wales,
Scotland, and Ireland. Some had been forcibly fed three times a day
for weeks, and prison doctors had been ordered to increase the dose
to four times a day. In Holloway Prison, when war—and an amnesty
for political prisoners—had been declared, a sly and much-resented
attempt was made to inveigle individual prisoners to sign a pledge
not to resume militancy. But Grace Roe, who had been forcibly fed

three hundred times, managed, though her throat was almost unbearably inflamed and her voice weak and hoarse, to shout from her cell a warning that no one was to do anything, that everything would be settled outside at high level.

Outside, on his own high but misinformed level, the Kaiser was said to be counting on the support of the suffragettes against the British Government they had done so much to shake and discredit.

The Recruiters

Two Novelists, a Nurse, and a Student

The first apparent lesson of the Great War was that when the country was in a tight corner, men were still indisputably cocks of the walk. As the author of *Soliloquies of a Subaltern,* a volume of best-selling verse published in 1915, put it in a poem entitled "The Women's Share":

> Ours but the waiting part, and ours to give,
> To patiently endure without a word;
> And if our dearest die, 'tis ours to live
> Though death may be a thousandfold preferred.
> The history of our times won't mention us,
> 'Tis so indeed that we would have it be;
> Let men have all that may seem glorious,
> Let us but feel our part is known to Thee.

While men did the fighting, it was women's role to say good-bye, bear dead heroes' babies, and lure or browbeat men into the forces. At Folkestone, the White Feather Movement was launched by peppery Admiral Penrose Fitzgerald. After delivering a patriotic speech from the bandstand, he assembled a squad of young women whose task it was to patrol the "front" presenting white feathers of cowardice to all young men in mufti. Jingo booklets by the dozen urged women to use their charms and wiles to increase the number of volunteers in Britain, which did not yet have conscription.

Baroness Orczy, the famous romantic novelist, founded the Women of England's Active Service League, whose manifesto an-

nounced: "Your hour has come! . . . You know me, don't you? Together we have laughed and cried over that dauntless Englishman,
the Scarlet Pimpernel, and thrilled over the brave days of his
League. Now we shall form ourselves into an Active Service League,
whose sole object will be that of influencing our men to offer themselves at once to the nearest recruiting officer." Members of her
League had to sign a form that read: "At this hour of England's
peril, I do hereby pledge myself most solemnly in the name of my
King and Country to persuade every man I know to offer his service
to his country. I also pledge myself never to be seen in public with
any man who, being in every way fit and free for service, has refused to respond to his country's call." The Baroness asked for one
hundred thousand volunteers. She got twenty thousand, and their
names and addresses were inscribed on an honor roll that was presented to the King.

Another novelist, Sarah Macnaughtan, went to work in a hospital
in Belgium. A few months later, she was writing in her diary: "I
think I have seen too much pain lately. . . . There is a peculiar
brutality which seems to possess everyone. Always I am reminded of
birds on a small ledge pushing each other into the sea. The big bird
that pushes another one over goes to sleep comfortably." Yet, despite her private doubts, she thought it her duty to return to Britain
and urge the munitions-producing masses to greater efforts in a
series of flag-waving lectures.

She began with the Vickers-Maxim works at Erith. Her audience
was easily stirred by her stories of suffering and self-sacrifice. She
noted: "In some of the hushes that came one could hear men crying." At Glasgow she had a tougher job. "Red Clydeside," as the newspapers called it, was the nerve center of socialist, or plain working-
class, resistance to a "capitalist" war. William Gallacher, chairman
of the Clyde Workers' Committee, told an enthusiastic audience: "We
are accustomed to hear Irish Nationalists declare that England's adversity is Ireland's opportunity; I say that the adversity of the capitalist class is the opportunity of the working class. Let us take advantage
of it!" In the Glasgow streets, the famous Kitchener poster—YOUR
KING AND COUNTRY NEED YOU—was scribbled over with
disbelieving doggerel:

Your King and Country Need You,
Ye hardy sons of toil,
But will your King and Country need you
When they're sharing out the spoil?

The Clyde Workers' Committee, which later included two women, had been formed to safeguard the interests of the workers in the great Glasgow shipyards and munition factories against the "treachery" of official trade union leaders, now collaborating closely with the Government. During 1915, backed by the threat of a general strike, it virtually dictated its own terms. Glasgow housewives, threatened with eviction because of their refusal to pay soaring rents, organized a no-rent campaign, and gathered in militant mobs to drive away rent collectors. When a huge procession of women and workers converged on the Sheriff's Court, rent restriction was hurriedly enforced. Ramsay MacDonald declared that a visit to Glasgow, with its bracing socialist priorities, was like a spiritual tonic. To Miss Macnaughtan it was a spiritual outrage. She set herself to "arouse slackers and tell rotters about what is going on out there," and addressed seven meetings in a week. "At one place," she wrote, "I spoke from a lorry in the dinner hour. All the men, with blackened faces, crowded round, some swung from the iron girders, others perched, like queer bronze images, on pieces of machinery." To her surprise, she found them polite and not inclined to interrupt, stunned into silence by the war horror photographs she displayed, and mindful of the three cheers due to a lady.

Sometimes she was puzzled by a feeling of unreality about the lecture campaign. But "England," she reassured herself, "did not realise the war, she did not realise the wave of heroism that is sweeping over the world, and I had to tell about it." In South Wales, another center of deep industrial unrest, she gave fourteen talks in less than two weeks: "Every day I used to have tea and an egg at five o'clock, and a motor would come to take me to different places of meeting. It was generally up the Rhondda Valley that we went. I spoke in chapels, from the pulpit, and this gave me the chance to speak my mind to these people and ask them and *teach* them what Power and Possession and Freedom really meant. Oh it was wonderful! The rapt faces of the miners, the hush of the big buildings, and then the sudden burst of cheering!" She remembered how at one meeting "there was a bumptious-looking man with a bald head. He took up his position just over the clock in the gallery, listened critically, talked a good deal, and made remarks. I began to speak straight at him, and quite suddenly I saw him, as I spoke of our men at the war, cover his face and burst into tears."

Under the chairmanship of Lord James Bryce, a celebrated jurist (and a determined opponent of women's emancipation), the Committee of Enquiry into German Atrocities spared nothing—and, perhaps in the interests of Allied propaganda, exaggerated—in its report. With grave reiteration, it piled up the evidence of atravistic horrors: pregnant women violated and bayoneted; women with their breasts slashed, their legs cut off; women publicly raped in the marketplace of Liége; babies bayoneted and crucified to doors by their hands and feet; whole families burned alive; civilians machine-gunned en masse; priests tortured and murdered. But it was the firsthand accounts of women who by some chance had been in the thick of the fight that played most tellingly on the twanging nerves of the supposedly torpid British public. Publishers and ghost-writers worked overtime to hammer their jottings into shape and sustain the calculated assault.

Sister Joan Martin-Nicholson, for instance, told of her experiences when stranded in Belgium by the speed of the German advance. Disguised as a peasant woman in borrowed skirt and shawl and sabots, she wandered about Brussels and Louvain ("I had to keep up a rather broad banter with the soldiers, and suffer the indignity of being chucked under the chin"). She claimed to have seen children run over by German military vehicles that raced recklessly through the streets, carrying senior officers to their destination and having a bit of sport on the way: "I heard screaming mothers brutally told, as they clasped their dead babies to their breasts, to teach their brats how to cross the streets in wartime." In Louvain, she wrote, the pavements were stained with blood. She saw charred corpses, old people sitting helplessly among the ruins of their homes. Turning a corner, she "tripped over something lying very still in the sun. Golden-haired, with her little face buried in the dust and her tiny fingers piteously outstretched, lay a little girl of about six, and between her shoulder blades shone a knife-edged bayonet. Sick at heart, I drew out the blade and cleaned the blood-stained face, and, covering her with an old sack, gently laid her to rest among some bushes at the end of a garden."

Ordered to work under the Germans at the Hôpital Militaire in Brussels, she found herself "the only woman in the place among more than a thousand of the enemy." The punctilious colonel in command allotted her a bodyguard who followed her everywhere with a fixed bayonet; he had her moved to another room because of the proximity of some slightly wounded German officers who had been given rooms near hers. "They have been in the war for six weeks, away from women," he said ominously. "I could not trust them even if you were behind steel doors!" Sister Martin-Nicholson said nothing: "I just looked the man in the eyes, bringing a dark flush to the stern cheeks, and turned silently to pack." Crossing the court-yard, a major jeered at her with a group of soldiers standing around: "He insulted my country, scoffed at my King, reviled my Navy. I got whiter and whiter with rage under the torrent of abuse. 'And your Army, ach Liebe Gott!' he almost screamed, and one soldier put his fingers to his nose and cried 'Schweinhunden!' There was one moment of breathless silence as they waited to see what the English-woman would say. . . . I left their Kaiser, their country, their Army and their Navy alone, but like a tigress I fastened on their Kultur, their honour and their faith. My words lashed and struck and drove the blood to their sallow faces. They silently made way for me to pass."

Perhaps the most provocative and vivid report was Phyllis Camp-bell's *Back of the Front*, a slim volume published early in 1915. When war broke out, Miss Campbell, who had been rescued by an aunt from her studies at a German university, was staying with aristo-cratic French friends in a large country house not far from Paris in the forest of Marly. When the news of mobilization came, the gay, flirtatious house party broke up, the laughter stilled. With her friends, she took a crash course in surgical nursing and reported for duty at a railway-*cum*-dressing station in the forest. Belgian refu-gees started to pour in. She saw a child with its head almost severed from its body, still held protectively in the arms of an old man crazed with grief. She wrote: "In one wagon, sitting on the floor, was a naked girl of about 23. One of her suffering sisters, more fortunate than the rest in possessing an undergarment, had torn it in half and covered the front of her poor body. It was saturated with blood from her cut-off breasts. On her knees lay a little baby, dead. There were women covered with sabre cuts, women who had been whipped, women burned alive escaping from their blazing homes, little boys maimed in the hands and feet, their wounds done up in sacking or any kind of old rag."

Then came the wounded soldiers from the front: "The train came slowly, crawling out of the forest, and before it came a low, awful crying. Some of the doors were shut, and a red stream slowly oozed under them. At one side of a door sat a soldier who had lost both his legs, and he was supporting a boy whose arms were gone. . . . One Highlander implored me to run away—'Get awa', lassie,' he said, heavily. 'They're no' men, they're devils!' His dying eyes seemed to look at an awful something beyond us. 'Oh, women, dear,' he said, but he could say no more. . . ." Delirious soldiers insisted that they had seen heavenly visions at Mons. One Tommy was caring for a small boy he had picked up on the road. He had been able to do this because of a lull in the headlong retreat caused by "a kind of golden cloud between us and the Germans, and a man on a big horse. . . . St. George it must have been. . . ."

At the big house, Pierre, the old forester, reported the fate of a solitary marauder, whom he had discovered torturing a kitten tied to a tree. "I killed the dirty Boche. Oh, I assure you, he died thoroughly, that one." Miss Campbell, tired as she was by her harrowing day's work, hastened to treat the kitten's wounds. "I sat down and bandaged the little black hand. Of all the devilish cruelties I had seen, none so brought home to me the utter depravity of the German soul. . . . It seemed to me that all the wickedness, all the fear and filthiness unimaginable that exists can be summed up in one word: GERMAN." She was convinced that Germans were a race apart. They even *looked* different: "When I saw the German prisoners and went about, like all the others, holding my nose, when they stood blinking in the sun with their square heads and putty-coloured faces, their colourless eyes and lashes, it suggested to me a creation of some monstrous spirit of evil. Is it strange that saints and angels should fight against this dreadful foe? I have seen no vision, but in my heart I believe that the Captains of God are leading the Allies to

Victory." And in this victory, France, apparently so corrupt and de-
generate, had a special part to play. She was going to wipe the stain
of conquest away; "France was suddenly stripped bare to the soul,
and behold! that soul was a pure white light of knightly splen-
dour. . . ."

2 ❧

The Pankhursts Change Fronts

In July, 1914, Mrs. Emmeline Pankhurst, emaciated and tottering
from the effects of her twelfth hunger, thirst, and sleep strike in less
than a year, crossed the Channel to join her friend Ethel Smyth,
who was vacationing at a small resort on the coast of Brittany. According to the British Government, she was a criminal on the run,
with a sentence of three years' penal servitude (of which she had
served only thirty days) hanging over her, and liable to rearrest and
reimprisonment as soon as she came back to England. While the
mannish Miss Smyth played golf, Mrs. Pankhurst swam in the
sea—a pleasure that she had not known for some twenty-five years.
Amazingly soon, the health and sparkle of this ailing but fantas-
tically resilient woman returned.

Christabel joined her at St. Malo. Both felt that the Liberal Government was on the verge of capitulation. Together they planned
the tactics of the final push. It was an exciting moment. Then came
news of the assassination of the Austrian Archduke at Sarajevo; and
a couple of days later, the German waiters, who had been placidly
serving their hotel meals, mysteriously vanished, and Europe was at
war.

The war might not last more than a few months, so perhaps, as
Mrs. Pankhurst said in an interim message to the WSPU, the time
could be used to rest and regroup for the suffrage battle that might
still lie ahead. Certainly Mrs. Pankhurst needed to relax. For years,
as the traveling evangelist of militancy, she had lived out of suit-

cases or in prison cells (the darling of wardresses, the terror of would-be forcible feeders). Her second son, Harry, had become seriously ill while she was in the United States on a lecture tour (her WSPU salary never exceeded £200 year, and it was always a struggle to make ends meet) and had died soon after her return. Her sister, Mary, a faithful disciple, had died as a result of her treatment in prison. There had been a rift with her Socialist daughter, Sylvia. When she considered the private wreckage left by her whirlwind public life, she must have longed to stop being a leader for a while.

Christabel helped to brace her mother for new efforts. Always she had been driven by a fierce, consuming shame at women's feeble acceptance of their degrading position in society. The spirit of revolt that forced women to fight for the vote was to her the important thing, for it signified the beginning of the end of the slave mentality. She had never been able to tolerate weakness and had roused many a suffragette audience by telling them in her clear, ringing voice: "You are already emancipated!"

Helped by Jessie Kenney and other devoted secretaries, she had (under the alias of Amy Richards) for more than two years generaled the movement from a tiny flat in Paris, despite an attempt— which the French Government had refused—to have her extradited. Week after week, articles for *The Suffragette* and plans of campaign had flowed from her cool and calculating brain and were smuggled by secret routes to the printers. For four months, after police raids had dislocated the work of WSPU headquarters in London, Jessie Kenney (alias Mary Fordyce) had stayed in Scotland to copy-edit *The Suffragette,* first in Glasgow, then in Edinburgh, while Grace Roe, the latest recruit to the WSPU's inner circle, schemed her way to and from Paris to bring back more copy.

Christabel was a strikingly attractive woman, with fresh colouring and a flawless skin, a plump and delicately featured face, heavily lidded, brilliantly blue eyes, and a smooth forehead topped by a mass of soft brown hair. But she did not encourage male admirers or even bother with anyone who could not advance The Cause in some way. She and Jessie, helped by influential French friends, had lived a life of conventual, almost claustrophic, dedication, a world away from the heckling and missiles of British by-elections, where the crowds had roared, "We want Chris!"

It was during 1913 that Christabel first began to make a serious study of the Bible. In the last prewar issue of *The Suffragette*, which appeared on August 7, 1914, a report on "The Inferno of Holloway" (where prisoners had been forcibly fed for periods ranging from three to thirteen weeks) mingled with the now familiar denunciations of the white-slave traffic and an exultant Old Testament interpretation of the causes of the impending war. "A dreadful warcloud," she wrote, "seems about to burst and deluge the people of Europe with fire, slaughter and ruin. . . . A man-made civilisation, hideous and cruel enough in time of peace, is to be destroyed. . . . This great war is God's vengeance upon the people who held women in subjection, and by doing that have destroyed the perfect human balance. Had women been equal partners with men from the beginning, human civilisation would have been very different. For that which has made men from generations past sacrifice women and the race to their lusts is now making them fly at each other's throats. Women of the WSPU, we must protect our Union through everything. . . . Let us strive unceasingly that the world may learn from the tragedy by which it is menaced, that for the sake of the divinity that is in the human race, women must be free."

She did not believe that the war would be short, but she saw that it would provide a new field for the exercise of her heaven-sent strategic sense. With her flair for leadership, she could bring women into the very heart of the war, into the places of power and decision. She could show men how to campaign with a total, unsentimental efficiency. What point was there in waging war on any other terms?

Apart from Christabel's enthusiasm, there were personal memories ready to catch at Mrs. Pankhurst's romantic sense of allegiance. Ever since, as a girl of fourteen, she had been sent to school in Paris just after the Franco-Prussian War of 1870, she had been vehemently Francophile. She had made friends with the daughter of a French Marquis who had been a hero of the Paris Commune and had learned the tricks of elegance that were to make her such a strikingly unfrumpish ornament of the suffrage movement. She would, indeed, have married a French writer if her father had been willing to supply the necessary dowry—and she continued to advocate the dowry system because of the financial independence it gave a woman. She had even been born on Bastille Day. Could it be wrong to fight for her beloved France, to fight for what Christabel insisted was the right—for could anything be imagined more repellent, more woman-hating, and more woman-subjecting than the spirit of Prussianism? In some such way did the old cause and the new merge and fuse in her mind.

Meantime, Grace Roe, Chief Organizer of the WSPU, was making arrangements for the exiled Christabel to return and outline her war policy. At the London Opera House, on September 8, 1914, Christabel faced her first large audience since her escape from London. Her admirers queued in the aisles to present her with bouquets that were arranged in a semicircle at her feet. The stage was hung with dark-green velvet, and on it Christabel appeared alone, in a flowing gown of her favorite pale green, slender, graceful, and dramatized by a shaft of limelight.

The time and money spent on fighting the suffragettes, she said, would have been better devoted to preparing to fight the Germans. A German victory would mean a disastrous check to women's progress toward equal citizenship. Militant women should be willing to go into the firing line if necessary, but at least it was their plain duty to rouse the militancy of men to match the self-sacrifice of France and Belgium. Talk of pacifism was a luxury, and "Socialists and advanced liberals must realise that the whole system of democratic government for men as well as women is at stake." They must not be sidetracked by talk of the Russian bogey, but must concentrate on one danger at a time. Above all, they must beware of the blandishments of "that vague cosmopolitanism which is detached from love of one's country. Our love for another country is absolutely worthless unless we love our own."

She was convinced that the war would have some beneficial results. It would, surely, "sweep away the jealousy, the suicidal folly, which have made of our country two opposing camps—enfranchised men in the one, voteless women in the other." If women had been trained for industry, there would have been no sudden industrial crisis, with its threat to the supply of munitions. "There must," argued Christabel, "be an end to class privilege, and a system of national rationing should be enforced to put an end to a state of affairs in which some people are starved out of patriotism."

She knew that the suffrage was as good as won, even if it was in cold storage. Her aim now was to swing the women of Britain into the bigger struggle of the moment, and, typically, she eliminated everything that might hamper victory, considered everything in the baleful but fascinating light of war. The WSPU as she and her devotees had known it was finished. Many in her audience were captured by her new realism, but others were puzzled by the apparent abandonment of even a "watchful waiting" policy in regard to the vote. Victor Duval, of the Men's Political Union for Women's Enfranchisement, interrupted her speech with the old cry of "Votes for Women!" To which she replied curtly: "We cannot discuss that now."

In the next four years, she and her mother, Mrs. Drummond, Annie and Jessie Kenney, Grace Roe, and other stalwarts of the new-style WSPU were to hear that cry from the past as they traveled Britain whipping up the war effort. For, as before, it was the *spirit* of warfare that engrossed Christabel, the heart of the whirlwind where she felt most at peace. She had to ignore those who were unable to move with the times, people like Alice Beale, for instance, a suffragette who continued to fight on the old, deserted front. Miss Beale declined to complete her National Registration Form and told the magistrate: "I refuse, without the safeguard of the vote, to help the Government in any way to build up the lost trade of the country on the forced labour and sweated work of myself and my fellow-women. I refuse to take part in a plot to force men, against their will, to give their lives in defence of this country."

As time went on, there were signs of wider revolt against the Pankhurst leadership. In November, 1915, members and ex-members of the WSPU held a meeting of censure. They complained that WSPU funds were being used for purposes outside the scope of its written constitution, and that no annual report or financial statement had been issued by headquarters since spring, 1914. It was, said these rebels, "a matter of the utmost importance that Mrs. Pankhurst, as Hon. Treasurer, should without further delay issue a report and a duly audited balance sheet and statement of accounts, showing especially how funds have been dealt with since the beginning of the war. In regard to Miss Christabel Pankhurst, it would seem obvious that the time has now come when she should resign her association with the Union as one of its leaders, or offer a clear explanation to the members of her continued absence from this country at a time when the services of all women of capacity are so sorely needed." A group led by Miss Charlotte "Charlie" Marsh, a veteran of well over a hundred forcible feedings, broke away to form what they called the Independent WSPU (duly repudiated by Mrs. Pankhurst), which concerned itself with the encroachments of the state acting through the Defence of the Realm Act and continued to agitate for the vote.

Miss Marsh was soon won back to the fold when, at Mrs. Pankhurst's suggestion, she became Lloyd George's official driver. As Minister of Munitions, he was keen to get as many women as possible into the nation's factories and, as a gesture of appeasement to the WSPU, on whom he relied to lead a recruiting drive, particularly asked for a suffragette chauffeuse.

One other critic got rougher handling. Miss Annie Bell, an ex-militant who interrupted a patriotic harangue by Mrs. Pankhurst at the London Pavilion, was shouted down as a "pro-German." She was refused admittance to the next WSPU meeting, and when she protested vigorously, according to the free speech formula laid down by her former leader, she was arrested, charged with obstruction, and sentenced to one month's imprisonment. She hunger-struck and was released after five days. The Pankhurst wheel had turned a full, ironic circle.

3 &

Pankhursts versus Huns

Emmeline and Christabel were, however, soaring far beyond the reach of minority criticism. They were scanning wider horizons. At the outbreak of war, the ever-buoyant Annie Kenney, Christabel's deputy since 1912, had been sent to the United States on a lecture tour. In this way, it was thought, one WSPU leader at least would be saved from the disaster (feared by Christabel) of a German breakthrough in France and a snap invasion of Britain. Short of money but full of charm and resource, Annie toured North Dakota, Montana, and Nevada; and when the last two states became the first in America to give women the vote, the Pankhursts could claim that the long arm of the WSPU had played its part in that victory.

Just as Annie Kenney ended her American tour, Christabel began hers, and the two met in a New York hotel to discuss Annie's next assignment. Her instructions were to learn as much as she could, as quickly as she could, about the Balkans, in order to launch a Save-the-Balkans campaign in England (Christabel already had strong ideas about Allied strategy). So Annie cabled back to headquarters in London excitedly: HAVE TO SPEAK ON BALKANS STOP GET ME ALL BOOKS POSSIBLE. After two weeks of intensive study, she made her first "Balkan" speech in Huddersfield.

Accompanied by an aide (Miss Olive Bartels, a young WSPU organizer), Christabel stayed for six months in America, making contracts at the highest level and talking about the war and women's part in it to enormous audiences in New York, Chicago, Washington, Indianapolis, Minneapolis, and, later, in various towns in Canada. She got a mixed reception on arrival. When the dutifully neutralist New York suffrage societies heard that Miss Pankhurst's speech was to be unashamedly pro-Allies, they were dutifully shocked. Mrs. Raymond Bacon, President of the New York State Woman Suffrage Association, refused to countenance her. But Miss Pankhurst was unrepentant. When reporters reminded her that President Wilson had asked all citizens not to enter into partisan discussions, she retorted: "If America is to take an intelligent part in the peace program at the end of the war, she must have an intelligent understanding of the conditions which brought it on. It seems to me time that America listened to both sides. I notice everywhere the activities of the German press bureau. It surely is not worse to hear partisan arguments than to read them."

Despite this brush, or perhaps because of it, Carnegie Hall was packed to capacity for the suffragette mastermind's first speech on October 24, 1914. Certainly her appearance was utterly disarming. "A pink-cheeked slip of a girl," said the *New York Tribune*, "with fluffy yellow hair, in a gown of white satin and pale green chiffon, she looked so dainty and appealing that more than one in the audience was moved to say she didn't see how Asquith could have done it." There was no undue disturbance, though a special squad of police officers was on duty outside.

Many of her listeners remembered the power of her mother's molten oratory, for Mrs. Pankhurst had several times visited America before the war. They discovered that Miss Pankhurst, though less passionate in style, was also a great and courageous speaker. When the strains of the "Battle Hymn of the Republic," sung by a massed choir, had died away, the elegant figure in the green-and-white gown did not hesitate to hammer home truths.

Serbia, she said, might be tiny and remote, but Serbia, too, had a soul and a love of liberty; and to preserve that liberty, the Balkan state was making sacrifices "almost unimaginable to the people of a nation such as this, who are living in safety far from the scene of war." Her speech was touched with a special emotion when she spoke of France, where for the first time she herself had known a measure of personal independence, a private life, and a home of her own. "France," she told her Carnegie Hall audience, "is in some senses the greatest and most glorious nation in the world." It was the duty of America, as well as Britain, to fight alongside her. "If you let that country be destroyed which has given so much to you . . . retribution will come upon you, freedom will desert this world. Be sure of that!"

Americans talked of the need for an international police force, but she maintained that the Allied Armies were acting as such. Germany had refused to submit her case to arbitration and certainly had no more love for America than for any other nation. If Germany conquered Belgium, France, and Britain, she would cross the Atlantic. Then what would happen to Americans, including those idealists who still went on saying that all war was wrong? "I challenge that statement," said Christabel fiercely, "with all the power I have at my disposal." Then she showed that gift of illustration that had made her one of the most feared and respected speakers in Britain. "Was *your* war against a British Government wrong?" she demanded. "As an Englishwoman, I say that when you fought us for the right of self-government, you did right. I am glad you fought us and I am glad you beat us. I think you taught us a lesson about governing that has cemented our Empire and its strength today. We lost you, but we gained so much else. We were as much in the wrong in that war as Germany is in the wrong today."

She even managed one of those near-epigrammatic flashes (the

Pankhursts were good at epigrams, whether original with them or not: "Give us justice or give us prison," "Give us liberty or give us death," they had told Asquith) that had delighted Max Beerbohm at prewar by-elections. The Germans, she said, appealed for *Lebensraum* because of an increasing birthrate. They ignored the fact that the Slav birthrate was even higher. And, in any case, could they seriously maintain that a high birthrate was the final test of a nation's position in the world? Quality was more important then mere quantity. "We cannot," she quipped, "be bullied by birthrates."

She had little difficulty in dealing with questioners. How could suffragettes cooperate with a Government that had so cruelly persecuted them and denied them their rights? "I have told you we are not fighting for the Government. We are supporting the country. The Government is the instrument through which the war has to be fought." To an irate questioner who wished she had spoken more about the rights of Ireland while she was talking about the rights of small nations, she replied that there was a Home Rule Bill on the statute books, and, after all, Irish men at least had the vote, and because of it they even held the balance of power in the British Parliament. How, then, could Ireland be compared with Belgium or Serbia?

It was a masterly performance, the first considered statement about Allied war aims—and possibly the best—made by a Briton in the United States.

When she returned to Paris, she established close touch with an old antagonist, Lloyd George—a man of destiny now in her eyes, by comparison with the tired and treacherous trio of Asquith, Haldane, and Grey. She began to move in a world of VIP's and special passes and powerful notes and smoothed paths. Alfred Harmsworth, Lord Northcliffe, acknowledged her ability and promised to put his papers behind the demand for votes for women. In Paris, she was able to keep her finger on the pulse of the war, to meet leading politicians and writers and military men, and to report on the balance of forces in France, on the latest rumors and the realities behind them. Seldom can Britain (let alone a slippery, visionmongering politician like Lloyd George) have had such a zealous and brilliant representative. She was blazing a trail in the hitherto closed jungle of male politics.

In April, 1915, *The Suffragette* reappeared, just in time to con-
demn the "folly" of the International Congress of Women for Peace
held at The Hague, and giving a new and characteristically clear-
cut lead to the loyal rump of the old WSPU. "This paper," trum-
peted Christabel, "has always sought to rouse women to a sense of
their personal dignity and importance and of their rights as individuals, so quite naturally and logically, in the present national crisis,
our appeal is to the patriotism of women. The supreme reason why
we fought for the vote is to make British civilisation even finer. We
suffragettes are no believers in that sham internationalism which is
really disloyalty and anti-nationalism. With Mazzini we believe that
'our country is the token of the mission which God has given us to
fulfil to humanity.' . . . Anti-suffragism in Britain is virtually dead,
but in a grosser form is glorified and enthroned and more alive than
ever in Prussia. A woman's deepest instinct and her reason tell her
that Prussia stands for all that is deadly to woman spirit in the
world. We will not be Prussianised!"

It was a sparkling tour de force, and Mrs. Pankhurst followed
up by giving a queenly press interview in London. "I believe," she
told reporters, "that the country is ready for national service. Now
we have a non-Party Government it will be possible for our women
to do something to help. We are experts in organisation, and can
also help to create the right sort of feeling among the people. This
is not the time for criticism, but for readiness to help. When we,
formerly implacable critics of the Government, say this, we hope it
will have some weight." She advocated the proclamation of a national state of emergency, of martial law. This should be done "in
a dramatic manner, from all the high places of the kingdom at the
same time, by mayors in the towns, officials in the country, in thea-
tres and churches—wherever the people gather together. I suggest
Empire Day would be a good time to do it."

Old admirers and old opponents were astonished to see her at
a Queen's Hall meeting in her new role. Mrs. Swanwick watched her
as she sat on the platform, apparently approving, while a male
speaker, a prewar reactionary of the deepest dye, maintained that
the stewards at prewar Liberal meetings had been Huns. "You will
remember," he shouted, "with what brutality they treated the

women?" Then, after a dramatic pause: "It was not for nothing that they spoke in a guttural foreign accent."

Mrs. Pankhurst was on the road again, speaking in music halls, in movie theaters, in civic halls in London and the main provincial cities. Men, she told them, had claimed the right to protect the nation and its women in time of war. Yet the men of Belgium, France, and Serbia, however willing, had been unable to do it, and it was sheer good luck that British women, on British soil, were still safe from the horrors of the Continent. The least, she thought, that men could do was to make sure that every man of fighting age redeemed his word to women, to save them from outrages too vile—and she had witnessed the results of them (she had been one of the chosen few admitted to an atrocity exhibition where, among other horrors, multilated Belgian babies, carefully preserved to make mute propaganda, were on view)—to think of. She told her audiences that women, eager to do their bit on the home front, were bitter when they saw men who should be in the firing lines skulking in factories. Surely it was better to die a glorious death in the defense of liberty, honor, and the national inheritance than to live a long, inglorious life? She was convinced, she said—and this sentiment always brought long and loud applause—that the war was a trial out of which "we shall emerge better and nobler and more worthy of our great traditions than ever we should have been without it."

It was a routine recruiting speech, but it was delivered with complete conviction in that extraordinarily thrilling voice, capable of every nuance of pathos and defiance, that had swayed vast crowds, given new impact to the suffrage movement, and melted hardened magistrates and policemen to tears. Taking her cue from Christabel in *The Suffragette,* she delivered violent attacks on progressives, pacifists, and all who refused to surrender to the mood of the moment. Ramsay MacDonald, whom she had long detested for his hostility to the suffragettes, was, she accused, with his talk of pacifism, in effect "more German than the Germans"; and so were the contemptible subversives of the Union of Democratic Control ("Norman Angell: Is He Working for Germany?" asked Christabel in *The Suffragette*) and such intellectual playboys as Bertrand Russell, who maintained that soldiers would be brutalized and morally

degraded and that gallant Serbia was in reality a murderous, barbarous backwater. This last contention particularly angered the
Pankhursts, who, helped by such experts as Professor Seton Watson,
the *Times* correspondent Wickham Steed, and, later, by the exiled
Czech patriot Professor Tomáš Masaryk (who in 1915 come to live
in London), had made a special study of the Balkans. Annie Kenney
and Mrs. Pankhurst featured the grievances of Serbia and Rumania
in their speeches, and Christabel, perhaps influenced by French
strategy, insisted on the military wisdom as well as the political justice of a great campaign of liberation in the Balkans. Annie even
visited newspaper editors to try to persuade them to give promi-
nence to these views, which were shared by Lloyd George, the
Pankhursts' new ally. Christabel was in close touch with another influential Czech exile, Dr. Eduard Beneš, in Paris, and determined to
air her inside information to good effect.

She supplied her little group of agitators with suitable ammunition. For Russell to accuse Serbia of being barbarous, said Mrs.
Pankhurst, was "a criminal piece of audacity on the part of a man
who belongs to a country which took off the head of Charles Ist."
And at one of a series of meetings held at the London Palladium to
urge the Government to establish Universal Obligatory National
Service for men and women (the most democratic method and the
most likely to speed victory), she contradicted Russell's estimate of
the effects of war on soldiers' morals. "From Lord Kitchener downwards," she insisted, "the officers of our splendid Army have impressed upon those of whom they are in charge the duty to keep
themselves clean and pure. Never in the history of our Army have so
many moral forces been at work as during this war." She may have
been right; on the other hand, she may have been influenced by the
knowledge that army chaplains were busy distributing Christabel's
booklet on the dangers of venereal diseases (a reissue of her *Suffragette* articles under the title of *The Great Scourge*) to the troops.

Illegitimate babies? She and Christabel did not believe there had
been any appreciable increase in their numbers, but they did pro-
pose to do something practical to help. Under an idealized picture
of children sprouting angel wings, *The Suffragette* announced that
the WSPU intended to adopt a number of "war babies," who would
be reared under model conditions and provided with a good general

education. Less guardedly, Mrs. Pankhurst, to whom this activity made a particular appeal, informed the press that about fifty little girls would be adopted.

In fact, only four were finally adopted, and the raising of funds for their upbringing was another burden for Mrs. Pankhurst to shoulder. Money did not roll in with the old ease. The WSPU offices at Lincoln's Inn House—the largest political headquarters in London—were rented, and smaller premises were taken in Great Portland Street. Even a world war could not lift Mrs. Pankhurst's spirit to the death-or-glory heights from which the problems of old age and an indefinite future had been too insignificant to be noticed. She looked urgently to Christabel to give her heart for the fight and defended her against the criticisms of old friends who found her bellicosity repellent. "I don't want her different," she said, "or liable to her mother's human weaknesses."

With the knowledge and encouragement of Lloyd George, now scheming for supreme power with a mixture of subtlety and impetuosity similar to that of Christabel, the WSPU continued to attack Asquith, Haldane, Grey, and other prewar targets, joining its now tiny forces with those of Lord Northcliffe, Sir Edward Carson, and other advocates of the "knockout blow." Week after week, *The Suffragette* repeated its demands for an intensification of the blockade of Europe in order if necessary to force neutrals into line with the Allies; for a massive attack on the Central Powers through the Balkans; for unified control of Allied war strategy with one overall warlord; for universal conscription; for the expulsion from public service of all persons of enemy origin or connections; and for canceling the naturalization certificates of all Germans, Austrians, Hungarians, and Turks in Britain.

In October, 1915, the paper was renamed *Britannia* and took on an even more reckless tone. There must be a clear-out at the Foreign Office. Sir Edward Grey, Sir Robert Cecil, Sir Eyre Crowe (Assistant Undersecretary of State) must go: "The Germans know that their hope of victory depends upon the British Foreign Office as at present constituted more than upon anything else!" Considering that Sir Eyre Crowe was the nephew of Admiral Henning von Holtzendorff, Chief of the German Naval War Staff, was it surprising that "our Foreign Office ordered that Germany's reservists should be allowed to cross the sea to fight Great Britain and her Allies, that Sir Edward Grey believes in the German principle of freedom of the seas, that cotton is allowed into Germany to feed her guns and kill our soldiers, that Serbia was betrayed and the German object of World Domination was thus promoted!"

Christabel demanded that the Allied diplomatic center should be moved from London, with its tainted atmosphere and illusions of peace, to somewhere nearer the realities of the war—Havre, perhaps, or Boulogne. At the London Pavilion, Mrs. Pankhurst spoke of her shame that France should be doing so much more for small nations like Serbia than Britain: "I am thankful that I am a woman and therefore do not share the guilt which rests not only upon the Government but upon the manhood of our country." She warned the Government that women might well go on strike and even riot if they were not given their full share of war work, especially as men were striking in ignorance of the real issues of the war, under the influence of "German international and socialist ideals" traceable to Karl Marx. She urged that the Welsh miners and their wives should be shown around the front and forced to read the Bryce Report. That might bring them to their senses. She even, at the urgent invitation of the mineowners, traveled to South Wales to deliver the same message to the miners in person—with considerable effect, for, as she pointed out, she herself was a rebel, but had set aside her grievances during the national emergency.

Early in 1915, Lloyd George, then Minister of Munitions, approached Mrs. Pankhurst to discuss the need to recruit women for factory work to overcome the munitions shortage. There was much opposition in the Cabinet and among trades unions, but he counted upon the WSPU to help him to bring pressure to bear. Mrs. Pankhurst, accompanied by Annie Kenney, agreed to do her best, but added stiffly: "If you feel it necessary to convert *men* to the need of munitions, we will have a procession and deputation of women. But please understand that *women* are fully aware of it already."

With the help of a £2,000 Ministry grant (about which questions were asked in Parliament), the WSPU began to organize a monster procession with an efficiency and verve last shown on the occasion of Emily Wilding Davison's funeral in 1913. WANTED! appealed *The Suffragette*, 700 BANNER BEARERS, 300 MARSHALS, 300 PA-

PER SELLERS, 400 YOUNG WOMEN DRESSED IN WHITE TO HELP IN AR-
RANGING ONE OF THE SPECIAL DECORATIVE FEATURES OF THE PROCES-
SION. Apart from contingents of nurses and other war workers, there
was to be "a section of girls dressed in white and carrying crooks
with red roses," as well as a Pageant of the Allies, led by a young
woman, in a somber, flowing gown and carrying a tattered flag, who
represented Belgium ("The Suffragette Nation"). At a special meeting at the London Pavilion on July 9, Dame Clara Butt, a celebrated
contralto, opened the proceedings by singing the National Anthem,
and Mrs. Pankhurst urged the need for women to be used far more
widely in war industry, as they were on the Continent.

On July 17, despite heavy rain and a tearing wind, the procession—125 contingents strong, two miles long, and accompanied by
ninety bands playing the "Marseillaise"—moved with a military precision, officered by red-sashed marshals and blue-sashed assistant
marshals. For two and a half hours it marched through crowded
streets to its final destination on the embankment outside the Ministry of Munitions, where a covered platform had been built from
which Lloyd George, accompanied by Winston Churchill, could re-
view the demonstration.

The flags of the Allies, including the Sun of Japan, and banners
with specially worked mottoes ("We Demand The Right to Serve,"
"For Men Must Fight and Women Must Work," "Let None Be Kaiser's Cat's-Paws") enlivened the scene. Recruiting tables had been
set up along the route, and a vast crowd—estimated at more than
sixty thousand—had assembled on the embankment when the
procession came to a halt. Mrs. Pankhurst, dressed with sober but
majestic elegance, stepped out at the head of the women's deputation and mounted the rostrum. In reply to her questions, Lloyd
George assured the deputation that munitions factories would be
controlled by the Government, which would see to it that women's
labor was not exploited, and that, as far as possible, there would
be equal pay for equal work. He produced a fine phrase, like a
resplendent rabbit, from his top hat. "Without women," he said,
"victory will tarry, and the victory which tarries means a victory
whose footprints are footprints of blood." He even worked in a
gracefully facetious reference to "the organizing capacity of women
of which I have been a victim on occasions," which brought some

dutiful laughter. As the rain beat onto the platform and the drenched processionists waited for a word from the great man, there was little time for serious bargaining, even if Mrs. Pankhurst had been in the mood for it. And perhaps she was not, for this was a moment of real personal triumph for her. Now the acknowledged Queen of Women Patriots, she cried to the assembled multitude: "Women are going to work. They are going to save the men in the trenches. Let us all unite in giving three cheers for the Army and the Navy—three cheers for the good old country that we mean to save!" Though thinned by the wind, the answering cheers were strong enough to warm her heart and convince her of her new mission.

For weeks afterward, WSPU headquarters in Kingsway were besieged by inquirers, and sackfuls of mail arrived by every post. Moved by the magic Pankhurst push, the ball of women's recruitment began to roll vigorously. This was the beginning of her remarkable alliance with an old enemy, Lloyd George. But Lloyd George was not yet Prime Minister (despite Christabel's editorials) and Asquith, still precariously in power, felt obliged to take some action against these women who continued to torment him. Under Government pressure, managers began to refuse to hire their halls to the WSPU. In the midst of a rousing anti-Asquith tirade in Trafalgar Square, Mrs. Pankhurst was taken to Cannon Row Police Station to cool off. It was quite like old times. At the end of 1915, attempts were made to suppress *Britannia*. For more than a year, the paper appeared at irregular intervals and in odd shapes and sizes. Often it was a defiant, dimly duplicated sheet run off by women once more on the run from the police.

Christabel, to whose Paris eyrie Grace Roe now traveled weekly for copy and briefing, editorialized: "We are not surprised that Sir Eyre Crowe and the Foreign Office should desire the disappearance of *Britannia,* the most outspoken, most persistent and most damaging of their critics. But BRITANNIA RECANTS NOTHING AND REITERATES EVERYTHING." In an article headed "Judas," she remarked that against treachery even the Son of God was helpless, so what chance had *Britannia* against the corrupt Foreign Office? She alleged that even before the war, the WSPU had condemned the Government's reprehensible neglect of "air flight." If women had had the vote, "Great Britain would be stronger in the air today."

Sometimes she showed a lighter, satirical touch; reminiscent of her celebrated raillery at by-elections. In October, 1916, appeared "An imaginary dialogue between Sir Everso Black [Sir Edward Grey], Sealand's Minister of Foreign Affairs, and Prince Humbugsky, Ambassador of Stodgeland."

PRINCE H.: We have, in countries overseas, thousands of Stodgelanders whom we should like to see return to the Fatherland in its time of trouble. You, with your keen patriotism, will sympathise, I am sure. But your fleet! There is the difficulty. How is it to be overcome?

SIR E.B.: Pray do not distress yourself. Our fleet will have orders to let them pass.

PRINCE H: Very good. But the real tragedy of the war will be the interference with the trade of neutral countries.

SIR E.B.: I will simply say that I am in agreement with you that neutral trade must be in every possible way protected from interference.

PRINCE H: Most reassuring! But still I fear that your public may insist upon strong naval measures . . . a blockade and all that sort of thing. . . .

SIR E.B.: Do you not know that we are even called the Too Foreign Office because of our resistance to such clamour? I can assure you that there will be no war fever at the Foreign Office. . . .

WSPU Patriotic Meetings continued to be held in the open air, at Hyde Park and Clapham Common in London, and Mrs. Pankhurst continued to demand action in the Balkans. "The war," she prophesied, "began in the Balkans and it will end there. Many people have allowed themselves to be hynotised by the Western Front." It was a pity, she thought, that Churchill's Gallipoli scheme had been preferred to Lloyd George's grand Balkan strategy. And early in 1916, aided by Jessie Kenney, she went on a tour of the United States and Canada to raise funds for Serbia and educate people about the Balkans. It had been arranged that certain days should be left free for her to speak on social hygiene (here she could draw on her wealth of experience in local government in Manchester) and that the proceeds should be devoted to the upbringing of her war babies. But she did not feel able to take advantage of this arrangement. She wrote to a friend: "Somehow I couldn't go in for personal money-making in wartime, so I stick to considering the lilies as usual."

While Mrs. Pankhurst lectured, Jessie Kenney organized—and made contact with a number of people in Christabel's ever-widening network. In particular, she had long talks with a M. Voska, another Czech exile who was working for Czechoslovak independence and keeping a close eye on German Secret Service methods in North America. She took several packets from M. Voska to Christabel in Paris, for delivery to Dr. Beneš.

Even after Lloyd George became Prime Minister in December, 1916, he could not always shield *Britannia* from the penalties of its own exuberance. Angered by what she regarded as the stupidity of the British Higher Military Command, Christabel accused Sir William Robertson, Chief of the Imperial General Staff, of being "Hindenburg's partner" and "the tool and accomplice of the traitors Grey, Asquith and Cecil." He "spelled compromise peace and the downfall of the British Empire." Did he believe, or had he advised, that Germany should be left as a strong buffer state in the near East? Was he the enemy of Russia?

Christabel printed a letter from the Secretary of State for War, which gave the Government's reasons for breaking up the type of this issue. The articles attacking the CIGS, said Edward Stanley, Lord Derby, were of a nature "calculated to damage our credit with our Allies, and the authority in the Army of the officer in whom is centred the supreme responsibility for advising our Government in regard to military operations. Lord Derby is not concerned to argue that the motives inspiring the promoters of these attacks are to be described as unpatriotic. He can only look to effects." The Government, he argued, had to step in, since Sir William was prevented by the Rules of the Service from taking any part in newspaper controversy.

Christabel's reply was characteristic: "I will begin," she wrote, "by saying that I have entirely failed to notice any lack of ability on Sir William Robertson's part to conduct offensive and defensive operations through the medium of newspapers. On the contrary, he has, in our opinion, displayed a quite unusual gift of press manipulation." Why should *Britannia* be singled out for victimization? Lord Northcliffe had not been raided when attacks on Horatio Kitchener appeared in the *Daily Mail* and the *Times*. "We cannot accept the suggestion that Sir William's military reputation and prestige ought to be maintained at the expense of the truth, and we notice that you do not in any way deny the truth of the statements made concerning his policy. We therefore consider your letter to be in itself a very complete justification of our campaign, which the recent raid was powerless to interrupt."

When the question of suffrage reform came up in 1916—the pre-war Parliamentary Registers had been made obsolete by mobilization, and there was agitation for "Votes for the Fighting Men"—the women's claim was raised, and Asquith admitted that their record in war work fully entitled them to the vote. This about-face brought a quick reaction from die-hard antisuffragists. James Bryce, George Curzon, and Rudyard Kipling wrote to the *Times* proclaiming their determination to resist any such measure. Sir Almoth Wright insisted that "a certain minimum personal vigour and muscular development were required to fit any individual to fight, and the same minimum should be required of the individual who aspires to the Parliamentary franchise—*even if this means debarring old men*."

The WSPU, busy shooting down the peace-proposal kites, which from the end of 1916 were flown in ever-increasing numbers, stayed aloof from this rather fusty flurry and from the ensuing Speaker's Conference held to consider the scope of suffrage reform. Christabel believed, in any case, that an attitude of detachment, if not distrust, would revive the Government's fears of a resumption of militancy and so act as a useful spur. Her mother, seething with patriotic zeal and self-sacrifice (and, it may be, anxious to keep the initiative with the WSPU), went a stage further. She insisted, to almost everyone's amazement, that Asquith was up to his old deceitful tricks again: "Before the war he used the questions of more votes for men to 'dish' the women. Now he reverses the process and uses the women to 'dish' the men, who are heroically sacrificing themselves in defence of the Nation. We indignantly resent his attempt to exploit, for his own political purposes, the women's cause, of which he has been, and still is, the determined enemy."

4 §

Pankhursts versus Bolsheviks

In 1917 there were many surprises and yet stranger enterprises for
Mrs. Pankhurst. On March 10, she made a curious reappearance on
the witness stand at the Old Bailey (London's central criminal
court). She did so at the end of a sensational five-day trial that resulted in the sentencing of Alice Wheeldon, her daughter Winnie,
and her son-in-law, Alfred Mason, for plotting to assassinate Lloyd
George with poisoned darts. During the trial, Mrs. Wheeldon, a vehement feminist, was alleged to have revealed that before the war
the suffragettes had schemed to murder Lloyd George and Reginald
McKenna. The idea, she claimed, was to get a suffragette employed
as a chambermaid at a hotel where Lloyd George was going to stay.
The "chambermaid" would then drive a poisoned nail through the
sole of the victim's boot. The conspiracy was thwarted when he
suddenly changed his itinerary.

Horrified at the implications (since in the popular mind suffragettes and the WSPU were synonomous), Mrs. Pankhurst was given
permission by the judge to state that it had never been WSPU policy
to take human life and that the WSPU now regarded the Prime
Minister, Lloyd George, as "of the greatest possible value in the
present grave crisis. Its members would, if necessary," she said, "lay
down their lives to protect his."

When, early in 1917, the Government decided to draft a bill to
give women the first installment of the vote, Mrs. Pankhurst went
with other suffragist leaders to see Lloyd George at 10 Downing
Street—whose windows she had broken a few short years before.
Now that Asquith had been ousted, she forgot her quibbling and
appealed: "Whatever you think can be passed in the war circumstances we are ready to accept. In this room where so many women
have come, one cannot help feeling that the spirits might be among

us of those who died without seeing the result of their labour and sacrifice."

To some of her old followers her attitude seemed unduly humble. But she was an elder stateswoman now, the confidante of the Prime Minister, who not long after arranged for her to go to Russia on a special mission. The French Army mutinies had thrown a greater strain on Britain's troops on the Western Front, and now there was the danger that Russia's collapse would release more enemy troops from the Eastern Front. It was widely believed by many people, including Mrs. Pankhurst, that the Russian Revolution of March, 1917 (which had forced the Tsar to abdicate and had brought the first glimmerings of parliamentary democracy), might be a blessing in disguise. It had probably gotten rid of the sinister pro-German influences that had corrupted the court, and perhaps now the tide—and the massive desertions from the Russian Army— might turn. Mrs. Pankhurst was to deliver a stirring appeal to the women of Russia to keep the men up to the mark and in the war, and she was to meet Aleksandr Kerenski, the head of the provisional government, and other important political leaders.

It was a unique opportunity, and Mrs. Pankhurst was honored by it. Yet she felt a certain reluctance to leave the house in Holland Park, which she had rented for the war babies. They were being looked after by Sister C. E. Pine, whose nursing home had, in days gone by, been turned into a convalescent home for suffragettes weakened by prison treatment. It was the first settled home Mrs. Pankhurst had known since she had left Manchester eleven years before. To Ethel Smyth she wrote: "I have got to love this home of mine, and pray heaven that I shall be able to keep it. Sometimes I feel appalled at the responsibility I have undertaken in adopting these four young things at my time of life. . . . However, who knows? I'll go on as long as I can, in the faith that help will come when it's needed. The cost of living increases from week to week. How the poor live God only knows."

She was beginning to feel her age and to wilt under the constant physical and financial strain. But the mission had to be fulfilled. Once more she was to be accompanied by Jessie Kenney, who at the age of nineteen had left Lancashire to be Mrs. Pethick-Lawrence's private secretary, and two years later became the WSPU's youngest national organizer. Like her sister Annie, she had been in the deepest confidence of the Pankhursts ever since. She went to Paris for a special briefing from Christabel, who also gave her £5 in a bag to tie around her neck in case of emergency and fitted her out with some new clothes from her own wardrobe.

Britannia, now back to its full format, had a cover picture that showed the two envoys solemn-faced and elegantly gowned. They were to sail from Aberdeen to Norway, and thence travel overland to Petrograd. Right at the start of their journey there was a pleasing omen. Mrs. Pankhurst had the satisfaction of seeing her bête noire, Ramsay MacDonald, turned off the ship by order of the patriotic Seamen's Union and so prevented from spreading his insidious pacifist poison in Russia.

In Petrograd, rooms had been booked for them by Christabel's friend Thomáš Masaryk, soon to become the first President of Czechoslovakia. He was in Russia to try to form the Czechoslovak troops, one hundred thousand of whom had deserted from the Austro-Hungarian Army, into independent divisions. Food was scarce and bad, but Russian admirers queued for hours to get a little white bread for Mrs. Pankhurst: the black bread was sour and indigestible, and she was in great pain with the chronic gastric trouble that was a legacy of her many imprisonments. When the epidemic of strikes spread to the hotel staff, Mrs. Pankhurst's new friends, mostly teachers and nurses, tidied the envoys' rooms and foraged for food and made tea on a little stove lent by a soldier. Three interpreters were assigned to Mrs. Pankhurst, and each day they brought the Russian papers and translated the main news items for her.

She and Miss Kenney learned that the Russian court had taken a great interest in the suffragette campaign, and the Tsar and Tsarina, then held prisoner at Tsarskoe Selo, sent a message expressing a wish to meet Mrs. Pankhurst. She had, regretfully, to refuse the invitation, since, as a semiofficial Allied ambassador, it was her duty to deal and work with the provisional government.

It was, in any case, difficult for her to leave her hotel, such was the press of visitors. Among them was a group of aristocratic officers of the Order of St. George, who were so concerned for her safety (there were street clashes between Bolsheviks and Loyalists, and the British Embassy was guarded by armored cars) that they suggested forming a bodyguard. Though touched by the offer, Mrs. Pankhurst told them that she had no fear of moving about freely among the people. She also laughed off a suggestion that it might be prudent for her and Miss Kenney to dress in "proletarian" clothes when they went out, in order to avoid bourgeois-baiters.

For a short time, Mrs. Pankhurst and Miss Kenny stayed in the Hotel Astoria, which had become the headquarters of the Allied military and naval staff in Petrograd. Their balcony, overlooking St. Isaac's Square, was, they were told, the very one that the Kaiser had threatened to use for a triumphal appearance when his armies had captured the city. Madame de Chabanov, President of the All Russian Women's Union, arranged a series of meetings in private houses, and Miss Kenney spoke at one large outdoor meeting of women factory workers, which took place outside Anarchist headquarters. Mrs. Pankhurst wanted to hold a whole series of mass outdoor meetings, but this was not allowed. Starvation and uncertainty and fear had created an atmosphere in which anything might happen, and though Mrs. Pankhurst was willing to take risks, the provisional government was not. It was a big disappointment. Anxious to make a supreme effort to energize the Russian people, she found herself restricted to preaching to the converted and entertaining the fashionable.

Journalists hurried to interview her, and she did not mince her words—this was her best chance of reaching a wider audience. "I came to Petrograd," she said, "with a prayer from the English nation, that you may continue the war on which depends the fate of civilisation and of freedom. I believe in the kindness of heart and the soul of Russia. In Britain not only men, but women of all classes are taking part in the work. Girls with a university education are working on factory lathes. Ladies of the highest classes are replacing the working women on Sundays. I have always been astonished at the materialistic aspect of Marxian Socialism. I cannot think of Socialism without a spiritual background. From the very beginning of my public life I was in the ranks of the Socialists, together with my husband. But I soon found how narrow were the interests with which I was concerned, and so devoted myself to the cause of women. I consider that as a revolutionist who has been 16 times in prison I deserve the sympathy of those people who have been at the head of the revolution in Russia."

The provisional government was now in a desperate situation. It included every shade of Socialist opinion except Bolshevism—and the Bolshevists quietly set about manufacturing chaos. Deserters continued to stream back from the fronts, and Kerenski made an extensive personal tour of the armies in an attempt to restore morale. White-faced and swaying on his feet with exhaustion, he drove from one unit to another, haranguing the troops. But words were all he had to offer, and incandescent as they were, the effect of them cooled as soon as his back was turned.

In a last effort to conjure an outburst of patriotism, he created the Women's Battalions. Would not the sight of them, with their cropped hair, smart uniforms, and eager faces, shame the Army into courage? Mrs. Pankhurst spoke with tremendous feeling at a large meeting held in the Army and Navy Hall to raise funds for these battalions. "I honour these women who are setting such an example to their comrades," she cried. "When I looked at their tender bodies I thought how terrible it was that they should have to fight, besides bringing children into the world. Men of Russia, must the women fight? Are there men who will stay at home and let them fight alone? One thing women say. We will never be slaves to Germany! Better that we should die fighting than be outraged and dishonoured like the women of France, Belgium and Serbia." In St. Isaac's Square she took the salute as a woman's battalion marched past. Its banners were blessed at an impressive ceremony. The battalion left Petrograd amid great excitement, but at the front its losses were heavy, and its presence was resented and even laughed at by the men whose sense of honor it hoped to revive.

Mrs. Pankhurst had hoped for great things from Kerenski. But when she and Miss Kenney had an interview with him in his enormous office in the Winter Palace, she was sadly disappointed. He seemed to resent her mission and was so wildly voluble (they spoke in French) that it was hard to make rational contact. There were other, pleasanter, occasions. It was nice to have tea with Georgi Plekhanov, the courteous and scholarly leader of the Menshevik Party. It was flattering to be presented with a Russian edition of her autobiography and to learn that it was being read in a girls' high school. It was interesting to have dinner with Prince Yusupov and to be shown the very spot where he had fired his revolver at Grigori Rasputin. It was delightful to go to the opera and to see the sights of the Kremlin. But all this did little to further her mission. She had not come to Russia as a tourist. Why could she not address the workers in the factories, where, she had heard, production was being crippled by a sudden mad proliferation of committees?

In August, she and Miss Kenney went to Moscow to attend the great congress to which workers' and soldiers' delegates and representatives of almost every branch of Russian life had been summoned. Still relying on the power of his oratory, Kerenski pleaded and threatened and promised in highly emotional speeches of interminable length. To Mrs. Pankhurst, who had never been in the habit of justifying herself to committees, it was a pitiful spectacle, and it convinced her that the provisional government could not last and that Kerenski, who had allowed Nikolai Lenin to return to Russia and had released Leon Trotsky and other Bolshevik leaders from prison, was a man of straw.

The Russian press was sharply divided about Mrs. Pankhurst. Left-wing writers saw her as a capitalist tool, a prestigious puppet. Right-wing journalists went into rhapsodies over her. "I wondered," wrote one of them, "if there was anything feminine left in this woman rebel. Yet she has remained essentially feminine. It gives her figure a soft, romantic character. She is not a chauvinistic Valkyrie. Her patriotism is impersonal and nationalistic, able to lift the soul to the highest summits of morality. She is a new woman. Are there any like her in Russia? Angry extremists will no doubt denounce her as a paid agent of the Anglo-French capitalists. These fools, however, do not spare anybody. All that is noble and romantic is, for that very reason, hateful to them."

When the two disillusioned envoys returned to Petrograd, Miss Kenney was badly hurt in a scrimmage between a pro-Kerenski and a pro-Bolshevist mob when she went to the railway station to say good-bye to a woman's battalion on its way to the front. Crushed to fainting point, she was rescued in the nick of time by a mounted officer of the Order of St. George, who lifted her clear and called a droshky to take her back to her hotel.

She and Mrs. Pankhurst liked to go into St. Isaac's Cathedral and sit there quietly, listening to the magnificent singing and watching the simple and unselfconscious devotion of the worshipers. Mrs. Pankhurst was fascinated by the way soldiers would touch the ground

with their foreheads and stay kneeling for many minutes, still as statues, gazing at the icons. Wistfully, she told Miss Kenney how lucky
she was to have had a good Christian upbringing—how wise her
mother had been to give that to her children. Old, sad memories
must have plagued her. Memories of the attempt made to bar the
Pankhurst girls from Manchester High School because their father
was an atheist and a republican; of the way Sylvia had been jeered
at for refusing to attend Scripture classes (was she a Jew? the other
children had mocked); of books being hurled at her youngest
daughter, Adela, because she was "different"; of her son, Harry, being found unconscious in the road after being beaten by other
grammar-school boys because he had spoken out against the Boer
War. Had it all been really necessary, the constant kicking against
the pricks of convention? She understood now the value of a simple
religious faith, had glimpsed the living truths that lay behind the
apparent deadness and fatuity of tradition. She saw things so differently now, and she could not help wishing that things had been
different.

But it was time to move on again. She had been in Russia for
more than three months. It was September, and the provisional government was tottering. Total chaos and mass violence were imminent, and Professor Masaryk warned her and Miss Kenney to leave
while there was still time. The Bolsheviks would soon be in control.
There would be a separate peace with Germany.

Mrs. Pankhurst traveled back in a somber mood, her depression
deepened by a severe attack of pleurisy. After a short convalescence,
she summoned her strength for two long interviews with the Prime
Minister, in which she impressed upon him the utter hopelessness of
the situation in Russia, the need for swift and massive Allied intervention to help the Cossack and Loyalist elements to regain power.

It seemed to her that the illiterate Russian masses had been
cruelly deluded by the lies and machinations of German agents, and,
in a series of press interviews, she bitterly denounced Kerenski's
weakness. She had, she said, found him feverish and vacillating, a
man ill in body and mind, whose elimination could only be regarded
with relief. Allied intervention, preferably by America and Japan,
was the one true hope. This was a theme she took up again in her

speech at a mass meeting in the Queen's Hall on November 7, and she added a scathing criticism of the committee mania that was paralyzing Russia and seemed to her likely to paralyze Britain. She would like, she said, to take the committee-worshipers to Russia to see the logical results of their theories. In one large factory, employing thirty thousand people, there was a committee of eight hundred who "sat all day deciding how the others are to do their work." There were committees of hospital patients who "decided whether they should take the pills ordered." Worst of all, there were committees of soldiers at the front who decided whether or not to obey military orders.

She flourished the Bolshevik bogey to try to frighten a slackening Britain into a new and sterner unity. In this she was joined by Christabel, who had at last left Paris and was living in a small flat above the new WSPU offices in William Street, Knightsbridge. Here, there was a band of highborn voluntary workers, including Lady Sybil Knox and Mrs. Peggy Macmillan, sister-in-law of Harold Macmillan, Britain's future Prime Minister, then serving with the Grenadier Guards. As usual, Christabel was crackling with ambitious ideas. She had adopted one of the four war orphans and now felt that the WSPU should, with the prestige backing it now commanded, open a full-scale day nursery run on Montessori lines. A large house—Tower Cressy, near Mrs. Pankhurst's rented home—was acquired and luxuriously furnished. Annie and Jessie Kenney were to live there, and their sister Jane, a trained Montessori teacher, was brought over from America (where she was teaching in a Montessori school in Washington) to run the place. But funds lagged, and apart from the four war orphans, few other children attended.

Christabel was busy with other schemes. With industrial discontent spreading, it was, she felt, essential to expand and intensify the WSPU's industrial campaigns, which urged women workers in particular to stand firm against Socialist "plots." Many industrialists —"captains of industry," as Christabel and Mrs. Pankhurst, incurably romantic, preferred to call them—had already found these campaigns useful and, headed by William Lever, Lord Leverhulme (whose country house had been set on fire by suffragettes in the early months of 1914), invited Christabel and Annie Kenney to address them at a special gathering. The speeches were so effective that a sum of £15,000 was raised, and the WSPU's industrial-campaign staff considerably increased.

Christabel now returned to the platform with frequency and zest. Every week, and sometimes twice a week, she delivered a brisk and wide-ranging commentary on current affairs at the Aeolian Hall, New Bond Street. The Prime Minister, she said, must be backed to the hilt in his drive to defeat those—anong them, in her opinion, Winston Churchill—who favored a compromise peace. Ramsay Mac-Donald she regarded as a complete fraud, a man who used to be the flunky of Asquith and was now "the flunkey and toady and tool of the Kaiser." Rather than consent to a craven peace, she told one audience, she was willing to see London destroyed. "After all," she said, "humanity is not the final expression of the Divine Will. Women realise the truth of the words: 'Fear not those that kill the body and have nothing more that they can do.' This war is in very truth a conflict between God and the Devil, and women's part must be to keep the spiritual side of this conflict uppermost."

With mingled feminist and Francophile gall, she bitterly complained that, though it was planned to erect a statue of Abraham Lincoln in London to mark a hundred years of peace between Britain and America, there was no move to put up a statue to Joan of Arc to celebrate the centenary of peaceful relations between Britain and France. She went so far as to claim that "the delay in erecting this statue will be a reliable measure of the strength of that pro-Germanism which is jeopardising British victory in this war." Her patriotic zeal led her to strange places and strange company: for instance, to an Anniversary of the Start of the War rally in the Great Pavilion at Llandudno, Wales, where, as the local newspaper reported, the county's Lord Lieutenant, Sir Polwett Milbank, delivered one of his "straight from the shoulder speeches." What he wanted was to see every German in the country shut up. He would send the whole jolly lot back or intern them.

Christabel, wearing a wide-brimmed hat and a filmy gown and looking as though she were going to open a charity bazaar, agreed with him. With her prejudices sharpened to the point of prophecy, she berated the Hun. The Kaiser, she said, was a hardened criminal, and the whole German nation shared his guilt. She did not believe in the possibility of a free Germany. Germans liked tyranny and took revenge on other people for their own servility. They resembled Uriah Heep—very humble until they got on top of their victims. She brushed aside any thoughts of democratizing the Germans: "We did not start this war to give freedom to a people who do not want it, but to keep freedom for ourselves and our Allies." Germans, she maintained, were naturally brutal: "No British officer would give the kind of orders that German officers have given, and British soldiers and sailors would be shot rather than obey them." At other meetings, she amplified her onslaught on Ramsay MacDonald, pro-German intellectuals, and conscientious objectors ("whose conscience," she noted, "always seems to guide them to the safe side, perhaps to some snug post in a Government Department") and warned her audiences that the Germans were making a pretense of starving "in order to damp down our war effort."

Meanwhile, the industrial campaign proceeded vigorously, with Mrs. Pankhurst (whose speeches were sometimes drowned by clattering plates in factory canteens), Annie Kenney, and "General" Flora Drummond as the star speakers. Men, they claimed, were more susceptible to insidious peace propaganda than women, who must therefore set them an example. How could the workers consider slackening their efforts against Germany's scientific barbarism? "Grievances," thundered the "General" in one factory-gate oration, "grievances! Of course you have grievances. But what about me? I'm out on ticket-of-leave at this moment!" At Newcastle, she told munitionettes that they should take the trouble to attend trade-union meetings, which were too often manipulated by small groups of Socialist subversives who had the audacity to present their views as those of the majority. Criticism of the Prime Minister must stop. "If you've got a better man than Lloyd George," she challenged, "for God's sake trot him out. If not, shut up."

In Glasgow, WSPU speakers, including Christabel Pankhurst, showed real courage in braving the proletarian lions of "Red Clydeside." In December, 1915, these sturdy socialists had drowned Lloyd George's public attempt to justify the regimentation of the Munitions Act with a rendering of the Red Flag, had told him to get his hair cut, and had insisted that "dilution," male or female, should be controlled by the workers, and that there should be equal pay for equal work. When Lloyd George came to Glasgow in June, 1917, to receive the Freedom of the City, he had to be provided with a strong police and military escort as he drove through streets lined with sullen crowds. Yet the Pankhurst preachers of industrial peace would go alone to factory gates, climb on a chair, and—perhaps because they were often so young and gloriously innocent—often got a good-humored hearing for their bourgeois message.

In South Wales, the WSPU was alarmed to find "a close connection between the shop steward movement and Bolshevism." Pacifists, it recommended, should be removed from industry and sent into the firing line. It was a scandal that "young men of military age were able to go from town to town defying constitutional trade unionism, and even boasting that they travel round keeping up a continual ferment of strikes." Annie Kenney, in a newspaper article, made a particular appeal to the women of her native Lancashire to thwart the German plot to cripple British industry. "They should beware," she wrote, "of internationalists, who are more dishonourable than foreigners, because they have no country at all. The Bolsheviks have tried and tested the centres of industry, but they are not sure of Lancashire. Women of Lancashire, you can foil them!"

By now the simple enthusiasms of August, 1914, had been muddied and complicated. The great Socialist Conference of June, 1917, in Stockholm marked a resurgence of labor internationalism. Then there was the famous letter written by Henry Petty-Fitzmaurice, Lord Lansdowne, once a Tory Minister, and published in the *Daily Telegraph*. Lord Lansdowne suggested that in the peace negotiations, though Germany must make suitable reparation and restitution, the British Government should ease the way by making it clear that there would be no attempt to crush Germany or impose a government upon her. "We are not going to lose this war," the letter reasoned, "but its prolongation will spell ruin for the civilised world. What will be the value of the blessings of peace to nations so exhausted that they can scarcely stretch out an arm with which to grasp them?" Like many members of Britain's ruling class, both Tory and Liberal, Lansdowne saw that the war was hastening the spread of socialism and the collapse of the old social order. He too was driven by a spirit of internationalism, the internationalism of the trembling upper crust.

But the WSPU would have no truck with such babblings, and *Britannia* attacked them heartily, from whichever direction they came. In November, 1917, the month of the Lansdowne letter, it was announced that the WSPU would thenceforth be known as the Women's Party, with a twelve-point program drawn up by Christabel:

1. A fight to the finish with Germany.

2. More vigorous war measures to include drastic food rationing, more communal kitchens to reduce waste, and the closing down of nonessential industries to release labor for work on the land and in the factories.

3. A clean sweep of all officials of enemy blood or connections from Government departments.

4. Stringent peace terms to include the dismemberment of the Hapsburg Empire.

5. After the war, the present Grand Alliance to be maintained.

6. National authority to be maintained in face of proposals for a League of Nations and international control.

7. Natural resources, essential industries, and the transport systems of the British Isles and the British Empire to be under strictly British ownership; Britain's public services to be manned exclusively by officials of British descent and wholly British connections; the naturalization laws to be changed to prevent Germans and their allies from acquiring and exploiting British nationality.

8. Irish Home Rule to be denied and the unity of Ireland maintained because of the German peril.

9. Industry to be run on the principle that the interests of the community as a whole came first, before those of employer or employee; Parliament, as the nation's representative, to settle disputes by specific guarantees about hours (a six-hour day was advocated) and wages. The attempt to run industry by consultative committees led to chaos, and "there was absolutely nothing inconsistent with personal dignity and individual liberty in submitting to discipline and obeying orders for a certain part of each day, provided that the individual is free to utilise ample hours of leisure according to his particular will."

10. On specifically women's questions, there must be equal pay

for equal work, equal marriage and divorce laws, the same rights over children for both parents, equality of rights and opportunities in public service, and a system of maternity benefits.

11. The educational system to be reformed so as to guarantee every child the general and specialized education necessary to render him a worthy citizen; welfare systems to be set up to ensure adequate food and medical treatment.

12. The problem of housing to be tackled on radical lines, involving the use of modern ideas of architecture, sanitation, and domestic economy; a system of cooperative housekeeping to be started "in order to avoid the present deplorable waste of women's economic energy, and enable standards of living to be enormously raised." To this end, there should be large blocks of flats set out in well-planned estates, with centralized heating and hot water; bulk purchasing of food, which would be cooked in communal kitchens; a communal laundry; hospital and health clinic services; and a nursery school, a gymnasium, and estate library.

In January, 1918, three days after the House of Commons passed the Women's Vote Clause by 134 votes to 71, Lloyd George invited Mrs. Pankhurst to breakfast with him to discuss the implications of the long-delayed victory. With an ardor intensified by the memory of her own struggles as a widow and the strain of caring for the war babies, she urged him to press forward with the Women's Party program. She still believed that the Prime Minister was a man of vision, above mere party politics, and she left convinced that they could work together to give the country a glorious new postwar deal. After the Reform Bill received royal assent on February 6, Christabel appeared at Albert Hall, urging women to rally to the suffragette leaders who had been the true architects of the vote. *Britannia* banner-headlined: BRITAIN EXPECTS THAT EVERY WOMAN THIS DAY WILL DO HER DUTY AND JOIN THE WOMEN'S PARTY.

With a General Election in the offing, Emmeline and Christabel traveled the country making propaganda for the new party. Mrs. Pankhurst urged her hearers not to vote for Ramsay MacDonald, Arthur Henderson, Philip Snowden, and other crypto-Bolsheviks, who, as she put it, "were trying to lure the newly-enfranchised women, whom they did so sadly little to enfranchise." *Britannia* published a blacklist of unsound MP's who on no account should be voted for. Christabel denied that the Women's Party was based on sex antagonism, but stressed that women did have a special contribution to make and should not sink their identity in men's worn-out parties. Unfortunately, in speeches and editorials, the more constructive proposals tended to be submerged in personal recriminations and Bolshevik-hunting. Pankhurst supporters heckled Asquith during a visit to Liverpool, and Christabel explained that this had been done because Asquith was more responsible than anyone for insufficient unity among the Allies: "His best service to this country would be to get out of the way and keep out of the way."

Germany's subtle ramifications must, Miss Pankhurst insisted, be carefully watched and scotched. There was even, for instance, a danger that German Jews might at that very moment be trying to manipulate Zionism for nefarious purposes. She continued to demand the resignation of Sir William Robertson and denounced the introduction of the Whitley system of staff-management consultation as a triumph of Bolshevism. The proposals of male trade unionists to exclude women from industry after the war were likewise inspired by Bolshevism. An Industrial and Women Workers' Section of the Women's Party was started in an attempt to wean support from Mary Macarthur, Margaret Bondfield, and other "Bolshevik" women trade-union organizers. "Germany," she shrilled in *Britannia*, "is preparing to take an active part in Britain's forthcoming General Election! What Germany wants is victory for British pacifists under the leadership of either Mr. Asquith or Mr. Bolshevik Henderson!" She suggested that all prewar books on economics and labor questions should be publicly burned, since they were "so full of right- or left-wing prejudice."

Striving for a slogan, she hit on "Abolish the Proletariat." This was much more sensible than the Bolshevist aim of abolishing the bourgeoisie, she said. Manual workers must have the same advantages as the bourgeoisie, so that the two, in effect, merged: "As Democrats in the best sense of the word, we of the Women's Party cannot tolerate the existing system under which manual workers are marked off from their fellow-citizens by peculiarities of speech and deportment, by uncouthness or unharmony, if not actual poverty, of dress, due to lack of advantages which are today the monopoly of the so-called 'upper' classes, but in reality the birthright of all."

The Women's Party, with its harsh war policy and opposition to industrial democracy, alienated women "progressives" (who were, in any case, anathema to Christabel) and appeared to many as a weird mixture of Lloyd Georgian rhetoric and Tory reaction. On the other hand, its proposal for a six-hour day did nothing to recommend it to the captains of industry. It fell, painfully, between a number of stools. Mrs. Pankhurst saw in it a means of realizing the ideals of her Socialist youth—a society scientifically organized to promote the greater happiness of the underprivileged—and of releasing the passion of pity which still possessed her and which she believed to be locked in many breasts by poverty, ignorance, and injustice. During the struggle for the vote, she had got into the habit of ignoring "details" like economic questions. Surely these could be solved easily enough by a blend of patriotism and goodwill? Christabel's grandiose outline, a sort of moral-rearmament version of national socialism, seemed to offer a framework within which these vaguely defined forces could operate. Both women inhabited a world of their own, tinted with the fantasies born of more than a decade of oversimplification, overwork, and the unstinting, uncritical devotion of subordinates.

But in June, 1918, Mrs. Pankhurst withdrew from the electoral turmoil to undertake yet another "special mission" to the United States. She was accompanied by Commander Maria Botchkareva, a refugee from the ill-fated Russian Women's Battalions, and she went not only to advise Americans how best to organize women in industry for the final push to victory, to warn of the horrors of committee control, to celebrate the vote and outline the aims of the Women's Party, but also to urge the necessity of Allied military intervention in Bolshevist Russia, preferably by Japan, since Japan was best-placed geographically. Successful intervention would relieve pressure on the Western Front and shorten the war. Bitterly she denounced the weakness of Kerenski, so bitterly that British newspapers demanded to know why "this woman should be allowed to pose as the special envoy of the Prime Minister." The *Daily Chronicle* commented:"It is unfortunate that this egregious person cannot keep her opinions secret. No sooner had the slanderer of Lord Grey landed in New York than she made mischief, attacking the Irish and giving a scurrilous interview about Kerensky." In the House of Commons, questions were asked. Did Mrs. Pankhurst represent the Government's point of view? Why had she been allowed to go to America, while permission had been refused to trade-union organizer Margaret Bondfield, surely more genuinely representative of workingwomen in Britain?

Ignoring hecklers on both sides of the Atlantic, she made her visit to America almost as memorable as any of her three prewar fund-raising tours, when she had wowed audiences with her famous opening sentence: "I am what you call a hooligan!" Nearly sixty, frail with the illness that plagued her till her death ten years later, she was still a formidable personality. Her tragic, smoldering eyes and deep, superbly modulated voice worked their old magic. "Always a fighter," said the *North American,* "she is fighting still with the bulldog tenacity of the English nation." On Boston Common, she addressed a crowd of ten thousand people. She warned them against class warfare that played into the hands of the enemy, against internationalism, and against the dangerous abstractions of Socialist intellectuals: "Men like Bernard Shaw, Sidney Webb and Mr. Graham Wallas, some of them very irresponsible—of the long-haired, pale-faced type: men who worked up all kinds of visionary ideas about human beings, but have had no practical experience of human life, of the working man or the employer." Only the women of England, she maintained, had kept the political truce and stuck to the job in hand of winning the war. She was sure American women would do the same.

In October, she gave an account of her tour in a speech at Queen's Hall, London. America, she reported, was sound: "Her whole idea is a Peace dictated in Berlin." During ten days in Canada, she had helped to launch a Women's Party with a program similar to Christabel's. There was no denying, of course, that both the United States and Canada had an immigrant problem:"You find whole villages which are entirely German. Well, the women of Canada are determined that there is to be no increase in that kind of thing in the future, that there shall be very drastic immigration laws." She reaffirmed her belief in the future of the British Empire: "It is the fashion nowadays to sneer at Imperialism, but it seems to me a great thing to be the inheritors of an Empire like ours." And she damned class-consciousness: "Now that we women have the vote, we are going to have a Government composed of the best people—drawn from the one and only class that we mean to have before the Women's Party has finished its work."

When Parliament gave women the right to be Members of Parliament—something that neither she nor any other prewar suffragist leader had dreamed of demanding—she girded herself for another bout of electioneering, on behalf of Christabel, the Women's Party candidate. Britons must "forget class," pull together, and put Christianity into practice. Everything else would follow. "The Women's Party is needed, gentlemen," she said to a male audience in Birmingham, "because you haven't made such a success of things in the past, have you?" Women were more keenly practical and aware of the insidiousness of Bolshevism. What of the "horrible decree of Lenin and Trotsky, declaring all women over 18 to be national property, subject to a system of free love? Where," she blazed, "'is the liberty of women here?" She stood up and read the riot act to the restless workers of the Clyde: "The spread of Bolshevism is part of Germany's next war. She is out to win on the Home Front in Britain what she lost on the battlefields of Europe."

Ailing but indomitable, tiny but a giant even in her absurdities, she soldiered on at her last and dearest war mission—to get her beloved daughter, Christabel the Anointed One, into the House of Commons as the first woman MP.

Noblesse Oblige

I 🙊

Patriotism in High Places

"Worked from 3 to 5 planting potatoes. Got very hot & tired," wrote Queen Mary in her wartime diary. The royal couple determined to set an example of self-denial to the nation by banning the use of alcohol in royal establishments for the duration and, when the German submarine campaign began to affect Britain's food supplies, by cultivating plots at Windsor and on the grounds of Buckingham Palace. The Queen also led the household at Sandringham in the harvesting of horse chestnuts.

A plan to turn Buckingham Palace into a hospital did not come to anything—the building was too old-fashioned, did not have an elevator, and was generally inconvenient for the purpose. But members of the royal household were released for active service, royal carriage horses were used in ambulance work, and royal carriages converted for the work of conveying the wounded from London's railway stations. The Queen also held special parties for convalescent soldiers at the palace.

Right from the outbreak of war, she did what she could to put women's voluntary organizations on an efficient basis. During the Boer War, as Duchess of York, she had been shocked by the haphazard and unrealistic efforts that had dispatched to the Cape almost anything but what the men really needed. So, in daring collaboration with Mary Macarthur, the Socialist Queen of women's trade unions, she reorganized her Needlework Guild so that instead of competing with sweated women workers, it offered them some

83

much-needed work through what were hastily christened Queen Mary's Workshops. This move came after a vigorous appeal from Miss Macarthur to "do everything in your power to stop those women knitting." The revamped Guild was allotted headquarters in St. James's Palace.

But one of her main and most exacting jobs was to encourage her irascible, easily depressed husband with at least one letter a day when he was away from home. Pressure was put on her to decree the use of a simple purple armband (instead of black clothes) as a sign of mourning, but she felt that this was going too far and might be construed as "interference with the liberty of the subject."

Life was often a grisly alternation between inspecting troops on their way to the front and dutifully visiting them in the hospital when they returned maimed, blinded, or otherwise afflicted. "We have rebegun visiting hospitals! ! !" she noted in November, 1916. "Oh! dear, Oh! dear." Or again: "Went to Milbanke Hospital to see 214 of our badly wounded soldiers. It was pathetic seeing so many men without arms, legs, eyes, etc." Sometimes the general hospitals were too empty for easy coverage: "I found the big hospitals of 700 beds or more only had about 25 patients from the last fighting, which meant going through endless wards to find a couple of patients. So I visited St. Dunstan's Hospital for the Blind instead."

Even York Cottage, Sandringham, a favorite country retreat, was not free from war's alarms. In January, 1915, one of her Women of the Bedchamber recorded: "We were all, maids included" (such was the democracy of the Great Emergency), "after tea sitting listening to the gramophone when Sir Charles Cust put his head in and said: 'Come, a Zepp can be heard,' so out of the front door we went, the Queen with the King's fur coat on. . . ."

While King George V was convalescing after being severely crushed when he fell from his horse in France in October, 1915, Queen Mary had to deputize for him on such occasions as the inspection of the 33rd Division on Salisbury Plain or the decoration of Indian naval officers. But from 1916 onward, the growing unrest among munitions and engineering workers meant that both these conscientious constitutional monarchs had to spend much time on extensive goodwill tours of industrial areas.

The Queen took the initiative in arranging to send presents at

Christmastime to men on the various fronts ("I have ordered for Sir Courtauld Thompson, to take to the Dardanelles, some wallets or packets and some small writing blocks for the wounded as a *personal* gift from me"), and other highborn women were quick to follow her example. Of these, Lady Fanny Byron was the most original in her interpretation of the personal touch. Scarcity of matches in the early days of the war ("such a dire disaster for the Tommy") inspired her to distribute one hundred thousand boxes with the slogan "A Match for a Matchless Soldier" on each one. Later, she arranged for the dispatch of hundreds of plum puddings and sent a thousand brown woolen sweaters to men of the 9th Buffs with "A warm greeting from Lady Byron" punningly inscribed on a card attached to each garment. Another of her happy thoughts was to send consignments of soccer balls to the fronts, being convinced that manly sport was the main foundation of the British character. Each ball bore a quotation attributed to Queen Elizabeth I: "Simple mirth keepeth high courage alive."

Many servicemen wrote to her giving detailed accounts of their lives and backgrounds, perhaps hoping, ultimately, for something more substantial than a matchbox, a woolen sweater, or a literary soccer ball. One particularly gratifying letter came from Seaman F. Skinner of HMS *Centaur:* "Well, dear Madam," he wrote, "it is a funny way I came into possession of one of your lovely boxes, and I can assure you I would not part with it for pounds. I was on the hospital ship *Soudan.* There was a chap who had been wounded had two of these boxes. One he had taken from a chap that had been killed at Neuve Chapelle. It was a very rough night and the poor fellow was dying fast. Just before he died I was placed sentry by his bedside and he said: 'Here you are, Jack, take that for luck.' And I am sorry to say he never spoke another word. I have been offered £1 for this box, but have refused every time. I look at it, it seems to put more courage into me and I think of what kind people we have at home to think of us like this. I can promise you, Madam, faithfully that I will never part from it until I die. . . . I hope you will excuse this writing, as I am anxious to write to you. . . . I am a lonely sailor, but I will fight for the rights of dear old Blighty. . . ."

Lady Byron also gave garden parties for convalescent soldiers and, more unusually, parties for lonely mothers of sons who were fighting. She served as Chairwoman of the Polish Relief Fund, was on the committees of the Serbian and Montenegrin and Italian Relief Funds, and, of course, was a keen supporter of the Tobacco Fund. Not content with this, in the fullness of her heart and wealth she established a rest home for nurses on leave on the edge of Hampstead Heath in London. Acting on her theory that blue is the color most soothing to the nerves, she had the house decorated throughout in various blending shades of blue and called it The Blue Bird's Nest—"in the anticipation that the happiness of Maeterlinck's Blue Bird will reign there." Byron cottage, her own home nearby, was turned into a sock-collecting center, and she made a point of personally acknowledging every gift.

The wholesale exodus of the Belgian civilian population from the advancing German armies faced France, Holland, and Britain with a tremendous task of relief, and once more the privileged women of Britain showed their capacity for efficient improvisation. Lady Flora Louise Lugard, the wife of the celebrated administrator of Britain's Nigerian colonies, set herself to sort the sheep from the goats among the Belgian refugees. In London, more than twelve thousand had been crammed into transit centers in a large general store and two exhibition centers—Alexandra Palace and Earl's Court. As one report put it: "With all the goodwill in the world, it was soon evident that in these great camps many men and women were living in the utmost discomfort. Here were members of the Belgian Court circle, the aristocracy of the country, men of former great wealth, and professional people, herded together with the flotsam and jetsam which forms a part of every country, Belgium not excepted. . . . One elderly lady, who had all her life been accustomed to every luxury and service that wealth can procure, was now trying, with failing eyes, and completely broken down by the horrors she had witnessed, to take her share in the rough, unaccustomed work of keeping Earl's Court clean. Imagine the hardship to any delicately reared woman. . . ."

Lady Lugard procured eleven large houses, each accommodating up to forty guests, in which refugees were segregated according to birth and occupations. In one, for instance, were former members of the court, in another broken financiers, in another university men and professional people and artists. Each house had a lady manager

and a suitable complement of servants. "What," inquired one manager, "will be my duties?" and Lady Lugard answered: "You must
imagine yourself to be hostess of a continuous week-end party, with
a gnawing desire to keep down expenses." By careful manipulation,
costs were kept down to an average of 14s. 4d. a week per head, to
which Lady Lugard's fund contributed 5s. 6d., the rest being supplied by the Government. In this way, what she liked to call "a
thousand *representative* Belgians" were entertained for the duration
of the war.

Other society women organized the finding of homes and jobs
for humbler exiles. The Hon. Mrs. Alfred Lyttelton supervised the
interviewing of Belgians on arrival in London, set up temporary hostels, got offers of hospitality from private homes, recommended hotels or lodgings to those able to pay their way, and started a labor
exchange. Miss Mary Bidwell, the daughter of Lady Selina Harvey,
was supervisor of the Allocation Department of the War Refugees'
Committee, which was responsible for dealing with more than
225,000 refugees. She and fourteen assistants placed an average of
500 a week in suitable homes, and Miss Bidwell showed a special
interest in the welfare of Belgian troops. She was Chairwoman of
the British Club for Belgian Soldiers in London, which she visited
frequently, talking to the men in fluent French. As one journalist
commented: "It is fortunate that these men return to become trench-
worn and tired with an impression of an Englishwoman such as
Miss Mary Bidwell to take with them. . . ."

On yet another Belgian tack was Lady Lowther, a Mary Pick-
fordish beauty in her wartime photograph. In an article explaining
why she had become President of the London branch of Relief for
Belgian Prisoners in Germany, she wrote: "These men were all
miserable, the most miserable: their homes destroyed, their wives
and sisters wanderers or worse, their country but a name. Our sole
aim is to send food and clothing to the half-starved and shivering
Belgian soldier. The articles are all packed at our roomy and convenient offices at London Wall. About 34 ladies and gentlemen work
at this exhausting task, with the splendid result that over 150 parcels
are despatched every day. . . ." And she concluded her message:
"Can one help feeling that war is not wholly evil when one can testify to the exquisite never-failing springs of charity which well up in

all hearts? If spirituality is our ultimate goal in this life, then surely this terrible war has been our gain. When a hungry, shuddering Belgian in the depth of a German prison is clothed by an eager hand in San Francisco or by a glowing heart in the Antipodes . . ." and so on, in the strain of a book (typical of the period) by a British nurse, which summarized, "Oh dolorous but holy times of war, which purify our youth, which summon up again all our effective faculties."

The Hon. Evelina Haverfield, one of the first and most vigorous of the upper-echelon suffragettes, stepped into the breach, and the breeches, with a will. She had gone to prison for rushing the Houses of Parliament, but before that she had shown signs of a restless and masterful temperament. A daughter of the third Baron Abinger, she was one of the most brilliant and daring horsewomen of her day, and during the Boer War she had accompanied her army officer husband to South Africa (despite a broken leg sustained in a hunting accident in Dorsetshire). There she organized a supply of remounts by collecting and reconditioning horses abandoned on the veldt. In 1914, she was a founder member of the Women's Emergency Corps, which offered gardeners, cooks, canteen hands, doctors, nurses, drivers, and messengers on motorcycles; was appointed Commandant in Chief of the Women's Reserve Ambulance Corps; and founded the Women's Volunteer Reserve. The Volunteer Reserve members wore felt hats and khaki uniforms of her own design, an ensemble that was the basis of all subsequent uniforms for women working with the Army. Later, she worked under Dr. Elsie Inglis with Scottish Women's Hospital Units in Serbia and Rumania and was one of the leading forces in the Serbian Relief Fund.

The Times History of the War told how Queen Amelie of Portugal "worked indefatigably as a checking clerk, while Lady Sophie Scott, Lady Beatrice Pole-Carew and other Society women worked long hours packing and sorting medical requirements." At Cliveden, the Astor country house near Maidenhead, American-born Nancy (later Lady) Astor, energetically presided over patriotic house parties. To one of these, rather unwillingly, went Sylvia Pankhurst, a left-wing Socialist and, unlike her mother and sister, a bitter opponent of a "capitalist" war. She hoped to enlist the aid of Mrs. Astor in raising funds for the toy factory and welfare services that she had started in the East End of London to give employment to the women of its poverty-stricken slums. It was a bizarre experience. Each enormous guest suite had its own fire and magnificent marble bath. In the drawing room, men in faultless evening dress lounged and sauntered, and A. J. Balfour, the Conservative leader, was the center of attention.

"He talked," said Sylvia, "with flippant, senile elegance. At last came the ladies, all with their delicate, flaxen fairness, in black silk gowns with delightful white ruffles. The dinner was sumptuous, with abundant meats. It seemed strange to me, in the midst of the Great War, to be filing out with the women while the men sat chatting over their wine, as they did in the time of our grandfathers. In the rush of an agitator's life, I had forgotten that such foolish customs still obtained." The endless small talk grated on her, and she had to look on, fuming, while the odious Balfour ogled a young actress "with compliments a trifle too fulsome, in the manner of a dying epoch, when women were merely toys." She decided to make herself small and plan her next anticapitalist article for her magazine, *The Worker's Dreadnought,* but she did not escape so easily: "A troupe of lovely beings bore down on me. 'What are you doing in war work?' 'Nothing!' I answered with passion, 'I am not connected with the War!' 'Of course we are *all* connected with the War!' one beauty answered haughtily," and the virtuous belles turned their pretty backs on her.

The following day, Sunday, brought more trials. After planning the destruction of the Hun over a breakfast of immense and epicurean proportions, the guests trooped off to morning service with their hostess. To while away the afternoon, Mrs. Astor suggested a visit to the military hospital on the grounds, but, to Miss Pankhurst's secret satisfaction, the matron refused admission to the party. Sylvia then embarrassed everyone by flatly contradicting an American journalist who had enthused about the wonderful unity he had found among all classes in the war effort, and Mrs. Astor aggravated matters by questioning Miss Pankhurst about her "interesting" work in the East End. "I hope," she said, "you teach the women to be good?" To which the reply was: "I do not consider that my province. They know as much of goodness as I do. I try to spur them to revolt against the hideous conditions in which they live."

Between fund-raising concerts and balls and parties, women of the leisure classes found an outlet for their surplus energy (that effervescence whose repression had, in Florence Nightingale's time and opinion, driven them mad) in Sunday relief work in munition factories. Sylvia Pankhurst complained that these perfumed part-timers got special treatment, were paid more than ordinary employ-ees (who worked all hours for from 8 to 14s. a week in the early, unregulated months of the war), and were often put in as super-visors at superior wages.

The *Manchester Guardian* ran the story of a lady of title who, having become a munitionette, gave a dinner party to celebrate her first month of work. The guests numbered a Duchess, the wife of a Cabinet Minister, and—*pièce de résistance*—a workingwoman who was introduced as "Mabel, my mate in the shop." The hostess and her mate wore print dresses, with handkerchiefs turbaning their hair —as was the custom in the shop—and the table was covered, can-teenwise, with oilcloth. The meal was brought in by a maid, but the hostess did the carving and the guests helped themselves to the vegetables. "It's the simple life," explained the hostess. "Mabel and I only get fifteen bob a week and it won't run to more." The butler had been sent to the theater to get him out of the way.

Britons continued, to the despair of Sylvia Pankhurst and other social reformers, to love a Lord—and the gamier and more flam-boyant, the better. Lady Constance Manners, wife of John Thomas Manners-Sutton, and her daughter turned the family mansion into a convalescent home for New Zealand officers, who were not only able to ride when they felt strong enough, but gloried in the knowledge that Lord Manners, who addressed them when they gathered around an Armistice Day bonfire on the grounds, had actually won the Grand National on his own horse.

2 ❧

Lady Muriel

The first thirty years of Lady Muriel Paget's life gave little sign that, in an age given to spectacular private charity, she would become

Britain's archimpresario of relief work. Indeed, it seemed unlikely that she would be anything more than a charming and slightly eccentric semi-invalid. She was born Muriel Finch-Hatton in 1876, and her father, Murray Finch-Hatton, became twelfth Earl of Winchelsea in 1887. Life at home—Haverholme Priory, a Victorian Gothic mansion in Lincolnshire—had its peculiarities, not the least being the presence of a young lion. The Earl had brought it back as a cub from a visit to South Africa, and its favorite resting place was the drawing-room sofa. The Earl's political activities were concentrated on improving the lot of the agricultural laborer, and he started a newssheet called *The Cable* with the object of drawing the "three strands" of country life (landlord, farmer, laborer) closer together in mutual understanding. Muriel's mother, Lady Edith Winchelsea, developed early into a professional hypochondriac who spent most of her time lying in bed or sending back long bulletins about her health from various Continental resorts ("I have been out for 10 mins. in a nice yellow bath chair, and am none the worse for it . . .").

Her brother, Viscount Maidstone, was a precocious child who, before he died at the age of nine, discussed with his father the founding of a Children's Order of Chivalry. Its members would each "adopt" a child of the poorer classes, corresponding with it regularly and helping it in suitable ways. Even after her marriage, in 1897, to Richard (later Sir Richard) Paget, an aristocratic inventor who designed one of the first electric phaetons, Muriel's health, always fragile, continued to give concern, and she accompanied her mother to the English seaside, to Bad Kissingen, St. Moritz, and Cannes in search of an elusive robustness. When she was strong enough, she played golf, rode, paid visits, and entertained. Having been taught that social privilege carried its own responsibilities, she dutifully agreed, in 1905, to become Honorary Secretary of the Invalid Kitchens, which had been started in the slums of South London. Her husband fervently hoped that this would take her mind off her own illnesses and give her a new interest in life.

And so it proved. She threw herself into the work with zest and, determined to enlarge the usefulness of the kitchens, rapidly emerged as one of London's most resourceful and effective hostesses and fund-raisers. She was a pioneer of charity balls, and the fame of her own charity grew so that Queen Mary agreed to be a patron and the Duchess of Gloucester to be President. Immersed in philanthropic schemes, she not only forgot her ailments, but found little time to take an interest in the upbringing of her own children, leaving that side of things to Sir Richard, who, as she told her friends, was "the best mother in London."

When war came, she further extended the scope of her kitchens and did her share of work for Belgian refugees. But this did not satisfy her. Hearing of the appalling casualty rate among the ill-armed Russian troops, she resolved to form a hospital unit of British surgeons and nurses to be sent to Russia as a gesture of goodwill. Her prewar contacts and experience stood her in good stead, and this dynamic invalid (who was still laid low for weeks by a common cold) had soon whipped up a title-studded committee with Dowager Queen Alexandra as patron. King George V and Queen Mary headed the subscription list, and contributions poured in. Lady Muriel made a lightning tour of military hospitals in France to gather ideas for her unit, interviewed nurses, and cajoled firms into donating equipment.

After this feverish burst of activity, she was too ill to accompany the unit to Petrograd. It was quartered on the first floor of the Grand Duke Dmitri's baroque palace on the Nevsky Prospect, the ground floor being occupied by the Grand Duke, the top floor by complicated swarms of family retainers and hangers-on. The work of conversion was costly—protecting the parquet floors, boxing in the many cherubic carvings—but a hospital of two hundred beds was finally organized. The whole enterprise was viewed with disfavor by Lady Georgina Buchanan, the energetic wife of Sir George Buchanan, the immaculate, monocled British Ambassador. She ran the British colony's hospital, had improvised a hostel for refugee children from the wood of old packing cases, and thought another British unit distinctly superfluous.

Progress, under these circumstances, was slow, and all the slower when the ship carrying the hospital stores got stuck in the hostile ice of the White Sea. Replacements had to be purchased hastily in Petrograd, where everyone shivered in the grip of a ferocious winter. Lady Muriel, on her bed of sickness in England, fretted at the delays. She cabled to her deputy, Lady Sybil Grey: COMMITTEE THINK

IMPORTANT FOLLOW ORIGINAL SCHEME HAVE HOSPITAL 400 BEDS FED
EVENTUALLY BY OWN THREE FIELD HOSPITALS. URGE ACQUIRING
ADDITIONAL BUILDING. But since there was a lull in the fighting and
ten field hospitals had been sent back from the dormant Northern
Front, nothing came of this suggestion. In January, 1916, however,
the Dowager Empress of Russia officially opened the Anglo-Russian
Hospital, and a trickle of wounded entered its impressive wards.

In the spring, recovered from her indisposition, Lady Muriel set
out for Russia to take over in person. At Oslo she had an audience
with the Queen of Norway, at Stockholm she met Sweden's Crown
Prince and was nerved to a new determination by the disgusting
sight of the German naval attaché, plump in a brown-and-green-
checked suit, dining gluttonously in a smart restaurant. Always a
magnet to odd situations (though sublimely unaware of their—and
her—oddness), she traveled with a British general who had been
put in charge of an unusual gift from Queen Alexandra to the Dowager Empress. It was a sitting of eggs, which had to be turned every
day.

In Petrograd, the sparks soon began to fly as the tiny, frail, de-
ceptively mild-mannered Lady Muriel clashed with the more obviously formidable Lady Georgina. The fronts had sprung to deadly
life again, and Lady Muriel was determined to form a field unit and
escape from the gilded cage of the Grand Duke Dmitri's palace. She
got her way, and the Grand Duchess and Sir George and Lady
Georgina were present at a grand ceremony of dedication, during
which the resplendently coped and magnificently bearded Metropolitan sprinkled holy water over personnel and equipment with a
liberal hand. The unit left Petrograd in June on a special train—
thirty-seven coaches, gaily festooned with greenery—and prepared
for sterner action.

But it was deposited, after a triumphal ride, at Voropayevo, the
least active part of the Northern Galician front. Keyed up for shot
and shell and plenty of casualties, Lady Muriel was infuriated by
such treachery. Back she went to Petrograd, to begin a ruthless pestering of the military authorities. Elderly Russian generals, unused
to such relentless wheedling, found that her memory was sometimes
so conveniently inaccurate that they insisted on a third party being
present during interviews to keep the record straight. But they ca-

pitulated. Having gotten her unit moved from its backwater, she wrote to her committee in London, brusquely demanding "a hundred ambulances to work in connection with our dressing stations; then we could be of real practical use, and the Russians would feel that, even if we were not holding the Germans in the West, we were doing our bit."

Obediently, the committee buckled to. A gala matinee was staged at the Empire Theatre in the presence of Queen Alexandra and the Grand Duke Michael. Stars like Phyllis Dare, Harry Tate, Gladys Cooper, José Collins, and Gertie Millar took part, not to mention the sixteen palace girls and some Russian peasant dancers, and more than £1,000 was raised. Lady Muriel suggested some highly effective gimmicks. Russian curios were sold in gift shops outside which Russian wolfhounds mounted guard. A lifeboat that had survived the sinking of the *Lusitania* was suspended in Trafalgar Square and picturesquely filled with girls in sailor suits rattling collection boxes. Debs in Russian costume sold flags in Piccadilly; and in the Palm Court of the Carlton Hotel, the comedian George Robey profitably auctioned a hand-painted imperial standard autographed by the ever-obliging Queen Alexandra. Civic authorities hastened to raise the £250 that would entitle them to have their coat of arms placed over a bed in the Anglo-Russian Hospital. Fetes, whist games, darts matches with the Kaiser's face as a target, cricket matches between teams of local ladies and convalescent soldiers (gallantly playing left-handed)—all contributed to the funds. The island town of Stornoway, in Scotland's Outer Hebrides, alone raised £500. The British Isles brought their tribute to Lady Muriel's expectant, tapping feet.

She herself accompanied the field hospital to its new, and more satisfactorily dangerous, quarters, and she wrote home a description of its bombing: "I found Old Whiskers [a Russian general] and asked if some of the patients suffering from shock could be moved, and he said no." She moved them all the same: "One they thought would have a haemorrhage on the way, so, fervently praying that it would not be necessary to use it, I armed myself with a tourniquet and for 2½ hours was wedged in between the stretchers in an ambulance, trying to calm a boy who could luckily talk French. You never saw such a heartrending sight as the outside of the hospital that night. As far as you could see, wounded men were lying in rows and heaps in the courtyard and along the roads, half-naked many of them." For bravery under bombardment, she was awarded the Medal of St. George, Second Class.

Visiting Petrograd again, she went to tea with the Tsarina and her children in the palace at Tsarskoe Selo. The Tsarina was studying the question of artificial limbs and said she would like to build a factory to make them. The tea, Lady Muriel reported, was excellent, and the royal girls so cheerful that they threw cherrystones at each other. Her own pleasure was slightly clouded when her committee, as it tentatively did from time to time, asked for more exact accounts of the spending of its money. She replied that she resented such "criticism" and threatened to resign forthwith if she was not "giving satisfaction." Having quelled her critics, she turned her attention to M. Khomyakov, a young aristocrat who had been attached to her unit as liaison officer by the Russian Red Cross. He presented a much more difficult problem. "He is utterly unbusinesslike," she analyzed, in the full flush of her self-vindicated virtue. "His interests are art, philosophy and religion. He is utterly bored with life and would like to become a monk were it not that he is shortly to be married. He will sit for hours drinking tea, smoking innumerable cigarettes, and dreamily looking into space. You have to be *at* him all the time. I find it hard to be patient and long to stick a pin into him. Then he looks at you with those eyes of his, a hundred years old, eyes whose lids come half over them as if it were too much trouble to keep them open. . . ."

Khomyakov and the onset of winter plunged her into a long bout of illness, and in November, 1916, she left for England—dancing a hornpipe (to the astonishment of bystanders) on the platform at Petrograd Railway Station to keep warm. Despite severe flu, she struggled up to London for meetings of the committee, busied herself with raising more funds, and was impatient to get back to Russia. She heard that in the comparatively mild outbreak of March, 1917, which deposed the Tsar and brought the first, and so quickly extinguished, glimmerings of parliamentary democracy, her hospital had been guarded by a special detachment of troops and had escaped damage. But she hurried back soon afterward, arriving at about the same time as another restless exile, Lenin. In Petrograd, where she met Mrs. Pankhurst and Jessie Kenney on their mission, she found time for some social life. She too had a night out with the Yusupovs. After dinner, Prince Yusupov sang folk songs to a guitar, and "at midnight we went down to the cellar and listened to the gypsies. An old woman sang wild songs in a big, deep voice, and the ladies sat on heaps of cushions on the floor, Princess Yusupov in red against green—lovely. Yusupov told me he sang one of those songs to Rasputin."

Thoroughly used to a hectic life and possessing a childlike faith in her own authority and personal immunity, she took the first Bolshevik uprising, in July, in her stride. She was dining out when the news of it reached her and insisted on returning to the hospital. In the streets she saw soldiers firing into the crowds and, turning a corner, found herself, as she put it, "looking into the mouth of a revolver with a fierce Russian behind it. I pushed the revolver away and laughed at the soldier, who let me pass. . . ."

As the German armies penetrated the demoralized Russian lines, the field unit worked at fearful pressure, coping with some five thousand casualties in less than ten days. Lady Muriel was there to see them come in and noted that "more than 300 had had their left hands shot off, so that they should not have to go back to the front. They used to put a loaf of bread on the muzzle of their rifle and their hand on top of it, and then fire. It was horrible." The field hospital was evacuated to Odessa in November, 1917, during the second and final Bolshevik Revolution. On the way, freezing Russian orderlies lit fires on the floor of one of the railway carriages, which burst into flames. It was a suitably apocalyptic climax to an almost slapstick career.

In Odessa, though tired and under orders to rest and recuperate her strength, Lady Muriel roused herself to give a cheer-up party for the despondent members of the British colony. Among the guests was a jockey who had been expatriate for so long that his English was almost impossible to understand, and even Lady Muriel's reckless gaiety could not for long distract the minds of lesser mortals from the murderous chaos around them. There was shooting and looting and robbing in the streets. Naval officers were hurled overboard by mutinous sailors, and terrified Jews paid protection money to the troops. Lady Muriel stayed long enough to help establish food distribution centers in Odessa and Kiev, and in February, 1918, she left Kiev on the long and perilous overland journey across Siberia to Vladivostok. In the train she met and made firm friends with Tomáš Masaryk, the exiled Czech nationalist leader. In Washington, she had an interview with President Wilson, reporting on the situation in Russia, and for a while worked with the British Military Mission. There was no holding her. Like some maddening, heartening top, she spun from one unlikely assignment to the next.

Shortly after the Armistice, Dr. Alice Masaryk, daughter of the first President of the freshly created Czechoslovakian state, appealed to her to organize a new fight—against famine and disease. She immediately began, in her own inimitable way, to recruit staff for a medical mission. One candidate, given an appointment for midday at a London hotel, arrived to find her prospective employer still in bed and decidedly nebulous about Central European geography and the probable duties of her nurses. When asked what the job would lead to, she grandly replied, "It will lead you to the Courts of Europe."

Perhaps she was already meditating on the tactics she would use when she went to Paris to beg backing from the Allied statesmen, still engaged on the godlike task of remaking the map of Europe. Her impact on them was sharp. *"Protégez-moi, protégez-moi de cette dame!"* cried Dr. Beneš, the bewildered Czech Foreign Minister, and the general impression was neatly summed up in a limerick composed by a British victim of her zeal:

> How lucky Lady Muriel
> Isn't in the pluriel.

Unperturbed by such resistance, she urged the British Government to help the starving children of Vienna, and she even wrote to Lord Northcliffe to enlist his support. "Dear Lady Muriel," he somewhat chillily replied, "Is it rude of me to suggest that there are many people in this country who badly need relief? Exactly why we should help the Viennese and neglect our friends, I am unable to divine. I am quite sure that my newspapers would not be at all inclined to support these enterprises." Even Dr. Alice Masaryk had to protest against Lady Muriel's extravagance. The poverty-stricken Czech Government could not be expected to pay the salaries of a team of fifty workers ("I am very sorry to have to tell you this, for I am thankful for your interest, and I love you").

Yet the Paget Mission, despite capricious methods of selection and an almost total ignorance of the Czech language, was remarkably effective. By 1920, Lady Muriel, with her incurable tendency toward expansion, was organizing relief work on an unprecedented scale—in the Crimea, the Baltic States, and Rumania as well as in Czechoslovakia. The Invalid Kitchens of 1905 were written large all over Europe. She herself ricocheted around her far-flung empire, skimming its vast surface like a sleepless swallow, always traveling with an assortment of fruit in a little net bag, always in too much of a hurry to listen to the problems of her often distracted staff. Employees found it best to waylay her in her hotel room and help her with her packing, the choosing of her clothes, even the running of her bath, in order to get a decision. One worker, based in Riga, had to run alongside Lady Muriel's departing train to get her last-minute instructions, concluding with, "And write to my family. I haven't got time." So powerful and all-pervasive was her influence that the Orient Express was held up for twenty minutes while she searched absorbedly for some missing false curls.

She continued her whirlwind campaign against the aftermath of the First World War until near her death. In 1932, welcomed by Soviet officials who remembered her wartime exploits, she returned to Petrograd (now Leningrad). It was her last mission, and possibly her weirdest. Its object was to do something for displaced British subjects (DBS's for short) in Russia, mostly elderly widows eking out a strange existence, in a world into which perhaps only Lady Muriel (herself perpetually hovering on the border line of fantasy) could have entered without offense. There was a Mrs. Brown, who thought she was the Queen of England or (sometimes) the Metropolitan of Belgrade, and a Mrs. Ambrose, a jockey's wife who was wasting away because she would not eat horseflesh. Mrs. Nora Macnamara-Zabczinski complained that she was tormented by the behavior of a mentally deranged neighbor who, as soon as she put out the light to go to sleep, hammered on the partition and yelled: "You are eating a decomposed cat, and I can't bear the smell!" Lady Muriel chatted with, and even kissed, these strange and often unkempt creatures, who lived in surroundings that turned the stomach of the British Consul who accompanied her.

She built a rest home for them in the countryside and managed to rent a large flat in Leningrad that served as a sort of DBS information and social center. She had thoughtfully brought with her five sets of false teeth, and these were given to those who found they fitted.

For nearly thirty years, she had got her way by saying, "Rubbish! Don't be so fussy!" to finicky administrative types. A legend in many countries, she was a comparative stranger in her own home. When she strayed from her warpaths for long enough to visit it, she found herself so out of touch. It was a saddening experience. "Why," she would lament, "why am I never told anything?"

3

Leila, Lady Paget

Friends were surprised when they heard that Leila, Lady Paget was taking a hospital unit to Serbia. Tall and rather pale, she was considered delicate and had led a conventional and sheltered life unsuggestive of such enterprise. The daughter of Mary, Lady Paget (formerly Mary Paran Stevens of New York) and General Sir Arthur Paget, she had grown up in a stately mansion in Belgrave Square, London, and had married her cousin, diplomat Sir Ralph Paget (who was much older than she was), soon after "coming out." In 1911, she accompanied her husband to Serbia, where he had been appointed Ambassador. In 1914, the Pagets returned to England. Sir Ralph had been appointed Undersecretary of State for Foreign Affairs, and they settled into a new and august social round.

When war was declared, she calmly, and with a hint of suppressed delight, announced her intention of doing something for the Serbs. Methodically and without fluster, as though ordering clothes for a new Mayfair season, she compiled her lists and issued her instructions. She was not concerned with making any feminist point, so hers was not an all-female unit (it included some of the leading surgeons and physicians in London), but it was the first unit to ar-

rive in Serbia, and it set up in Skopje in October, 1914. The first
wave of Austrian invaders had been driven back, but there was terrible chaos. Wounded were piled in schools, inns, and stables.
Typhus and smallpox swept the country. There were few doctors, no
nurses, and only Austrian prisoner-of-war orderlies.

Lady Paget amazed everyone by getting up at 4 A.M. and working with a will. She wore the regulation "germproof" uniform—
long white cotton underwear with the legs tucked into high Serbian
boots, topped by a smock with a tight collar and tight wristbands.
Over her hair she wore a close-fitting cap, and beneath the uniform,
around her neck and arms, bandages soaked in Vaseline and petro-
leum as a protection against the swarming vermin.

Most patients were infested with lice, but Lady Paget left her
administrator's office to scrub floors and help with funeral rites at
the bedsides of dying soldiers. She caught typhus and for weeks was
on the brink of death. She had already made such an impression
that when she left for England to convalesce, Serbs lined the streets
of Skopje and threw flowers and jostled to kiss the hem of her dress.
At the railway station, the Crown Prince presented her with the Order of St. Sava with a cross of diamonds—the highest decoration he
could bestow.

After two months' rest, and despite the protests of husband, relatives, and friends, she was back in Skopje. It was summer, 1915,
now. The typhus epidemic was at last under control. There had
been no fresh fighting or casualties since December, when the second Austrian invasion had been rolled back from Belgrade. It
seemed doubtful whether her unit was needed, but the Crown
Prince, certain that a third and even more overwhelming invasion
was imminent, begged her to stay. She brought her staff up to
strength by arranging the loan or transfer of members from other
units that were disbanding, and so saved the expense of having a
new staff sent out from England. When she had finished, her hospital was nothing if not international, with three hundred Austrian orderlies; Serbian interpreters and washerwomen; British, American,
and Danish surgeons; and British, American, Danish, Dutch, and
French nurses.

Soon came reports of the massing of troops—German, Austrian,
and Bulgarian—on the frontier for a triple assault. What followed

was told by Lady Paget herself in the report that she presented to the Serbian Relief Fund Committee a year later.

Despite the news, morale was high in Serbia. Skopje was be-flagged to celebrate the arrival of Allied troops at Salonika. Bunches of box—the traditional sign of rejoicing—were tied to the lampposts at the railway station, and rows of lanterns were hung either side of the bridge over the Vardar. Arrangements were made for the quartering of Allied troops, especially British troops (for surely they would hurry to help Lady Paget). But the days passed, and there was no sign of them.

On October 5, the bombardment of Belgrade, already twice captured and twice freed, began. A week later, wounded began to arrive at Skopje. The Germans and Austrians were advancing from the north, the Bulgarians from the east—where the Allies had been expected to hold the line. Lady Paget sped to Salonika to urge the Allied generals to take immediate action, and on the return journey she found panic at stations already crammed with refugees and wounded soldiers. As the train drew in, wounded and unwounded tried to rush it, clinging to the footboards and clambering onto the roofs. "Children," she wrote, "were trampled underfoot, and others were hurled by their parents over the heads of the affrighted crowds into the horseboxes, where sick and wounded soldiers were huddled. Many of the children were injured. Some passengers opposed the fresh influx, but I intervened and made them stand and give their seats to the wounded. Sick women, children and the badly wounded I took into my own carriage."

As the Bulgarians advanced on Skopje, she hurried to gather in badly wounded Serbs from outlying hospitals. At one, the Serbian staff had fled, leaving an English nurse in charge of more than a hundred men, who had no food or water and lay on the floor, some in a raging fever, others dying of hideous, septic wounds. Such was the fear of the Bulgarians that many sick and wounded troops attempted to take refuge in the mountains: "One man with a fractured thigh set out on crutches, another with pneumonia and typhoid forced us to give him his clothes, as he would otherwise have set out in his nightshirt." Some collapsed before they had gone more than a few hundred yards, and were fetched back by waiting ambulances.

As the troops evacuated the town, Lady Paget organized the distribution of clothes and blankets: "At first we handed them through the door, but soon every window had to be opened as well, and as fast as the bales could be ripped open, vests, pants, socks, etc., were thrown to the clamouring crowds outside. It was satisfactory to know that at least this small section of the Serbian Army was the warmer during its retreat through Albania."

Her ambulances continued to round up food and medical stores as well as patients. Hard liquor was ruthlessly disposed of: "At the Grad Hospital we found big barrels of wine in the vaults. It seemed a pity to see the clear, sparkling stream pouring down the face of the citadel rock as we staved in the casks, especially as we knew that later on it would be badly needed for patients; but we could not risk letting it fall into the hands of the victorious troops."

After the military had left, Skopje seemed like a city of the dead. Not a chink of light glimmered from any of the windows, not a sound came up from the streets, except now and then the howling of a starving dog. It was a time of gloomy tension.

Just before the Bulgarians entered the town, on October 22, Lady Paget went to complete the clearance of the Poloumesetz Hospital, which lay further down the river in the direction of the enemy's advance. Shells were falling nearer and nearer, and the wounded were literally flung into the ambulances. Such was the crush that one man was prevented from falling out, as they jolted over the rutted roads, only because Lady Paget twined her hand in his long, thick, matted hair. However, his joy at being taken to the English hospital was so intense that, between groans, he chuckled with pleasure.

By this time the rattle of machine guns was incessant, and shells began to explode near the hospital buildings, shattering windows. Retreating Serbian troops were shot down in view of the staff and struggled to reach the hospital—some on foot, some on ponies, some crawling through the mud. As a final touch of horror and confusion, so typical of the Balkan campaigns, Albanian guerrillas started potting at the wounded as they scrambled to sanctuary. It was a scene of scarifying futility and wanton cruelty.

As the battle swirled about the buildings, hundreds of Serbians were patched up, and two hundred taken into the wards. Sallying forth again to the Poloumesetz Hospital, Lady Paget, who paused to berate the astonished Albanian snipers, was angered by the refusal of the Greek doctor in charge to let his Bulgarian wounded be taken away. As her ambulances waited with their engines running, she tackled the obstinate, frightened man: "I told him that he would not receive much gratitude from the Bulgarians when they found that the majority of their men had died through lack of food and attention. There was a stormy scene, and we had literally to shout at one another to be heard above the shrieks and groans of the wounded."

Having gotten her Bulgarians, the next thing was to search for the Bulgarian commandant and ask permission to scour the battlefield for wounded. She found him fast asleep in an improvised trench: "Not having time for ceremony, I at once woke him up and put the hospital at his disposal and formally handed over the stores to him. I explained that we were a unit supported by a public fund in England to help the Serbians, and that I should have to account both to my Government and to my committee for everything I had done. I said we were willing to give help to the wounded Bulgarians until they could make their own medical arrangements, but I demanded, as soon as it was practicable, to be sent home with my entire staff." The sleepy commandant promised to grant her wish—as soon as the blown-up railway lines and bridges had been repaired.

Soon after she returned to her wards, an irate Hungarian first lieutenant appeared on the scene. He had been ill and a prisoner for some months in another hospital in Skopje, but now demanded the return of the three hundred Austrian orderlies. After some wrangling, he agreed to refer the matter to Vienna for a decision and, in the meantime, set about restoring military discipline. "His task," Lady Paget observed, "was not easy. He had to deal with a mixed lot of Austrians, Hungarians, Czechs, Croats, Slovenes and Moravians, many of them with strong racial antipathies towards one another, and towards himself as a Hungarian. To use his own words, commanding in the Austrian Army is a species of warfare in itself. He held a parade next day, and delinquents who had forgotten how to salute their officers were soundly cuffed."

She tried hard to win the confidence of the Bulgarians so that she could continue to help the Serbs. Famine had hit the town. The Serbian Army had taken most of the food supplies, driving flocks and herds before them, burning crops and smashing the railways.

The Bulgarians naturally sent what food they could find to their troops in the field, and the civilian population of Skopje, constantly swollen by refugees from the surrounding countryside, was in a desperate plight.

Lady Paget's hospital still had three hundred sacks of flour, some rice, and a lot of warm clothes, and the harassed Bulgarians were content to allow her to do what she could to cope with this problem. She organized a daily distribution of rations for Serbian refugees.

But the military governor was exasperated by her cool, efficient independence. He ordered her to go to the cemetery to watch the disinterment of some Bulgarians who were said to have been the victims of Serbian atrocities. Seeing photographers in attendance, Lady Paget was immediately on guard. She knew that any picture that showed her and the corpses together would probably be used for enemy propaganda, and she therefore maneuvered to keep behind the cameras. In a sequence of macabre comedy, the governor kept telling her to make a personal examination of the bodies, and she kept refusing on the ground that only expert evidence could be of any value. After much inconclusive sparring, the governor's objective was mercifully defeated when the photographer himself—a Serbian—with tactful clumsiness dropped and broke his two remaining plates.

In this war of nerves, Lady Paget received powerful support from a personal friend of prewar diplomatic days—Queen Eleonora of the Bulgarians, who sent money as well as telegrams that had a restraining effect on the governor. As her supplies of flour ran out, Lady Paget had to buy from small traders in the town. Fearing that their whole stock would be commandeered, they demanded secrecy and would only part with a few sacks at a time, which had to be collected after dark from one of the hidden subterranean storerooms in the labyrinthine Turkish quarter. Still grumbling, the governor claimed that Serbian soldiers disguised as women were joining the food queues to exchange information with the British hospital staff, and he posted sentries with fixed bayonets at the distribution points.

The cold was now biting, and the snow lay deep for weeks. Perhaps only the cold prevented the earth and the air from curdling with pestilence. Hundreds of carcasses of horses, mules, oxen, and buffalo lay where they had fallen. Their skins had been hacked off to make shoes, and the flesh, bloated and purple, was torn at by dogs and carrion crows. Ditches as well as a number of mortuaries were heaped with human corpses.

Refugees came in with frostbitten feet and open wounds caused by lice. Many were mad with hunger, having had no bread for nineteen days and no food of any kind for five. Food prices were skyrocketing, and not only the poor came to the hospital for relief—Serbian gentlewomen, wives of officers and officials, stood in the snow for hours hoping for half a kilo of flour or rice. In December the daily number of applicants had risen to more than four thousand.

Lady Paget opened an emergency clinic for the civilian population, who would otherwise have been totally without medical aid. Treatment was given free, and the seriously ill were taken into the hospital or visited at home by nurses. Despite every possible economy and a frantic search for new supplies, the food ran out, and the queues had to be turned away: "They received the news in silence, but a look of utter despair crept into their faces, and tears poured down their cheeks. They kissed our hands and our dresses, murmuring heartfelt gratitude for what we had done." In some cases, Lady Paget arranged to pay the rent to prevent some of the wretches from being turned into the freezing streets.

Overcrowding in Skopje was so appalling that the Bulgarians ordered all Serbian refugees to leave the town, whose population had grown within a few months from 30,000 to more than 130,000. It was a hard and a tragic decision, yet it must have been a relief to Lady Paget, for there were nearly eight hundred patients—Bulgarians, Serbs, and Austrians—to be cared for in the hospital.

The Bulgarians showed their growing confidence in Lady Paget by providing three hundred able-bodied Serb prisoners to take the place of the departing Austrian orderlies. The tension was easing, relations had improved wonderfully. Then, in December, the Germans, under General August von Mackensen, arrived to set up headquarters in Skopje. Lady Paget, as well as the Bulgarians and the Austrians ("We are fettered to a corpse," sneered the Germans of those allies), watched them with dismay. "They emerged out of the fog," she said, "with their spiked helmets and artillery and field-kitchens. Over a thousand quartered themselves in the outbuildings of the hospital; they stole our horses, burnt our firewood, exhausted our water supply and carried off all our hay. They took complete possession of the town, tore down the new Bulgarian street names and put up German ones. The principal square was re-christened Wilhelmsplatz."

The hospital, which the Germans coveted, found itself under a kind of psychological siege. *Gott Strafe England!* and other nasty messages were chalked on its walls. At this ominous juncture, it was the Bulgarians who worked out a plan to frustrate their allies. The Bulgarian flag was flown over the hospital, and a Bulgarian medical officer was made a nominal director of it.

The Germans hit back in various ways. General Mackensen complained that orderlies in uniform did not salute German officers in the town. Lady Paget was furious: "Considering that German soldiers never by any chance saluted Austrian or Bulgarian officers, who were their allies, I did not see any reason why our men should take any notice of German officers." But since she wanted her unit to leave as soon as possible, she got over the difficulty by instructing her orderlies to wear mufti when they left the hospital. When the Austrians and Bulgarians heard of this ruse, said Lady Paget, "they hugged themselves with delight."

The Bulgarians did more than applaud her resistance to German arrogance. They made special arrangements to transport the unit to Sofia. It would be dangerous for it to go by train, now that the railways were under German control, so ten large motor ambulances were put at Lady Paget's disposal for the journey across the frontier into Bulgaria.

The unit left before dawn on February 17, 1916, accompanied by a bodyguard of Bulgarian officers, the hackles of their honor bristling. Lady Paget was sorry to leave the hospital, but proud of her staff's achievement. "The hospital," she recorded, "had risen up out of the filth and disease in which we found it, till by degrees it had become one of the finest and best-equipped in Serbia. But it was being rapidly evacuated of Bulgarian and Serbian patients. The staff was worn out and our stores were gone. There had been 2,205 admissions since October 22nd. We had done all we could for Serbia."

In a last fling of spite, the Germans managed to delay the arrival of the special hospital train that King Ferdinand himself had ordered. "This," wrote Lady Paget, "resulted in our spending from one o'clock till six on the crowded platform at Sofia, our sick members lying on stretchers, until the Bulgarians, in a high state of indignation, hunted up carriages from different directions and made up another train."

This was not the last of Lady Paget's trials. Reaching England in April after a long and tedious journey, she found herself cold-shouldered for being too friendly with Austrians and Bulgarians. After such positively proconsular service, it was a little hard to be treated as a semitraitor, a feeble fraternizer.

4 ❧

The Mother of the British Army

The French and Belgian châteaux near the front, which provided good addresses for Allied generals and their staffs, provided also a fine array of bold and standard-guarding chatelaines. At the Château of Pronleroy in Picardy, from which the first victorious offensive of the French armies in 1918 was launched, the Marquise de Foucault saw that there were flowers in the bedrooms and in the dining room, that the food was good and elegantly served. She dressed with care for dinner, no matter how long the day had been, how near and noisy the enemy guns. She expected conversation at mealtimes to be casual and supple and civilized. There was a box on the table into which any officer who forgot his manners and spoke about the dreary, vulgar war had to drop his fine.

But perhaps the most charming and formidable of these ladies was the Flemish Baroness Ernest de la Grange, who specialized in British officers and looked after them so well that she became an honorary Britisher, a Commander of the Order of the British Empire. One of her favorite and most distinguished residents, Field Marshal Lord Edmund Allenby, the conqueror of Palestine, wrote, in a foreword to her wartime memoirs: "I am proud of the fact that I was the earliest British guest of the gracious lady who became so well known as 'The Mother of the British Army.' . . . Never has there been a finer gesture than hers in the early days of the war, when, urged to flight, she stood at her post—Chatelaine of La Motte au Bois—regardless of the advancing enemy, whose cavalry was sweeping through the surrounding Forest of Nieppe. Her example of intrepidity calmed the people of the village and restrained them from compromising their safety by panic action."

In those early, breathless days, she noted in her diary a rumor that Louvain had been destroyed ("What a crime against Civilisation, Art and Science! If this be the result of German Kultur, one would rather be a Red Indian!") and wandered, lonely but regal, through the enormous empty rooms. Hearing a plane buzz overhead, she went out to see if it was friend or foe, taking with her her little pet dog, Mino, a German basset hound. "Such," she reflected, "is the irony of things!" She had time, then, to ponder on the peculiarities of war: "The only beings who really like it are the pheasants in the forest. Since all guns were confiscated, there are no sportsmen and fewer poachers. The birds stroll peacefully on the lawn. . . ."

This illusory calm was broken by the news, in October, 1914, that General Allenby and his staff were to be quartered at La Motte au Bois. There was a great coming and going of orderlies, which the Baroness regarded with some alarm ("In spite of my patriotic pleasure I gave one despairing thought to my parquet"). Then came the great moment, the great man. "It was late when the headlights of a Rolls Royce threw their dazzling glare across our old walls, and one could hear horses snorting under the trees in the park. The Rolls made a half turn, and the aide-de-camp jumped out lightly. I admired the suppleness of body, produced by the practice of athletic games, and the cut of the uniform, which, if a man is not already a gentleman, gives the appearance of being one. Then the door of the car was opened and General Allenby's tall figure was silhouetted for an instant in the doorway."

She wondered whether to store the fine furniture in a safe place, but decided to leave things as they were, with the exception of four paintings of sentimental or commercial value: "the *Henri IV* by Porbus; the *Liseuse* attributed to the Italian School; the *Virgin with the Grapes* by Mignard; and the portrait of my grandmother, the Countess Tascher de la Pagerie."

She took to Allenby immediately, but had to complain to him about the behavior of some of his troops, who found it good sport to hunt calves through her woods. Then there was the delicate matter of the soldiers' habit of swimming naked in the canal. The Mother Superior of a nearby convent was most concerned at the effect on the maidens of the village. Allenby treated the problem lightly. "My dear lady," he said, "you know those signposts we put in yesterday? I wanted to see if they were all right, so I went there this morning. All your girls were there watching the bathing." As the Baroness strolled with Allenby along the canal, she was startled to see the Chief Surgeon, stout Major General Sir Menus William O'Keefe, costumeless in the water. He was about to climb onto the bank, but thoughtfully stayed submerged until his hostess had passed. After this, she stopped trying to treat the matter seriously.

The grandest occasion was when His Majesty King George V and the Prince of Wales came to decorate troops drawn up in the courtyard of the château. "The Prince," she wrote, "arrived first. He looks a mere boy, fresh, pink-and-white and charming. He examined the cars with great interest and made the officers' dogs jump over his stick." The Baroness watched discreetly from behind the hall curtains. She had gone to immense pains to arrange everything to the best advantage—"a big Louis XIV boule desk in the middle of the hall, and on it the visitors' book, hoping that the King might sign it. A few bottles of champagne and some biscuits on the sideboard. I put on the best dress I had in my wardrobe. The men who were to receive the medals were lined up under the lime trees, while on the card table I had lent were the cases containing the decorations. In spite of the extremely simple and modest bearing of the Royal Personage I felt rather overwhelmed."

Conversation was stilted. The King asked: "Madame, I hope you have no complaints against the British Army?" And the Baroness replied: "No, Sire. When one has the pleasure of receiving General Allenby as one's guest, it would ill become one to complain." She showed the King around, and he showed a keen interest in the trophies of the chase which antlered the walls and which her husband had shot in Canada: "He had not, he said, a single example of a cer-

tain great moose there. I would have offered it to His Majesty had it
not belonged to my son." To change the subject, she asked the King
his opinion of the outcome of the war. " 'My cousin William thinks
he will win, but he won't,' said the King, with an energy that delighted me. 'We shall conquer.' Then the champagne was poured
out and we drank good health to the Allies."

General William Pulteney, an older man, succeeded General
Allenby in due course. His aide, Gavin George, Lord Hamilton of
Dalzell, was, the Baroness noted, "very tall, with grey hair and fine
blue eyes. I should think he must be something of a lady killer."
The new regime was distinctly relaxed: "General Pulteney is what
we call a *bon vivant*, with a lively and twinkling eye. His Staff is a
very cheerful one, and I see extremely frivolous Parisian papers lying on the tables mixed up with ordnance maps and plans of attack."
There was a young officer who amused himself by devising curious
tableaux with cuttings from *La Vie Parisienne:* "He has arranged a
screen like a staircase. On each step are curious neighbours, as for instance Mr. Lloyd George with a modern Eve on his knees, or Lord
Balfour carrying on his shoulder a Venus well known to the world of
the grands boulevards! When I cross the office I lower my gaze
primly, but I manage not to miss a single detail of the screen all the
same."

During the biting winter of early 1916, the officers made a snow-
woman that was a kindly caricature of the Baroness, and she, entering into the fun, found some old clothes—a feather hat, a parasol, a
shawl, a skirt, and some boots—and dressed it up. At Christmas,
1916, General Sir Andrew Hamilton Russell, Commander of the
New Zealand Division, added an exotic touch to the festivities by
"putting some Maori dancers at my disposal for the general entertainment." After that, life went on without any remarkable incidents
—until midnight on June 5, 1917. The Baroness was writing in the
library when she heard a knock on the shutter of the vestibule. "I
called out cautiously before opening: 'Who goes there?' 'Friend,'
came General Allenby's deep tones. He came to tell me great news
—he is about to leave France for another front." The two corre-
sponded regularly (Allenby giving her his first impressions of T. E.
Lawrence), and when she heard of the death of Allenby's son, she
offered, with a loyal and possessive compassion, to have him buried

in the family vault at La Motte au Bois. To this proposal, Allenby replied, in February, 1918: "I am deeply grateful for your kind offer to receive my son Michael's body into your family vault. However, my wife and I would both wish his body to lie where it was placed by his friends and brother officers, close to the battlefield where he met his death."

During the German breakthrough, in May, 1918, the château was badly shelled, and the Baroness was at last persuaded to leave. It was a melancholy moment: "I let them help me into the car, with an extraordinarily varied heap of objects that I had rescued—some were on my lap, some on General [Beauvoir] de Lisle's." They passed a sad sight, surely a bad omen: "We saw a fair swan lying beating her white wings in death's agony! A shell had struck her mortally as she sat brooding on her nest."

Yet two months later, when the Allies had halted the German advance and launched their victorious counterattack, the Baroness returned to La Motte au Bois, to begin its restoration and to get the scarred and neglected fields of her domains into something like working order. A new and most obliging British general came to her rescue: "General [William] Birdwood has authorised me to choose from the British battery at Morbecque all the horses and men required to work every available plough. I have fifty horses, and seventy five men who before the war were agricultural labourers. Whatever harvest there is in this district in 1919 will be partly owing to them."

After the Armistice, her old boys and her adopted country did not forget her services. At Versailles in July, 1919, General Birdwood, with a wholehearted embrace à la française, invested her with the CBE, and then, on Bastille Day, she watched the triumphal entry into Paris of the Allies. "The British group," she recorded, "had at its head Field Marshal [Douglas] Haig and his Staff, and among them I saw General Birdwood and several of my other friends. They were looking up at the roof of the Automobile Club where I was— and then, in perfect unison, they suddenly saluted with their sabres! I could not restrain my tears. . . ."

Nine years later, she met the Prince of Wales once more, sharing a picnic lunch with him at the dedication of the British War Memorial at Ypres, and on Armistice Day, 1929, when she presented a copy of her memoirs to the Imperial War Museum in London, she wrote in her letter: "The Author would like her sentiments as well as her book to go down to posterity. . . . It was with my heart filled with hope that I watched the arrival of those splendid British troops in 1914. I saw them in action during five years. Officers and men rivalled each other in acts of heroism on the battlefields and gallantry towards the owners of the land on which they fought and where so many of them laid down their lives. It is on French land that they sleep their last sleep, those heroes who died in Flanders, Picardy and the Somme." She was proud of this, as glad of it as though it were some mysterious transfusion of courage, even of immunity. "This vast necropolis," she ended, "is the strongest safeguard against future aggression, and those thousands of white headstones are so many swords, ready to raise themselves against all those who would violate the Peace and Liberty of France."

Alas, poor Baroness, for such hopes. The dead did not rise from their graves to fight the battles of the living. They only provided reasons for the living to go to war again.

5

The View from Berlin

When Evelyn, the handsome daughter of Frederick Stapleton-Bretherton of Rainhill Hall, Lancashire, married Count Gebhard Blücher, a great-grandson of the German marshal who fought against Napoleon at Waterloo, she made a match that promised everything that she or her parents could possibly have desired. It had wealth, it had high social standing—and she loved her husband. For seven years, all went well. The couple spent most of the time in England (Count Blücher was a noted Anglophile), with occasional visits to the Blücher family estate in Silesia. At a court ball in Berlin shortly after Evelyn's marriage, the Kaiser himself spoke to the Countess and asked her to christen a new battleship—the *Blücher*

—at Kiel. There she met the Princess of Prussia, who reminisced about happy days with dear Queen Victoria and said how much she and her sister, the Tsarina of Russia, had enjoyed rummaging in the antique shops at Windsor. It was fun to go and stay with her father-in-law, the endearingly eccentric old Prince Blücher, a keen zoologist who lived on the diminutive Channel Island of Herm, where he devoted himself to breeding kangaroos.

So life passed, pleasantly if unspectacularly, as the Countess swung gently among the dense Teutonic ramifications of Europe's highest society, where, despite the deplorable *bêtises* of Kaiser Wilhelm, all seemed so safe, so solid, and so comforting.

In August, 1914, the Blüchers were staying at Rainhill Hall. Until the last moment, they refused to believe in the possibility of war, but when the impossible happened they hurried to London for consultations at the German Embassy. There it was settled that they must leave England, and they drove to Victoria Station with the Ambassador, Prince Lichnowsky, and his party. Friends who came to see them go stood with their heads bared, solemn and silent and mourning, and many people, among them Princess Lichnowsky, openly wept. They wept for the passing of a whole way of life.

At Harwich, the ambassadorial party was met by an admiral, who escorted it between rows of saluting sailors. Overcome by grief, Countess Blücher shut herself in her cabin. "I could not bear to look on the shores of my beautiful England fading from sight," she wrote in her diary. The journey was so swift, so efficient, almost as if it were part of a master plan in which everything had been foreseen, everything taken care of. At the Hook of Holland a special train waited to take them directly to Berlin. They passed train after train full of shouting, singing, laughing troops. The Countess was astonished by the holiday atmosphere. "I have at last seen the Germans stirred out of their morose dullness and what I used to think their everlasting heaviness," she commented.

In Berlin the Blüchers joined the colony of displaced notabilities at the luxurious Esplanade Hotel. Here, at dinner, the Countess was advised by Major Langhorne, the American military attaché, to wear an American badge when she went into the streets and on no account to talk English outside the Hotel or on the phone. Sunday Mass at the fashionable Hedwigkirche was a melancholy affair.

There were more tears, more forebodings. Poor little Princess Ratibor, who, the last time the Blüchers had met her, had been "the leading spirit in a gay romping set at a large shooting party, had all one side of her face plastered up, having been shot by mistake by her own Polish peasants when motoring to the station. Her car had been suspected of being one of the many said to be driving all over Germany filled with gold and spies."

News came that old Prince Blücher had been forced to leave Herm and his kangaroos. In fact, from the point of view of the Countess and other British-born wives of her acquaintance (among them Princess Münster, Princess Pless, and Baroness Roeder), the news was uniformly depressing. They had to read accounts of one British defeat after another and listen to patronizing remarks about British courage being useless without proper equipment and leadership. Trains taking troops to the Eastern Front were decorated with flowers, and, to the Countess's intense indignation, "stuffed-out figures of men dressed in the uniform of English Grenadier Guardsmen were fastened to some of the trucks." There were occasions when it was devilish hard to keep a stiff upper lip. October 12, the evening of the fall of Antwerp, was one of them. It had been agreed among the residents at the Esplanade that, for the duration of the war, it was bad form to wear coquettish clothes, and décolletage was definitely out. Yet one lady—an outsider, of course—arrived for dinner in "a transparent, low-necked dress, suitable for a grand ball at the height of the season. Some one remarked: 'You're very smart tonight, Madame.' 'Yes,' she said, with a beam of pleasure, 'I put this on to celebrate the fall of Antwerp, but wait until you see the dress I'm keeping for the day when England is beaten!' " The provocation was all but unbearable. "I think," wrote the Countess, "that if looks can hurt, mine must have penetrated to the marrow of her bones."

The air was full of rumors and atrocity tales. A German officer told her that if German troops had behaved brutally in Belgium, it was the fault of Belgian civilians. He knew of thirty officers, at that moment in the hospital, who had had their eyes gouged out by Belgian women and children as they lay wounded. Could the Army be blamed if it retaliated? This was bad, incredible, enough. But when one was seriously informed that British convicts were being let loose at the front and that British troops used dumdum bullets and car-

ried specially twisted knives for scooping out the eyes of wounded
Germans, one simply had to protest, even if in vain: "When I tell
them that these are knives carried by sappers to cut their way
through forests, etc., they only shrug their shoulders and say I am
pro-British."

It was most frustrating, but there were odd moments of light relief. When the Countess called on an old English lady detained in
Berlin, she was told to shut the door and keep her voice down. She
obeyed, and, with great circumspection, the old lady felt under the
pillow of her hotel bed and pulled out an ancient copy of the *Daily
Mail.* An American woman, a new arrival in the city, brought a
mountain of provisions with her, including two sacks of flour. Every
one laughed at her, but she explained that when she was in London
the newspapers had reported that Berlin was in a state of famine
and revolution.

The best thing to do was to keep as busy as possible. So the
Countess took a course in nursing (her husband was working for the
Red Cross) and spent most of her mornings in a military hospital.
Often she was tempted, as she helped to bandage patients' wounds,
to ask if they had committed atrocities on women and children. But
she restrained herself. Such curiosity was surely morbid. She did,
however, allow herself to talk to British prisoners of war working on
a road near Lichterfelde: "One very young sailor boy struck us so
much, he looked so unutterably sad and ill, and he was the only one
who stood up to attention and saluted as we left." But on the whole
the men seemed cheerful enough, and the wife of the camp commandant told her that, by contrast with French and Russian prisoners, who were slovenly and always grumbling, the British were clean
and smart and remarkably contented, especially if they were given a
ball to kick about.

She spent much time at the Red Cross office, compiling and typing British casualty lists and interviewing destitute German governesses and domestic servants who had been shipped from England
and now found work hard to get. Sometimes the old *Almanac de
Gotha* network still helped. One day as she hurried through the hall
of the Esplanade, an officer, a Count Welsczek, stopped her and
asked if she was related to Lord Edmund Talbot. She was, and he
told her that he had found Captain Talbot of the 11th Hussars lying

semiconscious in a ditch in France and had taken him to a casualty station. So she was able to send a telegram to Lord Talbot to say that his son, posted missing for weeks, was in a hospital near Lille.

There was the occasional morale-boosting diplomatic chore. In June, 1915, she entered in her diary: "Have been fearfully busy about the Reprisal Question. Winston Churchill has ordered all submarine prisoners to be put into solitary confinement. On hearing this, Germany ordered 39 English officers to be put into solitary confinement. Princess Münster, Princess Pless and I were told that as we all had relations among them, we could write to England and say that these officers would be released when Winston Churchill rescinded his decision." The Countess was, in fact, a model of versatile industry—a model, too, of tact, which was more than could be said for some people. The American women at the Esplanade turned very nasty after the sinking of the *Lusitania:* "One German turned to me and said: 'You and other English ladies have self-control, but these Americans do not care how or where they express their feelings.'" It was a well-earned, if slightly embarrassing, tribute.

As the war went on, the Countess—who became Princess in 1916, when Prince Blücher died and her husband succeeded to the title—became so used to the bizarre that she was seldom tricked into a display of emotion. There was, for instance, the case of the sinking of the *Blücher.* The captain, talking to the naval officer in charge of him, remarked that a photograph of the Englishwoman who had launched the *Blücher* had gone down when the ship sank. The officer answered that the Englishwoman happened to be his sister-in-law. It was a comforting incident. "Curious," wrote the Countess, "how small the world is." It seemed even smaller, and not quite so comforting, when Sir Roger Casement, an old acquaintance, turned up in Berlin in an abortive attempt to raise a brigade to fight against England from the many Irish prisoners of war in Germany. He had just been to the United States to try to recruit Irish-Americans for the same purpose. For once the Blüchers' tact slipped a little. They hinted that no one ever really trusted a traitor. Despite this rebuff, Casement contacted the Princess again in April, 1916, less than three weeks before the Easter Rebellion in Ireland. It must have been a trying interview, for poor Casement was in a highly nervous state. After he had left, the Princess noted that he "came into the room like one demented, talked in a husky whisper, and rushed round examining all the doors. I felt I was in the presence of a madman. He said: 'The German Foreign Office have had me shadowed, believing I was a spy in the pay of England, and England has had men spying on me as well.' He sat down and sobbed like a child. As he went out, he said: 'Tell them I was loyal to Ireland, although it will not appear so.' "

Perhaps this time the Blüchers were able to show some sympathy, at least to the extent of refraining from criticism. For they knew what it was to be spied upon. As casualties mounted and victory for the Central Powers seemed more and more remote, the standard of behavior at the Esplanade deteriorated lamentably. Dining-room conversations were noted, distorted, and reported, and in September, 1916, the Princess was summoned to military headquarters in Berlin to answer a charge of having spread lies about the treatment of prisoners of war. She was ordered to leave the city, but when powerful friends of her husband appealed to the Kaiser, the order was canceled.

The resident who had informed on her wrote a letter of apology, but the wretch was cut dead by everybody, and her husband had to resign from his staff job. It had been a nasty, if ludicrous, moment when passages from intercepted letters written by the Princess had been read out in court. "The Tennis Club is now open again," said one excerpt, "but it is not amusing, as everyone is in low spirits." This was interpreted as follows: "The writer evidently means to convey to her cousin that the German nation is depressed about the ultimate result of the war." The sentence "When the happy day of peace arrives, what a lot of nephews and nieces you and I will have to be introduced to" was clearly intended to convey that the writer was discontented with her life in Germany and wanted to return to England as soon as possible, and it "seemed to infer that she would like peace at any price." Meals at the hotel were becoming less and less palatable, but they were likely to be further spoiled by the presence of plainclothes detectives in badly cut suits who stared rudely at one and made civilized conversation impossible.

The casualties and the food and the spies were distressing enough, but far worse were the signs of social dislocation and upstart insolence. A fat parvenu war profiteer had made objectionable advances to the daughter of one of the Princess's friends in a first-class railway compartment. The hotel was stormed by a starving rabble who stole the bread supplies and had to be prevented by a strong cordon of police from doing violence to the residents. It was no longer sufficient not to talk English when one went out. The Princess, like Mrs. Pankhurst in Petrograd, was warned to make herself as inconspicuous as possible by wearing dowdy clothes. "All outward distinctions of class and rank," she wrote, "have to be avoided as much as possible. Even the few sorry carriage horses still permitted may not show any silver on their harness." When, in May, 1918, the Princess saw for the first time the red flag of revolution waving over the Russian Embassy, the plainclothes detectives and all the other petty humiliations faded. She rose above them on the powerful wings of class loyalty: "It must be such an unpleasant sight for the Emperor as he passes down the Unter den Linden." Members of the Russian Embassy, she was told, refused to mix with anyone except "the most blatant Socialists, and one hears strange stories of their manners at meals and their habits in private life, which are more or less what one would expect from the lowest class of Russian peasants."

On the Blücher estate in Silesia, the peasants were obliged to weave their own clothes from homegrown flax. The household depended on the Prince's marksmanship for food, and if he was successful, the surplus was bartered with the local tradespeople for butter, eggs, sugar, and clothes. It made one wonder if, after all, the war had not been fought against the wrong enemies. In Berlin there were street battles and what the Princess called "democratic excesses" when Karl Liebknecht, the Socialist leader who was her pet aversion harangued the mob from the same balcony where the Kaiser had stood and spouted at the beginning of the war. Was this what the flower of the nation's manhood had laid down their lives for? she wondered, as the poor Prince set out with his gun and his dogs and his beaters for yet another day's involuntary hunting. Now that it was beaten in war and threatened with occupation, "her" Germany seemed precious—as precious as "her" England had seemed when the ship had steamed away from Harwich four long years before. Both, but especially Germany, seemed menaced by the ogre of communism, the only real victor—and, as she (like other

members of Europe's ruling classes) now realized, the only real
enemy. "I have never felt so deeply for the German people," she
wrote, "the greater part of them fighting to guard some patch of
mother earth, a small cottage half-ridden in sheltering fruit trees,
ploughed fields rising on the slope of a hill up to the dark forest
pines. . . ."

The Individualists

The Western Front

I ৡ

A Thirst for Action

When the night of August 3, 1914, passed without any reply to Britain's ultimatum to Germany, London became the mecca for women volunteers, eager to make themselves useful and escape the boredom of routine middle- and upper-class lives. Committees sprang up like mushrooms and issued stirring Calls to Women. Uniforms, or hurriedly improvised semblances of uniforms, became a matter of honor and fashion, and if one could not manage a uniform, then an official-looking armband was *de rigueur*. In the music halls, the stars of the day belted out rush patriotic numbers, and strapping chorus girls dressed as sailors and soldiers stamped and saluted with mock-military precision. The Red Cross Society summoned its members to "mobilise at headquarters," and among those who answered this particular call was the novelist Sarah Broom Macnaughtan, tiny, quizzical, and trying hard not to be carried beyond all sense of proportion by the swirl of bizarre patriotism. She attended a drumhead service and marched off to first-aid courses, where the conveniently placed make-believe wounds of dragooned messenger boys were triumphantly bandaged.

After much drilling and bandaging, she was asked to join the hospital unit that Mrs. St. Clair Stobart was taking out to Brussels and sat on a committee interviewing other applicants ("They all spoke of AT THE FRONT as if it was one word, and all said they were strong and did not mind what they did"). On September 20, she left for Antwerp with the title of Head of the Orderlies.

After settling in at the Stobart Hospital, which had been improvised in a large concert hall, she hired a carriage and drove out to see the much-vaunted defenses of Antwerp. She was astonished to see laborers driving wooden stakes into the fields (to lame cavalry horses) while the Germans were preparing to shell the city from six miles away. "There seemed," she said, "to linger about Antwerp a notion of cavalry charges up to the walls. . . . The old stone forts looked to my ignorant eyes like remnants of medievalism."

When shells began to fall near the hospital and casualties poured in, she noted in her diary: "I had to pass 18 dead men. They were laid out near some women who were washing clothes, and I noticed how tired even in death their poor dirty feet looked." Shaken by the pathetic squalor of war, she went to seek comfort in the small chapel attached to the convent where the hospital staff was quartered. But she found little support in the conventional sentiments and trappings of religion. It was all too pretty and tender, and she began to feel rather enervatingly sorry for herself. Social pressures—considerations of what other people might think if one failed—were far more effective in bracing her, she discovered: "I had thought that the Flag or Religion would have been stronger incentives. But just to behave like a well-bred woman is what keeps one up best."

She was impressed by the invincible Cockney cheerfulness of the British troops during the retreat from Antwerp. When they were gassed, they were liable to joke: "All right, Allemands, put another penny in the meter!" When they passed some nurses, they yelled: "No, miss, not yet!" They chirpingly offered to bring Miss Macnaughtan the Kaiser's head as a souvenir. But she found the passion for souvenirs terribly depressing. "There are heaps of them," she wrote, "and I hate them all. I saw a sick Zouave hugging a German summer casquette. Our own men leave their trenches and go out into the open to get these horrible things, with their battered exterior and the suggestion of pomade inside."

By early 1915, she had, with a free-lance flexibility and determination characteristic of the time and place, set up a soup kitchen in the railway station at Furnes in Flanders. There she witnessed a scene that seemed to symbolize the tawdry yet moving theatricality of the early months of the Great War. A group of badly gassed

Tommies had just arrived, and, in tribute, a Belgian band struck up "God Save the King." The weary, disheveled men, their eyes covered with stained bandages, stood instantly to attention. As they did so, an armored train backed slowly into the station and a tiny airplane chugged across the sky. It was like some demented impresario's idea of a war spectacular. "At Drury Lane," she reflected, "one would have said that the staging had been overdone, that the clothes were *too* ragged, the men *too* gaunt and obviously wounded, and that by no stretch of the imagination could a band be playing God Save The King while a painted train called Lou-Lou steamed in, looking like a child's giant gaudy toy, and an aeroplane fussed overhead. . . ."

She visited Nieuport, a coastal town that had been the focus of fierce clashes. "It is as difficult to find words to describe Nieuport as it is to talk of metaphysics in slang," was her reaction. "The words don't seem to exist that will convey the haunting sense of desolation, that supreme quiet under the shock of continually firing guns." The pitted, pallid mud of the surrounding fields reminded her of "an immense Gruyère cheese." Yet, angered and touched as she was by it all, she strongly disapproved of the flood of indiscriminate charity that, in her opinion, was pauperizing the already demoralized Belgians. Things were being run on the wrong lines. Distribution should have been made through the Belgian Government and not through sentimental semiofficial agencies. "No lasting good," she complained, oppressed by the indignity, "ever came of gifts. Every child begs for cigarettes, and they begin smoking at five years old."

May Sinclair, another novelist—who had once rattled collection boxes on London street corners to raise funds for the suffragettes—got caught up in an even more eccentric eddy of individualistic effort. It was started by Dr. Hector Munro, a Scot, a Socialist, and a pioneer of naturist methods in medicine (to the accompaniment of scandalized press comment, he had started Britain's first nudist camp just before the war). He had formed yet another committee, with the object of taking an ambulance unit to Belgium. Apart from male doctors, stretcher-bearers, and drivers, he had, being an ardent feminist, decided to include four women—who would prove their sex's ability to serve in the most testing circumstances.

Distrustful of officialdom and its methods, he was not looking for fully trained, dedicated nurses, whose set ideas and expectations might not fit into his scheme. He wanted young women with a spirit of adventure and a willingness to work under fire and adapt themselves quickly to the changing demands of the battlefield. Of the four successful applicants (chosen from more than two hundred), three—Lady Dorothie Fielding, Helen Gleason, and Elsie Knocker —were in their twenties, and one, Mairi Chisholm, was a Scottish girl of eighteen.

Lady Dorothie, a daughter of Rudolph Feilding, Earl of Denbigh, had had some basic nursing experience in the Voluntary Aid Detachment; Mrs. Gleason, an American, was the wife of an American war correspondent already in Belgium and was anxious to join her husband; Miss Chisholm, a granddaughter of The Chisholm, Chief of Clan Chisholm ("There are only three The's in the world," goes an old Highland saying, "The Pope, The Devil, and The Chisholm"), had not long left school; and Mrs. Knocker, though a trained nurse and midwife, had not practiced her profession for some time and was better known as a pioneering lady motorcyclist. She and Miss Chisholm, also a keen motorcyclist and expert mechanic, had met at trials before the war and had come to London to work as emergency dispatch riders. All four were game for anything and willing to pay their own way (Mairi Chisholm sold her precious motorbike and put her quarterly dress allowance of £10 in the kitty).

May Sinclair was engaged to keep the accounts ("Heaven help them!" was her comment), write up the reports, and send articles about the doings of the Munro Corps to the newspapers in order to raise funds. Money was badly needed, in the absence of any official backing, an absence not surprising in view of the vagueness of Dr. Munro's plans. Someone had originally suggested that the Corps should dash across the battlefields on horseback, scoop up the wounded, sling them over their saddles, and bear them back to the dressing stations. This had finally been modified into a scheme for a motorized ambulance unit that could set up first-aid points as and where they were needed. Still the War Office was not impressed. Nor was the Red Cross—British, French, Belgian, or American. When, in the highest of spirits, the Munro Corps crossed the Chan-

nel to Ostend in September, 1914, it went as a Commission of
Enquiry, to report on the best methods of helping Belgian refugees.
For this purpose, the Belgian Legation in London had given pass-
ports and a modicum of official recognition.

But once in Ostend, events moved rapidly, and the Corps' terms
of reference changed—as everyone had hoped and prayed they
would. Short of personnel, the Belgian Red Cross accepted their
services, and the British Red Cross, relenting, provided two ambulances. Delighted, they piled into their new vehicles and drove from
Ostend to their first headquarters, in Ghent. It was a fine day. The
long, straight road ran through a quiet, sunny landscape of tall pop-
lars and pollarded willows and low Flemish houses with white walls,
green doors and shutters, and red roofs. It was beautiful and extraordinarily peaceful, but also excitingly ominous: a lull before the
storm of war and action that lay somewhere ahead, where the guns
were firing and the Germans, according to reports that they had
heard and read, were committing unspeakable atrocities in an attempt to cow Belgium into total surrender.

In Ghent, refugees from the north were packed dismally into the
huge Palais de Fêtes, normally used for annual shows and public
entertainments. But this was on the outskirts of the city. The city
itself, with its picturesque streets, its tall old houses with their delicate balconies, was not noticeably flustered by the German advance
or the tales of terror. Secure in its own venerability and in the fact
that it had been declared an open city, Ghent refused to panic. "The
very refugees," wrote May Sinclair, "have the look of a rather tired-
out tourist party, wandering about, seeing Ghent, seeing the Cathedral. . . ."

The Munro Corps was given excellent quarters in a luxury hotel
that had been converted into a hospital. Belgian doctors and nurses
bustled about the corridors, but not many casualties had yet been
brought in. There was little to do but hang around while Dr. Munro,
with his baggy tweed suit and shock of uncontrollable white hair,
tried to make contact with the authorities and get things moving.
The four chosen women particularly resented the enforced inactivity. They made angry entries in their diaries, tried to help in the
Palais de Fêtes, and looked on the mild attractions of Ghent with

unappreciative eyes. Why, they muttered among themselves, were they waiting? How much longer would it be before they could show their frustrated mettle?

2 §●

Mairi Chisholm's Story, or Valkyries in Knickerbockers

About two weeks after this, Miss Macnaughtan got her first, rather startled, glimpse of the Munro Corps. Ghent had fallen, and refugees of all sorts were jammed into Ostend. "Dr. Hector Munro," she wrote, "came in with his oddly-dressed ladies. At first one was inclined to call them masqueraders in their knickerbockers and puttees and caps, but I believe they have done excellent work. It is a queer side of war to see young, pretty girls in khaki and thick boots, fresh from the trenches, where they have been picking up wounded men within a hundred yards of the enemy's lines and carrying them on stretchers. Wonderful little Valkyries in knickerbockers, I lift my hat to you!"

During their last week in Ghent, the Corps had been through a baptism of fire hectic enough to satisfy the most exacting expectations. Its ambulances had been kept more than busy dashing to the scene of the vicious hand-to-hand battles that raged over the possession of the small towns and villages that stood in the line of the German advance. May Sinclair, who soon afterward returned to England (the unit's days seemed numbered, and, in any case, she had not the strong nerves and craving for violent action of the youngsters), had marveled at the coolness of the women in the fighting at Melle. There she watched Mrs. Knocker and Mairi Chisholm, who had already paired off to make a remarkable team, tending French, Belgian, and German casualties in a turnip field raked by enemy fire and then racing back to their ambulance through a hail of bullets. Mairi Chisholm, who because of her extreme youth was regarded with special concern by Dr. Munro and her other colleagues, she found quite breathtaking. "I simply cannot get used to it," she fretted, "it seems to me appalling that she should be here, strolling about the seat of War with her hands in her pockets, as if a battle were a cricket match at which you looked on between your innings, and yet there isn't a man in the Corps who does his work better or with more courage and endurance than this 18-year-old child."

Yet now, in the dreary limbo of Ostend (and, a little later, St. Malo), the adventure seemed to be finished. They were back where they had started only three weeks before. The German Army seemed likely to roll on inexorably. Then, amazingly, came the stand of the remnants of the Belgian Army and a scratch lot of French troops (including a brigade of Marines) along the Yser Canal. They miraculously stood firm on a line stretching from Nieuport through Dixmude to Ypres. A last tiny strip of Flanders was finally saved from German occupation when the dike gates at Nieuport were opened and the sea flooded slowly in to form a shallow but effective temporary barrier between the exhausted Allies and the frustrated Germans. The Munro Corps moved to the country town of Furnes, which had become the base for the Dixmude sector of the line. From here the ambulances went out, day and night, often in bitter weather, inching past oncoming convoys, driving around or over the corpses of men and animals, sometimes slithering off the raised paved road into the fearful glutinous mud at the side.

Back in England, May Sinclair (already at work on a book about her experiences in Belgium) wistfully dedicated a poem to the Corps:

> You go
> Under the thunder of the guns, the shrapnel's rain and
>   the curved lightning of the shells,
> And where the high towers are broken
> And houses crack like the staves of a thin crate filled with fire,
> Into the mixing smoke and dust of roof and walls torn asunder
> You go;
> And only my dream follows you. . . .

The casualty rate was frightening, but even more frightening was the lack of medical facilities, which turned the few available surgeons into butchers and Furnes into a shambles. Many men, often with superficial wounds, died in the jolting, overburdened military ambulances, and this gave Mrs. Knocker the idea of setting up a first-aid post right by the trenches, where men could rest and recover from shock and have their wounds properly cleansed and dressed before being taken to base. She was convinced that this could save many lives and, in the teeth of official disapproval, but with the backing of some Belgian Army doctors, actually set up her post in the ruined village of Pervyse. With her—and thrilling with pride because she had been chosen—went Mairi Chisholm, the baby and mascot of the Corps, which now, having amalgamated with a Scottish Women's Hospital Unit, moved to the Nieuport sector. Dr. Munro begged the two women not to leave. But they were not to be diverted. They had their own vision of service, a superabundant relish for danger, their own line to follow.

It took them, first, around the end of November, 1914, to a tiny cellar in Pervyse, just a few yards behind the trenches that had been hastily dug along the railway line. The cellar was about eight feet square, lighted and ventilated by a narrow slit in the wall. Night and day, by the light of candles, the women washed and bandaged, sleeping, when they could sleep, on straw, eating what the men could spare from their rations or shoot or scrounge in the abandoned fields. Exploring one day, Mairi Chisholm came across the corpses of an old man and woman sitting close together in chairs drawn up to a hearth now full of cold ashes and debris. Their heads had been blown off.

It was horrible, but, then, horrors were two a penny. Their drinking water passed through land where hundreds of troops had been buried, and even after boiling, it was green and tasted vile. Washing themselves was difficult, and their clothes began to stick to them. But they stuck to their job. Mairi Chisholm, taken on primarily as a driver and mechanic, had learned to bandage and apply a tourniquet, and she remembers how, in the freezing darkness, they carried hot soup and cocoa, brewed by an army cook in an old copper caldron they had found, to men at the outposts. So close were they to the enemy, so much like a game did war still seem, that sometimes they were tempted to shout across to the German sentries.

The cellar was not only damp and dreary. Being there involved a lot of awkward lifting of casualties up and down the narrow steps.

So, after a few weeks, the post was moved to a house a little further away from the trenches. Two ground-floor rooms were more or less intact, and a lean-to kitchen was built at the back. Belgian engineers kept repairing the sagging roof, but their efforts were invariably destroyed by the nightly shelling. Still the women carried on, lifting heavy, inert men in full fighting gear on stretchers through the mud. Gradually they won affection and respect—and official support, both Belgian and British. Orderlies and drivers were allotted to them, the base hospital, now vastly improved, acknowledged the value of their work, and when Mairi's father came to see how she was faring, he was able to report back to her mother that she was happier and even healthier than she had ever been.

She and Mrs. Knocker coped not only with wounded, but with all the "minor" ailments of trench warfare—especially devastating in the first terrible winter, when all was shortage and improvisation—swollen feet, septic cuts, boils, fever, mental and physical inertia. Until they were issued with British khaki, the Belgian troops' threadbare uniforms and split boots were pitifully inadequate to keep out the elements. Mrs. Knocker attended the more serious cases, while Mairi saw to the boils and the sores and even treated the quite frequent cases of venereal diseases ("How we didn't get infected," she says, "I don't know. I remember I wore long rubber gloves and we used a lot of mercury"). In those days, the Army had made no adequate provision for special treatment of VD.

Some patients had deliberately wounded themselves, shooting off fingers or toes. Others made themselves ill by various means—smoking cigarettes soaked in vinegar was a favorite dodge; this produced unconsciousness and high fever. "The Two," as they came to be known, soon learned to spot the shammers, but tried to treat them as real casualties, genuine victims of privation and boredom and of the constant, gnawing anxiety about what had happened to their wives and sweethearts and mothers and children in German-occupied Belgium. Sometimes a prisoners' company would be sent into the line. Convicts were offered free pardons if they volunteered for particularly dangerous raids or patrols and managed to survive. Mairi did not like to appear curious, but she did wonder what they had done and what they hoped to do in the future. The convicts, in their turn, must have felt some curiosity about her. With her fair hair, her wide, dimpling smile, her brilliant blue eyes, and a youthfulness so appealing that everyone wanted to protect her, she made even these men want to talk.

One day, when she was lancing a painful boil for one of them, he said to her: "Mam'selle, don't you ever wonder what we've done?"

"Why, yes, but I don't like to ask."

"Well, mam'selle, I killed my wife. She nagged and nagged, and finally I hit her with an ax."

"Do you feel sorry about it?" she ventured.

"No," he replied, "I couldn't stand that nagging, and what else could I do to stop it?"

He and nineteen others were sent to an advance post far in front of the main-line trenches. A German attack was expected, and the suicide squad might help to break it up. Mairi watched the attack, almost crossing her fingers for the wife-killer (she supposed he had been telling the truth, and yet he had seemed so gentle and shy). The fury of the battle was such that it did not seem possible that there could be any survivors among the twenty convicts. Yet late at night "her" murderer staggered into the surgery—the sole survivor, weary and shaking, but, he told her, with a great sense of peace inside him. She covered him with blankets and got water bottles—as Mrs. Knocker had taught her to do in cases of shock—and made him lie quietly.

While Mrs. Knocker, as the trained nurse, stayed on duty in the post, Mairi went out to help with stretcher cases, to run various errands, and, above all, to drive wounded men back to the base hospital fifteen miles away. At night, especially, this could be a terrific strain. "No lights," she wrote in her diary, "Shell-pocked pavé roads, often under fire, men and guns coming up to the trenches, total darkness, yells to mind oneself and get out of the way, a sickening slide off the pavé into the deep mud, screams from the stretchers behind one and thumps in the back through the canvas, then an appeal to passing troops to heave the ambulance back onto the road. . . ." Sometimes she found herself trembling hard for two hours after the more hair-raising drives. At "Suicide Corner," where the ruins of a convent stood and the road from Furnes joined the supply road that ran parallel to and behind the trenches, the shells fell thickest. She had to draw a deep breath and force herself to go on. After two or three night journeys, "one's eyes were on stalks, blood-shot and strained. No windscreen, no protection, no self-starters or electric lights to switch on when you got well away from the lines. You have to clamber out and strike a match and try to light the carbide lamps."

Early in 1915, "The Two" were given special permission to stay where they were—the only women allowed nearer than three miles to the front line. Their period of probation was over. Newspapers were already calling them "The Heroines of Pervyse" or sometimes just "The Women of Pervyse." In February came the great moment when Belgium, which they had come to love with a fierce possessiveness, recognized the services of these rebels. King Albert himself, towering over them, pinned the Star of the Order of Leopold on their tunics.

On their way back to Pervyse, their car got stuck hopelessly in the mud, and they stopped at a British officers' dugout in the Nieuport sector to beg a lift. There they met an American journalist, Mary Roberts Rinehart. She was immediately intrigued by their appearance and by the contrast of their personalities—the one so dark and nervous and imperious, the other so blonde and quiet and stolid. "Two very attractive young women came into the room," she wrote in an article. "Under a khaki-colored leather coat they wore riding breeches and puttees and flannel shirts. They had knitted caps and great mittens to keep out the cold." There was a blazing fire in the dugout, yet both refused to take off their leather over-coats, blushing when urged to do so. After much questioning and a good deal of chaffing, they confessed their secret:

"The jealously fastened coats were thrown open. Gleaming on the breast of each was the Star of the Order of Leopold II. . . .

" 'But why didn't you tell us?' the officers demanded.

" 'Because you have never approved of us. You have always wanted us sent back to England.' "

It was true. Their presence had been a source of embarrassment to British officers, who, when they were not facetiously gallant, tended to get irritated. But their fame had spread. It was the thing, now, to take them presents, some food perhaps, a crate of Perrier

water, or great slabs of chocolate. To visit "The Two" became almost as much a social ambition, even a social necessity, as to go to
tea on the barge at Adinkerke that Maxine Elliott and Lady Kathleen Drogheda had turned into a relief depot stocked with goods for
civilian refugees.

John Redmond, the Irish Parliamentary leader, wrote after a visit
to the post: "Here, in a half-ruined house in the midst of universal
ruin, we found two ladies living. . . . By the same kind of extraordinary coincidence as that whereby the crucifixes and statues have
escaped destruction in Belgium, so the portion of the little house
which these ladies have inhabited to this time has remained untouched. It is not surprising that the Belgian people look upon them
with a sort of supernatural and sacred love." Mrs. Rinehart found it
hard to believe that anyone could exist in Pervyse: "Walls without
roofs, roofs almost without walls, a street so torn up with shells that
walking was almost impossible." The table in the post's reception
room, which also did duty as a dining room and bedroom, was set
for supper when she arrived. An English officer and a Belgian major
joined them for a meal of mutton and potatoes, followed by fruit
and nuts (both officers had probably contributed something to the
meal). Miss Macnaughtan would probably have said that the whole
scene was stagier than the theater: Mrs. Knocker hurrying in with a
frying pan in her hand; Miss Chisholm following with the potatoes
in a saucepan; the major's devoted black Congolese servant boy
standing just outside the door; the major himself sitting down at a
shrapnel-scarred piano to play (in a moment of seriousness that followed the lighthearted chatter) the *Hungarian Rhapsody* and the
Moonlight Sonata.

"He played," wrote Mrs. Rinehart, "with a bulldog pipe gripped
firmly in his teeth, blue clouds encircling his fair hair. We sat silent.
His pipe died. His eyes, fixed on the shell-riddled wall, grew sombre.
When the music ceased, his hands lay lingeringly on the keys. . . ."

When the spell had been broken, Miss Chisholm put forward a
theory that the three shells that always came over in quick succes-
sion before the start of a German bombardment were a signal to
some spy in the area. But in the soft lamplight and with the glow of
the food and the music and the warmth and the pleasant talk upon
her, Miss Rinehart began to wonder whether all that she had seen

and heard could really be true. Was the noise at the end of the street really gunfire? Did these two young women really live amid such horrors? Pervyse had been taken and retaken in a half-dozen fierce skirmishes. Corpses had been thrown into shell holes and thinly covered with mud. Others floated in the stagnant water of the canal. The constant heavy rain of Flanders washed away the soil, exposing rotting limbs. How could they talk so matter-of-factly about it? When Mrs. Rinehart left at 11 P.M., the night bombardment was just beginning in earnest. She turned and looked back at the house (the women had called it "the sick and sorry house"): "Faint rays of light shone through the boarded windows. A wounded soldier had been brought up the street and stood leaning heavily on his companion by the door. . . ."

Not long after this visit, what remained of the sick and sorry house was finally shattered by several direct hits. "The Two" went for a short break to La Panne, a small coastal resort, where a fine military hospital had been set up and the Belgian royal family lived. They walked and rode over the sands where Queen Elizabeth and her children went for walks, and Mairi heard an amusing story about Dr. Munro. Continuing to practice what he preached, he had run up and down the deserted beach without any clothes on. The Queen, observing him from the window of the royal villa, telephoned the hospital and said that a shell-shocked patient had evidently escaped and was behaving most oddly. Two military policemen were sent to bring Dr. Munro under control. Shortly after this incident, he was drafted into the Royal Army Medical Corps, though he was even less suited to conventional military life than any of his Corps.

The third post in Pervyse (about four hundred yards behind the trenches) was a concrete structure built inside the shell of a house and well covered with sandbags. Layout, conditions of work, and equipment were all luxurious compared with the cellar days. For— thanks partly to a series of lecture tours in Britain and a determined press-correspondence campaign by the masterful Mrs. Knocker— funds and recognition were growing. On her home ground in Scotland, Mairi Chisholm, shy but determined, was featured. At Nairn and Inverness and Dundee, she explained the need to raise £2,000 so that the work (there were only the two of them, for no other woman could get permission to join them) could be expanded. They needed a new ambulance, and to keep the post going at all—and it was all done by voluntary contributions—cost at least £60 a month. By mid-1916, the Belgian Soldiers' Fund of Manchester was contributing to the post, and Miss Eva Moore, a well-known actress and charity organizer, had taken up the cause of "The Two." Their hastily written war diaries were used as the basis for a book, *The Cellar House of Pervyse,* the profits from which were used to forward the work.

One of their jobs was to go out with stretchers and search parties into the mud and craters of no-man's-land (the salt flood of 1914 had long ago evaporated or soaked into the soil) to find and bring back the bodies of crashed pilots of the Royal Naval Air Service and the Royal Flying Corps. This could be a sickening task, since in those days pilots had no parachutes. But one young man made a supply of miniature parachutes and tried to float down boxes of chocolates to Mairi as he flew over the lines. Often the women had to lay out corpses and nail them into coffins for transport to military cemeteries. But the slogging, unglamorous grimness was broken by a gay and unexpected event. Mrs. Knocker, the handsome widow whose brilliant achievements as a nurse had become almost legendary, became a Baroness—the Baroness de T'Serclaes. Her husband, a pilot, was a member of one of Belgium's oldest families, and the ceremony took place before a distinguished congregation in the chapel attached to the royal villa at La Panne.

"Gipsy" (as she was known to Mairi and other close friends) was given away by a senior officer of the 3rd Division of the Belgian Army, to which "The Two" were attached. Mairi walked behind with another officer of the 3rd Division. The band of the 1st Chasseurs played during the service, and another military band played outside the villa where the reception was held. Among the guests were HRH Prince Alexander of Teck (later the Earl of Athlone), head of the British Military Mission in Flanders; the general commanding the 3rd Division; the Russian military attaché; Lady Dorothie Feilding and her mother, the Countess of Denbigh; and Maxine Elliot, the American actress who had taken English high society by storm. It was an occasion of fizz and sparkle and photographers—the new Baroness wore a smart new dress and a great wide feathery hat—but after the few days of honeymoon were over, the Baron rejoined his squadron and "The Two" went back to business as usual at Pervyse.

There, a frequent and particularly welcome visitor was Commander Henry Halahan, who was in charge of the "Long Tom" naval siege guns at Nieuport. When, in 1917, the British took over the Nieuport sector from the French, these guns played a dramatic part in saving a desperate situation. General Henry Rawlinson planned an advance along the coast in cooperation with the British fleet, but when the attack was launched, the German artillery soon put Rawlinson's insufficiently camouflaged guns out of action and played murderously on the men of the King's Royal Rifles, deployed on what was known as "The Bristol Tunnel," a small and exposed strip of the east bank of the Yser. To hold the enemy in check, Commander Halahan ordered his men to fire "over sights" at very short range. So furious was the battle that their guns became dangerously overheated, and three of them blew up, killing the crews. That same night, the British artillery, which had moved up to support the Belgians in the Pervyse sector, was subjected to heavy shelling. It was a night of nights for Mairi Chisholm, who spent most of it driving up and down the shell-swept road to the hospital at La Panne, while the Baroness and her orderlies coped with a terrible spate of casualties at the post.

Mairi still vividly remembers the Belgians who were detailed to work with them. There was Gabriel, the cook, who once, with a macabre sense of humor, packed a freshly amputated foot in a cake box and took it to the men's dugout, saying, "Madame got this for you in Dunkirk." The driver, Joseph, was a little uncertain at times—he had been invalided out of the trenches, and his nerves were shaky. But her own main helper and particular friend was Octave La Meir, a tough, cheerful Antwerp dock worker who later became a prominent businessman.

"I was just a kid then," she says, "and full of high spirits." Her daredeviltry was a byword, and she remembers how one Irish colonel took her along when he was searching for a suitable observation post from which to direct his gunfire. Small and agile, she volunteered to be hauled up to the top of Pervyse's tottering church tower. Peering through binoculars, she shouted down that the view of the German lines was A-1. Just then a salvo of shells whistled past, and she was let down in a flash. Later, she was hauled up to test a three-plank platform fixed high in the leafless branches of one of the few trees that had escaped annihilation.

King Albert and Queen Elizabeth of the Belgians visited the first aid post, and Prince Alexander of Teck enjoyed going to Pervyse. Mairi saw him mostly in his official capacity and was startled and delighted when he danced a vigorous cakewalk with her during her twenty-first birthday party at Furnes.

In 1917, she and the Baroness were awarded the Military Medal —among the first women to be so honored—for their work, and in February, 1918, they went to London to attend a fund-raising gala matinee organized by Eva Moore at the Alhambra Theatre. "There was a packed house," reported one newspaper. "The Women of Pervyse were present, and relics brought by them from the fields of battle, and auctioned by Miss Violet Lorraine, added £250 to the results of the matinee—a handsome sum of £1,400, handed to the Women by Miss Eva Moore." The following day they went to St. John's Gate to receive the Cross of the Order of St. John of Jerusalem. Eva Moore reported the occasion for the *Evening Standard:* "The ceremony took place in the Chancery . . . and there was something wonderfully picturesque in the sight of the Baroness and Miss Chisholm in their khaki service uniforms standing in the ancient oak hall, with its lofty roof and old leaded windows, receiving the Cross of an Order which dates from the days of the Crusades."

Less than three weeks after their return to Pervyse, during the big German offensive of March, 1918, a mustard-and-arsenic-gas shell exploded near their dugout sleeping quarters. Both were badly affected. The Baroness had to go back to England for further treatment ("I felt as though a rope had been fastened round my neck," she told a reporter. "Miss Chisholm was rolling on the floor. My little dog Shot was killed. Ever since it happened I've longed to kill a German"). But Mairi recovered more quickly and returned to Pervyse. She was gassed again while using the field telephone, but she carried on, helping where she could, hoping that the Baroness would soon be back. Alas, it was not to be. Word came that the Baroness would not be fit for some time, and it was decided that the post must close down.

The adventure was over—"three and a half years of being privileged to work in danger alongside brave men, and to recognise the immense decency to two women in exceptional circumstances," as Mairi puts it. She made the last sad arrangements. The heavy steel door of the post, the furniture, the Red Cross flags, their uniforms —all were shipped back to London, to the Imperial War Museum, already confidently collecting relics of the "war to end war." At twenty-one, it was curious to feel yourself and your work turning into a museum piece.

When she arrived in London, it was not on a flying, triumphal visit. She had to plan a new future, yet her heart was still with her comrades in the ruins of Pervyse ("so strangely beautiful at night," she remembers, "when quiet reigned over the trenches"). Not long before, May Sinclair, who had kept in touch with her Munro Corps colleagues, had written of "The Two." "They will be known as the Women of Pervyse until the end of all memories of war." Now people congratulated Mairi on her escape and implied that she could relax now and enjoy herself; she had done her bit.

Certainly she felt tired, and the aftereffects of the gas shells were troubling her. She was grateful when Eva Moore and her husband, actor-dramatist H. V. Esmond, opened their house to her. Miss Moore, though she was appearing in a play and did not get to bed until late, would get up several times a night when Mairi had difficulty with her breathing. The care and kindness of the Esmonds, more than anything else, helped her to readjust to the unfamiliar demands of ordinary life, to shake off the nightmare and wonder of Pervyse.

3

Sapper Dorothy Lawrence

With Sapper Dorothy Lawrence, one enters a frisky fantasy world of larks and dares. "If that dear old Cathedral city in England had known of these escapades," she wrote later in an introduction to her memoirs, "I think my highly respectable guardian would have had forty fits."

A high-spirited young woman with a bouncy sense of fun, Miss Lawrence decided that she would try ("I'm hanged if I won't") to get to the front, and she wrote to several newspapers asking if they would commission her as a war correspondent and pay her expenses. Only one editor showed the slightest interest in her piquant proposal, and even he merely said that he would like to see how far she got and what sort of copy she managed to bring back.

So, in 1915, she crossed the Channel under her own auspices and, without any great difficulty, made her way to Paris. Her plan of campaign was clear in her mind. Thoughtfully she wandered the boulevards, searching the cafés for accomplices. After several hours and a number of old-fashioned looks, she found them. "Two soldiers, with the faces of clean-minded boys" were sitting opposite one of the railway stations looking lonesome. Quickly she stepped up to them with a hearty, "Hullo, boys!" but despite her antiseptic manner, it was, she admitted, obvious that "for a few minutes they wondered whether I was out for love! I told them bluntly: 'I want to get to the Front as a soldier. Will you help me?'"

They said they would. They agreed to steal a spare uniform for her, and they fixed a place and method for handing it over. She would pretend to be a French washerwoman to whom they were bringing their dirty laundry: "What a lark! I would approach, be saluted, walk a little way, hoist a parcel under my arm [the uniform was smuggled out in several installments], then jump on my cycle and ride away through the growing dusk to my hotel on the outskirts of Paris."

There she tried on her new clothes. To reduce her buxom figure to something like the right proportions, she bound herself tight in great swathes of bandages. To masculinize the line of her back, she padded it out with layers of cotton wool, over which, suspended by strings from her neck, she hung an apron of sacking. After much tugging and tweaking and pinning she contrived a passing semblance. Next, the two Tommies met her in a quiet side street for several evenings to give her some basic instruction in drill and army terminology. More important still, they got her a pass to go to Béthune. She claimed that it was common then for soldiers to make out their own passes, leaving a space for the commanding officer's signature—which Miss Lawrence, who now called herself Private

Denis Smith, filled in at random. She then went to a local government office, where, posing as a tourist who wished to make her way home as quickly as possible, she was given a safe-conduct to Calais. She had just one more need—someone to cut her hair to the regulation length and to smuggle her and her bicycle on a train to Amiens. Trusting to luck, she simply turned up at the appropriate railway station, and there, sure enough, she struck up an acquaintance with a military policeman. In no time at all, the big, softhearted darling had sneaked her into a quiet official nook and was snipping away at her auburn tresses with the scissors she had thoughtfully provided. Not only that, he helped her to stain her skin a would-be weather-beaten brown with a bottle of Condy's fluid, stowed her safely aboard her train, and returned to duty with her jolly secret locked in his manly bosom.

From Amiens, she pedaled out toward the front, wearing a floppy white hat that concealed her shorn head and sleeping rough in the woods at night. It was hot summer weather, and her ersatz tan was soon streaked with perspiration, but she dodged past some French sentries and waited for the right moment to change into her uniform, which was strapped to the back of her bike in a brown-paper parcel. On the road near Albert, she met a cavalryman who gave her an apple to eat and rode beside her into the town. Here, "two stalwart Scottish laddies confronted me, and one of them, lifting his head from a bucket of water [it was the hour of ablutions], stared at me." So far, so good. She had, in her own words, "pierced the lines of the 3rd Army, with its glorious names from the pick of Scotland's regiments." But she was immediately arrested. In a haze of excitement, she was marched off to see the senior officers, passing the famous statue of the Virgin that surmounted Albert Cathedral. Shaken by shellfire, the statue had tilted until it was almost parallel with the pavements. Troops playing soccer among the ruins paused to call out, "Bon jaw!"—to which she gaily replied, "Don't bon jaw me. I'm English!" She was given a room for the night at headquarters (an officer gave up his room for her) and had an excellent breakfast, during which she wore a full-length topcoat, kept her hat on, and told her amused hosts that she was looking for newspaper copy.

Though she was warned that she must leave the area, no one

seems to have made any serious attempt to expel her, and she wandered off on her own, hoping for another stroke of luck. Passing through a large camp, she was roughly accosted and handled by a soldier, whom she "hit till he desisted. That one incident only broke the rules of British chivalry." As a result of it, she found her next protector, Sapper Tom Dunn of the Royal Engineers, a Lancashireman. Shocked by his fellow soldier's lechery, he readily agreed to shield Miss Lawrence and get her into the line.

He found a hiding place in the cellar of a deserted cottage and smuggled food to her. Feeling the need for a good wash, she cleaned out a rusty old caldron, filled it with cold water, undressed —and was surprised by the sudden appearance of a French peasant (a looter, she supposed), who exclaimed reassuringly, "N'ayez pas peur, ma fille!" and rushed away. He returned with a jug of hot coffee, which she gratefully accepted. She passed the time for the next few days practicing quick changes, watching the troops, and, occasionally, under cover of darkness, mingling with them under Sapped Dunn's supervision. One thrilling night, he arranged for her to meet him outside a tavern where sappers were having a last drink (some of them, she noticed, were drunk) before going off to lay mines.

Falling in with them and sticking close to her mate, she descended, she says, to a depth of one hundred feet by ladders and steps cut in the wet clay and helped Dunn with his tunneling. It was weird, supersecret work, even more "authentic" than she had dared to hope, and when, in a moment's silence, she heard the *tap-tap* of Fritz working away on the same mission, she began to picture the look of admiration and gratitude on that editor's face when she delivered her copy. This was really, superlatively, it.

After nearly two weeks spent lurking in her uncozy cottage and hastily donning her complicated paraphernalia of male impersonation, the strain began to tell on Private Smith. Irregular and scanty food, the constant furtiveness, and the noise of the nightly bombardment were bad enough, but an attack of painful, half-crippling rheumatism made matters worse. She began to have fainting fits. Afraid of getting her accomplices into trouble (for others had had to be told about her), she came to the conclusion that the sergeant must be let into the secret, just in case she was wounded or became seriously ill.

The dastardly NCO promptly put her under arrest, and she was marched back to Albert and again brought before the senior officers. "Good Lord, Miss Lawrence!" they groaned. "You still here?" Sterner measures were now taken. Escorted by a staff officer ("Why don't you marry?" he asked her), she rode to a farmhouse, where General Rawlinson himself interviewed her. "Get her some decent clothes," he rapped, "and get her away from here." To which she replied: "Right-o!"

The military were not convinced that she was as innocent as she seemed. She was turned over to the Intelligence Corps and closely questioned by a crack interrogator. He got little information or respect from Miss Lawrence. "This funny little man," she remembered, "who struck terror in the hearts of German spies, evoked only laughter from an ordinary English girl." Her almost giggly reaction was taken for a brilliant ruse, and she next appeared before a board of *three* generals.

She repeated her story and complained of the sergeant's shabby behavior. "If he had been to a public school," she grumbled, "he would not have behaved like that," and her judges smilingly agreed with this. They got no further than their predecessors, and eventually, at the urgent plea of a certain Captain X, who happened to know Miss Lawrence from prewar days, she was released from the guardroom. After all, whatever she had done, she *was* a lady and should be treated accordingly. Captain X even took her to his own quarters and, with the aid of his orderly, rustled up a scratch set of female clothes (she kept his suspenders as souvenirs).

It was decided that, though Miss Lawrence might be giddy rather than sinister, she was nevertheless a very real security risk. It would never do to send her back to England to chatter away to those newspaper chaps about how she had fooled the British Army and actually passed as a soldier. So she was whisked off to an unknown destination, which turned out to be a convent at St. Omer. Here she was made very comfortable, and she noted with satisfaction that her gentle jailers were suitably wellborn. The Mother Superior, she discovered, was "one of France's old aristocrats." Young novices brought her enticing meals—fresh fruit from the convent garden and delicious red wine. Young officers came to speak to her through a grille and left books for her to read. In the long, walled-in walks, the nuns questioned her about her escapade, and she teased them about husbands and played with their pupils—for this was a teaching convent—in breaks between lessons.

After two weeks, she was released by special order of Sir John French, Commander in Chief of the British Expeditionary Force, and given a last scolding by Sir John Bunbury, Provost Marshal of the British Army. She calculated that he was the sixth general to have occupied himself with her affairs, not to speak of some twenty staff officers and various other officials. "Our Higher Command," concluded this lively butterfly, unscathed by her serial steamrollering, "surely lacked imagination and a proper perspective."

On the boat from Boulogne, she chanced to meet the great Mrs. Pankhurst, who asked her to speak at a recruiting rally in England —an invitation that she had to refuse because she was told it would contravene the Defence of the Realm Act. Examined again at Folkestone, she promised not to write any newspaper articles, since "the young officer asked this for the sake of the country." In London, she had to report to police headquarters at Scotland Yard and was given final clearance.

And that, for this rollicking Vesta Tilly of the Trenches (who later joined the Land Army), was that—until, when the war was over, she wrote a book about her experience. In case people thought she was inventing it, she prefaced her account with a letter of authentication. It was written in the Royal Berkshire Hospital, Reading, and witnessed by a head nurse:

"Dear Miss Lawrence," it said, "I once more take the privilege of dropping you a few lines, hoping they find you well and hearty to receive. . . . Well, for the moment I did not recognise you as you came down the ward the other day. You looked so different dressed as a girl, from the comrade-in-arms which at Albert in September 1915 you happened to be. I can hardly believe that three years have passed since then. It seems so short a time ago since you, looking so fine as a khaki soldier, joined up in our mine-laying company and spent ten days and nights within 400 yards from the Boche front line. . . . If the sergeant had not betrayed your secret you might have seen through as a trusted soldier the end of the first Battle of Loos as well as its early stages. I can see you now stealing along that wall by moonlight, ready to fall into line for the night shift, and prepared with the Buff regimental Badge as well as Royal Engineers equipment. Really I cannot help laughing at what happened later on. You kept in a French convent until whatever news you had gathered would have grown stale for use in the English papers. . . . I remain, Sincerely, Sapper T. Dunn No. 189467 R.E. . . ."

4 §◆

A Determined Mother

Lady Isabella St. John was a civilized, comfortable woman with a civilized, comfortable home on a fashionable street in Chelsea. Her son, a regular-army officer, had been moved from India to the front in France. Lady St. John did not question the rightness of the war, and she was proud that her son was in the thick of the fighting, for the war had brought to the surface a Kiplingesque patriotism that had always been latent in her, as in many other "sophisticated" Englishwomen.

It was, though, a bit of a shock when, during a tea party at a friend's house, someone told her that her son was missing, presumed killed. She might have been prepared to accept the fact, even to make a virtue of it, but she simply did not believe that it was true. *She* had not been notified, and though for the next few days she badgered the War Office, no one there could confirm or deny the story. There was only one thing for it. She must go and find out the truth for herself. So she set out in December, 1915, two months after Miss Lawrence had been shipped home, bound (like Miss Lawrence) for Béthune.

"Light," she wrote later, "was the order of my marching. An ordinary Foreign Office passport visé at the French Embassy, a small leather suitcase, a leather music case in place of the usual handbag, two warm coats worn one on top of the other [the weather was bitter and stormy], a woolly, mist-coloured hat that had seen much service in the London slums [she was a volunteer worker with the Soldiers' and Sailors' Families Association], and seven English sovereigns, hidden away in a secret place of my own contriving, constituted my travelling paraphernalia."

The Channel crossing was rough in more senses than one. The boat was crowded, and squeezed next to her on the deck was a Belgian soldier, cursing the Hun and vowing bloody vengeance. He was apparently convinced that his wife and two daughters, whom he had left in a Flemish village, had suffered a terrible fate. Lady St. John, trying hard to understand the man's very idiomatic French, was rather shocked by the violence of his tone. "Can two wrongs ever make one right?" she asked herself with the philosophic sadness of one who was still on the outer fringe of the muck and muddle and brutality of war and was inclined to lift her long skirt clear of it.

After shaking off the unwelcome attentions of a mysterious Englishman, a well-dressed young man with a sardonic manner who, she thought, should have been in uniform, she set about trying to get a railway ticket to Hazebrouck. This was pure impulse—she had little notion of the geography of the area and only the haziest idea of her son's whereabouts—but at the Calais station, a woman told her that she was going to visit her husband in a military hospital there. The booking clerk asked to see her permit. Firmly she told him that she had a passport valid for the *whole* of France, and, awed by the assurance of her tone, he capitulated and sold her a ticket.

She got into a first-class compartment, went to sleep, and awoke to find herself surrounded by French officers. It soon became obvious that they suspected her of being a spy. So, mobilizing her French again, she put them in the picture. She was English, they must know, the mother of a soldier, on her way to find her son. He had been reported missing, but she believed she knew where to find him—in some village beyond Béthune—and find him she would. Impressed by this spirited explanation, the Frenchmen broke into applause. "*Bravo, Madame!*" they said, and, "*Mon Dieu, quel courage!*"

With a sudden surge of patriotism, she went on to inform them that *her* courage was nothing; for, in her opinion, Britain had, in this war, not only attempted but accomplished the superhuman. Britons, she told her captive audience, "are determined that till the crying, bleeding wrong shall have been punished, until the nation that laid the mine by bringing up an entire generation of its people with war as the ideal before them, and fired the fuse of this universal conflagration, shall herself have paid the cost of it, there shall be no sheathing of the sword." Her gush of eloquence was rewarded with polite murmurs of *"La France n'oubliera jamais ce que l'Angleterre a fait pour elle."*

While these lofty and impeccable sentiments warmed the atmosphere of the compartment, the weather raged implacably outside. At Hazebrouck station, Lady St. John, mercifully protected, like the supertramp she was, by her two topcoats, descended into a storm of sleet and struggled along a waterlogged, windswept road until she reached a small, bricked-in yard, where she sought shelter. There she saw some British soldiers at work—"dear, fresh-faced, wholesome-looking Tommy Atkinses"—and listened gratefully to their Cockney banter. "'Ere, Johnnie, lend a 'and,' 'Slippy, there, Frenchie,' 'Old 'ard, matey!'" and similar expressions, she reported, "were in general use."

In a village just down the road, she persuaded an unwilling peasant to drive her to Béthune in a hard and bumpy horse cart. It took some hard bargaining, and she had to pay half her fare in advance, but off they went. After three hours, the man stopped at a dilapidated house for refreshment, leaving Lady St. John alone in a squalid room with chickens clucking about her feet. Munching the hard bread that she had been offered, she found a crack in the wall and peered through. A sad sight it was. Not only did she see the driver well provided with fresh bread and cheese and beer, but (could she believe her eyes?) two British soldiers sprawled over the table. Obviously they were exceptions to the rule of British respectability—"not fine, upstanding men these, such as I am accustomed to see in every Tommy's tunic, but bedraggled and degenerate-looking specimens, either very ill or very drunk."

When the nightmare drive was resumed, the driver confirmed that the men *were* drunk, but, perhaps taking pity on her shame, added that he had been surprised to find how many British soldiers were total abstainers. In any case, she was not left for long to dwell on the unpleasant memory, for suddenly the cart was surrounded by a great host of British troops, traveling to the front in requisitioned omnibuses, with nostalgic destinations (Piccadilly, she saw, and Walham Green) still visible front and back, and motor vans seized from well-known London stores (Harrod's, she noticed, and Waring & Gillow, and felt somehow strengthened for anything that might lie ahead).

When, outdistancing the mud-slowed convoy, they entered a thick forest of bare, shell-splintered boughs, the horse, tired as it was, raced in panic through the gloom and next caught up with a troop of Indian cavalry. Lady St. John felt very sorry for them— "utterly dispirited, sad beyond description, livid and leaden of complexion as of mood, the poor fellows looked. Seeing them was to realise how absolutely awful trench warfare, in Arctic conditions, must be to our Indian fellow-subjects." At this point, the horse went lame, but, providentially, an English officer passed within hailing distance. He stared hard at her, drenched but undaunted in her ignominious cart.

"How," he demanded, "in the name of all that is wonderful, did *you* get here?"

"Oh," she replied, "we just drove from Hazebrouck."

Did she realize that she had been in the firing line for most of her journey? No, she did not, but could he give her any news of her son? He could, and he commandeered a car and drove her to yet another village. In no time at all, he produced her son.

The poor boy was unwounded. He was also distinctly embarrassed by his mother's sudden appearance. "Well, mother," he jerked out constrainedly, "you had better come in. You can explain matters later."

It was anticlimactic, even rather hurting, but Lady St. John was soon romantically reasoning to herself that "war had set and sealed him, at this supreme moment of his life, to greater things than mere human relationships, save perhaps with the fellow-men who beside him daily faced death."

Next day, her son pleaded with her to leave immediately. His reputation, his promotion depended on it. But in order to make quite clear that she had come entirely of her own volition and not in response to any prompting from her son, she sought and obtained an interview with his commanding officer. He, a general, received her with the chilling courtesy of an abbot required to deal with a woman who had strayed, inexplicably, into the monastery garden. It would have been a serious matter, he told her, a very serious matter indeed, if any officer or man under his command had had anything to do with her being there. It was an immense relief that this was not so.

It seemed a pity to have come all that way only to turn back straightaway, so she was allowed to stay on for a couple of days. No one—least of all her son—had anything to do with her. She was left to her own devices, and, like Miss Lawrence, she made an effort to get to the front. She tried, by walking across muddy, empty fields, to have a peep at the trenches, but lost her way. Feeling guilty and unwanted, she tried to redeem herself by volunteering for work as a nursing orderly—in however humble a capacity. But no one would listen to her. Everyone wanted to get rid of her. She left. And her son breathed again.

Just five days after she had left it, she walked into her home in Chelsea. The younger members of her family were just finishing their luncheon and were duly amazed when she told them of her exploit.

Yet, think about it, joke about it, *understand* it as she might, her soldier son's behavior had soured her adventure. Almost everything else had been so grand, so climactic. She could make all sorts of excuses for her son, but could she ever really forgive him for his tiresome men's-worldliness? For in his eyes, at that moment of awkward truth, "I saw," she wrote, "no pleasure at all at my being beside him." It may have occurred to her that this was a minor manifestation of the kind of thing that that Mrs. Pankhurst and those tiresome suffragettes had been making such a fuss about before the war.

P A R T   II

Three for Serbia

From Odalisque to Women's Convoy Corps

When, on June 28, 1914, Gavrilo Princip, a young Bosnian student, shot Archduke Francis Ferdinand, heir to the Austrian throne, at Sarajevo, the idea of a world war caused by an incident in the remote, barbaric Balkans was ludicrous to British politicians and to the British public. Yet once war had been declared, Britons wholeheartedly backed the cause of "little" Serbia.

There was more than a hint of condescension, as well as sentimentality, about this change of attitude. A Society for Training Serbian Women in England announced that "since at least half the male population of Serbia has perished in the war, the present generation of women must carry on alone. As character-training is the basis of all good work, we bring them to this country, for the war has shown that, as a whole, the educated Englishwoman is more capable and has done more for others than the educated women of any other nation. The Serbs recognise this and greatly desire that their girls may be brought up in England."

If the Serbs did think so highly of Britain, it was due neither to such societies nor to military aid (which, as Christabel Pankhurst constantly grumbled, was tardy and inadequate), but to the efforts of a number of remarkable and unquenchably individualistic British women.

Foremost among them was Mrs. St. Clair Stobart. The daughter of Sir Samuel Boulton, Deputy Lieutenant of Hertfordshire, she had an unusual upbringing, never went to school, and refused to be pre-

150

sented at court. "Schools," she considered, "have advantages, but they are a necessary evil and stultify originality, one of the world's greatest needs. If the soul survives this ordeal, it is at best a group soul which is blind to the spiritual values that are not suggested in the curriculum."

Superhumanly energetic, she could never remember feeling mentally or physically tired. In the summer, she would get up at 5 A.M. and go for a long ride, play tennis or cricket with her brothers during the day, and dance all night (she especially reveled in the polka). When she and her first husband went to the Transvaal to farm just after the Boer War, they survived several terrifying veldt fires and a plague of locusts and lived for more than a year on tinned foods and tinned milk. She opened a Kaffir store—a corrugated iron shed where she sold a strange miscellany of goods (Jew's harps, plowshares, blankets, salt) to Swazis and Zulus. The natives developed a respect for "The Big Missis" and asked her to judge family disputes. She also gave medical treatment and made long, lonely treks, risking her life in territory agitated by tribal war, quite deliberately testing her powers of endurance for the special, but as yet unknown, task that (she was certain) destiny had planned for her.

When her husband died soon after the family returned to England, Mrs. Stobart plunged briskly into journalism. She had already written articles about fishing (she was a noted angler) and a little book on golf (she was a county champion golfer) called *How to Win at the Last Hole*. Now she tried her hand at political journalism. Convinced that Britain was making a big fuss about Belgian misrule in the Congo mainly as an excuse to annex the territory, she went to Brussels to interview leading politicians, who, not unnaturally, received her with open arms. There followed an extraordinary example of her talent for unconventional leadership. During a high-level dinner party, her host confided that he was worried about his waistline. Remarking that she knew an excellent way to lose weight, she got up and began to gallop around the dinner table on all fours. After a moment's stunned silence, most of the guests followed her example, bounding around the room, red in the face and guffawing with laughter.

This probably unique achievement did not satisfy her. Now that

her children had grown up, she felt free to realize her more serious
—feminist—ambitions. Her second husband, a retired Colonial Service judge, who sympathized with them, was kept firmly in his place.
She would retain her first married name, and he would be allowed,
if he wished, to take part in her new enterprise—but "always and
only, as understood between us, in the capacity of an orderly."

She was determined to prove that, despite popular prejudice to
the contrary, all-women units could be useful in time of war. Her
Women's Convoy Corps was launched in 1907. Its training program
was based on Royal Army Medical Corps methods, and its members
were given the use of the London Scottish drill hall at Buckingham
Gate, London. At an annual camp, they learned to pitch and strike
tents, dig trenches, and in general to improvise and live rough. In
1910, the *Red Cross and Ambulance News* reported: "Nearly fifty
young ladies, under the command of Mrs. St. Clair Stobart, arrived
at Swanage and marched the four miles to the camp they occupied
for a week. They were dressed in a very service-like blue-grey uniform and carried haversacks and water-bottles. Their kit consisted of
a divided skirt, Norfolk golf jacket, and helmet."

After five years of training and sporadic publicity, Mrs. Stobart
saw a chance of action when the Balkan War broke out in 1912. The
British Red Cross, however, refused her services, preferring to send
only men—who, in her opinion, "knew more about football than
hospital work." She hurried to Sofia and secured a personal interview with Queen Eleonora of the Bulgarians. The Queen was impressed, Mrs. Stobart sent a cable, and within a week a unit of
sixteen women (doctors, nurses, orderlies, and a cook) arrived to set
up a hospital in a commandeered house at Kirk-Kilissa in Thrace.
Allied with the Greeks and Serbs, the Bulgarians drove out the
Turks in a fast-moving six-week campaign, which was nevertheless
long enough to prove the unit's efficiency under extremely trying
circumstances.

The main struggle was with the shortcomings of Turkish sanitation. "A thoughtfully planned pipe," wrote Mrs. Stobart, "carried
excreta past the bedrooms to a cesspool partly covered with rotting
planks." She had to stand over Bulgarian orderlies as they dug new
channels under her direction. But this did not deter her. "All situations," she reasoned, "are interesting if you can either feel their sig-

nificance or see their humour. When both stare you in the face, life is a regalement."

Since the Bulgarians refused to open any windows in the improvised wards, she smashed panes of glass to let in some air. Spittoons were issued and attempts made to cure patients of the habit of throwing food scraps on the floor. After a short period of unavailing resistance, the soldiers grew to appreciate their reformer. When Mrs. Stobart went around the wards on Christmas morning, there was an atmosphere of suppressed, childlike excitement, and "the patients, all sitting up, shouted triumphantly with one accord: 'Melly Kissimas.' The night nurses told me that many of them had spent the night muttering the words over and over again in their anxiety not to forget them."

The expedition had been well worthwhile. "Imagine grey carts and white oxen," she wrote in her more purple style, "led in silence by Bulgarian and Turkish peasants in their grey clothing and white navishtas, defiling between the rocks of a narrow gorge, and freighted not with merchandise but with British women who, themselves emblematic of the dawn of a new day, had thrown off the shackles of civilisation. Betwixt Odalisque and the Women's Convoy Corps, what an interval!"

2 §❧

Inclined with Socrates

In August, 1914, Mrs. St. Clair Stobart founded the Women's National Service League, with the aim of "providing a body of women qualified to give useful service at home or abroad," and soon swirled into action again, despite a second refusal from the British Red Cross. The Belgian Red Cross invited her to set up a hospital in Brussels, but the German advance drove her unit out, and she herself was arrested in Louvain and tried as a spy. She learned afterward that her release was largely owing to the fact that her home was in Hampstead Garden suburb, which the German judge had visited and admired a few months before. She organized a hospital in Antwerp, and when that city had to be abandoned, she took her team to Château Tourlaville near Cherbourg.

This time there was no interruption. The hospital became a model of efficiency, and Mrs. Stobart became restless: "One day in mid-February 1915 I was walking in the woods. A warm sun was shining, birds were singing, purple and white violets carpeting the ground, and I felt a sudden sense of ineffectiveness. This place would be a paradise in the Spring and my job much too comfortable. I read that in Serbia typhus had broken out and there was a terrible lack of doctors and nurses. Clearly Serbia was my destiny."

The Serbian Relief Fund asked her to raise funds for, organize, and direct a hospital. She gathered another unit of twenty-five people, with seven doctors, eighteen trained nurses, cooks, orderlies, drivers, and interpreters. By this time, the Scottish Women's Hospital Units were in the field and women doctors were actually being employed by the War Office. The time had come when one could afford to make a few concessions: "The principle was firmly established, and I therefore thought that no harm could be done by accepting the services of a few male orderlies and chauffeurs."

In Serbia, her tented hospital at Kragujevac was a new departure. But the typhus epidemic was already past its peak, there was no fighting and therefore no new casualties, and Mrs. Stobart was restless once more. Looking around for something to keep her girls busy, she discovered that a third of Serbia's not very numerous doctors had died of disease or wounds and that the rest were in the Army. The result was that there was no medical service for the civilian population, especially in remote country districts, and disease was rampant. Here was her next installment of destiny. A chain of emergency dispensaries, she decided, must be opened immediately.

A bell tent was pitched on the fringe of the hospital encampment, and a notice board improvised from a packing case announced that if people would bring their own bottles, medicine and medical advice would be given free. Within a few weeks, twelve thousand people—men, women, and children—came to that dispensary, some in ox wagons, many walking distances of fifty, sixty, even seventy miles. They were ill, often riddled, with typhus, diphtheria, typhoid, smallpox, tuberculosis: "One man walked sixty miles there and sixty miles back to bring his daughter, who was suffering from swollen glands which needed an operation. The girl had no mother, and the father, who was going to the front, rejoiced greatly at being able to leave her in safe hands." Another little girl was suffering from the aftermath of neglected typhus. The bones of one leg were "as bare of flesh as if a dog had gnawed them clean, and her foot was a gangrenous mass of black pulp. Above the knee were huge holes and horrible sores."

Refreshments—tea or coffee, bread and plum jam—were provided, and the dispensary was such an overwhelming success that Mrs. Stobart cabled the Serbian Relief Fund in London for more material and personnel to start more clinics: "I should like 12 but I must have 6." Six she got, each staffed by one woman doctor, two nurses, a cook, an interpreter, and a driver—to take serious cases to the base hospital at Kragujevac. Permission had been granted to use the half-empty wards to treat civilians as well as soldiers. At first there was a great fear of going into the hospital ("Hospital!" said one woman of her daughter. "Why, she's much too ill to go into hospital!"), but this soon faded when reports spread of the luxury of life under the great tents, of the comfortable beds with their lovely clean white sheets. Patients clamored for operations and became quite angry if they were told they did not need one.

Well-to-do people came all the way from Belgrade to be X-rayed and consult the doctors, who had a high reputation for gentleness and tact as well as for efficiency. Serbian women found it easier to talk to a doctor of their own sex. One distraught young woman told Mrs. Stobart that her officer husband had infected her with venereal disease. She had refused to go to a male doctor and had been trying all sorts of folk remedies and cures she had read about in books. This was her last hope, and if something could not be done for her, she was going to shoot herself—with a revolver that she produced from her handbag.

The position of each dispensary was carefully chosen after detailed reconnaissance, and the opening ceremonies were impressive. Mrs. Stobart described one of them: "Upon the table was an old silver crucifix and a bowl of water containing a sprig of the national plant—boziliac. A monk put on a beautiful pale blue silk embroidered robe. The priest took an incense vessel and swung it in front of us all in turn. Then the monk, holding the crucifix in one hand and the holy plant in the other, suddenly came and stood in front of me. For a moment I was puzzled. But if in doubt in Serbia, kiss. I kissed the crucifix whilst he pressed the wet plant on my forehead."

A whole chain of clinics was now functioning smoothly, but before Mrs. Stobart had a chance to get bored, news came of the threat of an autumn offensive by the German, Austrian, and Bulgarian troops massing on the frontiers. The Serbs had been miraculously victorious in the comparatively minor campaigns of 1914, but now retribution hung over them. The door of a new opportunity of usefulness was opening, and Mrs. Stobart was through it in a flash, demanding that part of her unit should be allowed to go to the front as a mobile field hospital. Colonel Dr. Lazar Guentchitch, head of the Serbian Army Medical Services, by now almost mesmerized by this brilliant, willful creature, agreed, and she ignored the criticisms of her sponsoring committee in London, which was horrified when it heard of her latest escapade.

The colonel put her in sole charge of a full hospital column, with the rank of major—the first time in history, he believed, that such an appointment had been offered to any woman. Major St. Clair Stobart, however, decided, after careful consideration, that it might be best if she continued to be known as "Maika" (Mother). "The word Maika was already, to Serbian hearts, rich with impressions of the best qualities of the old-fashioned woman; it would do no harm to add to this a few impressions of qualities of authority and power not hitherto associated with women." Always and everywhere, she fought on two fronts.

The column journeyed at first by train, but it had no sooner reached the Danube than the order to retreat came. The retreat went on for three months, in bitter weather, over the mountains of Montenegro and Albania, with many confused and exhausting rearguard actions. It was the retreat not merely of the Serbian Army but of the Serbian nation. "Thousands of women, children and old men, driven from their homes," wrote Mrs. Stobart later in a magazine, "swelled the procession. Wagons were filled with household treasures, beds, frying pans, chairs, even geese slung head downwards at the back of the cart, or balancing themselves with curious dignity upon the uneven surfaces of indiscriminate luggage." She saw one

woman dragging two tired oxen that were pulling a wagon containing eight small children. Another woman was carrying two babies,
one on her back, one in front: "In one of the crushes which frequently occurred, the baby at her back was knocked off by a passing
ox."

For eight hundred miles and eighty-one days she led her column
on ponyback (journalists christened her romantically "The Lady on
the Black Horse"): "I always rode astride at the head of my company, by night as well as day, though other commanders urged me
to sleep in the carts or motor ambulances during night treks. I did
this, partly because it was the only way of always being on the alert,
and partly also in order that the soldiers should feel that I was not
asking them to do what I should not do myself."

She was fifty-three years old, small, and frail-looking. Clad in a
black riding habit and with her abundant fair hair hidden by a
large, floppy black hat, she seemed, like some God-sustained Cru-
sader, to draw on reserves of otherworldly strength. Her powers of
endurance must have seemed awesome: "We travelled slowly, an
average of one kilometre an hour, and I was surprised at the number
of hours it was possible to remain in the saddle without fatigue.
Once I was three days and three nights on horse-back almost con-
tinuously, with only an hour or two here and there of outspan for
rest and food for the animals."

Her column consisted of two women doctors, five nurses, five
male British drivers, and sixty Serbian orderlies and had for transport thirty ox wagons, seven horse-drawn wagons, and six ambulances. They inched through deserted villages and passed abandoned railway stations: "It was a world of shadows and of dreari-
ness, of wet and cold, of the creaking of wagons and the squish,
squish of oxen hooves pressing the glutinous mud." There were
hopeful rumors that the Allies were about to send reinforcements.
But no help came. The weather and the paths got worse, and the
mountains and the marauding bandits of the Balkans closed in on
them. Mrs. Stobart solved the problem of keeping the convoy together by sending the oxcarts ahead so that the horses were forced,
on the narrow roads, to keep their pace. Motor vehicles drove for
half an hour and then waited for the rest to catch up, or they started
well after the others had left.

The two Serbs who were in charge of foraging (she nicknamed

them "Sandford" and "Merton") were a dismal failure. They took no for an answer—an unforgivable sin to Mrs. Stobart: "We were near a town and hoped for some hay. But Sandford and Merton came back complacently with their dreadful 'Nema' ('There is none'). There is something inexpressibly exasperating about this word. It doesn't mean 'Very sorry, but I have done the best I could and failed.' It means 'Can't, shan't, won't, couldn't, wouldn't if I could.' It epitomises all the obstructive negatives capable of expression in any language. And 'Nema nishti Bogani' ('There is none, by God'), the Montenegrin version, was even worse. It invoked deific corroboration for assertions you knew to be untrue." Often, she and her faithful interpreter-bodyguard, Vooitch, had to do the foraging.

She had—as befitted a future chairman of the World Spiritualist Community—gloomy spiritual doubts and spectacular reassurances: "A German and a French aeroplane appeared, then, as though to hide from us on earth the prostitution of science to murderous ends, both birds of prey dived into a huge white cumulus cloud." Sometimes her faith wavered miserably: "How could I help asking, 'Where is God?' And immediately the answer came. The mountains in the East threw off the blackness of night. One daring cloud of brilliant gold spread itself in the shape of a great dragon across the sky. Glories and beauties everywhere, if we could only catch the meaning!"

About halfway through the retreat, the roads got so bad that it was decided to cut the four-wheeled carts in two and abandon half the hospital stores. Two days later, when the paths had become virtually impassable, Mrs. Stobart ordered the burning of the truncated carts, and the convoy pressed on as best it could with pack ponies and oxen. It pressed on "over passes 5,000 feet high, over snow, ice, boulders, unbroken forest, mud-holes, bridgeless rivers. And always those pitiless mountains. Mountains with steep, snow-covered slopes, or mountains of grey, bare rock, precipitous and shutting out all hope." Still her stamina held: "The only inconvenience I felt was from an occasional fit of sleepiness when nothing important had to be done."

Water could be obtained only by melting snow. There was no fodder for the animals, which had to be content with dead beech leaves exhumed from the snow. The human beings slept around fires and prevented themselves from slipping down the mountainsides by jamming logs at their feet. To take a wrong path would have meant disaster and death. But Mrs. Stobart was undismayed. "Life," she philosophized, "is a series of choices, and I risked prompt decisions to scale or descend this, that or the other height." Stumbling through a narrow gorge, they heard firing and screams in the distance. A party of Albanian bandits had attacked another convoy. There was a nasty moment when Mrs. Stobart caught her sergeant trying to shove a recalcitrant pony over a precipice to save time: "I dragged at the reins and saved the pony. I have never felt so angry in my life, and a vehement 'Damn!' saved me from bursting. I repeated it all the way down the hill, and it took me safely to the bottom."

The column arrived at Scutari, in Albania, on December 20, 1915. It was the only one to get through without any losses or desertions, and the Serbian Crown Prince himself was there to congratulate her. She was decorated with the orders of the White Eagle and St. Sava and was given tremendous testimonials. Colonel Guentchitch wrote: "You did not give up your command for one moment, and shared all the war inconveniences. You have made everybody believe that a woman can overcome and endure all the war difficulties. You can be sure, esteemed Madame, that you have won the sympathies of the whole of Serbia and that you have left the best impressions."

In London, however, her reception was cooler. The Chairman of the Serbian Relief Fund rebuked her for exceeding her instructions and leading her unit into unnecessary risks. But what did he, poor prosaic mortal, know of such things? She gave the proceeds of her writings and lectures about her Serbian experiences to the Serbian Red Cross, and in 1917, at their own expense, she and her devoted husband embarked on an extensive lecture tour in Canada and the United States. They traveled four times across the American continent from ocean to ocean, and Mrs. Stobart spoke at more than 150 meetings in churches, halls, clubs, theaters, and universities. She followed this mammoth bit of personal public relations—which yielded a sum of £4,000 for Serbia—by a blitz on Ireland ("Why not try and stir the inhabitants of the Emerald Isle to a more fervid participation?") that was cut short by the Armistice.

To those who asked for the secret of her impressive career, she replied: "I have all through life acted on the spur of the moment.

The world calls this impulsiveness: but I am inclined with Socrates to think that ideas can be impressed on us from other planes of life. Unless in our commonplace moments we act upon the suggestion of our inspired moments, we shall never achieve anything."

3 §⁊

The Clergyman's Wife

Mabel Dearmer was a remarkable person in her own right, though, at the last, it was her fate to be swept along in Mrs. Stobart's creaming wake. She had married the Rev. Percy Dearmer, an enterprising curate in South London, when she was nineteen and just out of the Bushey School of Art. But despite being a busy housewife, she had a full and vivid life of her own, writing and illustrating several books for children (including a *Children's Life of Christ*) and making friends with many writers, among them Henry Harland, Richard le Gallienne, Laurence Housman, Maurice Hewlett, and Stephen Gwynn. Later she published several novels, one of which, *The Difficult Way*, she dramatized for performance at the Court Theatre, with Lilian Braithwaite in the leading role. She founded a Morality Play Society and wrote several plays for it—*The Soul of the World* and *Joseph and His Brethren* were the most notable (and were praised by George Bernard Shaw)—but had most fun and most success with her children's plays, including *Brer Rabbit* and *The Cockyolly Bird*.

In the summer of 1914, the Dearmers bought a cottage in the Cotswolds, and Mrs. Dearmer went there for a complete rest. She was a vital and brilliant woman with a mass of bright-red hair and a tendency to exhaust herself by the sheer intensity and profusion of her activities. But at Oakridge Lynch, she luxuriated in the peace and the sunshine. "It is," she noted, "a wonderful plum year, and that means work—work or wasps." From the dawn, when she watched the sun rise "through the tangle of flowers overtopped by gigantic hollyhocks, on to the blue night when the primroses lit their lamps and the night-jar just ruffled the air with his purring," life was dreamily recuperative.

Then she got a postcard from Stephen Gwynn. It said: "There is war and we are in it." She was incredulous, even irritated: "I knew nothing of European complications and cared less. The murder of an Archduke meant no more to me than some tale of an imaginary kingdom in Zenda. I asked myself if any horrors could be greater than the horrors of peace—the sweating, the daily lives of the women on the streets, the cry of babes born to misery as the sparks fly upward."

Her friends did not come down to help with the plums: "They did not want to leave town, and a strange passionate excitement seemed to possess everybody. I could not enter into it. I did not hate the enemy. I hated the spirit that made war possible, and this spirit I seemed to catch in our own newspapers." Her younger son, Christopher, an undergraduate at Oxford, wrote from France, where he was on vacation, to say that he was hurrying home to enlist. His mother reflected: "If I had been a man I could not have fought, for the way in which I read the words of Christ is that the Kingdom of Heaven is gained by a different method altogether, a method never tried by diplomatists." Christopher was puzzled by what he saw as halfheartedness ("This is not like you, Mother"), but she could only answer: "If you feel you must go, you offer your life. That is always good. You can't do more."

She herself returned to London to produce plays for war charities and to do some volunteer work for the Belgian Refugee Fund, work that only intensified her conviction of war's futility: "One young woman I interviewed seemed strangely dazed. It was explained to me that she had lost her baby. She came by the last boat from Ostend and there was a great crush and she dropped the child in the sea. She had herself escaped death and outrage. She was young and pretty. She had only dropped her baby in the sea."

The Rev. Percy Dearmer volunteered to go to Serbia as chaplain to the British Army contingents there, and Mrs. Dearmer left rehearsals of *Brer Rabbit* to attend a farewell service held by him on March 26, 1915, at the church of St. Martin's-in-the-Fields in Trafalgar Square—for Mrs. Stobart's unit. "This," she wrote, "consisted of some forty women of varying ages dressed in a uniform of grey cloth and wearing a round black hat. Mrs. Stobart, whom I had known fairly well, wore the same with modifications. During the singing of the last hymn an idea struck me. Here was the work for which I had waited. I had no hesitation. The unit filed out of the church, all except Mrs. Stobart, who still stood in the aisle. I went up to her. 'Can you take me to Serbia?' I asked 'What can you do?' 'Nothing. But I am an ordinary sensible woman and can learn quickly.' "

Mrs. Stobart looked at her. Mrs. Dearmer liked pretty clothes and was wearing a green silk dress and a fur coat. She realized, of course, didn't she, that she would have to leave those sorts of things behind and accept discipline? When the quizzing was over, Mrs. Dearmer found her husband and told him that she too was going to Serbia, as a hospital orderly. If her husband was surprised, he did not show it: "He only said 'What fun!' and hailed a taxi."

A week later, she was on her way to Serbia. "We realised," she wrote in the first of a series of letters to Stephen Gwynn, "that there was a war on when we got to Boulogne, chiefly because all the Tommies came and kissed their hands to us. French soldiers were a lot more staid." At Malta the unit went ashore, and she met her elder son, Geoffrey, an Army subaltern. "Goats everywhere," she enthused, "*darling* goats and women in queer black veils stiffened in front into a kind of hat. I said to Geoffrey how lovely it all was, and he said: 'Oh, they are only Malts—*this* is the Club.' " Some of the Stobart nurses behaved rather skittishly, she noticed "They picked up escorts of stray Tommies and went round in large hilarious parties. I thought the best thing to do was for Percy to tell them that this must not be at other places. Accordingly Percy and the Cook's man have taken an enormous party to the Acropolis this morning."

In Salonika, the unit stayed at the Splendide Palace Hotel and did the sights: "We went up to the old Turkish town this afternoon. It is the most wonderful place with strange, dirty picturesque people. Some soldiers begged Mrs. Stobart to take a photograph of the group of them. Of course she did and there was a great deal of joking and laughter." They hired carriages and visited the mosques, attended a tea party on the roof garden of a big hotel, and saw a film at a picture palace.

Mrs. Stobart impressed upon everyone the need for hygiene: "Mrs. S. is frightfully keen on coming out of this without losing one of us. It would be *mean* to go and die and spoil the unit's chance of winning such a reputation, wouldn't it?" Temperatures were to be taken every morning when they reached camp, and there was to be regular Swedish drill. Like most of the others, Mrs. Dearmer pretended to be horrified at the thought of it all, but she was glad to reach the hospital site at Kragujevac, near Belgrade, in the north of Serbia: "It is wonderful to get into the air after the stuffy trains and the filthy, filthy sanitary arrangements of Salonika. We are on a sort of plateau with mountains on all sides and wonderful sunshine and wonderful evening skies. I have been put in charge of the linen tent for the whole camp and am, in addition, doctor's orderly. There are 62 tents in all."

A social gulf was fixed between her and her husband. "Percy and I are in quite different classes. He sits with the great—the doctors and Mrs. Stobart—and I with the common orderlies. That fills me with joy. It is like being at school—a very happy and delightful school, but still school—and one's virtues are school virtues and one's sins are the sins of schoolgirls."

On April 30, the first patients arrived: "The nurses are just passing my tent in their pretty blue dresses and white army caps. Mrs. S. and the others who are going into the receiving rooms are wearing their rubber suits, top boots and oilskin hats." By May 22, the weather had changed: there was wind and rain and mud, and Mrs. Dearmer was issuing what boots she had to ill-shod Serbian soldier patients: "We talk by signs and much laughter. They say, 'Dobra Sister' (Good Sister) and I say 'Dobra' and we all say 'Dobra'" She began to try to define her reaction to the sights and sounds of a war hospital: "I am not at all hardened to the sight of wounds. They don't make me feel sick or disgusted, only passionately pitiful, and I always get a little soppy and pat their hands and say 'Dobra voynick,' which means 'Good soldier.' The sight of a bad wound beautifully dressed is not repulsive."

She was proud of her work: "You make me laugh when you talk of my linen *cupboard*. Think of a tent, a sea of thick mud on the floor (in spite of the most careful trenching) with rough packing-cases and crates on their sides all round, filled with things that are nearly always wet, and all over the floor mattresses and hot bottles and air cushions and bedpans and cradles for wounded limbs. All my ingenuity is exercised in devising ways to keep things separate." She was annoyed by the fuss (which Stephen Gwynn had reported to her) about the sinking of the *Lusitania* by the Germans. "Of course," she snapped, "people are raving over it, but was there *ever* any real gilt on war? If I never saw you or Geoffrey or Christopher any more, I could no more be angry with the men or the nation that had taken you all from me than I could with an earthquake. It is all ignorance and folly, and we are working out through it to ordinary sense. *The only way to see war is from a hospital.*"

The hospital was quiet. The typhus epidemic was dying, the front was dead, and the unit was disgruntled: "Little groups of nurses come up to me and Percy, pathetically saying: 'What are we to do? We are wasting our training on wounds four to six months old.'" Mrs. Dearmer herself was in fact already ill with the beginnings of typhoid fever, but continued to work and to puzzle over the endless paradoxes of war: "We do live in odd times. The men go out to kill each other, and the women—well, if the women can't be ministering angels and brave dangers, they just become horrid little cats and break rules and squabble. I suppose God knows—oh I know God knows, but I wish He would make *us* know quicker. War is the devil's own. When I see these wounded here I have got a new obsession. I don't see you and Geoff and Chris hurt, but I see all the men that you and Geoff and Chris are going to hurt as these men are hurt, and *that* is the unbearable thing. This war will not bring peace, no war will bring peace, only terrific virtues such as loving one's enemy can bring a terrific thing like peace."

The Serbian wounded, when they got stronger, were always singing and dancing: "They dance in a ring, doing a sort of step all the time, and they sing long, long sagas of past wars in the strangest harmonies that are very beautiful." But as the mud got deeper and the fever sapped her energy, she found the Serbs less and less sympathetic: "Their whole talk is of fighting. They are human beings wasted. As soon as they are well they want to go and fight again. They are like fighting dogs or cocks. That is what war has done for them—killed their souls." And she added: "The hardest fight is to love the person you want to fight. It sounds a platitude, but today it is Christ or Kitchener. What chance would Christ have today? Crucifixion would be a gentle death for such a dangerous lunatic."

Despite all the precautions, typhoid was spreading. A Serbian interpreter, a nurse, an orderly, and Mrs. Stobart herself were isolated. Mrs. Dearmer felt so fit after roughing it in the fresh air for a few weeks that she was sure that even if she got typhus she would pull through. Even if she did not, "one has to stop some day, and personally I would rather stop here, doing this work, than anywhere else in the world."

On June 12, in a letter, she summarized her impressions of camp life. It was, she said, the lack of discipline, not the excess of it, that had irked her: "When I first came I simply never got a bath, for I felt I could not fight for hot water. I used to put my water on to boil and invariably somebody used to pinch it when I was gone to get my india rubber bath. Now I sit over my water and if I have to leave it for a minute I throw bricks at anyone who goes near it." One particular girl had got on her nerves, but she had refused to lose her temper: "Then it struck me one day that it was only a kind of rotten pride in me, so the next time she was intolerable I just shook her, saying 'Apologise to your betters for being a rude little pig. A-pol-o-gise!' She shrieked with laughter and was fearfully pleased, and in a way we have been friends ever since."

Three days later she sent a penciled note: "Yesterday I knocked under with this fever—typhoid. Don't worry. It may mean, though, that I come back to England at the end of three months."

She died on July 11, and her son Christopher, a pilot in the Royal Naval Air Service, was killed a few months later at Suvla Bay, Gallipoli. "One has to stop some day . . ."

4 ৡৡ

The Clergyman's Daughter

Flora, the youngest daughter, had always been something of a problem. As a small girl she kept saying she wished she were a boy, and as she grew up she showed no sign of changing her mind and marrying and settling down. She was born in 1876, soon after her father, the Rev. Samuel Dickson Sandes, Rector of Whitechurch in County Cork, moved to England to become Rector of Marlesford in Suffolk. Flora learned to ride and shoot and camp, and when her father retired to a house at Thornton Heath, near London, she rather unwillingly took a job as a secretary and let off steam by driving an old French racing car. In her spare time, she had some training as a nurse in the Ladies' Nursing Yeomanry, but was happiest in the kind of excercise that required her to gallop about some green English meadow that had been designated as a "battlefield" and dismount and scoop up "casualties" and heave them over the saddle and gallop to the finishing post in a kind of medical point-to-point.

Immediately after war was declared, Flora, a jolly, bouncing, buxom spinster of nearly forty, rushed to volunteer as a nurse, and on August 12, 1914, found herself en route for Serbia with six other girls. They had been selected, and were escorted, by Madame Mabel Grouitch, wife of the Serbian Minister for Foreign Affairs. Flora went through the worst of the typhus plague, and at Valjevo, just north of Kragujevac, since she was the only remotely qualified person still on her feet, she performed amputations in the operating theater. Such was her physical resilience that even when she caught typhus herself, she was up and about within two weeks.

Thornton Heath had never been like this, but even bigger adventures were to come. During the retreat of the Serbian Army in October, 1915, she was attached to the crack 2nd Regiment as a dresser. No coherent medical service was possible in the midst of a continuous rearguard action fought in rough and worsening weather. The commanding officer, Colonel Militch, lent Flora his white Arab mare, and she rode with him as he inspected the improvised trenches. She handed out some boots to men who, though soaked with mud to the knee, had nothing sturdier than "opankis" —leather sandals fastened with straps that wound about their legs. She distributed comforts: "I gave everyone a couple of cigarettes, and my orderly followed with half a dozen pots of jam and a spoon, the men opening their mouths like starlings to be fed."

She lived in dread not so much of the pursuing Bulgarians, rumored to be capable of any atrocity, as of being "packed off back to Salonika as a female encumbrance." Knowing her fear and seeing no reason why she should not be as effective a soldier as the Serbian peasant women who had enlisted in time of crisis, Colonel Militch made a soldier of Flora. In a half-joking ceremony, he took the little brass figure 2 off his own epaulets and fastened them on her shoulder straps. The new recruit was known as "Nashi Engleskinja" (Our Englishwoman) and was soon filled with romantic hero worship for her company commander, Lieutenant Janachko Jovitch: "He was a martinet, but the comfort of his men was always his first consideration. A good commander makes a good company, and he could make a dead man get up and walk."

The Serbs were driven from one hilltop to the next, and the twelve-hour ascent of Mount Chukus was one of the most grueling. Despite the cold, everyone was soaked with sweat. But it was a memorable night. The moon shone brilliantly, the ground was covered with white frost, and to Flora "it all looked perfectly lovely, with all the camp fires twinkling every few yards over the hillside among the pine trees. I lay on my back looking up at the stars, and when someone asked me what I was thinking about, I told him that when I was old and decrepit and done for, and had to stay in a house and not go about any more, I should remember my first night with the 4th Company on the top of Mount Chukus."

During the night, she stuck her feet too near the fire and scorched the soles of her boots. Next day, her company fired on the Bulgarians in the valley below, and Flora saw her first bit of action: "I had only a revolver and no rifle of my own, but one of my comrades was quite satisfied to lend me his and curl himself up and smoke. The bullets came singing round one's head directly one stood up, but they did not seem awfully good shots. It's a funny thing about rifle fire, that a person's instinct always seems to be to hunch up his shoulders and turn up his coat collar as if it were rain."

They ran out of bread and cigarettes and roasted corncobs over the fire and melted snow in billycans to get water. Flora slept on snowy mountainsides and in swampy fields and shared a hayloft in an Albanian village with fourteen officers—for she was a very special private. She rode as much as she could, on a pony that Lieutenant Jovitch had commandeered for her, sometimes walking to give the animal a rest. On Christmas Eve, there was a little celebration over the campfire—a plate of beans and some dry bread, a pull of brandy, and Flora playing "God Save the King" on the old violin she carried in her kit bag.

After a final march that lasted from five in the morning until eight at night, her regiment arrived in the town of Durazzo on the Adriatic coast of Albania. It camped on a hillside overlooking the sea, and Flora became a nurse again to deal with the hundred and one ailments that were the inevitable aftermath of the slogging retreat. On New Year's Day, to her delight, she was promoted corporal.

Shortly afterward, the regiment was shipped south to the Greek island of Corfu. It rained for six weeks without ceasing, and campfires were forbidden for fear the men might cut down all the olive trees. The damp, the cold, and inadequate clothes and rations brought a high mortality rate. Flora hitched a lift into the town of Corfu and, with all the Irish blood in her singing with resentment, badgered the British and French authorities to such effect that she returned to camp in triumph with a whole sackful of bread, another of bully beef, two large earthenware jars of wine, and a stack of logs. A few days later, despite daunting bureaucratic complexities, she managed to arrange for the issue of 3,250 uniforms and sets of undergarments for her regiment, which was the first Serbian unit to be fitted out in British khaki. Deeply impressed by this achievement, the NCO's and men of her company composed an address and presented it to their corporal. Flora had it translated as literally as possible. It read:

"To the high-esteemed Miss Flora Sandes!
"Esteemed Miss Sandes!
"Soldiers of the 4th Company, 1st Battalion, 2nd Infantry Regiment, touched with your nobleness, wish with this letter to pay their respects and thankfulness to you. . . . Serbian soldier is proud because in his midst he sees a noble daughter of England. . . . He will always respect acts of your kindness and remember them for ever. . . . You have often helped us to pass through hardships, buying food for us, and financially. . . . Thanking you in the name of all the soldiers, we, the committee, are greeting you with exclamation—
"Long life to our ally England!
"Long life to Serbia!
"Long life to their heroic Armies!
"Long life to noble Miss Sandes!"

When Lieutenant Jovitch added a note of commendation, Flora's happiness was complete. A few days later, at a special ceremony attended by the General of the First Army and by the Crown Prince of Serbia, she was promoted sergeant and given two months' leave. This she spent busily raising funds for Serbia and eagerly looking forward to the time when she could get "another whack at the enemy."

By mid-August, 1916, she was back with the 4th Company and was given charge of a *vod* (platoon) during a disastrous campaign in which the 2nd Regiment began with three thousand men and ended with five hundred. "Slept a bit," she wrote in the notebook that she carried in her tunic pocket. "About 1 A.M. the order came to go forward again. Cold, pouring buckets and blowing, awfully rough going on the hills. Got to the top of a stony rise where we lay on our tummies in pelting rain, with rifles and bombs ready, but nothing happened. Awfully cold at dawn and pretty wet, but managed to sleep for all that in my overcoat, no blanket—all that had to stay behind with the mule transport. Breakfast, cold stew, brought to us at 6 A.M. As soon as the sun got up, roasting hot, no shade. Stayed there till about 2 P.M."

In that hilly terrain, the shells made an appalling din, scattering rock fragments and waking a constant reverberation of echoes. Flora was lucky: the noise made her sleepy. The more there was of it, the more soundly she slept, and she needed all the sleep she could get to keep up with the men on the long hauls and the sudden dashes.

"I wish I could have seen the Western Front," she wrote in a letter home, "but I think I should like this better. Our casualties are slighter and we get more sport. They are all awfully good to me, and treat me like a kind of mascot. I don't carry anything except a cartridge belt, light carbine, revolver, water-bottle and a big square of light canvas tenting. We all wear those iron helmets; I hate mine when it is very hot, but love it when we get shelled and stones and shrapnel come pattering down on it."

Quite often, men were killed by stray bullets, and she spent much time in trenches and behind rocks. "I am sitting," she wrote in November, "in a hole about 7 feet by 4 feet and 3 feet deep, with two officers of my company. If anyone at home asks me to describe the War, I shall tell them to go into their back garden, dig a hole, and sit there for anything from three days and nights to a month, without a thing to read or do, and they can judge for themselves—minus the chance of being killed, of course." And she added: "If Mr. ⸺ thinks I ought to be a nurse instead of a soldier, tell him that when the men near me get wounded they generally get me to do them up, between shots."

She was "Brother" to her comrades now, completely accepted and completely at home. At night, when her company was in reserve, she played cards with the officers in a tiny hut lighted by two candles stuck in empty bottles. They drank red wine and played for small stakes, and the orderly kept bringing cups of thick, sweet turkish coffee. It was wild and wonderfully jolly and the answer to any tomboy's dream.

Lying behind a rock with Sergeant Miladin in pouring rain, her stomach rumbling with hunger, and the Bulgarians about fifty yards away, she recited "The Charge of the Light Brigade" to herself to keep up her spirits. She turned out her pockets and found "a forgotten packet of rather damp and squashed cigarettes. I divvied up with Miladin, and he turned out a miscellaneous assortment of odds and ends from his knapsack, and finally came on a very stale and mouldy chunk of breadcrust."

Such moments of copybook comradeship were very precious to her, but now and then the war that provided them could turn nasty, as when Jovan, another friend, tried to liven things up by sticking out his head and got a bullet through his tin hat. Flora clapped her palm over the spurting blood and fixed a rough bandage before the man rolled himself down the hill toward the stretcher-bearers.

On November 15, the five hundred effective soldiers of the regiment were sent in to help capture Hill 1212, the last strong point defending Bitolj, the capital of Macedonia. At dawn the Bulgarians made a surprise attack, routing the troops posted higher up the mountain and pursuing them until they reached the 2nd Regiment's lines. The confusion was made worse by a heavy mist. Flora and her platoon did not have time to advance more than a few yards when they were caught by a scattering of hand grenades: "I immediately had a feeling as though a house had fallen on top of me. Everything went dark, but I was not unconscious, for I realised that our platoon was falling back. I could see nothing, and it was exactly as if I had gone suddenly blind. But I felt the tail of an overcoat sweep across my face. Instinctively I clutched it with my left hand, and must have held on for two or three yards before I fainted. The Lieutenant who wore it told me later that he felt every button tear off, but had not the least idea what was dragging behind him." With her right arm and leg smashed, Flora was dragged to safety, and her mates poured half a bottle of brandy down her throat and lit a cigarette for her. When her wounds had been roughly bound, stretcher-bearers stumbled about for two hours in a snowstorm before they found the dressing station. Flora was glad she had had so much brandy.

Her revolver, she was told, had saved her life. A grenade had struck it and, though it had exploded two cartridges, had glanced off. As the surgeon probed for bomb fragments, Flora buried her face in the chest of a doctor who was standing at the top of the operating table: "He told me to shut up and remember I was a soldier, which had far more effect than any amount of petting would have done." She next faced a day's journey during which, on a stretcher slung beneath a handcart, she was pushed and pulled over bumpy country to another dressing station. Then came a slow, jolting ambulance trip to a hospital at Vodena, on the borders of Serbia and Macedonia, then a train journey in a cattle truck to a military hospital in Salonika.

She was put in a room with another wounded woman sergeant —a Serbian peasant girl called Milunka. A few days later, an aide-de-camp was sent to the ward by the Prince Regent. Flora was still in bed, but the smart young man bent over and pinned to her pajama coat the Kara George Star. This was the most coveted decoration in the Serbian Army, and with it came promotion to the rank of sergeant major.

At the beginning of 1917, she was sent to Bizerte, in Tunisia, to convalesce. Her leg acted up again, and she spent more than three months in bed. When she was out and about again, she found it hard, sometimes, to decide when she was supposed to behave as a lady, when as a plain sergeant. The Serbian military commandant seemed equally confused. "One night," complained Flora, "he invited me to dinner at the best hotel, and after treating me as anything but a non-com, he suddenly remarked, in his severest tone, that I had a small spot on my tunic, that my hair wanted cutting, and that he would send his barber round to me next morning."

She had reached the stage when it seemed to her a big joke to dress up in women's clothes and deceive the officers at a local camp. She wore a fashionable silk frock, a large picture hat with a veil, and very high-heeled shoes ("to which I was so unaccustomed that I toddled in them like a Chinese woman"). As the colonel began solemnly to introduce her as the sister of an English Red Cross worker, someone recognized her: "There was a howl of laughter, and they bore us into the mess for drinks and a gala luncheon with a military band playing."

When she rejoined her regiment, there were only sixteen of her old company left, and they were transferred to the 1st Company of the same battalion. Lieutenant Jovitch had been killed, but Miladin was still there. She had no chance to take up the old threads, for the wounds in her leg opened again, and, much to her disgust, she was sent on leave to England. There, she was such a success as a fund-raiser that she broke all records when she appeared at a gala charity matinee at the Alhambra Theatre. The garments donated as a result of her appeal eventually clothed the whole of the Moravia Division, of which her regiment was a part, most of the First Army, and thousands of other soldiers.

Just before she left England, Flora was summoned to an audience with Queen Alexandra at St. James's Palace. The Queen showed her a large oil painting of her husband, the late King Edward VII, and asked her to write her name in an autograph book. Princess Victoria admired her spurred top boots and asked if she carried a revolver: "I said I did always. 'Show it to us,' said the Queen. Though I usually carried the holster unfastened, that day I had buckled it securely so as not to make a lump under my tunic. 'Hurry up, hurry up!' laughed the Queen as I fumbled with the fastening. 'Supposing someone was attacking me, and you were all that time getting out your revolver!'"

Her wounds healed just in time for her to take part in the great offensive of September, 1918. It was wonderful to have the enemy on the retreat, but Flora sometimes had to restrain the exuberance of her men. Three of them invited her to compete with them in a shooting match. She asked what the target was, and they pointed to a vague heap lying under a rock about half a mile distant. When she realized it was a wounded Bulgarian, she threw down her rifle in disgust. "What plucky chaps you are!" she jeered. "Why don't you shoot at a man who can return your fire?" Awed by her blazing, if slightly incomprehensible, indignation, they stopped their game.

It was one long triumphal procession after another as they marched back through the towns and villages of Serbia after nearly three years of exile. Flora, by this time a sort of national talisman, was often singled out for affectionate mobbing.

In Belgrade, by a special Act of Parliament, she was promoted to the rank of lieutenant—the first woman officer in the fighting ranks of any modern army. After three years on coastal customs patrol (when she met her future husband, Sergeant Yurie Yudenitch, formerly an officer in the Tsarist Army), she was demobilized in 1922; and four years later, by another special order, she was made a captain. Serbia, now part of Yugoslavia, had taken her to its heart. In 1939, when the Germans invaded Yugoslavia, she was called up in the reserves. Six years later, the Royal Air Force flew her, an elderly and childless widow, back to England. She spent the last ten years of her life in a small cottage in a village in Suffolk, near the place where she had been born. She was poor but very cheerful, and when the Yugoslavian Embassy in London sent a hamper of food and drink, she would ask friends in to drink glass after glass of slivovitz (plum brandy), show them photographs of herself as a sergeant and a lieutenant and a captain, and pass around her old revolver so that they could see the dent made by the Bulgarian hand grenade.

Ministering Angels

Mrs. Pankhurst and her daughter Christabel in prison clothes, 1908.

RIGHT. *Christabel Pankhurst, in full finery, photographed after a WSPU get-together in a London restaurant, circa 1909.* BELOW. *Mrs. Pankhurst speaking in Hyde Park (shortly before she left on her Russian mission). Christabel at right.*

Mrs. Pankhurst in bed at "Mouse Castle"—the London nursing home run by Sister Pine (seen here) and Sister Townsend—after a hunger strike.

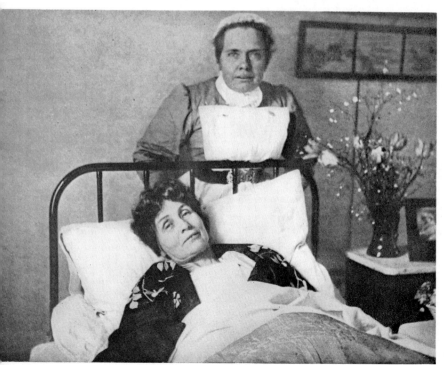

ABOVE. *Winston Churchill with C. P. Scott (editor of the* Manchester Guardian) *outside the Reform Club, Manchester, watching suffragette demonstrators, 1909.* LEFT. *Forcible feeding of suffragette prisoners began in 1908, and this is one of several WSPU posters that made a sensational appeal to public opinion. Note David Lloyd George as the "doctor" at right.*

"General" Drummond stands on a tank to make a typical fighting speech in Liverpool.

Mrs. Drummond opposite the terrace of the House of Commons addressing MP's, inviting them to the Hyde Park demonstration.

Suffragette "cavalry" in a parade in London, 1912.

Sylvia Pankhurst (second from extreme left) in the cheap restaurant that she opened in the East End of London.

TO SAVE THE COUNTRY

URGENTLY NEEDED

1. **THE RESIGNATION OF SIR EDWARD GREY,** whose war methods and sea policy for the future have proved to be a danger to the nation and to the Cause of the Allies.

   THE RESIGNATION ALSO OF LORD ROBERT CECIL, who is identified with the same dangerous policy.

   The disappearance from the public service of SIR EYRE CROWE, the principal permanent servant at the Foreign Office, who is connected with Germany both by birth and marriage.

2. **CLOSER CO-OPERATION BETWEEN THE ALLIES and improved co-ordination of their policy, especially in the diplomatic sphere !** (The Germans are rejoicing at the Allies' weakness in this respect, and see therein the chance of German victory.) This reform to be brought about by

3. **THE ESTABLISHMENT DURING THE WAR OF A DIPLOMATIC CENTRE FOR THE WHOLE ALLIANCE** which should be nearer to the storm centre than London is ; the advantages to be gained by such reform being

   (a) That the persons responsible for the foreign policy of each of the Allied nations shall be able to make daily and hourly personal exchanges of opinion, be so closely in touch that the Allies may speak and act as one, and

   (b) That the consideration of diplomatic affairs vital to Great Britain and the whole Alliance will be conducted, not in the atmosphere of London, which, owing to the efforts of the British Navy, is **artificially peaceful,** while War is raging but in an atmosphere of **reality.**

4. This also is urgently necessary : that decisions concerning NAVAL no less than Military and Diplomatic policy shall be made and announced by the Allies jointly, instead of being made and announced by Great Britain alone !

   As a result both Great Britain and her Allies will gain !

   Great Britain will gain by being relieved of the **sole burden** and the **unshared odium** of the inconvenience to which neutrals are inevitably exposed in the course of the Allies' War upon German Commerce.

   The Allies will gain by no longer having their naval and military and national interests dealt with by one Ally alone, as to a large extent they have been under the dangerously weak naval policy which has been pursued under the regime of Sir Edward Grey and his assistants.

   The country is in danger, our Allies are in danger, the liberty of Europe is at stake. Therefore individuals must give way before the interests of nations. The policy of Sir Edward Grey, assisted by Lord Robert Cecil and influenced by Sir Eyre Crowe, has been found wanting.

   As a people we owe it to ourselves, and to those who will come after us, to have the moral courage to decree that **this policy and its three authors shall give place to others.**

   We shall and must come through our present perils but the weakness of policy and act that has caused these perils would cause men responsible to retain their present office.

   Men are sacrificing life, women are giving sons, daughters, and husbands, and these Chiefs must at least be ready to vacate their positions if the country finds it necessary to call upon them to do it !

"*Britannia*," November 26, 1915.

FOR KING · FOR COUNTRY · FOR FREEDOM

Britannia

With which is incorporated "THE SUFFRAGETTE"

Official Organ of the Women's Social and Political Union

Edited by CHRISTABEL PANKHURST

No. 7.   Vol. V.   **FRIDAY, NOVEMBER 26, 1915**   Price 1d. Weekly

HOW CAN WE EXPECT TO WIN THE WAR

so long as the Nephew of

Admiral von Holtzendorff,

CHIEF OF THE GERMAN NAVAL WAR STAFF,

is at the

British Foreign Office ?

THIS NEPHEW IS SIR EYRE CROWE, AND HE IS SIR EDWARD GREY'S PRINCIPAL PERMANENT SERVANT!!

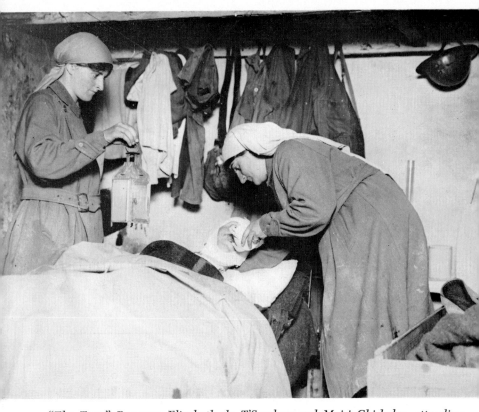

"The Two," Baroness Elizabeth de T'Serclaes and Mairi Chisholm, attending to a wounded Belgian soldier in their cellar dressing station, August 6, 1917.

Lady May Bradford, hospital letter writer, by the bedside of a patient in France.

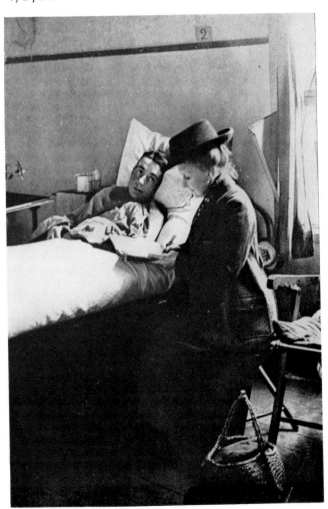

LEFT. *Enid Bagnold in the uniform of a driver of the First Aid Nursing Yeomanry, 1919.* BELOW. *Mairi Chisholm at Pervyse, 1915.*

VAD Nurse Vera Brittain with soldier patients, Malta, 1916.

MALTA . 1916

Baroness Ernest de la Grange with General Sir William Pulteney at Château de la Motte au Bois, 1916.

Commandant Mrs. Stobart and Siberian orderlies on horseback as she leads the column in the retreat, en route for Petch, November 22, 1915.

Sergeant Major Flora Sandes, an Irishwoman serving in the Serbian Army, wounded by a hand grenade, and afterward decorated with the Cross of Kara-George for bravery in the field. This photograph was taken when she was convalescing from her wounds, Salonika, January, 1917.

Members of the Women's Battalion of Death at play, Petrograd, September, 1917. At extreme left is Commander Maria Botchkareva. Photograph taken by Mrs. Pankhurst and reproduced by permission of Miss Jessie Kenney.

RIGHT. *Countess Markievicz in the uniform of the Irish Citizen Army, 1914.*

BELOW. *Commandant Allen (second from left) and other senior members of the Women's Police Service, just after the First World War. Left to right: Superintendent Goldingham, Commandant Allen, Chief Inspector Champneys, Inspector Barnet, Superintendent Sims.*

Keogh Bros.

Barratt's Photo Press, Ltd.

ABOVE. *Queen Mary talking to wounded soldiers in the St. John's Ambulance Hospital, Étaples, July 6, 1917.* LEFT. *Miss Douglas-Pennant (left) leaving the House of Lords, September 11, 1919.*

The Immaculate Dr. Inglis

Each morning, the Inglis children sat in front of their mother in a row, read verses from the Bible in turn, then knelt and repeated prayers after her. The fact that the family was stationed in India (Mr. Inglis was an employee of the East India Company) made the building and sustaining of moral and spiritual fiber all the more necessary, all the more intense.

Elsie, the eldest girl, was a great joy to her parents. Scrupulously honest and conscientious, she was also a natural leader, and she saw to it that games were constructive and practical as well as entertaining. She was fond of playing doctor. The other children would be set to paint red disease dots all over the household's forty dolls, and she would prescribe various forms of treatment. At appropriate intervals, she would instruct her sisters to wash off so many dots, until the patients' skins were clear and they could be pronounced well.

Such were the beginnings of Dr. Elsie Inglis, perhaps the most immaculate and conventionally noble heroine of the First World War. When her father retired in 1878 to live in Edinburgh, she edited the school magazine—and made it pay—and founded a group called the Six Sincere Students Society. It met at intervals and discussed bracing literature such as Ralph Waldo Emerson's essays on self-reliance and heroism.

It was not long before Elsie was troubled by male prejudice about women's part in the world, and she made up her mind to fight it with all her strength. As a medical student she made no attempt to conceal her feminist convictions. From Dublin, where she was taking a course in midwifery, she wrote to her always sympathetic father: "Did I tell you that Dr. B. and I had an awful argument? I never mentioned the subject again, for it is no good arguing with a man who has made up his mind. . . . However, right in the middle of an operation, he suddenly said: 'By the way, you are right about the suffrage, Dr. Inglis.' "

She was deeply angered by the stupid, lethal complacency of many husbands. From Glasgow, where she worked later, she wrote: "On my rounds I found one woman who ought to have been in bed, and discovered that she had been up all night because her husband came in tipsy. He was lying asleep there on the bed. I think he ought to have been horse-whipped, and when I have the vote I shall vote that all men who behave like that *shall* be horse-whipped. And if they make the excuse that they were tipsy I shall give them double. They would very soon learn to behave themselves."

Since women were barred from resident posts in Edinburgh's leading general and maternity hospitals, Dr. Inglis founded a hospital that for many years was the only maternity center in Scotland run by women. She helped to found the Scottish Women's Suffrage Federation and was its most tireless and effective speaker and organizer. It was she who, in August, 1914, suggested that Scottish Women's Hospital Units should be formed for service overseas, and she worked like a Trojan to get funds and recruits. She found the British War Office no more appreciative of her efforts than of Mrs. Stobart's. She too had to look for outlets elsewhere, in Belgium, France, and Serbia.

It was to Serbia that she herself went, in April, 1915. Scottish Women's Hospital teams had already been wonderfully effective in controlling the plague of typhus that had threatened to destroy the population. The Serbs planned a counteroffensive in the autumn, and Dr. Inglis set up three military hospitals in the north. Then came the triple thrust by a combination of German, Austrian, and Bulgarian troops under the supreme command of General Mackensen. Caught by the enemy advance, she and her staff decided to stay where they were and continue with their work. Dr. Inglis vowed that she would not leave until the last of "her" patients had been moved to hospitals in Hungary for further treatment.

Hospital accommodation in Krusevac, where she spent the next three months, had been designed to cope with four hundred men, but numbers rose to twelve hundred. Patients were put in the corridors, with three men lying on two beds pushed together. The men were starving, dirty, overcrowded, and exhausted, and a new epidemic of typhus seemed inevitable. But the women attacked the horrors of the hospital compound. They emptied the overflowing cesspool, buried rubbish, built incinerators, and, as Dr. Inglis put it, "cleaned and cleaned and cleaned. That is an Englishman's job all over the world." So impressed were the patients that when, late one evening, Serbian prisoners were put into the wards straight from the march and crawling with lice, there was great indignation. "Our hearts rejoiced," Dr. Inglis said. "If we have done nothing else, we have driven that fact home to the Serbian mind, that dirt and typhus go together."

Wounded prisoners for whom there was no room had to be left in the compound, where they huddled around meager fires. Dr. Inglis gave away all the bread that could be spared: "But we could not feed that enclosure of hungry men. We used to hear them coughing and moaning all night, and hid our heads under the blankets to shut out the sound."

In February, 1916, she and her unit were sent under guard first to Belgrade, then to Vienna, where, after the American Ambassador intervened, she was released and allowed to return to England. She offered the War Office a unit for service in Mesopotamia, where medical aid was urgently required, but once more she was rejected. So she answered an appeal for help from the Serbian 1st Division, then fighting with the Russian Army on the Rumanian front. The 1st Division consisted largely of "Austrian" Serbs, who had surrendered to the Russians in vast numbers.

She raised two units, complete with motor transport—a total of eighty women, with herself as Chief Medical Officer. They sailed from Liverpool on August 31, 1916, and a week later Dr. Inglis wrote the first of a series of detailed reports and letters to the Committee of the London Suffrage Society, which was financing the expedition. She complained about the shoddiness of the uniforms that had been supplied by a London tailor and outlined the daily routine. After breakfast came cabin tidying. Roll call was at 9:30 A.M., followed by cabin inspection. At 10 A.M. came drill—military drill, stretcher drill, and Swedish drill. During the afternoon, classes in Russian, Serbian, and motor mechanics were held. Sports were organized, and Dr. Inglis described how a Serbian officer reacted to this: "Watching an obstacle race where the girls squirmed under a sail tied down with ropes (it *was* a funny sight), he turned to me and said: '*C'est tout à fait nouveau pour nous, Madame!*' "

After nine days, they steamed south from the Arctic Ocean and arrived at Archangel, on the shores of the White Sea. It was a memorable moment. Anchored in the Dvina River, they gazed at a town of wooden houses that, with its towers and domes of blue and gold, red and gold, and green and gold, rose like an Oriental fantasy from a flat shore covered with scrub and young conifers. In the evening, as the last of their fifty tons of equipment and sixteen automobiles were unloaded, Russian soldiers sang and danced for them on the quay. Then came a two-week train journey, full of delays and alarms, south across Russia to Odessa, on the shores of the Black Sea. From here, they were to proceed to the Rumanian front, just across the border. Dr. Inglis and her senior staff members had tea with the officers of the Serbian 2nd Division: "The whole mess of two hundred men rose when we came in and cheered till we were nearly deafened. There were songs and dances. We sang all the national anthems, beginning with the British, and the list included three which we had never heard before—the Croatian, the Bohemian and the Czech—all three, especially the last, being most rousing tunes." The units were given fourteen boxes for a gala performance at the Opera House, and during the second intermission they lined up in the corridor to be inspected by Grand Duchess Marie Pavlovna. When they got back to their seats, the orchestra played "God Save the King" three times, and the audience cheered and waved their handkerchiefs.

It was a tremendous send-off, but when the units reached the front at Medgidia, some two hundred miles south in the Dobruja, they found that the Serb division had been so badly mauled in the recent fighting that it had been withdrawn from action. Two field hospitals with a total of more than one hundred beds were made ready for action within two days, but more than half the patients were Russians or Rumanians. This meant an awkward adjustment to different ways and different diets (Dr. Inglis's cooks had to learn to make kasha, a kind of grain mush much favored by the Russians).

After three weeks, the enemy broke through, and the retreat northward from the Dobruja began. For the next four days, all was chaos, and Dr. Inglis reported: "It was one continuous stream of carts loaded with luggage and children. Through it barged cannon and ammunition wagons and squadrons of cavalry." Like Miss Macnaughtan, she found the whole spectacle of war slightly unreal: "When we turned on our headlights it seemed like a well-staged piece of theatre." She was proud of the steadiness of her women under constant strafing and bombing. "I don't think it entered their heads to be afraid. In the middle of a panic, when people were throwing things off the carts to lighten them, and soldiers kept climbing onto our cars to gain a few minutes, our girls were picking up the thrown-away vegetables." It was very heartening: "I thought there might be something in what a Russian woman said to me—'There is no other nation goes into trouble laughing.'"

After a nightmare journey by train, truck, cart, and boat (on the Danube, where she saw corpses floating in the water), Dr. Inglis arrived in Braila. Here there were eleven thousand wounded and a mere seven doctors, only one of them a surgeon. The women took over: "It was a case of going on dressing blindly, and the wounded coming in and in. There were still men lying about in empty houses, and the horrible smell of sepsis from their wounds." In a way, she was glad to have such a test, for she had seen the uselessness of "talking about regular field hospitals to the men until they have tried our metal. The ordinary male disbelief in our capacity cannot be argued away. *It can only be worked away.*"

In the midst of all the blood and thunder, she found time to make detailed criticisms of some of the equipment that had been supplied. The disinfectors had been damaged in transit because of slovenly packing, and a large drum of chemical fluid had leaked for the same reason: "The hypodermic needles are worse than useless because they break. The supplier ought to replace them at his own cost immediately."

She admitted that there had been trouble with some of the staff: "I am sorry to hear that the Committee has been told about the disgusting habit of swearing which some members have adopted. I did not send anyone home on that account. In Serbia such a trouble would have been unthinkable. But on the other hand we had trouble there with girls flirting." But there was more than swearing. There was poor, puzzling Mrs. X, one of the transport drivers. She had gone peculiar, dressed like a man, bothered Russian soldiers, and lounged about in cafés smoking, talking to all and sundry, and giving the unit a bad name. "I think," wrote Dr. Inglis, "that it is all due to the shock she got when her husband was killed in India by a tiger—before her eyes."

One nurse had to be put full time in charge of Mrs. X, who, despite doses of bromide and appeals to her better nature, did not improve, going about "dressed in knickerbockers, with a Russian cap on, flourishing a whip and with revolver and cartridges." An attempt was made to persuade her to go home, but she reappeared after getting as far as Bucharest. Then came a new development: "One of Mrs. X's idiosyncrasies is to flirt with Rumanian girls! A Russian Red Cross Sister has been telling us about a ridiculous scene in a restaurant." After further unsuccessful efforts to rehabilitate her, Sir George Barclay, the British Consul at Jassy, had Mrs. X shut up in a mental asylum and cabled the Foreign Office in London to send out a mental nurse. Dr. Inglis was at her wit's end: "Sister Edwards *and* Nurse Ulph are visiting her daily. I cannot understand why her people did not come out. I wired for them *three* times."

But the problem of Mrs. X was soon swamped in other, vaster emergencies. The unit had fallen back to Galaţi, where badly wounded men poured in at the rate of about a thousand a day. The women worked for sixty-five hours on end, bathing, dressing, operating, with only two breaks of three hours for rest: "The night we opened we got 109 cases. We began operating the next afternoon at 2 o'clock and went on until 5 o'clock the next morning."

After a month of organized shambles, there was another move —a little way eastward along the banks of the Danube to Reni. Since the Serb divisions were in reserve and their Dobruja wounded in Russian hospitals, the Inglis units were asked to work for the Russians until the Serbs could be re-formed for action. Two hospitals were set up, one at Reni under Dr. Inglis, the other at Barlat under Dr. Chesney. Dr. Inglis, ill and exhausted, asked the committee to send out an administrator to lighten the load: "I know exactly the woman I need—a gentlewoman tolerant of other people's views, good at managing money and who can talk French well" (Dr. Inglis relied on her very English French in her dealings with the Russian authorities). She added: "Whoever comes must be as strong as a horse."

She was in urgent need of more orderlies, since some of them, having served out the six months they had signed on for, had gone home: "I hope all new members will sign on for a year. Six months means about three months' work here, what with the delay in getting off, the journey out and the journey home." She had strong views about the sort of recruits she wanted: "Get as good a class of girl as you can. The better bred they are the better they stand roughing it." She worried over each member of her unit. "Miss Clark," she reported, "wants a salary. The cooks are paid, but for some unknown reason the laundresses are not. It is not quite fair, as Miss Clark earns her living by her special work as much as the cooks do. She is excellent."

The zeal of the Hon. Evelina Haverfield, head of the transport column, had to be restrained. Her discipline was unreasonably harsh, and it was even said that it had been partly responsible for Mrs. X's breakdown. "Some of the girls," reported Dr. Inglis, "had not had a change of underclothing during the retreat. I tried to make Mrs. H. see that she was working for failure along those lines, and that the fact that men don't take off their clothes for a fortnight in the trenches had nothing whatever to do with women's army ambulance work. I took one case of flagrant injustice and made her see that you can be a beast but you must be a just beast."

Mrs. Haverfield agreed to resign and hand over her command to someone else, but that was not the end of the difficulty. Dr. Inglis herself was accused of obstinacy in her insistence that all the drivers should be women. She heard that Sir George Barclay had wired the committee to say that he considered it "criminal" to send out any more women to drive in such conditions, and some of the women apparently agreed with him. Dr. Inglis acted quickly to stop the threatened rout. "If you want me to stay here," she wrote, "will you back me up, and help me to keep the hospitals what they were intended to be, viz. women's organisations? And don't think I am the sort of fool who takes unnecessary risks. I haven't lost one bit of your equipment through the enemy, except one Ludgate boiler."

When revolution broke out in Russia in March, 1917, the spirit of rebellion spread to the Army, including the wounded soldiers in the hospital, who, in many places, elected committees that drew up timetables to suit their own convenience. But under Dr. Inglis's firm but imaginative rule, there were no outbursts of fanciful antiauthoritarianism. She purchased some icons, which, at a special service of blessing, were placed in the wards at Eastertide. "I am sure," she wrote, "the Committee will think the money was well spent, for it is a great thing in a foreign country to show the people that one has sympathy with their customs." The patients were so delighted with the gesture, and with the calm efficiency of the hospital, that they got one of their more literate comrades to write the following address: "To the much-honoured Elsie Maud, the daughter of John: The wounded and sick soldiers from all parts of the army and fleet of great free Russia, who are now for healing in the hospital which you command, penetrated with a feeling of sincere respect, feel it their much-desired duty to express our deep reverence to you, the doctor warmly loved by all, and also to your honoured personnel of women. . . . We bow low before the tireless and wonderful work of yourself and your personnel. . . . May England live! (Signed) The Russian Citizen Soldiers."

Her wrath about the tailor who had supplied defective uniforms still simmered: "I am exceedingly sorry that the Committee should have paid so much of Samuel's bill. He deliberately gave us shoddy. It does seem extraordinary that he should be allowed to subscribe to the funds some paltry sum after a transaction of that sort." In May, when the weather grew warmer, she sent someone to Galați to buy shady straw hats for the whole unit. Spring and summer were doubly welcome after the worst winter anyone in those parts could remember for at least ten years, but for Dr. Inglis the delicious relaxation held its own dangers. "Dances," she confided, "have unfortunately begun again; but the girls enjoy them and I am not sorry that they should have this little pleasure, even if it does involve chaperoning."

She fretted about the continued inactivity of the Serbian divisions: "Could the Committee do anything about getting the British Government to take over the financing and management of these

Divisions, and get us on to the Western or Salonika front—or to Mesopotamia? They are first-rate fighting men and worth their weight in gold." The Administrator chosen and rushed out by the committee was, she was sad to say, more of a liability than an asset: "Miss G. is quite, *quite* hopeless. She has resigned twice since she arrived in June. She can never put anything through, and then is annoyed because I do it myself." After twice withdrawing her resignation, Miss G. resigned for the third time in August, when the units left Reni and Barlat to rejoin the Serbian divisions, at last re-formed for action on the Rumanian front: "She accused me of sending her up to Odessa in order to get her out of the way, so that I could arrange this camp as I liked. I was absolutely dumbfounded, as I had only one idea in proposing she should go to Odessa, and that was to get the Store in order there (we none of us knew what we had and what we hadn't, things having been brought up at odd times during the winter). These deep-laid schemes are beyond me."

Mortally ill and desperately anxious to get justice for her Serbs, Dr. Inglis found it hard to understand or forgive human frailty that squandered itself in silly squabbles. Some months earlier, it had been discovered that she had inoperable cancer, but she had refused to return home for treatment. Her health had been further weakened by a terrible winter, by constant tension, and, now, by severe dysentery. She worried because the Serbian troops were short of ammunition, because the morale of the Russian Army was crumbling. Why should the Serbs be left to bear the brunt of a new disaster? They had not even gotten any proper winter clothing. Somehow they must be saved. When the committee suggested that the units had done all they could and should come back, she indignantly cabled: WE MUST STAND BY. IF YOU WANT US HOME, GET THE SERBS OUT.

Her fierce persistence was rewarded. She was told that arrangements were being made to ship some of the Serbian troops home with the units. On October 29, 1917, more than two thousand of them left on the special train that carried the units back to Archangel. For fifteen days, Dr. Inglis lay on an uncomfortable bench in a second-class compartment. Twice she walked for five minutes on a station platform, but even this utterly exhausted her. She lived on broth and gruel and often was unable to eat anything. At Archangel, two orderlies helped her to climb a twenty-foot ladder to the deck of the transport ship. Though in great and almost constant pain, her uniform was as impeccably neat, her gingery hair as carefully combed as ever. She spent the time in her cabin making plans to take another unit to join the Serbs at Salonika. She reckoned to be ready to start in six weeks and sent for each of her staff in turn to ask whether they would go with her. A sense of mission alone fueled her feeble body. She looked so deathly that it was like being summoned from the grave. Many of the women found it hard to restrain their tears in her presence.

On November 24, the day before the ship docked at Newcastle, her pain increased, and she could not sleep at all. But next morning, she insisted on getting up to say good-bye to her Serbs. "It was a wonderful example of her fortitude," wrote the nurse who had been attending her, "to see her standing unsupported, a splendid figure of quiet dignity, her face ashen and drawn like a mask, dressed in her worn uniform coat with the faded ribbons which had seen such good service. As the officers kissed her hand and thanked her for all she had done for them, she said to each of them a few words accompanied by her wonderful smile."

From a hotel in Newcastle, she sent a last message to the committee: "So sorry I cannot come to London. Whatever happens, do make sure that the Serbs have their hospitals and transport, for they do need them." Her sisters hurried to her bedside. "It will be grand, starting a new job over there," she told them (for to her heaven was no resting-place, but a zone of renewed activity), "although there are two or three jobs here I would like to have finished." At her request, one of her sisters read aloud to her from the New Testament: "Let not your heart be troubled. . . . In my Father's house are many mansions . . ." And, listening, she died.

On November 29, she was buried, with full military honors, in St. Giles Cathedral, Edinburgh.

In Serbia, a public fountain (a tribute to her characteristic desire that every village should have a supply of clean drinking water) was dedicated to her memory, with the following inscription:

> At Mladenovac still the fountain sings
> Raised by the Serbs to you, their angel friend,
> Who fought the hunger typhus to the end.

A nobler fountain from your memory springs,
A fountain-head where Faith renews its wings,
Faith in the powers of womanhood to bend
War's curse to blessing, and to make amend,
By love, for hate's unutterable things.

Until quite recently, a hospital in Belgrade bore her name, and
even today there are people in Yugoslavia who venerate her as a
Saint and old women in Edinburgh who talk with reverence of the
"wee sandy-heidit doctor."

2 ❧

"The Doctors Is Ladies"

Eighty-year-old Dr. Elizabeth Garrett Anderson had made a special
journey to London to be at Victoria Station that morning of September 14, 1914. Around her, a group of women in greenish-gray uniforms, their small cloth hats fringed with veils of the same color,
bustled about as the train got up steam. "I would be going with you
if I was twenty years younger," she told them. "If you succeed you
will put the Cause forward a hundred years."

The hastily but efficiently assembled Women's Hospital Corps
was on its way to Paris to turn the newly built, luxurious Hotel
Claridge into a hospital for Allied troops. Its two leaders, Dr. Flora
Murray, the Administrator, and Dr. Louisa Garrett Anderson (the
daughter of Elizabeth), the Chief Surgeon, had both been militant
supporters of Mrs. Pankhurst and had looked after suffragettes when
they were let out of prison under the just-repealed Cat-and-Mouse
Act. They approached this new task with perfervid missionary zeal.
Success in it was a religion, failure unthinkable. God forbid that any
man should be in a position, even remotely, to say, "I told you so."

Their dealings with the Home Office at the height of the WSPU's
militancy had taught them not to expect much of the official mind.
They had not bothered even to approach the War Office but, since
the French Army's medical arrangements were known to be in a

state of crisis, attacked the French Embassy on August 12. They were received by an official in a room full of red damask upholstery and stale cigar smoke. In slow, careful French, they explained that they wanted to raise and equip a surgical unit for service in France. Within a week the French Red Cross formally accepted their offer, and within two weeks £2,000 had been subscribed—sufficient in those days to buy equipment, cover preliminary expenses, and have a balance in hand. The only problem about the unit itself was who to turn away.

In Paris, workmen were hurrying to finish the interior of the Hotel Claridge. The windows were still whitened, the walls barely dry, the floors littered with plaster and other debris. Helped by some of the Belgian refugees lodged on an upper floor, the Corps immediately began to convert the ladies' cloakroom into an operating theater and to paste paper over the clear-glass partitions that separated the great salons on the ground floor. They had barely begun to get installed when a doctor at the American Hospital at Neuilly telephoned to say that he was sending over a batch of badly wounded British officers. The Corps' baggage was extricated from French customs only about an hour before the first patients arrived. Nurses and surgeons worked through the night while orderlies unpacked and sorted equipment.

News of this strange new hospital soon spread. Complete strangers brought gifts of money and warm clothing. Shopkeepers sent candy and cookies, and grocers added extras to their orders. Flower women invaded the foyer to press bouquets on staff members. While casualties were unloaded from ambulances at the hotel's grandiose entrance, elderly gentlemen elegantly dressed in silk hats and tailcoats and black kid gloves pleaded to be allowed to help carry the stretchers or the soldiers' muddy gear. Anxious to demonstrate their sympathy, they bought bunches of roses and violets for the ladies and cigarettes for the men. Now and again, some of them, in a state of high emotion, would insist on shaking or kissing the women doctors' hands.

The men were often in a shocking state when they reached the hospital. They lay on the platforms or (if they were lucky) in the waiting rooms of tiny country stations, on dirty straw in churches or stables, waiting for transport, so desperately inadequate, to bring them to Paris, where there were thousands of empty hospital beds. In a supply shed at Villeneuve, officers lay at one end, other ranks at the other. Sometimes sheds were roofless, and troops huddled under blankets or old sacks in the rain. After a day or more spent in such conditions, they were jolted over ill-paved roads to Paris and arrived with septic wounds, starving, dirty, and wasted with fever. The gilded halls of the Hotel Claridge seemed like a paradise after such experiences, and the fantasy was heightened by the presence of women doctors. Patients felt honored. "The doctors is ladies," British Tommies wrote home.

Dr. Louisa Garrett Anderson drove out into the countryside around Paris to see the wounded waiting for transport near Soissons, which was under bombardment. As she went down the main streets of villages and small towns, the stench alone told her where the wounded were. In the church at Braine, the smell of rotting flesh rose like the devil's incense. Dying men, dead men, delirious men were packed or heaped together. Horrified but helpless, she took back two walking cases in her car.

What with sepsis, tetanus, gas gangrene, and shock (some of the men had been shelled out of three hospitals), mortality was high. French soldiers tended to be in worse shape than British. Their equipment and clothing were poor, and, as Dr. Murray put it, "they were of a more intellectual and imaginative temperament." There were soldiers from all over France and the French Empire— Bretons, Alsatians, Provençals, Moroccans, Zouaves. It was impossible to cope with all the patois, but the Corps did its best to prepare tisanes and special dishes.

M. Casanova, the manager of the hotel, mourned the death of the tourist trade and the absence of the class of clientele he had been expecting, but did his best for his lodgers. Short, fat, pale, short of breath, and floridly courteous, he tried to glide gracefully but helpfully on the tide of suffering that had so suddenly engulfed his world. At night, if he heard a convoy arrive, he would put on a dressing gown over his pajamas and hurry down to play the host, his eyes full of tears and his long black beard quivering with emotion. "His sympathy and distress," wrote Dr. Murray, "combined with a desire to kiss the busy hands of the doctors, made him a touching figure."

French journalists, who got a great deal of copy out of this strange establishment, found it hard to accept the idea of a woman surgeon—a doctor perhaps, but not a surgeon. How could a woman bring herself to be so brutal? Oh, it was one thing to care for the wounded, but quite another to operate upon them. After being shown over the hospital, they would always ask the same question: "Who really does the operations?" One influential editor was allowed to look into the operating theater to see for himself. He rushed out of the building, gesticulating wildly and shouting triumphantly to some colleagues: "*Je l'ai vu! Je l'ai vu! Le couteau à la main!*"

On another occasion, a rather dashing young journalist stared hard at Dr. Cuthbert, who was young and pretty, and said: "*Et vous, mademoiselle, vous coupez aussi?*"

"*Mais oui, je coupe.*"

"*Incroyable!*"

It was all very exhilarating. To do one's duty was enough to make good propaganda for women. But Drs. Murray and Anderson made deliberate efforts as well: "We passed the conversational ball from one to another with skilful tact, intent on educating the officers on the work of medical women." Both of them wore the purple, green, and white badge of the WSPU, and this often provoked discussion. Most of the men were at least polite, but there was the odd exception, such as the Royal Army Medical Corps (RAMC) general who assumed the "semi-jocular, semi-familiar attitude which professional women so dislike in their colleagues, and permitted himself to say: 'I don't know anything about lady doctors. Do you bite?'"

It struck these determined women as distinctly odd that French medical women should be treated so unceremoniously, considering the fact that British women had had to go abroad to get their medical degrees during their struggle for recognition. But it seemed that on the Continent, university medical schools had not been closed to women because it was confidently assumed that they would not make use of them or, if they did, would not be allowed to make use of their knowledge. Experienced women doctors did the work of low-grade nurses. Were they content with this state of affairs? Would they not fight against such humiliation? After a few pep talks from the Englishwomen, they decided that they too must *faire un mouvement,* band together into a union.

After five months, the Corps had to move from the Hotel Claridge. M. Casanova could no longer get enough fuel to feed the five gigantic boilers in the basement, and despite the use of braziers, the wards were freezing. But Christmas had been a lively and interesting time. Many beds sported the Allied flags at each corner, and in one ward the Union Jack had been attached to a large blanket, with the words "The Flag of Freedom" written underneath in letters of cotton wool. Even in wartime, this was going too far. "Freedom!" snorted Dr. Murray, who only a few months before had been tending the casualties of the women's war. "There's no freedom for women under *that* flag!" In deference to her views, the men substituted "England" for "Freedom" and assured her that they were all for votes for women.

The Corps next opened a hospital in a large deserted villa—the Château Mauricien—at Wimereux, near Boulogne. Traveling by train, the senior doctors were obliged to reprimand a French nurse who was in the same compartment. She boasted that she always left German wounded to the very last and then made it clear that she resented helping them at all. One had lost both his hands, and when she fed him, she said, as she spooned each mouthful: "I do this, not for my own pleasure, but because God has so commanded me." Goaded beyond endurance, the wretched man spat out the food in her face. While the other travelers expressed horror at the brute's ingratitude and presumption, Dr. Murray stiffly criticized the nurse's unprofessional attitude to her work.

A Miss Fenn and a Miss Goodwin, a professional cook and parlormaid, were brought from London to run the Château Mauricien. They engaged a staff of Belgian girls for kitchen service and directed work by means of a basic French-English vocabulary pinned to the wall. In one of the wards, a nurse recognized a wounded ex-policeman as the man who had once arrested her during a suffragette demonstration in London. "I wouldn't have mentioned it, miss," he said with embarrassment. "We'll let bygones be bygones."

The military stalemate brought a drop in serious cases, and the château became little more than a casualty clearance station. By this time, hospital facilities in England were being greatly expanded, and it was decided that the Corps could be of greater service there. The senior doctors crossed the Channel to talk with Surgeon General Sir Alfred Keogh, Director General of Army Medical

Services, and found him, to their joy, sympathetic. He was prepared to give them charge of a hospital in London with more than five hundred beds. It was a tremendous prospect, a chance for a momentous breakthrough.

But the hospital was not yet ready for occupation. It was a question of converting the old workhouse of St. Giles, Bloomsbury (said to have been the one described by Dickens in *Oliver Twist*). The quadrangle was still divided into sections by iron railings, and the padlocked gates of the area where inmates had exercised were still labeled OLD MALES, YOUNG MALES, OLD FEMALES, and YOUNG FEMALES. The whole place reeked of male mismanagement and seemed to be waiting for a clean, progressive, feminist sweep.

The RAMC colonel in charge of the alterations was inclined to go slow (and even stop work) when he realized who was going to run the newly christened Endell Street Hospital. "Good God, *women!*" or, "God bless my soul, *women!*" was his only printable comment. He questioned the sanity of the War Office in allowing such a thing, left the room in a rage (unwilling to have anything to do with such "indelicate females"), and strode away muttering, with mingled relish and concern: "Oh, good God, what difficulties you will have!"

The quartermaster general, who shared his commanding officer's prejudices, pretended that he did not know his way around the buildings, so Drs. Murray and Anderson set out alone on their tour of inspection. On March 22, after a letter to Sir Alfred, the premises were handed over to them by the still-protesting colonel. From then on, the work of conversion proceeded with remarkable speed.

When the hospital opened in May, 1915, a staff of 180, including 100 handpicked orderlies, was ready. There was a RAMC detachment of one NCO and twenty men (mainly for unloading ambulances and difficult stretcher work), but fourteen of these were later replaced by women. Within a week, all beds were full, and extra beds were squeezed in. At times of extreme pressure, the number of patients rose to nearly eight hundred, and from August, 1917, wards were provided for members of the various women's services.

A total of some twenty-six thousand patients passed through the hospital. About five thousand were from Canada, Australia, and New Zealand, and there were a few hundred Americans. The staff developed a special liking for the Australians and New Zealanders, who began to arrive in August, 1915, fearfully thin and weak after the long and grueling voyage from Gallipoli. They must have been very grateful, or perhaps born diplomats, for Dr. Murray noted: "Their attitude towards the women was most friendly and chivalrous. They were almost the only men who wished to discuss the subject of the suffrage with the doctors and sisters."

Sir John Forbes-Robertson, Sir Henry Irving, Nigel Playfair, and Helen Haye were among the famous performers who entertained the troops in the Endell Street concert hall, whose Saxe-blue curtains were embroidered with the monogram WHC (standing for Women's Hospital Corps, but popularly construed as the What-Ho Corps or Wounded Heroes' Comforters). Proudly conspicuous above the stage was the WSPU motto—which was also the motto of the Corps—"Deeds Not Words."

In 1915, there was a terrible spate of bad head wounds, which decreased after the issue of efficient steel helmets; and there were always hundreds of compound fractures involving long-term nursing and surgical care. The complicated dressings were a terrific chore, since they had to be changed as many as six times a day, and the Corps, with its special incentive to excel, set very high standards indeed. Endell Street, though, was the first hospital to experiment with Bipp, an antiseptic paste invented by a Professor Morrison of Newcastle. Wounds treated with Bipp could be left alone for up to three weeks, and the undisturbed tissues tended to heal more rapidly. The amount of time spent on dressings was drastically reduced—by 80 per cent, in fact—and this was a quite revolutionary improvement. As a result of the trials at Endell Street, Bipp was at last considered for wider use.

Nurses and doctors were able to give more time to the many cases of gas poisoning, malaria, pneumonia, and mental disturbance in the medical wards, and the men boasted and counterboasted of the skill of *their* ward's doctor and surgeon. They were offered the chance of transfer to hospitals run by male medical staffs, but the offer was always refused. Before the hospital closed in 1919, more than seven thousand operations were performed in the theaters, and confidence in the Chief Surgeon, Dr. Anderson, almost amounted to veneration. She was scrupulous about explaining exactly what she proposed to do and why, and she made a point of not hurrying a patient into a decision. Many men wrote to her for advice after they left Endell Street, and war pensioners from all over Britain came to get her expert advice and assessment.

Average attendance in the casualty section totaled more than five thousand a year, and soldiers injured in accidents and brawls, or simply drunk, were brought in at all hours. It was all action. Yet in line with its general practice, the War Office denied the women either commissions or honorary rank and refused to allow them to wear any badges of rank. As Dr. Murray put it: "Having thus made it as difficult as possible, the authorities left the women to sink or swim." Women doctors overseas wrote to Endell Street outlining their difficulties. In some cases they were refused first-class traveling warrants, on the ground that they were "civilians." They were refused permission to drive cars or enter the officers' mess. One doctor working in East Africa reported that though one commanding officer had allowed her to wear badges of rank, his successor had ordered her to remove them, thus discrediting her in the hospital. Not until 1919 were the women given the right to be assessed under the service rate of income tax, and refund claims had to be dated back to 1915. Women in the medical services overseas—in Malta, Egypt, Salonika, India, France—were not graded or paid at officers' rates, but were given a flat rate that made no allowance for seniority.

At Endell Street, however, there was no difficulty about discipline. When a culprit was brought before Dr. Murray, she asked the sergeant to leave him alone with her, when "an appeal to his better feelings generally reduced him to tears. He then had to be detained in the office with more pleasant conversation till he regained composure sufficiently to meet the public eye." When the entire British Government had quailed before the determination of the suffragettes, what hope had a mere solitary soldier? And who could blame Dr. Murray if she took a certain pleasure in this knowledge?

Male chaplains had to be tolerated, but there was a certain contempt for them. Five were tried, but only one lasted for any length of time. The staff noticed that the men were acutely embarrassed by their attentions. Of one chaplain, a patient said: "He speaks beautifully, I'm sure, but I'm so afraid he's going to *kiss* me," and Dr. Murray commented that in his earnestness "the parson used to bend nearer and nearer, till the men became so nervous they almost screamed." Sermons in chapel could be painful ordeals, with the Bible topically referred to as a trenching tool, the prayer book figuring as an enameled mug, and the Twelve Apostles designated as staff officers. On one hilarious occasion, the chaplain, perhaps hoping to please the senior doctors, preached on the New Womanhood, exhorting the congregation not to regard those in charge of the hospital as "mere playthings," but as "their equals in every respect." Needlework classes run by volunteer ladies were considered far more therapeutic than the chaplains' spiritual inanities.

Disciplining visitors was more of a problem than keeping patients in order. Visitors came at all hours and were all determined to "speak one word of kindness to the poor fellows" or, as one lady wrote, "to bring one ray of pleasure into the lives of the poor mutilated darlings." Officers, Members of Parliament, ladies of title, colonels' wives, and VAD commandants—all had to be refused admission at one time or another. The orderlies on duty at the gate had to cope with some odd requests. "I've come to see my father's footman," said one imperious young woman. She could not remember the man's surname: "We always called him David, and he's in a Highland regiment."

The orderlies, some of whom stayed for four years, were on the whole a great success, and the few "disappointments" were grieved over in silence. Endell Street, despite its intense feminist zeal, must have been a good place to work. The management disliked rules, and none were drawn up ("it was desired that the staff should be free when off duty, and the trust was not abused"). Girls were expected to be friendly and charming but not flirtatious, and Dr. Murray felt able to record that "no man ever took liberties." Here again, as with the visitors, the real danger came from insidious outside influences. "Strange," observed Dr. Murray frigidly, "how parents thought it proper to control the actions of women well over age, and how younger brothers, uncles, brothers-in-law and the family doctor would think they had a right to interfere in their business and would invite the Doctor-in-Charge and the Matron to conspire with them. One could not help sympathising with healthy girls who were made to relinquish the work in which they were successful and a life which they enjoyed, because 'Mother was dull at home' or 'Father likes to have his girls with him in the evenings.'"

Most of the orderlies were too young to have been caught up in the suffrage movement, and attempts to "educate" them were not very successful. When, in February, 1918, women householders over thirty got the vote, WSPU and other flags were run up at Endell Street, and great was the rejoicing among the senior staff. The young women were polite but patronizing. "Simply topping about your bill," was the general reaction. They could not see that it had any real significance for them.

This was a little discouraging, but a letter from Sir Alfred Keogh about this time must have lifted their hearts. Writing to Dr. Anderson, he said: "Let me thank you and Dr. Murray, not only for what you have done for the country, but for what you have done for me personally. I should have been an object of scorn and ridicule if you had failed. . . . I think your success has probably done more for the cause of women than anything else I know of, and if that cause flourishes, you and I can feel that we have been sufficiently rewarded for our courage." There was, perhaps, a note of almost insulting relief in the letter, a tendency for the general to grab rather a lot of credit. But it was a useful testimonial, a well-earned trophy.

They had done well, no doubt of it. Three of them were made Commanders of the British Empire. Six doctors became Officers of the British Empire, and eleven Royal Red Crosses went to the nursing staff.

In October, 1919, the order came to close the hospital. No more convoys were coming in, and the wards were nearly empty. Completely relaxing for the first time in many years, the doctors dined together and had a night out at the Alhambra Music Hall. It must have been quite an occasion.

3 §☙

The VAD's

"The tube slipped out of the shoulder, all yellow and thick with pus, onto my kidney tray. The captain took the tube and pushed it right through the rotten shoulder. I felt my forehead wet and then heard a voice from a long distance saying, 'Put your head down, girl. . . .'"

The Great War destroyed or horribly damaged so many human bodies that thousands of hastily trained nurses and orderlies had to be rushed into service hospitals. Between 1914 and 1918, Voluntary Aid Detachments, started in 1909 at the request of the Army Council, supplied twenty-three thousand nurses and fifteen thousand orderlies. Most came from the cloistral ignorance of upper- or middle-class homes, in which they might, but for the war, have remained until marriage brought release. Upon them the medical horrors of the war had a particularly traumatic impact. Small wonder that some failed to survive for long and that others fainted occasionally.

Miss Vera Brittain was just beginning her studies at Somerville College, Oxford. When war came, she got the day off to say goodbye to her fiancé, who had volunteered for the Army. They traveled back together in the train, but the rules forbade him to accompany her to her college ("it was inexpedient for a woman student to be seen in Oxford with a young man who was not her brother"), so they parted at the railway station.

A few months later, to the disgust of her tutors, Miss Brittain volunteered for nursing duties and began work at a hospital near her home in Derbyshire. Training was a tough round of dreary chores and long hours, but like other such volunteers, she performed the most menial tasks in a redeeming glow of patriotic emotion. She felt somehow "worthier" of her fiancé, and she positively gloried in emptying bedpans and disposing of fearfully soiled dressings. Actually to *see* men's bodies—in authorized defiance of the tradition that a woman should see nothing but their faces and hands and clothes—was in itself a liberating experience.

When she went to work as a VAD nurse in a London general hospital, she found herself in an uncomfortable hostel at an inconvenient distance from the wards, where the ill-concealed contempt of the professional nursing staff created an icy atmosphere. Hours were from 7:30 A.M. to 8 P.M., with three hours off duty and (if you were lucky) a weekly half day. Night duty was from 8 P.M. to 8 A.M. and ran for two months at a stretch. Pay was £20 a year, plus a tiny uniform allowance and the cost of laundry.

The Hon. Monica Grenfell, daughter of Lord and Lady Desbor-
ough, was a guest at Badminton, the Duke of Beaufort's country
house, in August, 1914. The pleasures of the annual horse show were
shadowed by the news of war. The Duchess assembled the guests to
watch her turning a photograph of the Kaiser (who had presented it
on the occasion of a recent visit) to the wall. The smart young men
talked of sending their magnificent horses to the war, and Miss Grenfell parted with her own beloved hunter when she went to train as a
probationer nurse at the London Hospital, Whitechapel.

There, she dusted and polished and polished and dusted and
stood at attention while the ward nurse inspected her or knelt while
she conducted religious services. She worked among Belgian
wounded, two of whom, to her distress, pretended that they were
cripples, holding their caps out for alms, singing lugubriously. The
soldiers presented the nurses with military buttons and badges,
which they pinned on their outdoor cloaks. But this was war at a
remove, war strained through a sieve of field hospitals, and kept at a
distance from newcomers by a still-rigid system of seniority and
taboo.

But in December, 1914, Miss Grenfell got nearer to the heart of
things in a small hotel at Wimereux that had been converted into a
Red Cross hospital. She was the only half-trained nurse there
("friends at the War Office had somehow got me out; I think some
mention of kitchen work was put on my passport"), and her parents
accompanied her and stayed for two days at a small boardinghouse
in the village.

Each nurse was presented with a Christmas box of chocolates
from Princess Mary, with the Princess's profile on the lid, which was
nice. A stock of popular music-hall records and a gramophone had
been bought to entertain the men. But the hospital, flimsily built for
the summer trade, was freezing cold in the bitter winter, and the
aftermath of the first gas attack at Ypres was horrific. Men poured
into the hospital, blistered, gray-faced, and wheezing. Their wounds
had turned appallingly septic. "When I undressed," noted Miss
Grenfell, "all my clothes, down to my chemise, reeked of pus." No
one knew whether any of the men would live or, if they recovered,
what the long-term effects would be. There was the fear that the
whole of France would be devastated before any form of protection

could be devised. Yet a routine of treatment was established, the panic died. Miss Grenfell was moved back to London Hospital, where her favorite patient was a burglar who had slipped while jumping from a balcony and broken his leg.

Miss Enid Bagnold, drudging away in a military hospital near London, enjoyed the novelty of the experience. The daughter of a high-ranking officer in the Royal Engineers, she had spoken for the suffragettes at meetings in Hyde Park, studied art in Walter Sickert's studio, and decided that she wanted to be a writer. Now life as a VAD gave her her first subject. "I like to be part of an institution," she reflected. "It gives me more liberty than is possible among three or four observant friends." Dodging the amorous attentions of re-cuperating officers could be trying, but one soon learned the knack. The hospital routine, surprisingly enough, had its aesthetic aspects: "I lay my spoons and forks. 65 trays. It takes an hour to do. 13 pieces on each tray. 13 times 65. 845 things to collect, lay, square up sym-metrically. . . . I love the long, the dim and lonely corridors, the light centred in the gleam of the trays, salt cellars, yellow butter, cylinders of glass." She even found it soothing to pad splints in the ward, where she could be quiet and merge into the background and listen: "It is like listening to a kettle humming, bees round a bush of flowers, the ticking of a clock. I know how the waves of pain come up and recede; how a little sleep just brushes the spirit but never absorbs it; how the arms will struggle up to their air, only to be cov-ered and enmeshed again in heat and blankets."

She found the Tommies' wards more to her liking than the offi-cers'. There was less reticence and false dignity: "They will take nearly anything from each other. The only thing that cheered Rees up as he was being wheeled away was the voice of Pinker crying, 'Jer want white flowers on the coffin? We'll see to the brass 'andles.' " Like other healthy young women, she felt somehow guilty in the presence of so much and such majestic pain. She shuddered to watch the doctors as they redressed deep wounds: "Six inches deep the gauze stuck, crackling under the pull of the forceps, blood and pus leaping from the cavities."

The first batch of wounded that came in had been lying for days between the lines in France. The emergency was so great that oper-ations were done in the wards and amputated legs stuck in buckets in the corridors outside. When some nervously gushing visitors had left, Miss Bagnold imagined them boasting at home about what they had seen (*"What* an experience! My dear, the actual *wounds!"*) and reflected bitterly: "When one shoots at a wooden figure, it makes a hole. When one shoots at a man it makes a hole, and the doctor must make seven others."

When the surgeons had done the work and the volume of pain had been distributed evenly throughout the building, she became aware of more curious, less "noble" cases: the officer who had come up from the ranks, for instance, and had contracted VD in France. He had been to a Harley Street specialist and paid for his treatment like a gentleman. He had been told he was cured, and now he lay in a public ward, grievously ill and staring up for hours at his bed rail: "I only pass him on my way to the towel cupboard, twice an evening. Tonight, as I went quickly past, his blind flapped a little, and I saw the moon, shaped like a horn, behind it. I pushed his blind back: 'Mr. Wicks, do look at the moon.' Obedient as one who receives an order, he reached up to his supporting handle and pulled his shoulders half round to look."

She was particularly distressed by the way personal dignity, the sense of personality itself, tended to be whittled away or ignored. At first she held senior nurses in some awe, but soon she was writing: "One should never aspire to know a Sister intimately. They are disappointing people, without candour, without imagination. Yet what a look of personality hangs about them!" Her head nurse refused to bandy words with mere privates. She gave them injections and medicines without comment or explanation, apparently unaware of the resentment this caused. How different from the attitude of an old lady who was one of the official visitors: "She treats a man as though he were an individual, as though he had a wife and children, a house, a back garden and responsibilities. That is the difference. That is what the Sisters mean when they say 'the boys.'"

Lesley Smith, the eldest of three daughters of a comfortably off middle-class Scottish family, had been prevented, by the conventions of the time, from training for a serious job after she left school. Her parents had opposed her decision to become a VAD, and if they could have visualized the kinds of jobs she would have to do, their opposition would have been even stronger. Her first spell of night duty was in a VD ward in Royal Sussex Hospital, Brighton, and shortly afterward she was posted to a field hospital in France. The carnage was on a scale beyond anything she had imagined: "Day after day we cut down stinking bandages and exposed wounds that destroyed the whole original plan of the body. One man had had both buttocks blown off, one arm had been amputated at the elbow, and he had a host of smaller wounds from flying metal. Another lay propped on sphagnum moss to absorb the discharge from two large holes in each thigh."

The high-speed butchery of the operating theaters after a new battle had its own horrors: "The leg I was holding came off with a jerk and I sat down still clasping the foot. I stuffed the leg into the dressing pail beside the other arms and legs. The marquee grew hotter and hotter and the sweat ran off the surgeons' faces." After a gas attack, "the burned and sightless eyes made all the faces look like a ghastly row of masks, and the utter silence completed the illusion of being surrounded by puppets."

It was difficult to come to terms with such blasphemy. The temptation to take refuge in a hearty cheeriness, an impersonal chumminess ("How are you today, old man?") was overwhelming. Matrons got up hockey teams to keep the girls' minds occupied and their bodies exercised. Some girls cracked under the strain. Most did not. But they did become very superstitious. If no one happened to die on the day that you had bathed everyone's eyes four times, it became vitally important to bathe everyone's eyes four times a day from then on. If on the day when a nurse had ducked under the tent ropes at the entrance to the dressing station, the surgeons did a particularly skillful job, that nurse would make a point of always ducking under those ropes. Nurses became convinced that it was unlucky to give a dose of medicine unless the bottle was held in a certain way. If one took an odd instead of an even number of steps (or vice versa) between one tent and another, the whole day or night might be poisoned with foreboding.

In blustery weather, the great marquees bellied and creaked in the wind, and they sometimes collapsed altogether, causing unimaginable chaos. In the winter of 1917–1918, they froze stiff, and nurses scraped their skin opening the door flaps. Under their inadequate blankets, "the men lay still and dumb, afraid to lose the slight warmth that surrounded them by an unwary movement." Clothes were rigid and unwearable in the morning if you did not sleep on them at night, the steel handles of knives and forks in the canteen burned your fingers if you did not wear mittens.

In the summer the sun heated the canvas roofs to stifling point, and even when the sides of the tents were furled up "not the slightest breeze came through to blow away the smell of burned flesh that thickened the air. The gassed men lay and panted through their black, crusted lips and fumbled on their lockers for their bowls of lemon squash."

Dressings soaked in picric acid stuck on the huge burns, and nurses busied themselves adding castor oil to the acid and tailoring the lint in advance so that the whole dressing could be put on at once with the minimum of fuss and pain. The Allied offensive of autumn, 1918, brought more casualties, longer hours, nerves more tightly stretched—and the end seemed as remote as ever. When the news of the Armistice reached Lesley Smith's hospital, "the camp buglers sounded the Cease Fire and we all stopped work for a few minutes and watched the orderlies trying to play Rule Britannia on mess-pot lids. I was dressing a man who was covered with painful boils, and he looked at me dully and said: 'It's over, then?' "

The Armistice, the mere cessation of fighting, could not immediately dispel the talk, the atmosphere, the mystique of war. Lying in their beds, the wounded continued to relive the moment of their wounding. It was the central fact of their lives. VAD Bagnold listened to them: "One and all they know the exact hour and minute in which their bit of metal turned them for home. Sometimes a man will whisper 'Nurse . . .' as I go by, and when I stop I hear: 'In ten minutes it will be a twelvemonth!' I don't know whether I should be sorry or glad. They think I understand: for when they tell me in that earnest voice that the minute is approaching, they take for granted that I will share some sacrament with them."

After such a sharing, it was not easy, often, to break off and go back to one's class, one's appointed station in life, as to a waiting kennel. The prospects of peace were not all pleasant. On the boat back to Dover, a professional nurse remarked to VAD Smith: "Well, I suppose you're going to settle down at home now and buy clothes and do the flowers for mother?" VAD Brittain had had a taste of things to come when (much against her will) she had broken her contract, left France and the punctiliously polite German officers she was helping to nurse, and returned to England to look after her father. Her mother was in a nursing home, and it was, he considered, his daughter's obvious duty to rally round. In 1919, when she resumed her studies at Oxford, she found the university authorities (disturbed at the sudden influx of potentially disrespectful "veterans") intent on forgetting the war.

But the war and its scarifying, sacramental insights could not be buried. The Battle of the Twenties lay ahead, and thousands of ex-VAD's joined the fight against humbug and lunatic tradition.

4

Tommy's Little Mothers

Between 1915 and 1919, some six hundred performers traveled the various fronts, and one of the chief organizers of this rush of entertainment was Lena Ashwell, before the war a leading light of the Actresses' Franchise League and an active suffragist. She was a cultured woman, and she gave careful thought to the way in which the troops should be distracted from the nastinesses of war. Certainly not by libidinous nastiness on the stage. She approached the problem on what today would be considered an absurdly highfalutin level. "Orpheus," she explained, "with his lute was also a Fisher. Does not the playing of music incite men to lay aside their cares and the turmoil of the daily struggle; to let something beautiful, invisible and healing cleanse and beautify their souls?"

The first parties came under the auspices of the YMCA and so were expected to be respectable and uplifting, even if popular. A then unknown young composer, Ivor Novello, played and sang a new song, "Keep the Home Fires Burning," which was an immediate and enormous success ("as we drove away in the dark and rain and mud, from all parts of the camp we could hear the refrain of the chorus"). But the tendency was to repeat, or adapt, old (in some cases centuries-old) favorites: "We had a quartet from *The Gondoliers* and then *Van Tromp Was an Admiral,* only this time of course he was Von Tirpitz and Sir John Jellicoe admirably filled the place of Admiral Blake. . . ." Miss Ashwell was delighted to find that, in those days before the mass media had massacred local and regional cultures, the taste of her soldier audiences was unexpectedly sound: "They loved the old folk songs. For instance, they never tired of *Annie Laurie* and were very appreciative of the old English catches —*Would you know my Celia's charms?* but above all *Drink to me only with thine eyes.*"

She herself began by reciting humorous verse, but soon switched to more ambitious things. Surely desperately ill, frightfully wounded men needed something more than vulgar jollity? She watched the eyes of heavily bandaged patients (casualties from Neuve-Chapelle) following every movement hungrily through their two eerie funnels, and she noted how "the last movement of the Mendelssohn Concerto and the Intermezzo of Cavalleria Rusticana and Handel's Largo were always much loved in hospital." So she learned "Abou ben Adhem" and a series of Elizabethan love lyrics and tried the effect of them. She was nervous at first, but soon gained confidence when she experienced the "deep interest and very real response the men made."

May Bradford, too, was determined that the Tommies should have the advantage of such culture as she could offer. For her, the war did not provide a glorious escape from a state of girlish or suffragist frustration. The capable, middle-aged wife of an eminent medical man—Sir John Rose Bradford, Consulting Physician to the British Expeditionary Force—she simply made up her mind to be of some service during the emergency.

And so, late in 1914, she arrived in Boulogne, having been officially appointed hospital letter writer for troops who were either too ill or too illiterate to write their own letters. As casualties poured in from the fighting at Ypres, she was kept busy. "Men shot in the head and face," she recalled, "were so bandaged up that often only the mouth could be seen, and one had to go very near to hear the faintly-uttered address given in response to a request."

Even if they were not severely incapacitated, the men were not always very good at expressing themselves, so Lady Bradford used her own initiative to convey the maximum of accurate information to relatives alarmed by the skeletal details of an official telegram: "After giving the medical report, I used to describe the ward, tell what the man had eaten during the day, and then give all his personal messages and love and 'barbed wire entanglements,' as they called the xxxxx put for kisses." When she had finished, she read the letter aloud for approval. She introduced many a soldier to the niceties, the small tendernesses of civilized correspondence: "To one man I said, 'Shall I begin with My dear wife?' He quietly answered: 'That sounds fine, but she'll be wondering I never said that before.'"

The men were impressed by the fact that she did not wear a uniform and did not have to submit letters to the censor (though she effectively cut out anything that in her opinion might be a security risk or otherwise undesirable). They nicknamed her "Tommy's Little Mother" and quite often consulted her about family problems: "In many cases such worries obviously retarded recovery. Sometimes it would be an epileptic child who could not be placed in a home. By writing to the clergyman of the parish, the difficulty was often removed." A private in the Loyal North Lancashires surprisingly remarked: "You are just the size my wife could knock out in one round," and explained that his wife was a formidable prizefighter who took on women or boys for a penny a round and "could knock out anyone up to six stone eight [ninety-two pounds], which I take to be your fighting weight." He had enlisted, he said, to get away from his wife, but could not prevent the woman from drawing allowances from his pay. Lady Bradford suggested an attempt at reconciliation and succeeded in tracing the wife and persuading her husband to drop her a carefully worded line. In due course, the man received a present of a slab of tobacco: "He looked upon it as quite satisfactory, remarking 'It's my favourite shag.'"

Sometimes her job was almost unbearable in its pathos: "One day a youth was brought in with both eyes shot away. After all his messages to his wife and children had been written down, he put up his hand to try to find mine. 'Sister,' he said, 'is it a fine day, and are the birds singing?' I pictured it all to him. 'Well,' he answered, 'I have much to live for still.'" One man, a mechanic who had been badly mangled by the propeller of an airplane, had "a curious selection of endings for his epistles. Among them were: 'Yours to a cinder,' 'Yours till hell freezes,' 'Yours until the sands of the desert grow cold and grey,' and 'Yours till I kick up the daisies.'" Other clients, she found, had a more limited vocabulary, like the man who dictated: "On the way back the wounded bloke was hit twice, and the officer once, and the bloke that carried the wounded bloke was not touched. The wounded bloke had been lying out from Monday till Friday." But perhaps she sensed that it would have been hard to improve on this as an expression of the brute boredom of a war of attrition, and she left it alone.

She had little personal pockets of specialized knowledge ("My love of birds was greatly gratified by seeing the golden oriole twice in 1917 and several times in 1918") that she could turn to good effect in an emergency. When told by a flustered nurse that a man with a serious head injury was moving restlessly about and muttering, "O Llefara, O Llefara!" or some such incomprehensible gibberish, she at once recognized the opening line of a well-known Welsh hymn: "I repeated the verse slowly. The man became quite still and gave me his mother's address."

Sometimes relatives or fiancées were suspicious of the woman who signed their man's letters. A mother wrote to the matron of the hospital: "Would you kindly tell me who May Bradford is? My son is very susceptible." And one private, badgered by his girl, pleaded: "Would you mind saying you're not young? That would soon put it right."

So she wrote and listened and educated, moving later to Étaples, where the voices continued to call, "Write for me, Sister!" and, "Don't leave me out!" and she would feel her dress clutched by patients afraid of being forgotten. It wasn't always that they wanted a letter written. Often they would ask "Mother" to go under the bed and get a pipe or some other item from their kit. They would swear that she was the "spit" of their own mother and would show her a photograph to prove it: "I always told them I was glad that I reminded them of anyone they loved. One poor fellow, terribly wounded, used to watch the door, and, as soon as he caught sight of me, he would call out 'How are you, Mother? I do love you.'"

A keen botanist as well as an expert bird watcher, she found the district around Étaples rich in flora and listed some 650 different species seen in the sand dunes and pinewoods near the hospital. She told the men of her hobby, and it was not long before they became interested and began to note and pluck the plants that grew from the sandbags against the walls of the wards: "They would say, 'Have you got this little fellow, Mother?', handing me two minute green leaves."

Quiet and methodical, with her erect, confidence-inspiring carriage, her good but unpretentious clothes, her writing case, and her campstool (which she sat on to take dictation), May Bradford was a credit to the ruling classes, the old school tie, the Lord and Lady Bountiful values that Sir Edward Grey feared would be swamped in the socialism and anarchy let loose by the war. Well did she earn her place among the Officers of the British Empire.

The Servicewomen

I ℘

Women Police

Germany was the first country to try to make use of women police —in 1905—but public reception of the experiment was so hostile that it had to be abandoned. In Britain the police were kept so busy battling the Women's Revolution that the idea of enlisting females was considered a joke in poor taste. Mrs. Pankhurst, and others striving for a saner, healthier society, urged the need for policewomen, in the interests of decency as well as efficiency. But it was the Great War that again, like a perverse, backhanded Santa Claus, gave the chance to infiltrate this man's world.

A concern for the moral welfare of young girls provided the first excuse and the strongest impetus of a movement that had strong overtones of the upper-class do-goodism that had driven such diverse women as Lady Muriel Paget and Mrs. Emmeline Pethick-Lawrence to dip into the depths of the vast, poverty-stricken underworld of Edwardian society. In the early months of the war, Lady Codrington and Mrs. Creighton (a bishop's widow) of the National Union of Women Workers, alarmed at the drunkenness and disorder prevalent around large military camps, suggested a system of voluntary patrols. Their aim, as outlined in a letter to the *Times*, was to be "neither police nor rescue workers, but true friends of the girls, in the deepest and holiest sense of the word."

Already harassed and embarrassed by problems of moral welfare, the authorities welcomed the suggestion, and a Patrol Committee circularized the Headmistresses' Association and the Federation of University Women for suitable recruits, who were asked to give a certain number of hours each week to the work. Distinguished by a neat badge and carrying an official card, they launched a determined attack on what was known as "khaki fever." For as the *Times History of the War*, perhaps rather naïvely, explained: "When quite ordinary men donned khaki, they became, in the eyes of a number of foolish young women, objects to be pestered with an attention very few of them desired."

Patrols were active in public parks, and the War Office gave permission for them to do what they could to discourage "provocative loitering" near military centers. Reports from local organizers give a graphic impression of the kinds of situations they dealt with during the next four years:

A military policeman came up, evidently very perturbed, and said he had been watching a couple (man a civilian) for some time, and would the lady patrols try and get the girl away? They found the couple indicated partly screened by bushes, but with other couples all around and in disgraceful position. . . . Yet later, when the patrols passed the same spot, they noticed that all the couples, though lying on the damp grass, were in decorous attitudes. . . .

. . . We came across a young girl one night struggling with a Canadian soldier among some bushes, and were able to save her. With the consent of the Chief Constable I am now ordering such couples to come out into the open, and have met with no refusals or resistance of any kind from the men, who always look extremely ashamed and sheepish. The girls try to brazen it out, but always do as they are told in the end. I really feel ashamed that the men should never stand up for the girls, it seems rather cowardly, though very convenient from our point of view. . . .

. . . One night patrol intervened when a soldier was about to strike his wife. He is going with a girl, and the Rescue Worker has visited and warned her, and has also spoken to the Commanding Officer at the barracks of this man's behaviour. . . .

. . . A special duty from the very first was to turn girls and lads out of the deep doorways and shop entrances. This is a job the police constable did not care to do, owing to the amount of abuse he got. But we never have any difficulty. Indeed the rule now is that as soon as we appear, out they all come of their own accord, some sheepishly touching their caps with the remark: "All right, Miss." And yet we have not said a word. . . .

. . . At a public house we watched three girls get into conversation with a sailor. Soon he beckoned to another and all five walked away. We followed until the girls, seeing us behind, turned sharply and left the men. We spoke to them, and they took it in good part. . . .

. . . Patrols noticed a girl, obviously the worse for drink, standing up against a wall outside a public house. A group of soldiers were surrounding her. Eventually the patrols were able to support the girl home, where she turned and thanked them for their help, flinging her arms around their necks. . . .

. . . One evening two patrols were stopped by a party of soldiers, who said they had been looking for someone to help them get rid of a young girl who *would* bother them. . . .

. . . May 1916. An outstanding feature of this month has been the effect of the new order for darkening the streets at 8:45 P.M. Men of unpleasant character have appeared in the crowded better streets and speak to women freely. Large numbers of giddy girls find the novelty exciting, and gather in dark corners giggling and shrieking. . . .

Nine patrols undertook a special investigation of cinemas in London. About three hundred were visited in three weeks, and reports stressed inadequate ventilation, as well as the dangers of dimming the lights between films and of employing very young girls as usherettes. The Patrol committee opened a series of clubs, where soldiers were encouraged to take their girl friends, and gradually organized a "follow-up" system of aftercare. By the end of the war, nearly two thousand patrols had been at work—more than four hundred of them in the London area. An organizer was sent to South Africa to help start a Voluntary Patrol force there, and it was reported that during the Irish disturbances of 1916, the women's patrols alone were allowed to carry on without interference, "being passed through both by the revolutionary party and by the soldiers."

The Women Police Volunteers (WPV), founded at the same time as the Voluntary Patrols, was more ambitious. It aimed to provide a full-time body of uniformed policewomen, ready to be posted to any part of the country, and hoped that this would form the nucleus of a permanent service that would be an integral part of the nation's police force. Its founder, Miss Margaret Damer Dawson, was a woman of wide cultural and administrative interests. She had studied with distinction at the Royal Academy of Music, was an experienced Alpine mountaineer and an expert motorist, became Organizing Secretary of the International Congress of Animal Protection Societies, and was a member of the Criminal Law Amendment committee—one of the first organizations in Britain to press the need for policewomen.

When war came, she played an important part in shepherding the tens of thousands of Belgian refugees who poured into London. Then, with the encouragement of the Chief Commissioner of Police, Sir Edward Henry, she began to recruit her Women Police Volunteers. Like the Voluntary Patrols, it was conceived as a *corps d'élite*. She wanted women of good education and social background, and she interviewed candidates at her house in Cheyne Row, Chelsea. Among the first to apply was Miss Mary Sophia Allen.

Miss Allen had been a suffragette from the early days of the WSPU, which she joined after hearing Annie Kenney speak near her home in the West Country. Her outraged father ordered her to leave his house, but nevertheless sent her a generous allowance, which meant that she could work for The Cause in an honorary capacity. She soon became a front-rank militant. In 1909, she was imprisoned three times: once for marching in a deputation to the House of Commons, once for breaking windows in the Treasury in Whitehall, once for breaking windows in the Board of Trade Offices in Bristol. In prison, she embroidered VOTES FOR WOMEN around the tails of men's shirts she was made to stitch and was one of the first suffragettes to go on a hunger strike and be forcibly fed. Six wardresses held her down while prison doctors beat up an egg in one and a half pints of milk and poured the mixture through a tube in her nose. Her health suffered so badly that Mrs. Pankhurst gave her a "desk" job as an organizer of militant tactics. In 1914, she was sent to Edinburgh, where she planned a series of efficiently executed "outrages," including the burning of empty houses. Such was Asquith's fear of the suffragettes that when he came to Scotland just before the outbreak of war to address a large political meeting, he arrived at the hall crouching on the floor of his carriage under a large blanket. Miss Allen ran forward and tried to thrust some WSPU leaflets under the blanket before she was seized and hustled away by the police. It was her last militant action before Mrs. Pankhurst called a truce.

She wanted to serve the nation, but had no relish for conventional women's war work. The WPV, though, sounded almost ironically ideal. "A sense of humour," she wrote later, "had kept me from any bitterness. I was quite as enthusiastically ready to work with and for the police as I had been prepared, if necessary, to enter into combat with them."

A number of other suffragettes joined the force, which firmly believed that women should be protected by women. An intensive training course included (apart from a close study of existing police textbooks) first aid, drill, jujitsu, signaling, and police-court procedure. This last item, though vital to a proper understanding of the work, was not always easy to come by. The conservative instincts of some magistrates were so outraged by the presence of these unwelcome innovations that, war or no war, they took every opportunity of having the court cleared, especially if a case contained a hint of sexual offense—though this was the very type of case with which the WPV was to be particularly concerned. The raising of funds, too, was a problem, for at first the WPV (rechristened the Women's Police Service early in 1915) depended entirely on voluntary contributions. This meant constant propaganda, and Miss Damer Dawson traveled constantly to address innumerable meetings. Not until 1916 did the Government agree to make a grant, and even then it was too small to relieve constant anxiety about money. Many Chief Constables, unimpressed (and unbound) by the Chief Commissioner's enthusiasm, were skeptical of the value of policewomen, arguing that a woman's lack of physical strength would expose her to danger and force her, in moments of crisis, to rely on the help of a policeman— though it was well known that, under pressure, one constable often called on another for support.

So Miss Damer Dawson's pioneers were at first limited to work in the London area, where they were entrusted with cases involving women and young girls that needed "delicate handling." Clad in a uniform of dark blue, with a hard felt hat (a modified form of which was later adopted by the Voluntary Patrols), they gained experience in dealing with chronic drunkenness, suspected lunacy, and first offenses of theft. The appearance of a "lady copper" was often much more effective in quelling disturbances than the intervention of a beefy constable, and it was found that raids on disorderly houses tended to be much more orderly when carried out by, or at least with a sprinkling of, policewomen.

Grantham, in Lincolnshire, was the first provincial town to make use of the WPV. After a persuasive address by Miss Damer Dawson, a Women Police Subcommittee was set up, and it guaranteed to maintain two policewomen. Miss Allen was one of those selected for this important breakthrough; the other was a Miss Harburn, a keen suffragist who had been responsible for running London County Council special schools for deaf and mentally handicapped children. Very conscious that they were marked women, the two left London late in November, 1914. It was dark and drizzling when they arrived at Grantham, a small town whose population had been almost doubled by the establishment of a camp of eighteen thousand troops on its outskirts. They were depressed by the squalor of the streets they passed through on their way to their lodgings and by the sights and sounds of a community that had no entertainment to offer the strangers in its midst except cheap drink and cheap whores. Lenient local magistrates made the situation worse by a patriotic determination to overlook the "peccadilloes" of young soldiers. When Miss Allen and Miss Harburn went to help a woman who was trying to lug a hopelessly drunken youth along the pavement, she told them that it was her son. He was like that almost every night, she said, but the magistrate wouldn't give him anything because he was a soldier. If only he could get a month's hard labor, it might do him a world of good, she thought.

The policewomen's instructions from the military provost marshal, from whom they took their orders, were to "keep an eye on alleys, courts, yards, passages, and public houses." To avoid the stares, giggles, and catcalls of a half-hostile, half-amused populace, they wore plain clothes during the day and spent long hours visiting the homes of women and girls in an effort to persuade them not to loiter about the camp. Often they were on duty for twelve hours at a stretch and plodded back to their rooms at midnight or later. They were on call to accompany military police on searches for missing troops, and the strength of their vocation was tested by the oaths and blows of many a brothel brawl. Stallmen in the market that had grown up around the camp had to be carefully watched, since they supplied liquor and acted as pimps. Women pretended to be taking in washing in order to gain admission to the camp; and if a strange man was discovered in their house, they would swear black and blue that he was a relative. Mothers would promise—and keep on promising—to reform their daughters. It was a heartening change when one prostitute begged Miss Allen to do her best to persuade a young girl she knew from taking to the streets. But such interludes were few. It was an uphill, a dirty, and an exhausting job, but gradually Miss Allen and Miss Harburn got results—and recognition. In November, 1915, a meeting chaired by the Bishop of Grantham urged that policewomen should be given national as well as local support. A month later, they were made full members of the local police force, which meant that they worked to the orders of the Chief Constable and were paid from police funds. They had driven in the thin end of Miss Damer Dawson's wedge. All female prisoners, all cases concerning children were now considered their special province.

Hull now followed Grantham's lead. It asked for two policewomen to supervise the forty Voluntary Patrollers already in action there, and Miss Allen and Miss Harburn were transferred for this purpose. One of the most trying chores was the controlling of crowds during air raids. Since there were no underground shelters, people simply rushed out of their homes into the public parks, taking their favorite possessions with them. The ground was littered with large framed pictures, birds in cages, huge ornamental vases, bedding, bundles of clothes, and bags of knickknacks. The policewomen were expected to prevent pilfering and to restrain lechery in the general blacked-out panic and confusion. They were also given the doubtful privilege of arresting drunk and disorderly women and of dragging or carrying them to the police station—a performance that usually attracted the attentions of a ribald crowd.

In 1916, at the request of the Admiralty, the WPS trained a policewoman for special duties. Disguised as a prostitute, she proved remarkably useful in helping to expose the drug traffic that battened profitably on nerve-shattered troops and in breaking a spy ring that had passed on valuable information about British naval movements at Scapa Flow.

Also in 1916, at the recommendation of Sir Edward Henry, the Ministry of Munitions asked the WPS to supply policewomen for work in munitions areas. The factory and specially constructed township at Gretna, near Carlisle, was the first big assignment of this kind. There were nine thousand female and three thousand male workers, eighty-five hostels, and quarters for five hundred married couples and their families. By June, 1918, more than 150 policewomen were working there, under the command of two male superintendents. They searched women workers to make sure that they were not taking penknives, cigarettes, matches, hairpins, and other forbidden articles into the workshops. Operatives were especially inclined to smuggle in hairpins and would pass the word along the production line: "Look out, girls—'air raid!'" Policewomen were at hand to break up the brawls that often flared between Scots and Irish and to rescue women who rashly removed their caps and got their hair caught in the machines. They checked passes, controlled canteen and payday queues, took charge of women prisoners, and attended court hearings. By the end of the war, nearly a thousand WPS-trained policewomen had been posted to munitions areas, and it was generally agreed that, apart from anything else, they greatly improved the "moral tone" wherever they went. There was much less profanity, and less time was lost through secret trysts in formerly unscrutinized nooks and crannies.

Moral-welfare patrolling continued to form a large part of the duties of the WPS in the many large towns that now began to call on its services. Its members had little difficulty in dealing with turbulent Tommies. Civilians and officers were much more likely to damn their impudence for interrupting their shady pleasures. One officer, asked to move on, insisted that the girl with him was his fiancée. But by this time, the policewomen had a ready answer to such prevarications. "That," he was briskly informed, "is what I thought. I also thought you would be glad, when she is your wife and you have daughters of your own, to know that they will be protected, as we are trying to protect her."

In London, which was crammed with troops of many nationalities, policewomen braved showers of stones and threats of physical violence as they went about their unpopular work. But the threats were never carried out. As the *Evening News* put it: "In many cases the policewoman does not even have to speak. She just looks, and he who is looked at melts thoughtfully away." Doubtful cafés, hotbed hotels, suspected brothels, public houses, music halls, and dance halls were watched, and the many tricks used by prostitutes to smuggle clients past patrols were unmasked and foiled. Men were disguised as old women, in shawls and shabby coats, or small children were sent to hold their hand and call them "Daddy." Sometimes policemen hauled a tipsy soldier to safety while a streetwalker fought savagely over her customer. Sometimes, after breaking up a near riot in a tart-infested slum, they would emerge from the back streets to find a constable, blissfully unaware of what had happened, strolling along on his routine beat with a large Airedale guard dog by his side.

Women caught soliciting were cautioned and, if they were the worse for drink, were escorted home and later visited by members of the WPS Benevolent Department. During six months in 1917, more than five hundred women picked up on street patrol, often far from home and in dire poverty and distress, were given immediate help, and a home for unmarried mothers and their babies was opened at Aldington in Kent. Policewomen did their best to ensure that mothers did not exploit their children, but too often poverty or the desire for extra money for little unaccustomed luxuries was stronger than any pressure that the WPS could bring to bear. Many girls and boys of ten or eleven got up at 4:30 A.M. to do milk and newspaper rounds or to help in coal yards before they went to school. Children of three to five years were encouraged to follow soldiers and beg for money. Bands of children roamed the streets at night stealing food from grocers and general stores, and in winter, carrying sacks at the ready, they stealthily stalked carts delivering coal.

Four policewomen—two based at a Canadian YMCA building, two at the Eagle Hut, a center for American troops—operated in the Strand, in the heart of the West End of London. Lined with music halls, theaters, and bars, filled with pickpockets and prostitutes and troops on leave, the Strand was the scene of such violence, licentiousness, and drunkenness, especially in the months that followed the Armistice, that the WPS nicknamed it "The Devil's Promenade." The organization helped many destitute men and women to get home or return to camp and directed others to an emergency relief center at the nearby church of St. Martin's-in-the-Field at Trafalgar

Square. Tributes flowed in—among others, from the Charing Cross Vigilance Association, formed for rescue work in the scarlet West End; from the British Empire League's Country Club at Richmond Hill ("we were much troubled by the loose women of Richmond, but thanks to the exertions of the WPS we have nearly eliminated this class"); and from the vicar of a church in North London, who was most gratified by the results of a two-month antivice drive. "Most of the women," he wrote, "have disappeared from the neighbourhood, and the rest reformed. With regard to the soldiers, who were mostly overseas men, a good work has been done, and many were deeply grateful for the warning given them. I would strongly recommend any brother faced with a similar state of things to apply to the WPS."

By 1918, WPS women were on duty in Edinburgh, Birmingham, Glasgow, Bristol, Belfast, Portsmouth, Plymouth, Brighton, Nottingham, Southampton, Folkestone, Oxford, Cambridge, and Reading, as well as London, Grantham, and Hull. But their status and their pay varied according to local regulations and the attitude of the Chief Constable. Where they were not sworn in as full members of the local police force, they could not make arrests, and this led to embarrassment and loss of face. Sometimes face was saved by allowing the WPS to arrest a woman and bring her to the police station, where a constable would read the warrant. Next day, on the witness stand, he would claim that he had made the arrest.

Despite several influential demands that policewomen should be given official status, the battle was far from won. Like many other employers, the police hastened to put back the feminist clock when the emergency was over. When Commandant Damer Dawson and Subcommandant Allen asked the new Chief Commissioner, Sir Nevil Macready, to recognize the WPS—five hundred trained women were still in uniform—as a permanent part of his force, he flatly refused. He preferred, he said, to recruit and train his own women—if the Home Office considered them necessary. Miss Damer Dawson's women were, he thought, too "educated." They would only irritate the men, and he did not want any unnecessary friction.

In February, 1920, insult was added to injury when summonses were issued against five members of the WPS—Commandant Allen (she had taken the top job when Miss Damer Dawson died), Superintendent Goldingham, Chief Inspector Champneys, Inspector Barnett, and Sergeant Sims—for wearing a uniform too similar to that proposed for Metropolitan Women Police Patrols. After a four-day hearing at Westminster Police Court, it was ruled, although Chief Commissioner Sir Edward Henry had approved the uniform and although the Women's Police Service had been recognized as an agent of the Government, that the uniform must be altered and the title of the corps changed.

As the Women's Auxiliary Service, it continued for some years, before the official policewomen got into their stride, to be in considerable demand, notably in Ireland during the Troubles and with the British Army of Occupation on the Rhine. But its days were numbered.

It was as Mrs. Creighton had forecast at the annual general meeting of the Voluntary Patrol Committee in 1917. "The policewomen of the future," she had said, "will be taken from that class of women who are forced to earn their living by it, and not so much from the educated women who now take smaller or no pay for the sake of helping on the work." Like Mrs. Pankhurst and Christabel, Miss Allen found herself out in the cold of a postwar world that took the *achievements* of the suffragettes for granted, but regarded suffragettes as historical monuments rather than as human beings with a living to make.

2 &

Army Auxiliaries

Between 1917 and 1919 more than one hundred thousand women passed through the auxiliary services, replacing soldiers, sailors, and airmen. Of these, about thirty-two thousand served in the Women's Royal Air Force (WRAF), about three thousand in the Women's Royal Naval Service (WRNS), and some five thousand in the

Women's Legion Motor Transport Section. But by far the greatest number—fifty-seven thousand—served in the Women's Army Auxiliary Corps (WAAC).

At first the services were unwilling to admit that they needed any help from women other than nurses, but by 1915 Lady Edith Londonderry's Women's Legion was providing a pool of cooks and waitresses from which the Army could staff cookhouses and officers' and sergeants' messes. Not until the end of 1916, when the shortage of manpower was glaringly obvious, did the Army think of enrolling a certain number of women for duty in back areas in France, where too many fit soldiers were doing "soft" jobs in what were known as the Lines of Communication. Acting on a report from Lieutenant General Sir Henry Lawson, Brigadier General (later Sir) Auckland Geddes, Director of Recruitment at the War Office, proposed to form a uniformed women's corps. He called in his sister, Mrs. Chalmers Watson (the first woman to receive the degree of Doctor of Medicine from the University of Edinburg), for consultation. She was appointed Chief Controller (Home), with overall supervision of the new corps, and at the end of January, 1917, addressed a conference of representatives of women's societies called by Lord Derby, Secretary of State for War.

The WAAC was to be very different from the improvised wartime women's services that had gone before. Though officered by women of education and (if possible) breeding, it was to consist largely of women of the working class. They had already proved their worth in the factories, but now, daringly—dangerously, as some thought—they were to be posted overseas.

Much, clearly, depended on the choice of the Chief Controller (Overseas). It fell on Helen (later Dame Helen) Gwynne-Vaughan. The elder daughter of Captain the Hon. A. H. Fraser of the Scots Guards, she had been educated at Cheltenham Ladies' College and at the University of London and was already well advanced in a successful academic career. For several years, she has been head of the Department of Botany at Birkbeck College, one of the pioneering coeducational centers at London University, and had carried out some important research into the structure and development of microscopic organisms. After her husband's death in September, 1915, she had attended a course in medical bacteriology. "That," she wrote later, "seemed the direction of war service most appropriate to my civilian experience. I think I had visions of a mobile laboratory on some really dangerous front."

She was interviewed at the War Office by the Adjutant General, Sir Nevil Macready. It was a much pleasanter meeting than that experienced by the leaders of the Women's Police Service after Sir Nevil had become Chief Commissioner. Mrs. Gwynne-Vaughan remembered that he had been adjutant of the Gordon Highlanders when she "came out" at their ball in Aberdeen in 1896. She asked to be allowed to go to France in some capacity, even if she were not chosen for the senior post. A week later came the news of her appointment. Her task was officially defined as "the posting of women in offices, cookhouse and stores in the Lines of Communication, wherever they may be needed." She and Mrs. Chalmers Watson both ranked equivalent to a lieutenant colonel.

As a keen social worker, Mrs. Gwynne-Vaughan had made contact with women of different backgrounds in girls' clubs and just as important, had been in what she described as "perhaps the only sphere in which at the time young men and women worked freely together—the laboratories of a modern university." She and Mrs. Chalmers Watson were now faced with the problem of forming sensible regulations for the WAAC. They agreed that a feminine equivalent to "Sir" would have to be found, and they decided on "Ma'am." Mrs. Gwynne-Vaughan was convinced that one of the main advantages of this was that young officers would find it easier to disagree with their seniors behind the formal shelter of a title of respect.

The War Office did not give the WAAC full military status. Women did not enlist, therefore; they enrolled—and they were punishable for breaches of discipline only by fines or by action in the civil courts. They were, in fact, still regarded as civilians. Saluting was neither officially authorized nor officially forbidden. WAAC officials (it was decided not to call them officers) were usually saluted in the army areas, less frequently at bases. This ambiguity created many unnecessary problems, but Mrs. Gwynne-Vaughan soon found that there was little ambiguity about the attitude of many senior army officers to the employment of women. They knew little of the social evolution that was going on in Britain, and what they did know, they clearly did not like. At one early conference, a majority of those present agreed that it was better that "members" (the generic term for the WAAC rank and file, who were divided into "forewomen" and "workers") and soldiers should walk out together with official blessing rather than surreptitiously. For all that, one general protested that when all these women arrived, the Army would have to wire all the woods in the Lines of Communication. This remark exhausted the Chief Controller's patience. "If you do, sir," she replied, "you will have a number of enterprising couples climbing over." The woods were not wired.

But it was difficult to protect the WAAC against the insidious attacks of malicious gossip or the buffetings of comparatively innocent ribaldry. The French called them *les soldates* or *les Tommettes;* this had a skittish sound that bore little relation to the somber routine of their lives. They were quartered in camps, usually in huts that held eight women (sometimes up to thirty) and had a cubicle at one end for the forewoman or assistant forewoman (the WAAC version of sergeant and corporal). Though the girls slept in dormitories, an attempt was made by curtaining to give each her own washing cubicle. As a visiting journalist put it after an interview with Mrs. Gwynne-Vaughan: "For the class from which the greater part of the WAACs are drawn, privacy in ablutions ranks as a greater thing than privacy in slumber."

Uniforms were hurriedly designed. Skirts were full and, though a mere twelve inches above the ground, were considered almost scandalously short. Small, tight-fitting khaki caps with khaki crepe-de-chine veils were soon replaced by less seductive peaked caps. Here again there was some confusion. Apart from their issued uniform, "workers" were allowed to buy some additional garments, and the results could be bizarre. Jacket collars, deliberately made to circle the neck demurely, were sometimes tucked into a V-shape and fastened with brooches. It was not easy for "officials," backed only by a system of fines, to instill a sense of military pride and etiquette. Jewelry-bedecked Tommettes were apt to stroll arm in arm with Tommies, for all the world like parlormaids on their half day off. As novelist Miss Tennyson Jesse, sent to France under the auspices of the Ministry of Information, solemnly reported: "It is the first time most of these girls have had a symbol held before them. We of the upper classes are brought up with many reverences—for our superiors, our elders, for traditions; but the classes which, for want of a better word, I must call lower are for the most part brought up to think themselves as good as anyone else, and their rights as the chief thing in life." She blamed the defective curricula of the elementary schools, which did not place sufficient emphasis on the teaching of history, so that the girls were left "without proper standards of impersonal enthusiasm and imaginative daring which should be the inheritance of us all."

There was controversy, too, over mackintoshes. The War Office ordered that "officials" should wear belts on their raincoats and "workers" should not. This caused much grumbling before Mrs. Gwynne-Vaughan got it canceled. She herself made a point of sharing the same conditions as the rank and file. She slept without sheets, with a towel folded along the top of the blankets—"where they tickle one's chin." When headquarters were moved from Abbeville to St.-Valéry-sur-Somme, she found the run through the fresh air to a cold bath a "great luxury" and saw to it that all her staff and visiting Deputy Controllers did physical exercises every day in the garden.

Though tough with herself and determined that her officers should set an example of physical fitness, Mrs. Gwynne-Vaughan was not a stickler for petty discipline. Occasionally she had to reprimand young officers for walking out with WAAC "workers" (this was against the rules; but the subordinates were apt to reply that "they never thought such nice young girls *could* be anything but officers") or had to tell one of her own senior staff not to be too impatient with staff officers who tried to teach them about mess arrangements ("My dear boy," one Deputy Controller had snapped, "I was housekeeping long before you were born"). But such minor irregularities did not cause her much concern. What did concern her were the widespread rumors of immorality between Tommettes and Tommies.

"Immorality," she reflected later, "is an excellent stick with which to beat a corps of women. It was to be expected that, as censorship revealed, enemy agents should start stories. Indeed, we were proud that it was so, and took it as a compliment, much in the way that the old Regular Army did the term Contemptible." But when

she went home, early in 1918, to speak at a series of recruiting meetings, she found that the rumor-mongers had done an all too effective
job. Outraged mothers suspected the WAAC of trying to inveigle
their daughters into a nest of vice, and she had a lot of explaining
to do. Naturally, some pregnancies did originate on active service,
but they were very infrequent. Almost as many girls had been pregnant before they arrived in France, and when this was discovered,
Mrs. Gwynne-Vaughan reported on the following lines to the Adjutant General: "It is submitted for the favour of your consideration
that No. 1234 Worker Smith, being pregnant, is unfit for active service. It is recommended that she be returned to home establishment.
This condition appears to have supervened about 1st May 1917. The
woman reported for duty in France in August 1917." Sometimes she
was able to add, significantly: "This woman proceeded on leave
simultaneously with her husband on [date]. . . ."

She noted that it was not usually the pretty girls who got into
trouble. They were used to flattery and knew how to cope with it,
but "the older, plainer women might find it intoxicating to be the
cause of competition, and gratitude for this fillip might be her undo-
ing." The problem—if it could be called a problem—was well under
control, but the popular press had blown it up into a "crisis" that no
amount of common sense, or even cold statistics, could dispel. The
authorities decided to send out an investigating committee of five
ladies, specially selected by (of all things) the Ministry of Labour,
and Mrs. Gwynne-Vaughan, smarting under the indignity, was ordered to meet them when they disembarked at Boulogne in March,
1918. She conducted them to GHQ, where they sat rather awk-
wardly in a row in front of the Adjutant General's desk. Producing
a recent copy of *The Sporting Times*, he read aloud an example
of the kind of joke that was now so distressingly familiar. "Would
you," ran the caption to a rambunctiously suggestive drawing,
"rather have a slap in the eye or a WAAC on the knee?" This, he
said briskly, was the kind of thing that he was sure that the members of the committee could be relied upon to prevent after they had
seen the WAAC camps for themselves. Mrs. Gwynne-Vaughan did
not believe that even if there had been anything wrong the committee would have discovered it. But she arranged for the women
to see anything they asked to see, after which they produced

an excellent and exonerating report—which, of course, had little or no effect.

Miss Tennyson Jesse had already been on a tour of investigation and had studied the official statistics for the period from March, 1917, to February, 1918. In that time, she was assured, fourteen women had been sent home for incompetence, twenty-three for lack of discipline, and something like two per thousand because they had become pregnant after landing in France. "Compare this," she indignantly demanded, "with the morality of a village in England —or anywhere else in the world—and then (if you dare to be so obviously dishonest) say that there is any reason why the Women's Army should be aspersed." In her opinion, its members were far more effectively shielded from sexual temptation than they had been in civilian life. No WAAC could go anywhere without permission, she had to be in camp by eight o'clock at night, and she was liberally provided with healthy recreations such as Swedish exercises, morris dancing, and hockey. "In short," she concluded, "she is now looked after and guarded as young girls of the educated classes are normally."

Yet as late as 1930, in a book called *The Woman's Story of the War*, the anonymous author (who claimed to have been a WAAC) painted a different picture. "One became," she wrote, "so used to hearing coarse language and filthy stories that one no longer felt even disconcerted. . . . I came several times upon spectacles which before the war would have upset me very much. They made me realise how little removed from animals men and women are."

Rumors or no rumors, the WAAC's got on with their work, mostly in kitchens or behind desks, sometimes as gardeners in the vast war cemeteries. Their efficiency and calm during the great German offensive of spring, 1918, brought them much praise—and exalted approval. In the words of the official announcement of April 9: "As a mark of Her Majesty's appreciation of the good services rendered by the WAAC both at home and abroad since its inauguration, and especially of the distinction which it earned in France during the recent fighting on the Western Front, Her Majesty has been graciously pleased to assume the position and title of Commandant-in-Chief of the Corps, which in future will bear the name of Queen Mary's Army Auxiliary Corps" (QMAAC).

Here was vindication with a vengeance. And when eight WAAC's were killed during the bombing of one camp, journalists prepared to make amends with stories of WAAC heroism and Hun brutality. Mrs. Gwynne-Vaughan would have nothing to do with such male sentimentality. At a press conference, she made it quite clear that WAAC's had only been doing their duty—as they always had—and that since they were in France as replacements for soldiers, the enemy was quite entitled to try to kill them. It was a very satisfying moment for the Chief Controller.

In July, 1918, a QMAAC team was chosen to help organize the files of the Central Records Office of the American Expeditionary Force at Tours. The supervisor of the team, Unit Administrator Olive Bartels, had (though no one knew her secret) been a leading suffragette. When Grace Roe had been arrested in 1914, Miss Bartels had taken over her job as Chief Organizer of the WSPU. Under the pseudonym of Margaret Cunningham and heavily disguised as a widow in mourning with a thick black veil over her face, she had moved from one hiding place to another in a desperate—and successful—attempt to outwit the police. In October, 1914, she had accompanied Christabel Pankhurst on her tour of the United States. After such a record, it was hardly surprising that the War Office, where she worked in the coding and parliamentary branches from October, 1915, commended her for her ability and initiative or that the American headquarters at Tours mentioned her work in dispatches and was deeply impressed by the efficiency of her unit.

Mrs. Gwynne-Vaughan had every reason to be pleased with the progress of her Corps. But she was not given long to savor its new respectability. Toward the end of August, Dame Katharine Furse, Director of the WRNS, mentioned to her the possibility that there would be a vacancy for a senior officer in the Women's Royal Air Force. Unwilling to leave her present command, she emphasized the qualifications of Rachel (later Dame Rachel) Crowdy, Commandant of the VAD in France and Belgium. But at the beginning of September, she was ordered to proceed to the War Office, where she was told that she had been appointed Commandant of the WRAF. She accepted the situation with regret ("I was sick and sorry. For nearly two years I had lived with and for the Corps in France. I knew every officer and very many of the women").

She had a brief meeting with her predecessor as Commandant of the WRAF, Miss Violet Douglas-Pennant. "I had met her," she recalled, "once before in connection with a recruiting meeting in Cardiff. We were very polite and said nothing that mattered."

And thereby hangs a most extraordinary tale.

3 §✷

The Strange Case of the Hon.
Violet Douglas-Pennant

A handsome spinster in her late forties, the Hon. Violet Blanche Douglas-Pennant, sixth daughter of George Sholto Gordon Douglas-Pennant, Lord Penrhyn, a Welsh peer, had had a distinguished career, an unblemished war record, until the fateful day when she became associated with the Women's Royal Air Force (WRAF). From that moment, her life turned into a tragicomic nightmare. There were those who thought she had only herself to blame, but it was not as simple as that.

The decision to form the Royal Air Force (RAF) by amalgamating the Royal Naval Air Service (RNAS) and the Royal Flying Corps (RFC) met with determined resistance, and the Air Ministry was the scene of bitter interservice rivalry. This rivalry involved women as well as men, since the Women's Royal Air Force, which was to provide auxiliary services for the RAF, was scheduled to take over personnel from both QMAAC and the Women's Royal Naval Service (WRNS). Someone possessing an unusual mixture of tact and authority was needed to see the WRAF through its birth pangs, and the Air Council apparently thought that Miss Douglas-Pennant was that someone.

Before the war she had been a prominent member of London County Council education committees, Vice-President of the Association of Women Clerks and Secretaries, active in girls' youth clubs, and a Governor of the University College of South Wales. Most impressive of all, in 1911 she was appointed a National Health Insurance Commissioner for Wales at a salary of £1,000 a year, which made her probably the most highly paid woman in Britain.

A Tory of comparatively liberal tendencies (she was a member of the Workers' Educational Association), a devoted churchwoman (she was a friend of the Archbishop of Canterbury), well connected, and well meaning, she was one of those whose mission in life was to convert the whirlwind of indignation generated by suffragettes and women trade unionists into a gentle zephyr of reform that would aerate, without damaging, the fabric of society. Deeply aware of the privileges that she helped to confer, deeply aware of the privilege of being an honorary member of the Masculine Establishment, her career had followed an unruffled and unruffling course.

During the war she had been Chairwoman of a committee that selected nursing staff for the Scottish Women's Hospital Units in Serbia and a member of the South Wales Belgian Refugee Committee. She had helped to form the first official women's auxiliary corps, the WAAC, and had made recruiting speeches for the WAAC, the WRNS, and the Women's Legion. When a group of political opponents of the Prime Minister, Lloyd George, decided to mark their appreciation of his war services, Miss Douglas-Pennant had been invited to make the presentation—and a well-turned little speech about the value of cooperation between the parties.

When, late in April, 1918, she was approached by Major General Sir Godfrey Paine, the RAF's Master General of Personnel, to become Commandant of the WRAF, she asked for a "month's look round" before committing herself. What she saw, on a tour of RAF stations, shocked a mind used to the orderly calm and decorum of the Higher Civil Service. Because of a lack of volunteers from the WRNS and QMAAC, some stations had few, if any, WRAF officers. There were rumors of irregularity, even immorality. Despite Air Ministry promises that women who joined the WRAF would, after a month's probation, receive new uniforms and a special bonus, neither had been forthcoming. New recruits had no uniform of any kind—they had not even been issued with overalls and had to perform a variety of dirty jobs in their own civilian clothes. Dissatisfaction expressed itself in a series of strikes, and RAF officers treated Miss Douglas-Pennant as an unwelcome intruder. Headquarters in London seemed to be staffed largely by women friends or relatives of officers in M.3, the RAF's Department of Manning, to which the Commandant had to apply in order to implement most of her decisions. To make matters worse, the officers of M.3, including Acting Lieutenant Colonel William Bersey, her liaison officer, were men of undistinguished social background, many of whom, in the haste of a new and rapidly expanding service, had been steeply promoted overnight. Bersey himself, though he listened amiably enough to her complaints, did nothing about them—an attitude that his boss, Major General Guy Livingston, seemed to encourage.

Braced for a task of national importance at a time of crisis (the Germans, in a last fling, were breaking through on the Western Front), she was startled to find herself in an atmosphere of cheerful, even flippant, confusion. She had to reprimand three civilian clerks for what she called "hysterical horse-play in deshabille" long after they were supposed to have left the office. One commanding officer complained to her that when he telephoned for some women drivers, he was asked: "What sort do you want? Front row of the chorus or ladies of title? We stock them all—take your choice." Miss Douglas-Pennant was given no secretarial help, had difficulty in getting the use of a staff car for official journeys, and saw little or no sign of a filing system or proper office procedure. Furthermore, she received a cold welcome from her immediate subordinates. The Deputy Commandant, Edith Pratt, had formerly been Deputy Chief Controller of the WAAC in France. Rose Beatty, one of the two Assistant Commandants, had been transferred from the WRNS on the recommendation of its Director, Dame Katharine Furse. The other, Katharine Andrew, had transferred from the WAAC on the recommendation of its Chief Controller, Mrs. Burleigh Leach. It seemed to Miss Douglas-Pennant that all three had done, and were doing, very little to save the WRAF from total disintegration. It even crossed her mind that they wanted to disintegrate it.

Under such circumstances, surely the only sensible course was to refuse the job. So she wrote to Sir Godfrey Paine: "I am very sorry to be obliged to decline the appointment of Commandant. You will remember that I accepted provisionally on the clear understanding that I should be responsible to you for the general administration of the WRAFs. This was apparently not made clear to others concerned—I found myself in the difficult position of seeming to assume responsibilities to which I was not entitled, so I was blocked at every turn. The work that General Livingston requires from the Commandant could well be fulfilled by a subordinate clerk or a well-trained Matron. Please do not think that I care twopence for my own position. I only care about getting the work done smoothly, and I hope you will forgive me for saying that you will never get this force onto a sound footing unless the Commandant is treated with confidence and given due authority."

Sir Godfrey begged her to reconsider her decision and promised to have F.S.14, the relevant RAF Order, amended so that her rank and responsibilities were made quite clear. She allowed herself to be persuaded. But she still had her doubts. "I resigned," she wrote, "because I thought it was intended that I should. I do not feel, after what has happened, that I am the right person. However, as you are so good as to say you still have confidence in me, I will try my best not to disappoint you. Nothing would have induced me to take on this job, except for the feeling that one must try to justify one's existence, when all of you are slaving away. It is odious being a woman in war time."

Certainly it was odious being the Hon. Violet Douglas-Pennant during the next two months. Matters, alas, did not improve. To speed the flow of new officers, she had, through her influence with the London County Council, arranged for the use of Berridge House, a former Domestic Economy Training Center. This suggestion cut across plans already drawn up by M.3, and though it was approved by Sir Godfrey, Colonel Bersey pleaded a multitude of delays in getting the necessary authorization and equipment. Nor was this all. The Commandant was criticized for not answering certain letters—which she said she had never received. She had no success in obtaining uniforms. The cloths she selected were found, at the last moment, to be either unavailable or unsuitable. She had the mortification of watching, from a balcony at Buckingham Palace, a march past of women's auxiliary services in which the WRAF was unable to take part for lack of uniforms.

No one seemed to take any notice of her, even when she threatened to go to Lord Weir, the Air Minister, or to the Prime Minister himself. In an attempt to bring some order into the increasing chaos at headquarters, she borrowed the services of W. G. Hayward, a senior clerk with the National Health Insurance Commission at Cardiff, and worked late into the night ransacking files, answering letters, and drawing up schemes for improvement. Firmly she told five applicants for senior posts—including a sister of General Livingston and the wife of an old friend of Colonel Bersey—that because of their lack of qualifications she could offer them only junior positions or places in the officer-training course. All five indignantly refused. Her actions were deeply resented by Miss Pratt, Mrs. Beatty, and Miss Andrew, who handed in their resignations. These were accepted, and—probably to the Commandant's relief—all three refused to obey orders to stay on for a month. The fact that they had shown themselves in their true colors as "deserters" seemed ample proof of her dark suspicions, which were amplified when Dame Katherine Furse not only reinstated Mrs. Beatty in a senior position in the WRNS, but recommended her for a decoration.

Miss Douglas-Pennant now carried on virtually alone, aided only by Mr. Hayward and by two personal friends, an Air Force officer and his wife, who came along after office hours. In this situation of spiraling farce, she tried to keep calm. Everything, she was sure, would be all right when "her" officers were trained, and this was what, with her characteristic silvery laugh, she told anxious inquirers. But officer training was virtually at a standstill. Since the Berridge House scheme was still held up, training was left in the hands of QMAAC and the WRNS. Pressure was put on trainees to bypass the WRAF and enter one of the "senior" women's services. One of them was told by Mrs. Burleigh Leach that since it had been decided that Miss Douglas-Pennant must go and since, until she did go, the WRAF would continue to be in a state of disorganization, a trainee would be well-advised to stay with QMAAC, at any rate for the time being.

Miss Douglas-Pennant herself asked Lord Weir not to allow WRAF's to be posted to any more new stations, and the recruiting of the rank and file, theretofore inordinate, was drastically cut. In desperation, she arranged for a London County Council teacher-training college at Eltham to be used for officer training during the summer-vacation period. It was hoped that the training center would turn out 150 new officers at two-week intervals. Here, surely, was progress at last. But there was little gratitude for her initiative. On August 6, in the House of Commons, a Member of Parliament asked a series of questions that, Miss Douglas-Pennant could not help suspecting, had been inspired by the insidious Mrs. Beatty and Miss Andrew.

What, he demanded, were the Commandant's qualifications for her job? Was it true that a Mr. Hayward was Assistant Commandant of the Women's Royal Air Force, and was he of military age? Was the Air Ministry aware that there was a feeling of dissatisfaction in the Force, and would it set up a full inquiry into the causes of this? In reply, Major John Baird, Parliamentary Secretary to the Air Ministry, stated that the Air Council had every confidence in the Commandant's ability and outlined the distinguished career that had led to her selection.

This was something at least, but Miss Douglas-Pennant, now in a state of extreme mental and physical exhaustion, could no longer consent to be the quarry of such a determined hunt. Once more she tried to resign. Again Sir Godfrey Paine refused to accept her resignation, assuring her of his continuing confidence. He did more. Colonel Bersey was transferred and a new liaison officer brought in.

Lord Weir did not share Sir Godfrey's confidence. His doubts about the Commandant's suitability were intensified by an interview that, rather surprisingly, he granted to Miss Andrew—and the circle of disapproval was widening. Margaret, Lady Rhondda, a former suffragette who was now Director of the Women's Department of the Ministry of National Service, asked by her chief, Sir Auckland Geddes, to report on the state of the Women's services, was keenly critical of the WRAF—though she made no attempt to consult Miss Douglas-Pennant on the subject. Impressed by Lady Rhondda's findings, Geddes wrote to Weir: "I will, I am afraid, have to embargo recruiting for the WRAF if things are not improved. What in my opinion is required is (i) a complete reorganisation of your Central Women's Department, with new personnel, and (ii) a temporary transfer of local control of WRAF personnel to the WRNS and QMAAC." Weir, getting the message, replied: "I have made up my mind to supersede Miss Violet Pennant, and she will be told of this to-morrow."

The doomed Commandant, oblivious of all this, had on August 23 (the very day when, in France, Dame Katharine Furse was telling Mrs. Gwynne-Vaughan of the impending change) been introduced by Sir Godfrey Paine to his successor as Master General of Personnel, General Sefton Brancker. A monocled ex-artilleryman noted for his heartiness and a liking for the gay life, Brancker was exasperated by the prospect of being plunged straight into a women's squabble. His opinion of Miss Douglas-Pennant was not improved when he heard that she was trying to interfere with the administration of the WRAF's Motor Transport Depot at Hurst Park, near London. She complained that Colonel Samuel Janson, the commanding officer (a friend of Brancker), was encouraging two junior WRAF officers—a Miss Livesay and a Miss Gwenda Glubb—to issue night passes in defiance of the Hostel Administrator and was giving certain favored women drivers special permission to live in lodgings without supervision.

Convinced that all he had heard about Miss Douglas-Pennant's meddlesomeness was true, Brancker was now given the job of sacking her—only a few days after her resignation had been refused. On August 27 he was unable to do it, because Miss Douglas-Pennant was away in Berkshire settling a strike of several hundred WRAF's who had still received neither uniform nor bonus. On August 28 he saw her and brusquely told her that she must go—not because she was incompetent (she was he thought, efficient enough), but because she was "grossly unpopular" with everyone and had caused the resignation of an efficient staff. Brancker had chosen the one method—summary dismissal—that was certain to bring repercussions. White as a sheet, rigid with resentment, Miss Douglas-Pennant bowed stiffly and left the room. For five days—even more humiliating to Brancker than to her, for he had to seek her advice on many points—she stayed on, then the name of her successor was announced.

There was quite a tussle over this. The choice lay among Dame Katharine Furse, Mrs. Chalmers Watson (Sir Auckland Geddes' sister), Mrs. Gwynne-Vaughan, and Mrs. Pankhurst (favored, curiously, by General Brancker). Mrs. Gwynne-Vaughan was chosen, and with a speed that seemed more than coincidental to the ex-Commandant, uniforms appeared and the move to Berridge House went with a swing.

This was not, in Miss Douglas-Pennant's understandably jaundiced view, the only suspicious circumstance. It seemed odd that she had been dismissed so suddenly, just when she was about to probe allegations of immorality at Hurst Park (from which Janson, Miss Livesay, and Miss Glubb were soon afterward moved), and that one of her archenemies, Dame Katherine Furse, and the sister of her archexecutioner, Sir Auckland Geddes, had been in line for her job. Some WRAF officers were so shocked by her dismissal that they threatened to resign in sympathy. Miss Douglas-Pennant had the pleasure of dissuading them and of receiving a small presentation—some photographs of the training school at Eltham and a violet leather writing case.

But already she was busy with the problem, soon to become a crippling obsession, of clearing her name. Lord Weir begged her not to press for an inquiry and assured both her and the Insurance Commissioners that there was no reflection on her efficiency or character—it was just that "she appeared to be confronted with a combination of circumstances which would take too long to clear away, and the only solution, therefore, was a change." Lloyd George, though refusing the inquiry that she demanded, offered her back her old job as a National Health Insurance Commissioner. It was notable, too, that Lord Weir had been dropped from the Government and that Brancker, though knighted, had rather suddenly left the RAF to work in civil aviation.

Such oblique recognition of the wrong done to her only strengthened Miss Douglas-Pennant's determination to have a public and ceremonial cleansing. Already she was being turned into a symbol of military injustice, the victim of an English Dreyfus case. In vindicating herself, people told her, she would be doing a public service. If such high-handedness was not resisted, what protection would there be in the future for those in Government service who became the object of slanderous attacks from unprincipled people who had the ear of heads of departments? Oliver Arthur Villiers Russell, Lord Ampthill, in a letter to the *Times,* declared that if her case was not fully investigated, "we are at an end of honour and justice in public life." A letter in the *Daily Telegraph,* recapitulating her grievances, was signed not only by Lord Ampthill, but by Lord Henry Cavendish Bentinck, MP, Mary Macarthur (the great women's trade-union leader), and J. H. Thomas (Secretary of the National Union of Railwaymen).

In the spring and summer of 1919, the House of Lords and the House of Commons debated, with increasing acrimony, the pros and cons of the case. Winston Churchill himself, now Secretary of State for War and Air, intervened to say that Lord Weir, after supporting Miss Douglas-Pennant in "a constant series of difficulties and complaints," had decided to make a change. "That," he concluded, "may have been a harsh decision, but it is a perfectly reasonable and comprehensible one in time of peace or in time of war. Lord Weir decided that Miss Douglas-Pennant should be superseded. He did that in the interests of the Women's Royal Air Force." But as MP's and (next morning) the press were quick to point out, the Commandant had *not* been superseded—she had been humiliatingly dismissed without notice. There were loud cries of "Shuffling!" and in a lead article, the *Morning Post* scolded: "As for Mr. Churchill's statement, the man of candour blushes when he approaches it." Lord Henry Cavendish Bentinck claimed that Miss Douglas-Pennant was the victim of a corrupt intrigue by men who were obstructing her in the performance of her duty and that Lord Weir, instead of supporting her, threw his influence on the side of the obstructors. "Will you," he shouted at Churchill, "give an Inquiry into that or not?"

In Wales, the case had become a national issue. Bishops and Free Church leaders addressed public meetings, at one of which a trade-union official argued: "If this injustice goes unchallenged, the principle for which the war was fought will be lost. Our liberties are at stake, and what has been done to Miss Douglas-Pennant may be done to the working classes!" Encouraged by such demonstrations, the ex-Commandant pursued her campaign from her new headquarters, a suite in Jules Hotel, Jermyn Street. She was soon outmaneuvered. Winston Churchill led her to believe that she might be granted an inquiry if she could establish "a prima facie case of corruption or malice against named individuals." Believing that she was protected by official privilege, she wrote a long letter naming Livingston, Brancker, Bersey, Mrs. Beatty, Miss Andrew, Lord Weir, Geddes, and Dame Katharine Furse.

"Having attempted," she claimed, "to carry on the work of the

WRAF upon right principles and in the best interests of the Force, I became the object of a bitter attack. . . . I was warned that an intrigue was on foot to get rid of me because I was too just and straight." This letter was, suddenly and without her consent, published in a Government white paper that included the text of Churchill's reply. He still maintained that there was no sufficient basis for a public inquiry: "No charge of any kind has been made against you. You, on the other hand, have not hesitated to make a series of extremely disagreeable accusations against a number of persons whose reputation and character stand every whit as high as your own. You were a very difficult person to work with in official relations, and a source of friction and embarrassment to the work of the Air Ministry."

This was not, as the Air Ministry must have devoutly hoped, the end of the affair. On July 30, after a lengthy debate, the House of Lords resolved that a Select Committee of its members should be appointed "to examine the circumstances connected with the dismissal of Miss Violet Douglas-Pennant from the Women's Royal Air Force." This had been carried out, said Lord Ampthill, "in a manner in which none of your Lordships would dismiss a scullerymaid." It was, he fumed, "an act of so arbitrary a nature that it can only have been conceived in a very unwholesome atmosphere."

On October 14, before a committee of four peers under the chairmanship of Lord Wrenbury, a Chancery judge and Government nominee, Miss Douglas-Pennant's leading counsel, J. A. Hawke, KC, opened her case. His preliminary statement lasted one and a half days, and Lord Wrenbury burst out irritably: "I am really appalled at the length of your opening." Certainly Hawke had an unenviable task. It would have been comparatively simple to prove that the manner of his client's dismissal had been illegal; it might even have been possible to maintain that she should not have been dismissed at all. But to prove intrigue and to describe it without tedium and bathos ("Was there not an occasion," one witness was asked, "when Miss Pennant said: 'Take those vulgar flowers out of your hat?'") would have been beyond the powers of most barristers. It was certainly beyond the powers of the plodding Mr. Hawke.

Miss Douglas-Pennant's evidence and cross-examination lasted five days. Her counsel labored to present her as a conscientious woman with a fine record of public service ("In all those years, have you failed to work cordially with the people with whom you have been associated in your various duties?" "People have been most awfully nice to me"), but the brilliant Patrick Hastings—for Colonel Bersey—and Rigby Swift—for the Air Ministry—soon demolished this image and substituted that of a querulous snob. "I put it to you," rasped Hastings, "that you said to Miss Pratt that she and the other two were not ladies, that they had apparently never met a lady before, that you were a lady, and that they had treated you abominably."

As in a nightmare, the ex-Commandant felt the ground slipping from under her and saw the villains of her imagination—Lord Weir, General Livingston, Sir Auckland Geddes, Dame Katharine Furse, Mrs. Beatty, Miss Andrew, Colonel Bersey, Sir Sefton Brancker, ex-Colonel Janson, and Lady Rhondda—on the witness stand. She heard Lord Weir assert that Major Baird's support for her in the Commons in August, 1918, had been a "parliamentary answer" calculated, in the interests of morale, to keep the real state of affairs from the public. She heard Brancker, spruce and ebullient, say that "she did not seem to have any real grasp of the situation."

Sir Godfrey Paine alone stood by her, maintaining that any success the WRAF had achieved was largely due to her spadework. It had, he explained, been very hard for her to verify cases of immorality in the camps, since she had no jurisdiction over their commanding officers. He believed that the women who had resigned had tried to "put her in the cart" and had done so in hope that she would be relieved of her post and that they would be reinstated.

But Sir Godfrey alone could not stem the tide, which had turned strongly against her. The first bright glare of the twenties lay mockingly upon her maidenly face and her spinsterly ways. People were not impressed—indeed, they were amused—when they heard that it was during dinner with the Archbishop of Canterbury that she first heard reports of immorality at certain camps. Her description of the high jinks at Hurst Park sounded hilariously prim. "The girls," she said, "were allowed to lead very improper lives. They were given night passes when they should not have been given them; they were taken up to London in Government vehicles; they were brought down drunk in the early hours of the morning;

an officer in command of the station was behaving most improperly with a certain officer down there, and the same was true of other camps."

Such sympathy as may have survived for this by now desperate woman was squandered by her insistence on pressing evidence about immorality that, she alleged, had occurred between Miss Glubb and Colonel Janson in a London lodging house some months after her own dismissal. Harold Morris, Miss Glubb's counsel, produced a doctor to testify to his client's virginity. While an avid hush fell upon the crowded public gallery and members of the committee grew hot under the collar, the doctor explained in clinical detail: "I found the hymen—a membrane enclosing the entrance to the vagina—was unbroken; the aperture in the centre was oval in shape, just admitting the tip of the little finger. Of course," he cautiously added, "there is no definite physical sign of virginity, but the condition here is such that I am of opinion that there has never been penetration of this girl."

But Miss Douglas-Pennant was adamant. With an imperious little nod, she bade her counsel continue. The committee members, perceptibly restless, had to listen while the landlady told how she had found Miss Glubb's hot-water bottle in Colonel Janson's bed and had seen Miss Glubb emerge from his room one morning. They had to sit there while Miss Glubb, the daughter (they were informed) of General Sir Frederick Glubb, a young woman with a fine war record (she been through the Dobruja retreat as a Scottish Women's Hospital driver), was examined and cross-examined. She had, she explained, given Janson the hot-water bottle because he was ill with a recurrence of trench fever and had gone into his room in the morning to take his temperature.

After this sensationally embarrassing episode—such a cruelly far cry from the decency and dignity of the Higher Civil Service—the press turned, with banner headlines, upon Miss Douglas-Pennant. She was a traitor to her sex, a slanderer of the innocent girls entrusted to her care. CRUEL AND WICKED CHARGES, shrilled the *Evening Standard*, GIRL'S HONOUR AT STAKE. The majestic, malevolent breakers of a whole series of closing speeches descended crushingly upon a woman whose aspect and behavior gave credence to the theory, now widely whispered, that her mind was unbalanced. Patrick Hastings ("I venture to think that there was not one single person in this room except Miss Pennant whose blood did not boil at the thought of the indignity of that young lady sitting there") dwelt upon the ordeal of Gwenda Glubb, but it was left to Harold Morris to press home this particular attack. Injured vanity alone, he submitted, could have led Miss Douglas-Pennant to such lengths of vindictiveness: "She cared not about the good name of others. Yet Miss Glubb's honour, her good name, her whole future happiness are at stake. She asks assistance and protection, and I trust she will not be disappointed."

After eighteen much-publicized sessions, the committee adjourned to compile its report. When, in December, this appeared, it had little that was good to say of Miss Douglas-Pennant and little that was bad to say of her opponents. "She enters upon the scene," it sneered, "in the character, in her own opinion, of the saviour, eager to find evils which do not exist." She was "a woman full of zeal, much impressed with her own importance; very reckless in her imputations upon others, and a person not at all likely to get the best out of those with whom she had to work." The story of an intrigue against her "originated in her distortion of events and from her incapacity to see things in their true perspective." As for Colonel Janson and Miss Glubb, they had perhaps failed to observe conventional forms of behavior, but during the war men and women had been "so thrown into daily contact with each other that conventional notions of a certain reserve as between the sexes have been very largely modified." Miss Douglas-Pennant's evidence about Hurst Park, said the report, was, "as a substratum for the vast superstructure of immorality, connivance and encouragement, contemptible."

It was not so easy to explain away the manner of Miss Douglas-Pennant's dismissal, and here much play was made with the fact that, due to inexplicable delays, F.S.14 had not—as Sir Godfrey Paine had promised—been revised during her time in the WRAF. "The fact was," ran the bland, jesuitical reasoning, "that Miss Douglas-Pennant had not been appointed to any office at all. It remains that her employment was a temporary employment by way of loan. The Minister could dispense with her services at any time if, in the honest exercise of his discretion and in the interests of the public service, he thought he ought to do so."

Presenting the report to the House of Lords, Lord Curzon denounced its victim with a bitterness that, some thought, was a measure of the relief of the Establishment at the destruction of so awkward an enemy. She had, he said, under shelter of privilege, brought charges that were grossly defamatory and untrue, but "rarely, if ever, has such an attack met with such complete refutation and exposure." Livingston and Bersey both sued Miss Douglas-Pennant for libel, and she had to pay substantial damages. But she was not without support. Welsh sympathizers assured her that she had won a moral victory. A well-known surgeon wrote: "You assail the cancer which, if it is not eradicated, will drag the old country down." A Douglas-Pennant Committee was formed and made two determined unsuccessful attempts to persuade the Government to reopen the case on the basis of fresh evidence. Mrs. Beatty, it alleged, had been revealed as the main source of the slanderous accusations that had led to her Commandant's dismissal, and Miss Andrew had boasted that she and her friends could "make Weir eat out of our hands if we wished." The committee financed publication of *Under the Searchlight,* a book that gave Miss Douglas-Pennant's side of the story in minute detail. "In spite of the apparent triumph of evil," she concluded, "I am convinced that truth will prevail and that underhand methods, slander and perjury will be exposed."

She had little time now, even if she had had the opportunity (and some of her old committees refused to accept her resignation), to do much public work. But, then, what work could be more important than the great and thankless struggle to which she was pledged? By some strange providence she had emerged from a private hell to lead a crusade of national purification. Yet love mingled with hatred in her attitude toward her days as Commandant of the Women's Royal Air Force. When, many years later, one of the women who had given evidence against her in the House of Lords unexpectedly met her in the ladies' room at Claridge's Hotel, this ambivalence (perhaps indeed symptomatic of a radical ravage of the mind) showed itself startlingly.

At first she met a polite if formal greeting with frigid hostility.

Then, with her back to the door, she roundly abused her ex-subordinate for daring to criticize *her*, the Hon. Violet Douglas-Pennant. Then, with eerie suddenness, her face and manner changed. The charming smile reappeared, the pleasant, persuasive voice. Miss Douglas-Pennant stretched out her hand and, like an old comrade at a reunion, said: "But we *did* have good times together, didn't we?"

Women in Factories

The Munitionettes

After six days in the factory at Hayes, near London, Mabel Lethbridge volunteered for service in the Danger Zone, where high explosives were poured and packed into the shells. Only seventeen, she
had lied to her mother about the kind of work she was doing, had
lied about her age to get into the factory at all. But it was better
than staying at home, and she got a glimpse of the "outside world"
from which it had been her mother's ambition to protect her. There
had been soldiers with fixed bayonets at the factory gates, and in the
inspection shed she and about fifty other newcomers had had to
strip off their clothes and be searched for vermin: a strange introduction to munitions work, but stranger things lay ahead. In her hut
in the Danger Zone, she volunteered to work one of the antiquated
"monkey machines" that forced a mixture of amatol and TNT down
into the 18-pounder shell cases. Four girls hauled on a rope to raise
a massive weight (the "beater") and then, at a signal, let it drop on
the mixture, until it was packed tight. This cumbersome method had
caused a number of accidents already and had been condemned by
the Ministry of Munitions, but the new machinery had not yet
arrived.

Toward the end of her shift, as Mabel gave the signal to lower
and the "beater" descended on yet another shell, there was a frightful explosion. The workers were blown to bits or burned alive, and
she was the sole survivor. Appallingly wounded, she was unconscious for ten days; her left leg was amputated, and surgeons cut

and stitched and grafted away at her shattered body. For her bravery, she was awarded the CBE (one of the first five to be gazetted when this order was created). Today, nearly fifty years and forty-five operations later, she remembers every detail of that terrible day.

Several hundred women died in similar explosions during the Great War, but for many of the hundreds of thousands who entered the munitions factories (and war industry in general), it was a question of long hours, monotony, tedious traveling, and a constant fight for tolerable conditions. Until proper precautions were worked out, women handling high-explosive powder found their complexion turning a deep canary yellow. Some died or had their health wrecked by a type of pernicious anemia. The veils that they were issued gave little protection, and many did not bother to wear them. They treated the phenomenon as a joke or a badge of honor (after all, didn't the troops have to put up with worse?) and sang the popular ragtime songs of the day to keep up their spirits, while scientists poisoned countless rats and mice in the search for an antidote.

At the Government-run Woolwich Arsenal, there were only fourteen thousand workers—and not one woman—when the war began. By 1916, there were nearly one hundred thousand workers at the Arsenal and its satellite factories, and half of them were women. Entire workshops were taken over by women, with a handful of male mechanics to supervise maintenance and repairs. Journalists, apparently forgetting that hard labor had always been the lot of working-class women, were duly and continually astonished by it all. Hall Caine, the best-selling writer, described a visit to a "shop" as large as Trafalgar Square, where two thousand women were at work. "There is something incongruous in the spectacle of women operating masses of powerful machinery (or indeed any machinery more formidable than a sewing machine), but it is surprising how speedily they have wooed and won this new kind of male monster," he wrote. He found the girls' uniform—a khaki-colored overall belted at the waist and a hair-confining cap—becoming. "If," he vowed, "there is any man in London who can pass through the workshops of Woolwich without thinking that he has seen some of the best-looking young women in the world, it is certainly not the present writer." At another factory, he was stirred to enthusiasm by the sight of men and women working side by side: "A brave camaraderie. An old Roman writer tells how the wives ground the swords of their warrior husbands and exhorted them to deeds of valour. What else are these daughters of Britain doing?"

Novelist Arnold Bennett watched women controlling overhead cranes and driving electric trucks and was impressed by the elegance of women in peg-top trousers worn to exclude high-explosive powder: "These last piquant creatures start with two minute points near the ground and often finish near the top with an elaborate corsage and a flowing, glowing scarf." He saw a girl checker "delicately rolling a 9-inch shell with her foot, her fashionable glacé kid boot showing beneath her overall. These things, happily, will peep out."

Arch amazement and coy compliments of this kind formed a stock journalistic response to this industrial and social revolution. But for the upper- and middle-class women who took part in it, often as a specially trained elite, setting standards for the machine-minding masses was a serious business. Miss Lilian Barker, Lady Superintendent at Woolwich, watched the welfare of her girls like a benevolent hawk and braved unpopularity by forbidding the use of cosmetics. The "ladies" were often regarded as spies of the management. Tongues were stuck out behind their backs, their tools were hidden, and walls chalked with disparaging messages. Class warfare broke out over trifles. If a "lady" spread a newspaper on a bench before sitting on it to eat her sandwich, it might be construed as a silent reproach. If something went wrong, a "lady" was blamed first. So the ladies gritted their teeth, took their virtue as its own reward, and waited for the social thaw. When production eased in 1918 and work was short, the lady workers gave themselves the sack. "I suppose most people would call my mates rough girls," one of them told a reporter, "but if their ways were a bit noisy and their voices loud and rasping, they were so kind to me. 'She ain't half bad for a lady,' they said. But you must play your friends true. I am not dependent, as they are, upon my weekly earnings, so I have clocked in for the last time."

But the most efficient, most inspired female superintendent of female labor was not a lady by birth. Lilian Barker was one of a large family born and reared in near poverty in Kentish Town, London, where her father, a former butler to the Bishop of Salisbury, kept a tobacconist's shop. In her first job, as a florist's apprentice, she worked for twelve hours a day sorting and arranging flowers in the damp, dark basement beneath her employer's shop. Later she became a schoolteacher, and showed a remarkable ability for coaxing "problem" slum children, abandoned as hopeless by her colleagues, into an unsuspected willingness and ability to learn. By 1914 she was well known for her miracle-working, not only as a schoolteacher but as the head of a progressive club which sought, with a success almost entirely due to her rambunctious, convention-busting personality, to broaden the knowledge and horizons of working girls apparently stultified by long hours and slum surroundings.

With her plain yet vivacious face, cropped hair, severely tailored suit, and working-class background, she was a type of the "new women" who determined to transform the human slag heaps of Britain's *ancien regime,* and her sayings and doing were widely reported in the press. Though no Socialist, and appalled by the unfeminine tactics of the suffragettes, her hatred of injustice was based on personal experience and a radical, deeply felt Christianity. She startled the clergy on the platform of a meeting to raise funds for "rescue homes" for "fallen" girls by describing unmarried motherhood as a very human, even a generous sin, which contrasted favorably with mean sins, such as hypocrisy, whose consequences all fell upon other people. Journalists gleefully retailed the *mots* she struck off in the heat of her anger. For instance: "I am afraid," she said, "that people who take up rescue work are those who have never been tempted, but they are the very last people who should touch it, for they will do more harm than good."

In November, 1916, after organizing the Cookery Section of the Women's Legion, Lilian Barker was appointed Lady Superintendent of Woolwich Arsenal. As male workers were conscripted into the forces, 30,000 women flooded into the huge arsenal, which covered more than nine square miles, at the rate of 400 a day. Some had worked in offices and shops, many more had come from domestic service, others had been ladies of leisure. Yet somehow the Lady Superintendent—soon known as "Lady Barker" or "Good Old Lil"— managed to steer or switch them to the right jobs and to generate a cheerful *esprit de corps* which overcame grievances and class barriers. Notices drafted and signed by her and headed "Thoughts for Munition Workers" set the bracing, uncomplex tone.

Motive for Work: Patriotism. A munition worker is as important as the soldier in the trenches, and on her his life depends.

Aim: Output. Anyone who limits this is a traitor to sweethearts, husbands and brothers fighting. One minute lost by 60 girls means the loss of one hour's output. This includes slacking at meals and at closing time.

Happiness: If any worker does not like her job, she should give it up; she will be of no use, and probably a bad influence.

The girls worked a twelve-hour shift, but the Lady Superintendent, determined to make this gigantic feminist experiment a success, worked harder. In her office from eight in the morning to eight at night, she often returned to see the night workers. She organized concerts and drama groups, classes in gymnastics, fencing, painting, debating, and embroidery, and—in the teeth of much opposition—mixed clubs where her girls could bring their soldier boy friends. She also inaugurated a benevolent fund to raise money by concerts, bazaars, and fêtes, and with the proceeds opened convalescent homes in the country and at the seaside, homes for mothers and babies, and day nurseries where mothers could leave their children under proper supervision while they were at work. In newspaper articles she castigated those employers who regarded a smattering of "welfare" as an excuse for longer hours and lower wages.

She fiercely defended her girls against widespread rumors that they were overpaid, wildly extravagant (according to some reports, every other girl had a fur coat), and immoral. She caused consternation by refusing to order the immediate dismissal of single girls who became pregnant, unless the man concerned, if he was an arsenal employee, was also sacked.

The popularity of this bluntly spoken woman, who told girls to "take that muck off your face" if they wore cosmetics, and looked more bulky and masculine than ever in her round hat and double-breasted khaki uniform jacket, grew until it reached almost mythical proportions. When the time came for demobilization, many of her girls wept at the ending of what they now saw as the happiest and most purposeful days of their lives. All the women filed into her office to be thanked and advised about their futures, and to shake hands with "Good Old Lil." She shook hands so often, and with such characteristic vigor, that she had to wear her arm in a sling for two weeks after leaving Woolwich.

But Lilian Barker was an exceptional phenomenon. In a war which became more and more total, there was, inevitably, confusion and inefficiency and injustice. No one was prepared for the scale of the nation's involvement. Employers used the emergency as an excuse for lethally long hours and pitifully small wages. New machinery divided and subdivided processes in the interest of foolproof production until the whole structure of industry was altered. It was hard to define how far a woman was a "direct" substitute for a prewar man, difficult to say what was meant by equal pay for equal work as old boundaries became blurred. The idea of welfare—of cloakrooms and rest rooms and canteens and proper sanitation and ventilation and psychological insight being as important as efficient machinery—struggled into being. The Government, which ran only four munitions factories in 1914, was gradually edged into massive participation. By 1917, the Ministry of Munitions owned more than a hundred factories and "controlled" wages and conditions in more than four thousand others. It built whole townships to house migrant workers in remote areas and, against its unsocialistic will, fumbled toward a new system of industrial relations, a new concept of state responsibility.

In the frantic improvisation and cruel dislocations of the early days of the war, it needed a clear and courageous and class-busting person to see and set the pattern of the revolution in industry, to force a realization that the new army of women and the absent army of men had the same interests. Mary Macarthur was that person. Still only thirty-four, she was a veteran of industrial tactics and organization. In the eleven years, crackling with action, that had passed since she left her well-to-do father's drapery business in Ayr, the hometown of Robert Burns, to become the Secretary of the Women's Trade Union League in London, this remarkable Scot had amassed an unrivaled knowledge of the problems and needs of women in industry. A convinced and ardent Socialist (she married Will Anderson, a leading Labour politician, in 1911), she had burst with rude provincial zest into the still ladylike, semiphilanthropic atmosphere of the League.

She knew that few women got a living wage—as late as 1912, it was estimated that the average adult woman's earnings were 10s. 10½d. a week as against a man's 25s. 9d.—and she tackled the seemingly impossible task of energizing them, downtrodden and often apathetic as they were, to improve their lot. "Women," she summarized, "are badly paid and badly treated because they are not organised, and they are not organised because they are badly paid and badly treated." To break this vicious circle, she traveled the country in a passion of urgency, preaching the necessity of unity to hosiery workers and boot- and shoemakers in the Midlands, textile operatives in Lancashire and Yorkshire, jute workers in Dundee, tailoresses and telephonists and cigar rollers in London. "A trade union," she would tell them, "is like a bundle of sticks. The workers are bound together and have the strength of unity. No employer can do as he likes with them. They have the power of resistance. They can ask for an advance without fear. A worker who is not in a union is like a single stick, easily broken or bent to the will of her employer." In one whirlwind week in Dundee, she enrolled three thousand members in a new Jute and Flax Workers' Union, and by the end of 1906 she had affiliated more than two thousand groups to the National Federation of Women Workers (NFWW for short), of which she was founder, President, and (later) Secretary, combining this with the Secretaryship of the League. In two years, the League membership rose from fourteen thousand to seventy thousand, and though this was no more than a stage army, a tiny fraction of the total number of women she longed to help, her brilliant flair for publicity made it, and her, a force to be reckoned with, especially when she could rely on the support of a Parliamentary Labour Party.

As vehement and turbulent and uninhibited a personality as Mrs. Pankhurst herself, Mary Macarthur forced the press to sit up and take notice of the women's trade-union movement and did not hesitate to beard editors in their dens—and even burst into tears before them—if she thought it would help her cause. She launched and edited a vivid and lively weekly paper, *The Woman Worker,* and went into the streets to sell it. She spoke at street corners and factory gates, in rain, shine, or snow, went on picket duty before dawn, inspired an entire new generation of women Socialists, and organized innumerable strikes. A strike, with its tensions and its crises of decision, brought out the tender, fighting best in her. Her fiery yet intensely practical oratory (she knew it was details—the price of thread, for instance, and whether employer or employee should find it—that interested working people, whose lives were dominated by such details) lifted many cowed spirits and made them realize that even if their masters were monsters, they were vulnerable monsters. She was like a gale of fresh air in a stale and dreary atmosphere. "Keep on, miss," pleaded one woman, to whom, as to many others, the words of "Our Mary" came as a revelation. "Keep on, miss, it's better than t' seaside."

She was deeply moved by the spiritual as well as the physical ugliness of poverty. In one article, she wrote of the tormenting appeal of the children of Britain's teeming slums, with "their foul rags falling from shrunken, stunted limbs. Their white, wizened faces, the faces of little old men and little old women. They are mere babies, but they have never been young. Poverty of body is bad, but there is a poverty of mind which is infinitely worse. It is tragedy to have no flowers in one's life. It is death never to have known the desire for them. There are those in our midst who have lost the capacity for joy or sorrow. The sense of suffering is the last to go. When that goes, all is gone."

Her wrath and her pity gushed out on the spur of many a moment, splashing audiences into a revived sense of being part of a wider human family. Life, she proclaimed, could and should be wonderful and expansive, and trade unionism should be valued as much for its social and educational as for its financial benefits. Children should play in green fields, wear warm, comely clothes, be fed on pure milk and butter and eggs and fruit. She strove to draw the two strata, the privileged and the underprivileged, closer together, to irrigate the one with the excess wealth of the other. She told fashionable audiences of the babies of five, four, even three years old who toiled far into the night in Birmingham slums, linking hooks and eyes in an attempt to balance the family budget; of girls who earned only 2d. an hour for exquisite needlework on wealthy folks' clothes; of the East End seamstresses who got 6d. for blouses that sold in London's West End for 30s.

She organized a great and influential Exhibition of Sweated Trades, and when a Select Committee of the House of Commons began an inquiry into sweatshops, she not only gave evidence, but brought representative workers with her. She sought out a girl lace-maker who was making baby clothes by the dozen at 1*d*. a garment. Unknown to her, the girl was sickening with diphtheria, and through handling the garments, Mary contracted the disease and was seriously ill for weeks. Her illness stressed in the most sensa-tional way the widening ripples of the evils of sweating and helped to hasten the formation of the first Trade Boards, with power to fix minimum rates.

The women chainmakers of Cradley Heath in Staffordshire had been the focus of her Trade Boards campaign. Many earned no more than 6*s*. a week working (with their children) for unscrupu-lous middlemen in the backyards of the hovels in which they lived. When, in 1910, a Trade Board fixed rates giving workers a net in-crease of 150 per cent, a number of contractors outside the manufac-turers' association refused to accept the decision. So Mary Mac-arthur called a strike and put the resources of the NFWW behind it. So wide was her fame, so plain did she make the justice of the cause that money poured into the strike fund from all sections of society. After ten exhilarating, nerve-racking weeks, the contractors capitu-lated, and Mary was on a new pinnacle of achievement and adula-tion.

As much as, and perhaps more than, any other single person, she had stirred Britain's conscience to the point where the first glimmer-ings of a state welfare system became not only thinkable but in-evitable. Those who feared such an innovation alleged that the new Health Insurance Act encouraged malingering, especially among women, who were said to be making excessive claims. Quick and adroit as Christabel Pankhurst to turn their own chosen weap-ons on her opponents, she worked up a press campaign that forced an official inquiry into these allegations and gave her the chance to show the real significance of those claims. "The Act," she told the committee, "has shown this country what poverty really means. It has shown that people who are underfed, badly housed and over-worked are seldom in a state of physical efficiency, and it has ex-pressed in terms of pounds, shillings and pence the truth that where an industry pays starvation wages, it does, in literal, sober fact levy a tax upon the community." To the fury of Lloyd George, who had piloted the act though Parliament, she insisted that, far from being too radical, it was a pale shadow of what was really needed. There must be a proper system of maternity care, a state preventive medical service, and, ultimately, state control over the entire field of insurance and pensions. In the meantime, she demanded and got an extension of the Trade Board system to cover more sweated trades.

2 §▶

Mary Macarthur

To Mary Macarthur, the war was sheer destructive idiocy, a tragic interruption of humanity's most vital and urgent endeavors. In the last months, she and her husband spoke out against such madness, pleading with the masses to make their voice heard. When war did come, Mary was still recovering from the shock of a stillbirth and was pregnant again.

But it was not long before she was in action. The Trades Union Congress, the General Federation of Trade Unions, and the Labour Party declared an industrial truce, and the women's trade-union organizations followed suit. Mary was asked by Queen Mary herself to help relieve the frightening unemployment that swept the country before the nation's economy could be adjusted. The cotton and "luxury" trades collapsed, and by the end of September some two hundred thousand women were out of work. Thousands more were on short time, and their plight was made worse by an administrative chaos that meant that soldiers' separation allowances were terribly slow getting through to wives and other relatives.

To the surprise of those who expected such matters to remain in upper-class hands, Mary Macarthur was made Honorary Secretary of the newly formed Central Committee for Women's Training and Employment and given virtual control, under the chairmanship of Lady Margaret Crewe, of Queen Mary's Work for Women Fund. Labor leaders, slightly startled by this strange conjunction, joked about "the strange case of Mary M. and Mary R.," but, in fact, the two women, in their meetings at Buckingham Palace, recognized each other's qualities and shared a resolve to do the best they could regardless of convention. Eight years before, the Queen (then Princess of Wales) had been impressed and distressed by a visit to the Exhibition of Sweated Trades. Now, she regarded the brilliant, volatile, Socialist agitator as the mentor, acknowledging her own ignorance and reading the books that Mary Macarthur recommended as basic to an understanding of the complex situation. Words were not minced; delightedly, Mary told her colleagues at the Women's Trade Union League: "The Queen does grasp the whole situation from a Trade Union point of view. I positively lectured her on the inequality of the classes and the injustice of it."

Lady Crewe and the other members of the committee soon recognized her as the vital spark and natural leader. She was especially valuable when it came to battling with the civil servants of the Treasury, for she had a healthy disrespect for bureaucracy and refused to be bothered with carefully filed correspondence. She had always been the unpredictable terror of her own office staff, and she did not now change her ways. Her contacts with the press ensured that the work got full publicity, and if, as in the case of Lord Northcliffe and the *Times,* she felt that not enough notice was being taken, she hastened to put this right by personal interview.

A string of Queen Mary's Workshops was established to give work to unemployed women at 3*d*. an hour for a maximum of forty hours (and 10*s*.) a week. Some of the more dogmatic Socialists denounced this as sweating (just as they had denounced the Trade Boards, run by "enlightened" employers, as a capitalist dodge), but Mary justified the arrangement on the ground that wages must be kept slightly lower than those paid to women in regular employment. Something was better than nothing, and she had the task of pushing the committee to the limit of its prejudices.

This stopgap relief lasted only until the early months of 1915, when the problem changed completely. The double necessity of expanding the industrial war drive and releasing men for the fighting services brought an appeal from Lloyd George, now Minister of Munitions, for a massive recruitment of women. Mrs. Pankhurst answered the appeal with processions and without qualifications. Her object was simply to get women into the factories. But Mary Macarthur was just as concerned with what happened to them after they got there and with the whole long-term pattern and prospect of trade unionism. The replacement of men by women in industry was known as "dilution," a term that she loathed, and the country was divided into forty-three districts, each with three Senior Dilution Officers, whose job it was to whip up recruiting. The Ministry launched a *Dilution Bulletin,* which painted a pleasant picture of industrial life and printed carefully selected items illustrating women's aptitude for it. To such blandishments, Mary Macarthur was immune. "We women," she wrote in *The Woman Worker,* "have always had in our minds a lurking suspicion that we were, after all, as clever as the men, and it is pleasant to hear Mr. Lloyd George say so. But there is a conclusion to be drawn from all this. If girls are as important and as clever as the men, then they are as valuable to the employer. If this is so, it becomes a duty of the girls to see, now and always, whether in government work or not, that they receive the same pay as the men. Otherwise all their cleverness and all their intelligence go to helping the employer and bringing down the wages of their husbands, fathers and brothers."

Employers welcomed this new source of cheap labor, but the success of dilution depended on the attitude of the trade unions—especially the long-established and exclusive engineering unions. Perhaps that emollient word "dilution" was intended to soothe their natural suspicions: they feared the undermining effect of cheap female labor on men's wages after the war, and Mary Macarthur shared their forebodings. Lloyd George had promised that women would get the same piece rates as men, but the vast majority of women worked for time rates, and he had made no pledge about these. This left employers a free hand in fixing women's wages, and when the NFWW carried out a special inquiry toward the end of 1915, it discovered that the best ordinary rate was 15s. a week, and the average much lower. The excuse of the emergency was used to break all the rules of prewar Factory Acts, which had limited hours to ten and a half a day in most factories and had forbidden night and Sunday work.

Two twelve-hour shifts (instead of the three eight-hour ones favored by Government inspectors) were universal, and often women worked up to eighty hours a week in factories where there was no proper sanitation or provision for the most elementary comfort—and for wages as low as 9s. a week. In Parliament, the case was cited of a factory where girls were working ninety-five hours a week. One firm, given Home Office permission for "moderate overtime," worked girls for thirty hours at a stretch, and when the case came into court, the employer's defense counsel called the prosecution "a fatuous piece of folly, only justified by supreme ignorance," and suggested that instead of bringing action, the Home Office "should strike a medal for the girls. Now is not the time to talk about factory acts." This particular employer was put on probation, others were given fines so small as to be derisive.

Employers defended lower rates for women by saying that they now realized that the men had been paid too much, and they pleaded that women's wages should be cut to pay for the cost of buying and installing expensive new machinery. Small wonder that, with the red danger light winking so furiously, the formerly stand-offish Amalgamated Society of Engineers approached Mary Macarthur. A close alliance was forged between it and the NFWW, and Mary's aim of securing a definite minimum standard wage for women was accepted as the only practical solution. There followed a period of intense activity and hard bargaining. The Munitions Act, hastily drafted and erring blatantly on the employers' side, had at least one virtue. It placed the responsibility for the regulation of wartime industry squarely on the shoulders of the Government and, in particular, of the Ministry of Munitions. A Ministry and a Minister presented a handier target than a lot of firms and a plethora of industrialists. Reasoning thus, Mary Macarthur, once described by a journalist as "the quick firer of the Labour Party, her sentences bursting from her as though she were a Maxim-gun incarnate," sniped away at Lloyd George with grim determination. In person and in print, she banged away at the one clear and inescapable point that not even his verbal smoke screens could obscure. Strikes were forbidden, and a Leaving Certificate System made it virtually impossible for workers to change their jobs to better themselves: "If you tell women that they are not to leave their employment, then it is up to you to make their conditions of employment decent."

Her persistence resulted in a Committee of Inquiry—the Labor Supply Committee. She herself was a member of it, as the undisputed spokeswoman of one and a half million otherwise voiceless women, gagged by the Defence of the Realm Act and hampered by a growing network of barbed, legal wartime wire. After much discussion, women's time rates were fixed at £1 a week. The Ministry sent out a circular recommending the adoption of this rate and urging the importance of adequate lavatory and cloakroom accommodations. It had little or no effect. Most employers, including the Admiralty, ignored it. So Mary had to use other tactics. The Munitions Act specified that if a case was referred to the Board of Trade for arbitration and no ruling was given after a certain length of time, then it was permissible to call a strike. When there had been the requisite (and customary) delay in dealing with a dispute involving some scandalously underpaid Glasgow women workers, Mary threatened to call a strike. The firm gave way, and in the *Daily News,* she drew the moral: "The methods of the Ministry in dealing with the whole question of wages seems part of its deliberate policy of placating whatever may be the most powerful interest at the moment. In cases where, driven by desperate over-fatigue and under-payment, women munition workers engaged in vital work have revolted and refused to continue, it has been found possible to do more for them in a few hours than had been done for the mass of silent, uncomplaining women in a year."

The NFWW continued to spotlight cases of injustice, such as the factory that persisted in an eighty-two-hour week for grenade-core makers, and Mary described the six-month bout of political infighting that had preceded even the present unsatisfactory concessions. "The full history of it," she wrote, "will never be known—a struggle carried on largely in the twilight of Government buildings and Trade Union offices—sometimes even in the sanctity of Ministers' Rooms, where one is choked by a suffocating mist known as the official atmosphere, worse than anything ever experienced on Scottish moors." It was a world where no one took the final blame: "Wages are no more than figures to bureaucrats. The matter does not rest with Mr. Lloyd George himself. He makes the eloquent speeches, the silver promises, but to others is left the performance. The little Minister is surrounded by hide-bound officials, loyal servants of the State, but for the most part entirely lacking in the divine spark of sympathy and understanding. Minutes pass from hand to hand, while weary weeks slip by. And so eternal vigilance be ours."

A colleague, Margaret Bondfield, generaled a drive to form new trade unions among the wartime "birds of passage" (a point much stressed by employers), many of them the wives or widows of serving men, many of them never having worked before. Total membership was increased from 360,000 in 1914 to nearly 2,000,000 in 1918, and more and more, "Our Mary" was able to argue and plead from a position of numerical strength. Her nominal empire was vast. Dilution had seeped into many staple industries, involving more than a million women apart from the six hundred thousand directly engaged in munitions making. Women planed and molded and mortised and dovetailed in sawmills; they made barrels in cooperage works; ground rags and minded the beating and breaking machines in paper mills; drove trucks in flour and oil and cake mills; made upholstery and tire tubes; bottled beer and manufactured furniture; worked in cement factories and foundries and tanneries, in jute mills and wool mills; broke limestone and loaded bricks in steelworks and worked as riveters in shipbuilding yards. You found them in car factories, in quarrying and surface mining and brickmaking. They worked as porters and carriage cleaners on the railways; in power stations and gasworks and on sewage farms; as policewomen and park attendants and street and chimney sweepers. Only underground mining, stevedoring, and steel and iron smelting were still all male.

In June, 1917, Dr. Christopher Addison, who succeeded Lloyd George as Minister of Munitions, told the Commons that between 60 and 80 per cent of all machine work on shells, fuses, and trench-warfare supplies was carried out by women. A British Mission to the United States made much of the example of a former kitchen maid who was now operating a 900-horsepower steam engine without assistance. The *Dilution Bulletin* continued to lavish compliments, listing factories where output had increased since women took over (though this must have been partly due, in most cases, to improved production methods). At an east coast airplane factory, twelve women made twice the number of pulleys formerly made by sixteen men. The output of a horseshoe factory had increased by 7½ per cent since ninety women had replaced the same number of men.

Yet women's wages were always smaller. By the end of the war, the flat rate for male workers in National Shell Factories was £2 19s. 3d., and bonuses raised their weekly pay to £4 6s. 6d. The equivalent figures for women were £1 12s. 8d. and £2 2s. 4d. In National Filling Factories, there were some twenty-eight thousand women operatives and only about twenty-five hundred men. Yet while the men's rate was £2 and their total earnings £3 7s., women got £1 12s. 7d. and £2 2s. 4d. A foreman took home £5 1s. 10d., a forewoman £3 8d. On the Great Western Railway, men clerks averaged £4 3s. a week, women £2 6d., and women porters got the minimum rate paid to men of the same grade and less than half a man's bonus. In munitions factories, a woman's cost-of-living bonus was about half a man's.

What, complained Mary Macarthur, had happened to the glorious promises made by Lloyd George in the summer of 1915, "when Mrs. Pankhurst, accompanied by a number of ladies in fancy dress, many brass bands and £600 of banners, escorted a procession of women to interview the Minister of Munitions?" His circular was being ignored, and he had no power to enforce his own recommendations. Under pressure, the Ministry now took the power to enforce its recommendations. But this was only part of the picture. What of the hated Leaving Certificate System, said to be the only clause in the Munitions Act popular with all employers? Under it, an employer could withhold the certificate without which no employee could get work elsewhere for a period of six weeks, unless exemption was granted by a munitions tribunal. Until the composition of these tribunals was altered as a result of prolonged NFWW criticism, they consisted entirely of men and very rarely contradicted the employer's will. Mary commented in *The Woman Worker*: "The first Munitions Act came quietly, like a thief in the night, and not one woman worker in a thousand knew of its coming. Their shackles were rivetted while they slept. The foreman's reply to the complaining one is no longer: 'If you don't like it you can leave it.' She can't. . . . The other day a munitions worker who was being paid 12 shillings a week had a chance of doing the same work for another employer at £1 weekly, but was refused permission to make the change. Thus we have a concrete case of the State turning the key in the sweaters' den."

Even the newly constituted tribunals were erratic. Women were sacked for union membership, and the NFWW secured compensation for three girls who had been dismissed for joining it. Sometimes employers fired "troublemakers" *and* refused a leaving certificate. Not until the NFWW and the men's trade unions told the Government in 1917 that they could no longer answer for the discipline of their members while the system was in force, were leaving certificates abolished; and even then, the new Munitions Minister, Winston Churchill, had to intervene to break up a new and unofficial system whereby employers circulated blacklists of "undesirables."

Through its many branches, the NFWW constantly pinpointed grievances—firms that still paid less than the Ministry rate or worked employees excessive hours; the justice of the claim for "danger money" made by girls working on ladders fifty feet high as "holders-up" for riveters on airships. It maintained its vigilance to such good effect that Lloyd George was nettled into sneering that since women workers had never had it so good, their real grievance must be the *absence of grievance.* Such complaints as there were, he alleged, did not arise spontaneously, but were manufactured by the NFWW and, in particular, by its Secretary. "Once more," said *The Woman Worker,* now edited by Susan Lawrence, "our Secretary has put the cat among the pigeons."

The NFWW kept a sharp eye, too, on accommodation. Many women and a large number of boys and girls were sent to work long distances from their homes. As early as 1915, fisherwomen were moved from the enforced idleness of the east coast of England to the humming jute mills of Dundee. In February, 1917, alone more than five thousand women from two hundred different areas were brought to eight large munitions centers, more than fifteen hundred were drafted from sixty-three districts to a single munitions factory in Scotland, and to another in the Midlands nearly eight hundred were imported from places as far apart as Aberdeen and Penzance.

Ultimately, the Government introduced (and subsidized) compulsory billeting at fixed rents. It built its own clean, dormitoried (and usually unpopular) hostels and its model factories, miles from anywhere, but offering isolated munitionettes organized entertainment and classes in morris dancing, singing, elocution, hairdressing, dressmaking, and piano playing. But conditions could be grim. At the beginning of 1917, the Health of Munition Workers' Committee, well-primed with NFWW evidence, reported: "The arrival of mothers in a town accompanied by quite young infants, having travelled long distances, is becoming more and more common. . . . The sudden influx has so overtaxed accommodation that houses intended for one family are now occupied by several. Beds are never empty and rooms never aired. Beds, like the occupants, are organized in day and night shifts." In a Midland town, Rebecca West, then a young journalist on the Socialist *Clarion,* found that girls on a twelve-hour shift were often lodging one and a half hours' journey from their factory, so that their working day was augmented to fifteen hours: "To get a roof over their heads they have to endure dirt, bad cooking, rowdy companions, and above all extortionate charges. The poor can also cheat the poor. I have known the wives of foremen earning over £5 a week to charge a girl 15 shillings for bed and breakfast."

The NFWW, like other progressive women's organizations, urged the need for a thoroughgoing welfare system in industry. Too often, the welfare supervisor was a friend, or even the wife or daughter, of a director and was automatically viewed with suspicion by employers. Under these circumstances, a promising new profession sometimes degenerated into meddlesome condescension, so that, as Mary Macarthur said, "welfare is the most unpopular word in the terminology of the factory workers." In her opinion, it was hypocritical to try to wheedle the workers by a little "personal" attention, when their wages were disgracefully low and Ministry regulations about sanitation and other facilities flagrantly disobeyed.

Structural improvement in factories, she thought, must be laid down by Parliamentary legislation and enforced by an adequate number of state inspectors. Wages and hours must be agreed on by collective bargaining between employers and trade unions. The welfare worker's function must be clearly defined, and it was certainly no part of it to act as a "sympathetic" slave driver. Workshop committees were, in any case, preferable to welfare supervisors. In one factory, a workers' welfare committee (on which management was represented) had been elected at a general meeting. Workers had agreed to a deduction of 10 per cent from their wages, and this was used to relieve cases of distress and to provide medical treatment, entertainments, and a supply of newspapers and magazines. Mary Macarthur disliked the Lady Bountiful, *de haut en bas* approach.

She wanted to see more and more workers taking an active part in the shaping of their own destinies. To her, Christabel Pankhurst's leaders-and-led philosophy and her captains-of-industry fixation were anathema—and, of course, she was anathema to (and freely anathematized by) Christabel.

She eagerly publicized the findings of the Health of Munition Workers' Committee, which urged a return to prewar hours, the discouragement of Sunday work, and the restriction of overtime. The committee concluded that "for women engaged in moderately heavy lathe work, a fifty hour week yields as good an output as a sixty hour week, and a considerably better one than a seventy-seven hour week." Night shifts should be abandoned as soon as practicable, and no one should work for longer than four hours without a break.

Relentlessly, she chivied the authorities about wages, pointing out that although food prices were 120 per cent above prewar level, the Ministry of Munitions had, in July, 1916, fixed a rate of 4d. an hour. This was "equivalent to less than 2¾d., or lower than the lowest minimum wages fixed in any sweated trade under the Trade Boards Act. . . . In radiant words Mr. Lloyd George envisaged a great move forward for women workers. They have waited patiently for the protection of a legal minimum wage, and find themselves held down by a maximum. It will not do. Pledges solemnly given must not be carelessly broken." She complained that arbitration tribunals were still procrastinating, that awards were delayed for up to six months, and that when they came they were not retrospective. In April, 1917, the Ministry raised the rate in Government and Government-controlled establishments by 1d. an hour, and the standard rate for a 48-hour week (by them recognized as the norm) from 20s. to 24s.

But it was easier to jockey the Government into action than to get any improvement in the sweated trades, many of which were not even regulated by Trade Boards. *The Woman Worker* demanded the application of a national minimum-wage system here as well. The Trade Boards had never been more than an interim measure, and now the state must intervene to bring a semblance of justice. Thousands of women were still struggling to exist on 1¼d., 1½d., or 2d. an hour. After prolonged pressure, the Tailoring Board raised its rates to 4½d. an hour in 1917, with a special rate of 6d. for highly experienced women cutters who had directly replaced skilled men. Confectionery firms and tin-box manufacturers raised wages from 14s. 1d. to 16s. 3d. a week, and negotiations began for a minimum rate of 19s. 6d. Mary Macarthur appealed to the women to stir themselves. "Don't Blackleg Your Man in Flanders" was one of her slogans.

But though she was no pacifist-at-any-price and accepted the needs and implications of a war of nations, she remained true to her basic principles. She often went out of her way to help enemy aliens frightened by jingo fever, to befriend a conscientious objector, or to stand up for "troublemaking" Socialist shop stewards. She never allowed her view of the war machine to be blurred by a golden fuzz of patriotism, as did Mrs. Pankhurst and Christabel. It had to be shaped and tamed and used for the purposes of the peace, not glorified.

In summer, 1918, she was the first woman to be adopted as a Parliamentary candidate. Characteristically, she said: "Women did not ask for the vote or for the right to stand for Parliament as reward for services rendered—a decoration or a ribbon to wear in the coat, although it is rather in that spirit that these civic rights have been given to us. We asked for them because of our desire to render service as citizens." As soon as the war ended, preparations were made for a General Election, but before she began her electioneering, there were other things to attend to. Early in the year, the war industries had begun to slow down. Big orders from Russia had been canceled, stockpiles grew for lack of shipping space. Winston Churchill, as Minister of Munitions, had to consider moving workers from slack factories to busier ones. By June about fifty thousand women were out of work, and attempts were made to absorb some of them into the Women's Army Auxiliary Corps, the Women's Royal Naval Service, the Women's Royal Air Force, and the Land Army. They had become a problem, an administrative headache. The public and the press began to be less complimentary. "The idea," rasped the *Daily Graphic*, "that because the State called for women to help the nation, the State must continue to employ them is too absurd for sensible women to entertain. As a matter of grace, notice should be at least a fortnight and if possible a month. As for young women formerly in domestic service, they at least should have no difficulty in finding vacancies."

The *Daily Mirror* foresaw the return of thousands of soldiers' wives now in factories to the proverbial kitchen sink, and the "extravagance" of munitionettes (their fondness for a drink, for pretty clothes, and other "luxuries") was widely criticized. At a public meeting, Mr. Joynson-Hicks, MP, and Mrs. Bramwell Booth, wife of the General of the Salvation Army, spoke of the unfortunate habit of smoking common among the girls. There was little doubt that spiritual interests had been sadly neglected, and Mrs. Booth feared that "if this kind of thing does not stop, we shall see mothers of the future puffing out clouds of smoke into their babies' faces."

In some places, factory girls still demonstrated their patriotism by forgoing their Easter vacation and by sending perky messages to the front via Lord Northcliffe's newspapers. "Tell the boys," said one girl, "not to be downhearted, but to stick to it, and us girls will do our bit and stick to our machines so that they won't be hung up for shells." But Mary Macarthur, who knew the large-scale misery that could follow the pricking of the wartime bubble, had very different messages to give to any papers that would print them. Taking the long view, as she consistently did, she argued that this was not just a matter of temporary improvisation, but involved the whole question of Government planning for the demobilization of some 3 million civilian workers in the war industries. The demobilization of 5 million soldiers had been worked out in detail well in advance, so surely it was high time that the Ministry of Reconstruction worked out a detailed plan for the army of civilians? A free railway ticket home was no solution, nor was 7s. a week unemployment benefits, which in any case could be drawn only by workers in the few industries where there was a scheme for compulsory insurance. Unemployment benefits at *subsistence level* must be given to workers, at least in Government and Government-controlled industry, and everyone should have a month's vacation at existing rates of pay. In the interests of public health, the nation could not afford not to give their women some rest after the perpetual strain of more than three years, endured without any break save through illness.

The Government at last promised £1 a week unemployment pay; but this was not backdated, as Mary Macarthur had demanded, to the time of discharge. Awkward gaps and administrative breakdowns provoked many mass meetings and demonstrations up and down the country, and six thousand women from Woolwich and other London munitions factories marched, through dense crowds, on Whitehall, carrying banners with slogans such as "Shall Peace Bring Us Starvation?" Mary and some of her colleagues hurried from the Women's Trade League offices to meet the marchers, and Mary herself led a deputation of twenty shop stewards to the Ministry of Munitions, where tea was hastily prepared for them. After a tense period of waiting, she emerged with the news that the Government had promised unemployment pay at 25s. a week for thirteen weeks, as well as a month's vacation with pay for women discharged from factories under Government control.

It was her last personal blitz of the war. But her influence and inspiration permeated the deliberations of the War Cabinet Committee on Women in Industry and of the Ministry of Reconstruction's Women's Employment Committee, both of which had for some time been sifting evidence and preparing reports.

Mary's leaven was working—and to this day is working—busily. She now faced an election campaign in which Mrs. Pankhurst and Christabel, by whose side she had spoken in the stirring by-election fights of the early days of the WSPU, would vilify her as a Bolshevist, a traitor, a pro-German. Yet, perhaps more than anyone else with comparable strains and responsibilities, she had, despite an emotional temperament, kept a level head, a sense of human balance. Contrary to some reports, she had not been in any way "corrupted" by her contacts with high society. In all companies, she continued to uphold the ideal of social justice, telling one great lady that in the more equitable society of the future, her fine country house and its lovely grounds would be turned into a rest home for workers.

In the desert of war, she continued to desire and to fight for the flowers. She fought so hard that it shortened her life, and one opponent at least realized the extent of her victory. When Mary R. asked to include Mary M. in the first postwar Honors List, she was advised (almost certainly by Lloyd George, who never abated his detestation of "Our Mary" and all her works) that Miss Macarthur and her husband had been far too radical in their views to make such recognition desirable.

Our Sylvia

Cattle to the Slaughter

Sylvia Pankhurst's original ambition was to be "a painter and draughtsman in the service of the great movements for social betterment." Pale, dark-haired, withdrawn, but showing almost ferocious powers of concentration, she won prize after prize at Manchester Art School, including a traveling scholarship, which she used to visit Venice and Florence.

By 1905, she was a student at the Royal College of Art in London, and for a short time she acted as Honorary Secretary of the then tiny London branch of the WSPU. Mrs. Pethick-Lawrence found her a baffling personality—"the impersonation of what I imagined those young Russian students to be who, in the last decade of the 19th century, had given up career and status to go amongst the masses of the people in order to instruct them, and so prepare the ground for the revolution which they believed some day would take place."

Her suffragette associations made it difficult for her to get commissions as an artist. She was desperately poor (she says she lived on lentils, cocoa, and water) and shabby—which her mother and Christabel, great ones for appearances, deplored. But to her, this shabbiness was a matter almost of pride, a passport to the great proletarian underworld that fascinated her both as an artist and as a social reformer. She went to Cradley Heath, the scene of Mary Macarthur's victory, staying with an old woman who kept a confectioner's shop, drawing the women at their backyard forges and writing articles about them. She studied the conditions of work of migrant Scots fisher lasses and of casual potato pickers hired by the day from the slums of the border counties. She observed these women closely, the old and the young barely distinguishable, their skins were so ingrained with dirt, their eyes so inflamed, their clothes so ragged. "I heard their stories," she wrote later, "sordid and grey, with the workhouse as the inevitable harbour of old age." In Glasgow, she lodged in a tenement, painting by day, writing at night, speaking for the WSPU as opportunity arose.

Her increasingly outspoken socialism (her idol was Keir Hardie, founder of the International Labour Party) brought her into conflict with her mother and with her sister Christabel, who were determined to keep the WSPU free of any party alignment. But in 1912, the WSPU helped her to open a branch in the East End of London. With a few devoted helpers, including Zelie Emerson, a young American suffragette whose skull was fractured in an affray with the police, she set up headquarters in a vacant baker's shop in Bow, with VOTES FOR WOMEN written in letters of gold above the entrance. Sylvia's "clients" were the sweated, anonymous workers of London's slums—ropemakers, waste-rubber cleaners, cookie packers, chicken pluckers. Sylvia was shocked by squalid tenements, starvation wages, exorbitant rents, and the meager charity of the Poor Laws. She redoubled her pressure for the vote, and her hunger-and-thirst strikes in prison set new and terrifying standards of self-mortification. "Our Sylvia," as she was known to thousands of Cockneys, was carried about, in the interludes between imprisonment, on a stretcher, borne aloft, emaciated but indomitable, above a sea of curious heads, like a medieval saint in a procession.

Articles by her in the left-wing *New Statesman* told of magistrates who sent mothers, distraught with poverty and starvation, to prison for not looking after their children. "A woman I know," she revealed, "who supported a paralysed husband and three little children was only allowed 5 shillings a week by the Poor Law Guardians. Her children have to go to be weighed every five months to see that they are fat enough, and a male officer pays surprise visits and turns down their beds to see that they are clean."

In Bow, she made friends with George Lansbury, the editor of the Socialist *Daily Herald*, who had lost his seat in Parliament and gone to prison for his suffragette sympathies. In November, 1913, she spoke at the Albert Hall, the scene of many triumphant suffragette rallies, with him and other radicals, in a meeting to demand the release of Jim Larkin, the Irish trade-union leader. The *Daily Herald* commented: "Every day the industrial rebels and the suffrage rebels march near together."

Soon after this, Sylvia, accompanied by her faithful lieutenant Norah Smyth (a woman of considerable private means, she held a Cambridge degree and had once been Mrs. Pankhurst's chauffeuse), went to Paris to discuss the future with her mother and Christabel. There she was faced with the choice of severing her links with socialism or leaving the WSPU and losing its financial support. She decided to go her own way.

Sylvia's fame and that of her East London Federation of the Suffragettes spread rapidly, and suffrage organizations in Finland, Denmark, and Norway invited her to their countries to speak. She herself had forsworn "violent" tactics in the fight for the vote, but her speeches urging the workers to rise and demand their rights ("No Vote" ran one of her slogans, "No Rent") were fiery enough to land her in prison on a charge of incitement. Again and again she hunger-struck, again and again, under the Cat-and-Mouse Act, she was released and rearrested. Out for the seventh time, she wrote to Prime Minister Asquith asking him to receive a deputation of workingwomen and listen to the arguments for a really democratic measure of suffrage reform. (Asquith maintained that the limited measure demanded by most suffragists was "too narrow," and he implied that a wider view must be taken. Sylvia demanded the vote for all men and women over twenty-one.) She would neither eat nor drink again, she said, until he had agreed. In June, 1914, after another imprisonment, she had herself driven to the House of Commons and was laid on a stretcher on the pavement, fearfully pale and surrounded by a weeping, indignant group of woman from the East End.

Asquith gave way and received a deputation of six women. He listened to the ugly facts of life among the poor. Mrs. Ford, who had started working when she was eleven and struggled for years to provide for a sick husband and two children as a needlewoman and trouser-maker's presser, described how she had been sacked because

she would not let the foreman seduce her. Mrs. Parsons spoke of
packing thirty-five hundred cigarettes a day for a wage of 10½d.
a day. Jessie Payne, a shoemaker, told of the time her mentally defective daughter had been removed to a padded cell in Poplar
Workhouse. When Mrs. Payne tried to remove her, the authorities
told her that she had no say in the matter—her husband must apply:
"If my girl had not had a good father, I could not have got her
out. . . . We come from the East End and we have the voice of the
people that they want the vote for women over 21, and also for you
to release Miss Pankhurst. . . ." Asquith promised to give the matter his "mature consideration." He had, he said, been most impressed by the individual evidence, and he agreed that "if you are
going to give the franchise to women, you must make it a democratic measure. It is not good tinkering with a thing of this sort."
Though condemned by the WSPU as an untimely intervention, the
deputation was widely believed to have won a real victory. Sylvia,
still terribly weak, followed it up with a personal interview with
Lloyd George.

In the interests of her weekly paper, *The Woman's Dreadnought*
(the title symbolized the fact that "women who are fighting for their
freedom must fear nothing"), Sylvia made wide journalistic forays.
In August, 1914, she traveled to Dublin to investigate reports that
British troops had fired on women and children in the hysterical atmosphere of impending civil war between the Ulster Volunteers of
the North and the National Volunteers of the South. Then, as she
visited the victims of the shooting ("a little boy shot in the back, a
girl with her ankle shattered, a father lying dead"), came the news
of the declaration of war. She hurried back to London, on a cross-
Channel steamer crammed with troops, many of them singing
drunk. The noise, the spectacle, saddened her. "Men," she remembered, "going to die without heed to the beauty and purpose of life,
untouched by the cleansing fires of enthusiasm, going like cattle to
be slaughtered, mere pawns in the hands of those whose identity
was unknown to them. . . . Throughout Europe would be a vast
widowhood, the cries of fatherless children . . . a gigantic arrest of
human progress, a huge vanquishing of the higher life of culture, the
finer processes of thought." Lying in her berth, she put her hands
over her ears to shut out the noise of the soldiers' bawling.

2 §♥

The Battle of the East End

Sylvia determined to fight the Great War—its causes, its hypocrisies, and its results. She would tell the truth about it, whatever the cost —and an important part of the cost was a further, and final, postponement of her career as an artist. People must be made to see the war for what it really was, the creation of financiers, company promoters, armaments manufacturers, forcing the masses to dance to their devil's tune of greed. "Dear women," she wrote in *The Woman's Dreadnought* as prices and unemployment rose in the first weeks of war, "are you prepared to go on tamely starving, as though you and your children did not matter? The men in power have plunged us into war for their commercial interests. They pass bills in the interests of financiers. What will they do for you? Demand not paltry doles but adequate food for the children of poor mothers in this crisis. Demand that our Government shall take over the entire food supply of the country and distribute it in the interests of all the people."

She further insisted that the Government should protect women from being exploited by low wages; that the wartime moratorium on debts should be extended to debts under £5 ("the poor need relief as much or more than the rich"); that the Government should provide free medical services, at least while the war lasted; that working women should be placed on all committees concerned with fixing food prices and providing employment and relief; and that all adult women should be given the vote so that they could "help in minimising, as far as possible, the horrors of war." To back these demands, she continued to urge a no vote–no rent strike and was gratified to see a rhyme crudely painted on a strip of calico strung across a street:

> Please landlord don't be offended.
> Don't come for the rent till the War is ended.

The dislocation of industry in 1914 meant that men as well as women were thrown out of work. Starving mothers with starving babies crowded around Sylvia's door. Couldn't she do something? Couldn't she get the Army separation allowances, still at the old Boer War rates, increased? Couldn't she make the bigwigs understand what war meant to the poor? National insurance applied to only a few trades.The Poor Laws were not intended to help the able-bodied and their dependents. A Soldiers' and Sailors' Families Association (SSFA) gave temporary financial help, but the whole ramshackle system was about as impotently archaic in such a crisis as the charge of the British cavalry against machine guns at Mons.

National Distress Funds were channeled through local authorities, and Sylvia joined George Lansbury (also vehemently anti-war) on the Bow Committee. Dashing in from a hectic series of street-corner meetings, she found the pace and tone of the deliberations, under the guidance of an obstructive mayor, quite intolerable. There was little sense of urgency, and wrangles between Conservative, Labour, and Liberal members took up much of the time. The committee consisted for the most part of "thick-set middle-aged men, clad in broadcloth, with gold watch-chains and protruberant corporations." The few women there were, she thought, too ladylike, hesitant, and subordinate in manner. Susan Lawrence, who was to be a Labour Minister in the 1920's, was a capable administrator, but lacked fire. Miss Wintour was an inaudible Liberal. Mrs. Clement Attlee (wife of the future Labour Prime Minister) seemed "a middle class fish out of water." Why should they sit there pretending to represent workingwomen? Why shouldn't the workingwomen sit there themselves?

In the *Dreadnought,* which she herself sold in the streets and in pubs, she blazed away at such impertinences as police investigation of serving soldiers' wives and relatives, to see whether they were "worthy" of their separation allowances. The snooping of the SSFA, the Poor Law Guardians, and the local committee came in for criticism. Case after case of suffering and privation (". . . a woman with six children under 13 . . . her twins only a month old, fed on boiled bread, having no other food in the house, and but little of that"; "one woman with six children, deserted by her husband, went four days without food") was exposed; full details of sweated wages and bad working conditions—and employers' names—were given. The *Dreadnought* was a useful weapon. When Sylvia saw an old woman hauled before the committee and threatened by a local parson with the loss of her free meal tickets if she did not stop drinking, she rapped: "If this happens, I shall expose it in the *Dreadnought.*" The counterthreat was effective. "Angry voices," she noticed, "subsided, benignity began to reign."

Just so had Mrs. Pankhurst, when she was a Poor Law Guardian in Manchester in the 1890's, raged when she discovered that the little girls in the Chorlton Workhouse still wore eighteenth-century dresses with low necks and no sleeves and that they had no nightdresses or underclothes—because the matron and some refined female guardians had been too shy to mention such garments to the male members of the board.

But the committee would not be pushed into large-scale action. "It was steeped in the method of the Poor Law—to provide small doles, mainly in kind, postponed as long as possible." It was content to wait for orders from the Cabinet Committee, and if no orders came, no action was taken. So Sylvia, primed with East End household budgets and home truths, took a deputation to interview Walter Runciman, President of the Board of Trade. Melvina Walker, a docker's wife (and former lady's maid) who had gone to prison as a suffragette, reported the visit for the *Dreadnought*. She noted, disapprovingly, the opulence of the surroundings—thick carpets, massive furniture, well-padded, well-dressed bodies—and, approvingly, the officials' obvious respect for Sylvia. "We addressed these men," she wrote, "in the same way and with the same simple language as we would address our own men, and forgot that Mr. Runciman was a man holding Cabinet rank. We went there to look upon him as our paid servant, to give him our orders and see that he carried them out."

Charlotte Drake, a former barmaid, read out the budget of a widow with eleven children who received 11s. a week from the Poor Law and a 4s. grocery ticket. She also demanded nationalization of the land and strict food rationing for all classes. Other women stressed the need for equality of sacrifice on the home front, and, as tempers rose, Mr. Runciman was roundly accused of deliberately helping to "starve the men into enlisting"—a theory with which Sylvia did not hesitate to bludgeon the mayor of Poplar.

She took another deputation to the War Office to complain about the miserliness of pensions and separation allowances and their tardiness in coming through. A mother of six, officials were told, had had to pawn or sell most of her belongings and go for days without food while waiting for her allowance. Another with five children had been told by the SSFA that she ought to show her patriotism by selling her furniture and moving into one room before coming to them for help. Why, asked Sylvia, weren't common soldiers paid at least as well as industrial workers if they were expected to take over the state's responsibilities by supplementing the money paid to their wives and relatives?

But Sylvia, the Terror of the Ministries, reserved her bitterest attack for Mary Macarthur and the policy of Queen Mary's Workshops. It seemed to her iniquitous that a professed Socialist and trade unionist should be associated with a scheme that was apparently designed to rub the workers' noses in their own sweat. By offering wages that ranged from 6s. to 10s. a week (and less for girls under eighteen), Queen Mary's Workshops were, she maintained, encouraging employers to persist in their meanness. She coined the slogan "Queen Mary's Sweatshops," and after some delay, Miss Macarthur agreed to receive a deputation at the swagger headquarters of the Central Committee for Women's Employment. When Miss Macarthur welcomed them, she was eyed critically. "A large lady," wrote Sylvia acidly, "in old-gold silk, she came with a rustle of petticoats and white forearms advantageously displayed." Her main argument was that since the average national wage for women was only 7s. 6d., it was unreasonable to expect the workshops to pay more than 10s. Perhaps disconcerted by the hostile silence, she showed the deputation some babies' woolens set out on a table. They had been made in the workshops, she said, and some of them might well find their way to the East End. It was a tactical error. "I would rather take poison than them!" was the general reaction, and out swept the deputation.

But though it was a duty, and often a pleasure, to badger authority, Sylvia determined to set the lagging state an example by creating a network of welfare services in her own little kingdom. First of all, she appealed for milk and turned the meeting hall behind the Federation's headquarters on Old Ford Road into a distribution center. Here, watched impassively by plaster casts of Homer, the Delphic Apollo, and the Venus of Milo, with which Sylvia had attempted to evoke the riches of their cultural heritage, the women queued. They almost took it for granted that Miss Pankhurst would work another of her wonders. They knew that though she was so tenderly, so vociferously, among them, she was not of them. She had connections in the well-warmed, well-fed, money-snug, outer, upper world, and they had come to expect her to tap them. She watched "her" women with the yearning possessive eyes of the idealist, with the eye of a painter too: "poor young mothers in their starving fortitude, with faces of ashen pallor and sorrowful eyes dark-ringed; beautiful in their fading as pale lilies in the moonlight, to those who had eyes for their mournful loveliness . . ."

It was found that the babies were so ill that they could not digest the milk. So Sylvia opened four mother-and-baby clinics, run by two women doctors, notably Dr. Barbara Tchaykovsky, who before the war had organized the White Cross League to safeguard the health of the children of families involved in the great dock strike. The headquarters hall soon served also as a cost-price restaurant, with rented gas stoves and boilers. Wood for tables was given by Willie Lansbury, George Lansbury's son (who was now in charge of the family timber business), and the tables were made by members of the Rebels' Social and Political Union, a band of local men who before the war had helped in the struggle for the vote. Free meal tickets were issued to the destitute, and the restaurant was soon feeding more than 150 people at a sitting.

Helpers—including Zelie Emerson, who had come back from America to be with Sylvia in this crisis—were rushed off their feet. Miss Emerson opened a clinic-*cum*-soup kitchen-*cum*-milk center near the vacant stable where she and Sylvia had hidden one night when they were "mice" on the run from Government "cats." Next on the list was an employment bureau, then came the opening of a toy factory (with day nursery attached) to give work to local women at a wage of £1 a week—the same as the men's minimum wage in the district. Lady Sybil Smith managed the nursery for four days a

week, leaving a Mayfair home and seven children to live up to her
Tolstoyan principles. Lady Sybil also arranged meetings in the
homes of her wealthy friends—including Mrs. Nancy Astor—at
which Sylvia appealed for funds for her proliferating enterprises;
and when there were financial gaps, Norah Smyth, taciturn but generous, dug deep into her private means.

The toy factory prospered. The import of German toys had
stopped, opening a wider market for British goods, and Amy Brown-
ing, once a fellow student of Sylvia's at the Royal College of Art,
taught drawing and painting. Herr Niederhofer, a German crafts-
man, was taken on as foreman. Like many Germans, he had been
thrown out of work, and even George Lansbury was afraid to employ him in case his business was wrecked by jingo mobs. It gave
Sylvia keen pleasure to gather him into her progressive fold and to
watch what she called "the happy cultural influence of the factory
upon women starved of beauty and opportunity."

As rocketing prices drove more and more mothers into the rapidly expanding munitions factories late in 1915, Sylvia decided that
the day nursery must be enlarged. She brought it and an infant clinic
together in a converted pub, once The Gunmaker's Arms, now felici-
tously rechristened The Mothers' Arms. A motif of red caps of liberty decorated the exterior, and inside were a doctor's consulting
room, a bathroom, a dressing room, a kitchen, and a scullery. Up-
stairs was the day nursery, and the flat roof made a pleasant play
space when the sun shone. Toddlers were taken for walks in Victoria
Park—the scene of lively meetings and bruising scuffles with the police in the past, the scene of more controversy as the war dragged
on.

Montessori methods were used in the nursery, and grants were
made by the Ministry of Health and the Ministry of Education.
Press publicity was frequent and, on the whole, favorable. Dr.
Tchaykovsky's memorable statistics kept the funds rolling in. She
contrasted Britain's military casualties for the first year of the war—
seventy-five thousand killed, or some 2½ per cent of the combatants
—with infant mortality in the same period, when Britain had lost
more than one hundred thousand (about 12½ per cent) out of eight
hundred thousand babies born. During 1915, nearly one thousand
mothers and their babies were seen at the Federation's clinics, about

seventy thousand meals were served in the cost-price restaurants, and more than £1,000 was spent on milk alone. Dr. Tchaykovsky cited some of the cases treated at The Mothers' Arms. One applicant was supporting a blind and invalid husband with the help of a grant of 7s. a week from the Poor Law Guardians: "The case came to our knowledge the day after the birth of a fourth child. We supplied milk and dinners, and the baby came into the nursery when the mother went back to work." One seven-month-old baby weighed only eight and a half pounds when he was brought in, but improved after being given seawater plasma injections.

The Federation's Christmas parties for the children of Bow and Poplar and Canning Town were gay and delightful, complete with costumes and decorations designed by Sylvia. Bernard Shaw judged a children's essay competition and wrote a humorous report for each entrant. If Sylvia had been content to concentrate on her welfare work, she might have stayed respectably on the crest of a wave of well-earned approval. Bernard Shaw advised her to do so. "How," he quipped, "can you hope to convert the public, when you can't even convert your mother and Christabel?"

But Sylvia would not be deterred. The death of Keir Hardie in September, 1915, was a bitter blow to her. The first Labour MP, he had been almost the only one to stick to his pacifist principles in wartime. This consistency made him the target for criticism—not least from the WSPU. *The Suffragette* reproduced a *Punch* cartoon that showed Hardie obsequiously accepting a bag of money from the Kaiser, with the doggerel caption:

> Also the Nobel Prize (though tardy)
> I now confer on Keir von Hardie.

When Sylvia saw this, she wrote to her mother to say that Hardie was desperately ill. She believed that "her old love for him must flame out against further insults, did she know his state." Mrs. Pankhurst did not answer, and the WSPU sent Flora Drummond (who had formerly so revered Hardie that she named her son Keir) to his constituency, Merthyr Tydfil, to speak for the war-supporting Labour candidate who hoped to succeed him as MP. Hardie's persecution and death made Sylvia resolve to speak and work more boldly against the war.

In the *Dreadnought* she wrote: "Keir Hardie has been the greatest human being of our times," and she hit out harder than ever at the iniquities of capitalism. Under the terms of a prewar patent, she claimed, the British Government continued to pay the Krupp family, the German armament manufacturers, 1s. for every fuse made, so that German industrialists actually made money out of the frightful campaigns in which tens of thousands of British troops were being killed and maimed. The British-owned Whitehead Torpedo Company, she said, had a branch at Fiume, then part of Austro-Hungary, where torpedoes, submarines, and floating mines were made for use against the Allies. She alleged that grain merchants had forced the Government to abandon plans to control the purchase of grain because this might reduce their profits.

Week after week, she gave details of sweated pay and bad conditions, badgering Lloyd George by letter and in person about woman's rates in munitions factories, publicizing the case of women workers in a Limehouse food factory who complained that their pay was low, that the basement where they worked was damp and steamy, and that the food was often stinking and in a state of decomposition. Action followed quickly, and Government factory inspectors begged her not to publicize such cases in the future, but simply to notify the Home Office (it transpired that the firm was the official purveyor of turtle soup to the royal household). She refused, but sent a copy of the *Dreadnought* regularly to the Factory Inspectors' Department.

While, at great personal effort and cost, Mrs. Pankhurst had adopted four "war babies," Sylvia firmly maintained that they should be the responsibility of the state and not left to "the fluctuations and caprice of private charity." Marriage by proxy should be allowed, as it was in other countries at war, and separation allowances should be paid by soldiers to the girls they had seduced. For some unmarried mothers, she found work in her toy factory, where the babies could be left in the day nursery; for others, she found foster parents; and she personally located at least one absconding father and scolded him into doing the decent thing. In an open letter to a "war father" who had said that he could not marry the girl he had gotten with child because she was not "the right class," she wrote: "You should have considered what sort of girl she is before you entered into intimate relations. But in what are you better than she? Nature has placed the heavier share of the burden on the woman, whether the child be born according to our little lawyers' rules or not, but man-made society has added to the burden. Some day the children of our country will have protection, as in Norway, where a man must maintain equally *all* his children, whether born in or out of wedlock, and an equal moral standard will be established for men and women. . . ."

The contrast between harsh reality and her vision of a cooperative society glowing with fraternity and selflessness must sometimes have been almost unbearable. But even Sylvia's idealism knew some bounds. Approached by Lucy Thoumaian, a keen Swiss suffragist married to an Armenian, to help raise a Peace Expeditionary Force of a thousand women, who would make their way to the front and fling themselves between the opposing armies, she, usually so helpful to lost causes, demurred at last. Mme. Thoumaian came to her later, confessing that no one had volunteered. But she urged Sylvia to go to the front with her—perhaps the two of them could do something, somehow. Sylvia was moved, but she stayed put. She was, though, one of 180 British women delegates prevented by an embargo on shipping from going to the Women's International Peace Conference at The Hague in April, 1915.

As the Government moved toward conscription by instituting a scheme of registration for men and women, she was quick to warn her readers, suggesting the following comprehensive answer to the official questionnaire: "I do not think it right to do Government work unless I have a guarantee that I shall be paid the standard rate hitherto paid for the kind of work I am asked to undertake, with the addition of any War Bonus or increase in wages that may be granted owing to the war, and that if the work is unskilled and the wages hitherto paid have been low, I shall not be engaged to do it at less than 7d. an hour. I consider that women's labour should be safeguarded by the possession of the Parliamentary vote."

At Caxton Hall, where the WSPU had held its famous "Women's Parliaments," she organized the first of several Exhibitions of Sweated Wartime Labor, with actual homeworkers on the stands, stitching kit bags and trousers or finishing military overcoats, with the price they were paid per hour clearly placarded.

3 ❧

The Battle of the East End
(Continued)

In the weeks before Registration Sunday, August 15, 1915, Sylvia redoubled her efforts. She spoke at four street-corner meetings every night, lashing out at the hypocrisy of conscription (what kind of National Service, she wanted to know, could there be under makers of private profit?) and urging the people of the East End to join her in a procession to a protest meeting at the Portman Rooms in Baker Street (the manager of the Queen's Hall had refused to rent it for such purposes). Sylvia exulted in being there among "all the rebels of those days in London . . . socialists, anarchists, individualists, trade unionists, left wing industrialists, pacifists . . . those who hated compulsion and capitalism, those who opposed the War." In a passionate speech, George Lansbury warned that registration was the first big step toward conscription, which would mean cheaper soldiers, smaller (or even no) allotments or separation allowances, no pensions, workers shot or imprisoned if they asked for higher wages or better conditions.

He and Sylvia went in a deputation to see Reginald McKenna, Chancellor of the Exchequer, at the Treasury. Lansbury, who had had time to cool off, seemed to Sylvia much too apologetic and conciliatory in his approach. What, said McKenna blandly, could one expect? There was a *war* on. There was bound to be suffering, hardship. But not, said Sylvia, when her turn came to speak, gross inequality of sacrifice and blatant class distinction. Why, she demanded, didn't the Government nationalize the coal mines? Why didn't it take by forced loan the superfluous money owned by the rich? Why not, for that matter, take *all* income above £500 a year? The rich, said McKenna, would not submit to such treatment. Would they, said Sylvia, prefer to submit or give up the war? And Charlotte Drake, with tears of anger in her eyes, firmly supported her leader. "If a man made more than a certain amount of profit," she blazed, "I would have him hung!" As the deputation left, McKenna (who had introduced the Cat-and-Mouse Act and had been Home Secretary when Sylvia, after a month's hunger-and-thirst strike and forcible feeding, gained release from prison by stumbling up and down her cell for twenty-eight hours on end) hurried after Sylvia. "I must shake hands with you," he said, in the sporting upper-class manner that reduces everything to a game. "You are the pluckiest girl I ever knew." Sylvia refused to play: "Never would I surmount the barrier between the people and the governing classes while the masses starved on the other side."

Racing about her world of underdogs, Sylvia was forever turning on the oppressor, snarling and bristling. Unmarried mothers, war babies, sweated workers, soldiers' impoverished families—these did not exhaust her aggressive compassion. There were the children turned out of schools commandeered by the military and "released" for labor on farms—where twelve-year-old boys worked a forty-five-hour week for 3s. 6d.—or in factories. There were prostitutes, once more the scapegoats of an army attempt to control venereal disease. It was proposed to commit them to hospitals or reformatories and to bar them from public houses. It was poverty, said Sylvia, that pushed people into immorality. "The sweated pay of women in industry and Queen Mary's Workrooms," she charged, "will always bring recruits to the sad army of prostitutes." She decided to investigate in person charges (made, notably, by Sir Arthur Conan Doyle, the celebrated novelist) that innocent young soldiers were being "preyed upon and ruined by harpies." Walking along the notorious Waterloo Road one night, she saw nothing more objectionable than tipsiness and concluded, possibly as a result of personal experience, that "police constables were so harassed by charges of laxity in apprehending prostitutes that respectable women are in danger of arrest."

She detested the victimization of enemy aliens—and especially of their British wives, who were deprived of their nationality, rejected by employers, and insulted by petty relief clerks when their husbands lost their jobs and were interned. After the sinking of the *Lusitania* and the first air raids on London, German-owned shops were wrecked and looted, and the WSPU demanded, "Intern them all!" The *Dreadnought* reported the case of the wife of a German waiter, Wilhelm Sprick, who, because her husband could find no work, was driven to prostitution. Sprick was sentenced to six months' imprisonment for living on her immoral earnings. "But," wrote Sylvia, "the shame of such a story lies with a nation which offers women a choice between starvation and prostitution." A shop-girl who had shot at her defaulting lover was not punished because her lover's name happened to be Goldschmidt, and, as the judge remarked: "Such behaviour was just what could be expected from a man of his original nationality." Sylvia was not the one to let this go without comment. "Mr. Justice Avery," she wrote, "has created a precedent which enlightened women will expect to see followed in other cases. We cannot assent to the view that a woman has only a right to demand fair dealing from a German, and that an English-man should be allowed to betray and desert a woman and go scot-free." She was angered when the executive committee of the Woman's International League (which arose from The Hague Peace Congress), of which she was a member, excluded the British-born wives of aliens from membership, for fear of controversy.

There were so *many* injustices to put right. Why should South Wales miners who went on strike be punished under the Defence of the Realm Act, when employers, who, according to Runciman himself, were profiteering, went unpunished? It was the old story—one law for the rich, another for the poor. Down to Wales went Sylvia to speak and sell copies of the *Dreadnought,* writing articles for the next issue on the train on the way there and back. She told the men not to be dismayed by the suggestion that they were betraying their brothers in the trenches. On the contrary, they were defending their brothers' true interests, for the fight against capitalism would continue long after the squabble with the Central Powers had ended.

Sylvia met the miners' leaders at the Aberystwyth Café, a little tea shop in Tonypandy in the Rhondda Valley. Among them was A. J. Cook, hoarse from incessant oratory, who had been singled out for special attention by the WSPU (at one meeting in Cardiff, they collected money to send him to his "spiritual home," Germany). At Sheffield, Glasgow, and Leeds, in diametric opposition to the WSPU's industrial campaign, Sylvia urged shop stewards to stand firm against profiteering and conscription and to take strike action when necessary.

These strenuous forays, with their heady excitement and the warming comfort of being among birds of her own feather, were like a tonic to Sylvia, giving her new vision, new strength, and more money to go back to London and shoulder her self-imposed burden of multiple misery. She had taken the lead in forming a League of Rights for Soldiers' and Sailors' Wives and Relatives, which hoped to "spur the women to stand up for themselves and each other, instead of remaining inarticulate, to be dealt with by others as mere 'cases.'" This involved her and her small band of helpers in a tremendous amount of work. Hundreds of letters were written to the War Office and other military authorities on behalf of her "clients"—many of them, as time went on, disabled soldiers and soldiers' widows. Separation allowances were often cut off before a pension began, and the moneyless gap brought harassed women to the verge of despair and starvation. No pension was awarded unless the cause of death or disablement was certified as "wholly and directly due to war service." A woman whose husband was killed when he fell off the tail gate of an army truck did not qualify. When men's minds broke under the strain of trench warfare, officials probed into their past for "civilian" reasons for the breakdown. Other men were crippled with arthritis through exposure, and complicated quibbles followed about just *how* disabled a man was, how *permanently* crippled, where to place him on a sliding, actuarially calculated scale of suffering.

All this heartless administrative expertise sickened Sylvia, as did the Royal Warrant of February, 1916, which gave the military ample scope for prevarication. It stated that "a pension or gratuity for the dependants of a deceased soldier shall not be granted as a right. It shall not be granted or continued when the applicant is considered to be unworthy . . . or unless the soldier's services are such as to justify the grant. . . . our Army Council shall have power to vary or revoke any grant, and their decision in any case shall be final." The East London Federation battled on, typing dreary, semi-legalistic letters, interviewing distraught men and women to get the facts, presenting them in the most telling way, acting as people's advocate for bewildered illiterates. One young soldier of twenty-one who came for help had been shot through the lungs, and his speech was badly affected. He had been refused full pension, had had to find a job, and had collapsed after two months' work in a chemical factory. He turned down the offer of another job because he was too ill, and was punished by having his pension reduced. The Federation appealed to the local War Pensions Committee to raise his pension of 12s. 6d. to nearer the 25s. awarded for complete disablement. But it was objected that since the man had married since his discharge from the Army, his wife "could not expect to be kept." Yet, as Sylvia protested, the newspapers were at the time appealing to "patriotic" girls to marry "war-broken heroes."

She hurried to comfort the parents of a young Jewish conscript who had been shot for desertion, and she wrote to the War Office protesting against the brutality of executing a lad of eighteen who had endured eight months in the trenches and had recently been in the hospital suffering from wounds and severe shock. She published his letters home in the *Dreadnought* and made them into a telling pacifist pamphlet. After this sad chore, she organized yet another deputation, this time of old-age pensioners, a group of whom she escorted from the East End to the House of Commons. Though food prices were at least 65 per cent above prewar level, the 5s. old-age pension had not been raised, and some even advocated cutting or abolishing it as a wartime economy. The pension was reduced if income exceeded 10s. a week and was canceled altogether if it exceeded 12s. 6d. Some old people had been driven into the dreaded workhouse because they could not exist on their pension outside. One veteran of the Crimean War drowned himself on his way to the workhouse. Such were some of the facts and figures that Sylvia marshaled for the occasion. And a curious occasion it was. Some members of the deputation were in their eighties and nineties, tottering in the August heat, but determined to go through with their mission.

A sympathetic Member of Parliament gave them tea on the terrace, where they admired the view of the Thames, the spotlessly white tablecloths, the hovering waiters, the sight of real butter spread thick on thin slices of bread, the liberal supply of white sugar (in the East End, they had to queue for small amounts of black, unrefined stuff). They produced their budgets, carefully written out, and were heartened when Asquith promised that the Government would look into the pensioners' case. Later, it was announced that special grants up to 2s. 6d. a week would be made to "those suffering from special hardships," but there were long delays in putting even this meager concession into practice.

Sylvia grieved over the plight of schoolchildren. The war had created a shortage of teachers, a shortage even of flowers and plants for nature study. Somehow she found time to appeal to country dwellers to send contributions from their lanes and gardens, and she distributed their offerings to a dozen schools in her district. "Yet how small," she fretted, "are our efforts. Strive as we may in every direction, we can touch only the fringe of the need. Oh, for a great united effort for happiness, for culture, for plenty for all—not, oh not, for destruction and carnage!"

In the summer of 1916, the Federation (now rechristened the Workers' Suffrage Federation) organized a festival for children in Victoria Park. Sixty children were chosen to dance in specially made dresses of white muslin decorated with little garlands of flowers made of paper and wire. Sylvia was deeply moved by the sight of them in their cheap, improvised finery: "As I saw the long bedraggled line of them, hasting down the Old Ford Road, my eyes filled with tears. My dear little darlings, your poverty—oh your appalling poverty!" . . . "Where's my Mary? I want to put a flower in 'er bloody 'air!" cried one mother as she ran to catch up her daughter. Sylvia made allowances. "Harshly the ugly word smote me," she wrote, "but it fell from her unconsciously, as she ran in her happy excitement to bedeck her little one."

She yearned over the children the more intensely because she saw them as potential cannon fodder for the war that was reaching out to snatch and smudge everything that was good and wholesome and hopeful in life. When conscription came in April, 1916, she keyed up her peace drive to a higher pitch. "Often," she wrote, "as I rode home in the sad darkness in the crowded bus, I looked up at some young soldier lad who had given his seat to me or another woman and stood there steadying himself by the hanging strap, his slim wrist as yet unfit for heavy labour, his throat still childish-looking and smooth, his head drooping under the weight of his knapsack and greatcoat. Anguish almost unendurable would seize me, that this slender boy, here within touch, should be going out to the slaughter, and that all we adults should slavishly allow it."

She appealed to mothers not to allow Lloyd George to whittle away British liberties. "Conscription," she sweepingly forecast, "means immorality, venereal disease for youth, smaller allowances for dependants." It was bound to lead to industrial conscription, but of course the wealthy would find ways of evading the draft. Mothers should stand by their sons if they were conscientious objectors: "Refuse to allow them to be driven to fight against their will! Do not allow them to be persecuted as shirkers and cowards. It often requires the highest courage to refuse to fight at a time like this."

She traveled to Glasgow to take part in a demonstration demanding the repeal of the Conscription Act, joined the National Council Against Conscription, and marched in a deputation to the House of Commons. But in the main, she concentrated on reporting the absurdities and bullyings of local conscientious-objector tribunals and organizing a big procession from the East End to an anti-conscription rally in Trafalgar Square. The press called the rally "an act of open sedition" and invited patriots to break it up. This advance publicity brought big crowds. Some shouted, "Good old Sylvia!" Some women, weeping, ran out to shake hands with her and wish her luck. The meeting was soon ended by a rush of Anzac troops, who, hurling packets of red and yellow ocher (a tactic formerly used by suffragette "raiders"), drove the speakers from the plinth of Nelson's Column. Sylvia was comforted by kind words from the flower girls at Charing Cross, who, she noticed, shouted abuse at the soldiers and refused to sell them any flowers.

When Rose Rogers, a friend of hers, refused to register the birth of her baby in what she called a "conscript state" and was sentenced to a month's imprisonment in Holloway, Sylvia reported Mrs. Rogers' action prominently in the vain hope that thousands of mothers would follow her lead. She published a report by Dr. Ella Scarlett Synge (a sister of the Hon. Evelina Haverfield), who had visited prisoner-of-war camps in Germany and insisted that, contrary to the officially fostered belief, conditions were quite good. The *Dreadnought* also featured a report by Emily Hobhouse (who during the Boer War had exposed the shortcomings of British concentration camps) on conditions in Belgium; she claimed that atrocities and destruction had been greatly exaggerated. In yet another attempt to make jingo-blind eyes see, Sylvia eagerly printed a series of letters from the relatives of prisoners in Knockaloe Internment Camp on the Isle of Man.

"No one believes that prisoners-of-war in England are anything but luxuriously treated," wrote the English wife of a German school-master, "yet I hear from my husband that men in his compound have been driven by hunger to kill and eat a stray cat. My husband was struck on the head with a bayonet by a drunken soldier, and the Commandant refused to hold an enquiry." Sylvia also contrived to help conscientious objectors on the run. A woman in Bow, who had gone to prison as a suffragette, succeeded in hiding her husband and brother-in-law until the war was over. One local youth hid in Epping Forest, eating roots, berries, and the bark of trees, supplemented by food from relatives and friends handed over at night when he stole into the East End under cover of darkness.

While the Central Powers' Peace Note of December, 1916, was being considered, the Workers' Suffrage Federation launched yet another educational drive, distributing leaflets from door to door, chalking pavements with details of meetings. The reaction was stormy. Hecklers, mostly (insisted Sylvia) well-to-do middle-aged men from outside the district, broke up a meeting outside the gates of the East India Docks, where T. S. Attlee, brother of Major Clement (later Lord) Attlee, Sylvia, and other speakers were torn from the chair that served them as a platform. All were fined £2, and though Sylvia fully intended to go to prison, her fine was paid by a friend. Still she persisted with the peace campaign, in the teeth of mounting violence and local opposition. Some women, embittered by bereavement, interrupted with howls for revenge; young boys threw refuse from street-market stalls or paper soaked in the gutters (and sometimes in public urinals) and even hurled stones through the windows of the clinics.

4 §

Sylvia Sees Red

But Sylvia was back in Trafalgar Square on Christmas Eve, selling *Dreadnoughts* at a peace service held there. Australian troops laughed and jeered, but at least one bought a paper. "I think you're going to make me sad, girlie," he said. "I came 10,000 miles to do my bit, and I'd rather not be discouraged. But I'll read it." Other soldiers expressed sympathy, and not for the first time Sylvia noticed that men who had been in the trenches were much more amenable to reason than bloodthirsty civilians. Some soldiers wrote to her, some even sent donations. Funds were badly needed, for the Federation's peace campaign frightened off many wealthy subscribers (including Mrs. Nancy Astor) who had approved of Sylvia's doing good works for the poor, but could not stomach a double dose of pacifism and rabble-rousing.

But somehow the money came, and when it did not, Norah Smyth made some more "loans." Sylvia was, in any case, too busy worrying about the vote to worry about balancing the books. In 1915, she had forced herself to seek an interview with Lord Northcliffe, a pet aversion of hers, in an attempt to persuade him to give press backing for her demand for universal adult suffrage. In 1916, when, at her initiative, a conference of women's suffrage societies was held, the majority was against universal suffrage. But she did not accept this defeat as final. To counterbalance what she called "the Old Guard," she proposed that the Workers' Suffrage Federation should call another conference, this time inviting industrial and cooperative organizations to send representatives. For once, Norah Smyth put her foot down. It was a good idea, no doubt, but someone else must put it into practice. The WSF simply did not have the money to do it. So the conference took place under the auspices and on the premises of the Women's International League, where Sylvia had a friend in Mrs. Pethick-Lawrence.

Strong support for universal suffrage was gained, and there followed a string of public demonstrations in the provinces, with Sylvia and George Lansbury as the star speakers. After this, it was a question not so much of fighting the Government as of combating the imperious self-denial of Mrs. Fawcett and Mrs. Pankhurst, both of whom, rivals in patriotism, declared that the men, the voteless soldiers, must come first. The women could wait until the war was over. The infuriated Sylvia sent relays of workingwomen to lobby MP's about the franchise. They got short shrift, and it was galling to see a party of French munitionettes, brought over by the WSPU as a gesture of Allied goodwill, ushered into the inner citadel with much ceremony.

During 1917, the *Dreadnought* continued to expose ill-treatment of conscientious objectors—and of ordinary serving soldiers. From France came a letter reporting the frequency of No. 1 Field Punishment at certain military centers: "The soldiers are strapped onto the crucifix in the main road, regardless of the weather, and compelled to hang there in this degrading manner in full view of the French people, for two hours each day." In one of her immensely long, far-ranging editorials, Sylvia comments: "No intelligent person can still be under the delusion that the Central Powers alone caused the war, or that any of the Great Powers are fighting a war of liberation and freedom. People tell us that our agitation for peace can make little difference: but should it hasten the end of the War by a single day it will save thousands of precious lives. The people can end the war if they will. We address ourselves to them."

She lashed out at renewed attempts to regulate prostitution in the interests of the nation's health. It was up to the public to make such legislation impossible by changing and broadening its attitude. The unmarried mother was shunned by society, "but the underworld is organised to receive her. Shall the State take a hand in perfecting the underworld system, giving to the woman a certificate which permits her to sell her wares on the road to hell, and to the man a false sense of security which lulls his misgivings with the thought that this sort of thing is just a matter of business?" To Sylvia, progressive but puritan, the whole tone of capitalist society was corrupt, and she stressed the point with an article on "Being a Waitress"—long hours, wages of 7s. a week, a degrading dependence on tips, and the certainty, if you were at all pretty, of being treated like a potential tart.

In February, 1917, in a regular weekly feature called "Parliament As We See It," she reported, in her best republican manner, that "the King opened Parliament with the usual pomp and ceremony. The King's Speech was wholly confined to the War, containing the ominous statement that 'the accomplishment of the task to which I have set My hand will entail unsparing demands on My subjects.' The high and mighty possessive tone of it could hardly be outdone by the Kaiser. We notice that the King offers to make no sacrifice on his own account." Monarchy was an anachronism that must be swept away. So—when one realized that no one but a few amoral industrialists stood to gain by it—was war, and she mounted a new peace campaign. After one meeting in Hyde Park, Melvina Walker was arrested, fined £5, and enjoined for twelve months from repeating her offense. She had asked why Britain should go on spending £6 million a day on the war, while little children in the East End were dying of hunger. Why, Mrs. Walker further demanded before being parted from her soapbox, should mothers' sons be sent by the thousands to murder other mothers' sons?

The *Dreadnought's* most telling scoop was the publication of a letter from Second Lieutenant Siegried Sassoon, MC, DSO, of the Royal Welsh Fusiliers. Lieutenant Sassoon was a young writer of distinction who, despite his unimpeachably gallant war record and his impressive decorations, had become a bitter critic of the military mind. His statement was made, he said, "as an act of wilful defiance of military authority, because I believe that the War is being deliberately prolonged by those who have the power to end it. . . . It has become a war of aggression and conquest. . . . I can no longer be a party to prolong the sufferings of the troops for ends which I believe to be evil and unjust. . . . This statement may help to destroy the callous complacence with which the majority of those at home regard the continuance of agonies which they do not share and which they have not sufficient imagination to realise."

This issue of the paper, in which Sylvia urged her readers to paralyze militarism by whatever means they could devise and praised the righteous sabotage of conscientious objectors and mutinous troops, provoked the first of three police raids on the *Dreadnought* offices. The issue of October 6, 1917, which advocated a peace referendum among the troops on the various fronts, was destroyed and the type broken up, but its main contents appeared later in pamphlet form. One firm that had been criticized for sweating its workers successfully sued for libel, and Sylvia had to appeal for money to pay costs and damages.

Buoyant as ever, she bobbed up again in Parliament Square with pickets carrying banners inscribed with such slogans as "War Is Murder," "Stop This Capitalist's War," and "Bring Back Our Brothers." The Socialist half of the Pankhurst family was on the move with a vengeance. For at about the same time, in Australia, Sylvia's sister Adela and Jennie Baines (once one of the WSPU's most effective organizers) were arrested for leading processions of the Socialist Women's League to demand an equitable rationing system and the safeguarding of the health of women and children. The last of four marches on Parliament was dispersed by a police charge, and Adela and Mrs. Baines were sentenced to nine months in prison.

The Russian Revolution, which began its tortuous and dramatic course in March, 1917, put new hope and spirit into Sylvia and her battered band. At last the people had called their rulers' bluff and dared to guide their own destinies! It was bliss, suddenly, to be alive in such a dawn. Surely this would be the start of a chain reaction that would transform the world. With the full gush of her impetuous, frustrated idealism, Sylvia welcomed the tremendous event. When would the workers of Britain follow Russia's shining example? The Leeds Conference of Labor, Socialist and democratic organizations hailed the Revolution, and at the International Socialist Conference in Stockholm, Europe's renegade labor leaders showed some signs of redemption. But by now Sylvia was as distrustful of conference chatter and limp intellectuals as her mother and Christabel had always been. The Bolsheviks, to her mind, had the right idea. It was no use tinkering with an outworn system or parleying with it. You had to smash it and start afresh. Sylvia approved of the Bolsheviks as intensely as Mrs. Pankhurst disliked them. She was not afraid of the masses, for she had lived among them and considered herself one of them. Why this fetish about parliamentary democracy, which was only, in essence, a device for perpetuating middle- and upper-class rule? Didn't the fools realize that "under Socialism *we shall all be the proletariat?* There will be but one class. The tide of Socialism, bringing all power to the workers, is sweeping over Europe. Sidney Webb and those who hold the reins of power in the Labour Party shrink from it, trembling. Unconscious lackeys of the capitalist system, instinctively they fear that system's fall. Is there no spirit in their soul to answer the call of the Socialist fraternity? It seems not."

It was saddening that British workers—"jaded and dull-eyed from overtoil, and gulled by a capitalist press"—did not realize that they had the power to save the Russian workers' republic from military intervention and lay the foundations of a Golden Age of Socialism throughout the world. Because they lacked the Bolshevik spirit, British trade unionists still went to conferences "with minds befogged by the impression that they have some quarrel with the conscript workers who are fighting their own conscript sons." For the same reason, the poor women of Britain, standing patiently in food queues and paying their exorbitant rents, listened to Lloyd George's infamous lies about the need for more sacrifice and, pathetically, believed that the profiteers who really ran the country were out to save them from the working people of Germany, Austria, and Turkey. "Somehow or other," muttered Sylvia, "the British Labour movement must be aroused to demand the Bolshevik Peace Terms and the Bolshevik way of dealing with the world."

She cried out against the attempt, in April, 1918, to introduce conscription in Ireland, and in October, with the war obviously dying, castigated Czechoslovakians, Hungarians, and other misguided nationalists who insisted on battling on for their right to self-rule. The thought of Europe being littered with *more* tiresome little nations was ridiculous. To Sylvia, the small nations so vehemently championed by Mrs. Pankhurst and Christabel were a dangerous bore. Surely the aim must be to minimize this nationalist nonsense? In any case, it was easy for Britain to show sympathy for the Balkan countries. When her own interests were involved, it was a different story: "British soldiers who are forced to fight for Czech independence may also be forced to fight *against* Irish or Indian independence." Suppose the American Negroes or Indians were to set up a claim like that of the Czechoslovakians? How much sympathy would they get?

Speaking at Creswell in Derbyshire at the invitation of the local Labour Party, she condemned Allied intervention in Russia and advocated self-government for India. Other topics included the disgraceful inequality of food rationing in Britain, the urgent need to bring in a system of child allowances, the dangers of secret diplomacy, and the inevitability of capitalist clashes over oil supplies. Why, she asked, did people see the Bolsheviks as bogeymen? They had been harassed and provoked by Allied military intervention, but were, in essence, nothing more sinister than Russia's majority Socialist Party. She spoke of the need for a massive nationalization of industry in Britain, and when asked if she would compensate the expropriated owners, she replied: "No, I would not. I would offer them work at a decent wage. What more do they want?" For this speech, she was fined £50 and costs, with the alternative of three months' imprisonment. The fine was paid by the Derbyshire miners, who had been hugely entertained by Sylvia's hard-hitting oratory.

So she remained at liberty to relish the bus girls' strike for equal pay, which was supported by male public-transport workers, and forced the Government to set up a Cabinet committee to inquire into the whole question of women in industry. Even more heartening was the strike of London's police force for better pay. "Spirit of Petrograd," whooped Sylvia in the *Dreadnought*, "the London police on strike! After that, anything may happen! You belong to the working class army now, policemen. You have gained class-consciousness. Army officers [this was in September, 1918] look on grimly as you march. 'The Tommies will be striking next,' say some. Who knows? Who can foresee what will happen in this cataclysmic, revolutionary time?"

Dancing around what seemed, to her sanguine eyes, the grand and final bonfire of the rubbish of the *ancien régime*, it was hard for her to focus on the parochial politics of the vote. "Some women," she brought herself to say, "have been given the vote, for the new measure enfranchises 6 million out of a total of more than 13 million, and by its University and business franchise the Act still upholds the old class prejudices, the old checks and balances designed to prevent the will of the majority, who are the workers, from being registered without handicap."

Her best energies went into organizing a series of Hands Off Russia protest meetings and into demanding the repeal of the Defence of the Realm Act and the immediate release of political prisoners and conscientious objectors. They, her comrades, would be needed in the *real* war for freedom and social justice that was only just beginning. New and huger horizons beckoned her, and it was her job now to make not only her East Enders but all the workers of Britain stand up straight and see them and march toward them with pride and determination. For a start, she brought out a special edition of the *Dreadnought* devoted to a survey of Soviet Russia, her land of hope and potential glory, her outsized underdog surrounded by yelping capitalist curs. Like Mrs. Pankhurst and Christabel,

Sylvia had come a long, long way since the Manchester days. She had carved out a kingdom for herself in London. Now she wanted to be a citizen of the world.

Yet even in the intoxication of the end of 1918, in the heat of her ecstatic honeymoon with communism, she had misgivings. "It is the open, progressive mind," she wrote, "the tender heart, the fearless, comradely spirit which are needed and are so difficult, so infinitely difficult, for poor faulty human beings to attain."

War and Peace

The Lady in the Black Mantilla

Just as concerned as Sylvia Pankhurst with the "innocent" victims of war—the women and children—was the venerable but combative Charlotte French Despard. Seventy years old in 1914, she had for nearly twenty-five years been working among the poor of South London. The second of six daughters (her father, Commander John Tracy William French, RN, was of Irish descent, her mother Scottish), she had a strenuous childhood. Both parents died when she was young, and she helped to bring up the other children, including the only boy, John (later Field Marshal Sir John French, Commander of the British Expeditionary Force in France).

During the twenty years of her marriage to Maximilian Despard, there was little to indicate that she would become one of the most revered leaders of the movement for women's emancipation and a Socialist and pacifist of deep courage and conviction. Her husband's business took him abroad frequently, and she traveled with him. She visited India three times and wrote a successful romance, *The Rajah's Heir*, under a pen name. She also visited America, Australia, and Egypt. Her husband, long an invalid, died in 1890 on the voyage back to England from Tenerife and was buried at sea.

After his death, Mrs. Despard became a virtual recluse. She had no children, but found consolation in theosophy and planchette. Persuaded to take up social work, she served as a Poor Law Guardian—one of the first women to do so—but after a year launched out on her own, founding a club for workingmen and boys (and later a child-welfare center) in Battersea.

A woman of considerable wit and natural authority, her popularity and her fame were enhanced by a superbly striking physical presence. Tall and slightly built, her features combined Tennysonian strength with a kind of Shelleyan ethereality—indeed, Shelley was her favorite author, and his poetic republicanism and romantic rebellion against convention had first fired her to break with family traditions. Her long, startlingly pale face gave her the look of a benevolent witch, and her brilliantly white hair was always surmounted by a black-lace mantilla. A long, flowing, priestly black gown and slender feet shod in sandals completed an unusual and arresting exterior.

Mrs. Despard was something of a dress reformer, believing that women must free themselves from the absurd and sometimes crippling embellishments forced upon them by Victorian and Edwardian fashion. From her welfare centers, both before and during the war, she distributed what she called "hygienic" clothes, made from designs inspired and approved by herself. She was also a strict vegetarian. In her view, food reform and dress reform were just as important for female (and male) emancipation and right thinking as getting or having the vote. How could people be said to have any real dignity when they were slaves to idiotic fashions or depended upon the wholesale slaughter of innocent animals for their food?

When Mrs. Despard joined the WSPU in 1906, she was already a national figure. But it was not long before she left to form her own militant organization, the Women's Freedom League. Though her admiration for Mrs. Pankhurst and Christabel was still strong, she could not accept the necessity for their autocratic management of the WSPU and attempted to run the Freedom League on more democratic lines. She did not approve of acts of destruction and set an example of passive resistance by refusing to pay income tax or fill in census forms. For all her scrupulous nonviolence, Mrs. Despard was a wholehearted fighter. She toured Britain in a caravan to put the women's case to audiences of all degrees. She went to prison for the second time for holding a meeting of protest against Mrs. Pankhurst's sentence at the Old Bailey trial of 1913.

The war brought her into close contact with Sylvia Pankhurst, for whom, though sometimes dismayed by the dervish disarray of her emotions, she felt affection and respect. When war came, Mrs.

Despard promptly declared herself a pacifist, "in the sense that all women should be pacifists. Their fight should not be with weapons of war, but with spiritual darkness in high places. Women," she claimed, "could stop war if they chose." She joined Sylvia in founding the League of Rights for Soldiers' and Sailors' Wives and Relations and spoke with her at peace meetings. She never quailed before rowdies, nor did she hesitate to rebuke them. Surrounded in Victoria Park at Easter, 1917, by shouts of, "We don't *want* German peace terms! We want *our* terms!" she answered: "You will have neither their nor your own terms. You will have *God's* terms." For a moment there was a puzzled silence, then shouts of, "You'd better go before you get hurt!" Standing there like some proud, invulnerable old ghost (a journalist wrote that she seemed to belong to an age of samplers, embroidery, and wax fruits, to have strayed from the pages of *Cranford*), she cried: "I am not afraid of Englishmen. None of you will hurt me."

She went in the deputation with Sylvia and George Lansbury to protest to McKenna about registration and increasing regimentation of the people. In the Freedom League magazine, *The Vote*, which she edited, she pleaded for a sense of proportion and warned her readers to resist the insidious effects of war fever: "We know that there is a force in the long run more potent than armies or navies. It is spiritual. It manifests itself in the love which binds life to life. Actuated by this, we shall have no bitterness in our national feeling." To realize the sufferings of enemy aliens, to do everything possible to help them, was particularly the duty of women suffragists, who had received such generous hospitality from women abroad. "Never," wrote Mrs. Despard, "can those present at Budapest Women's Suffrage Congress last year forget the reception accorded them." Upon women and upon the workers of both sexes rested a tremendous responsibility: "If these combine, if they hold fast to the truth and refuse to hate, it will be in their power, perhaps in the near future, to stop war." Trying to look on the bright side, she foresaw the creation of a European Federation or, better, a Federation of the World. The Great War was itself the result of social injustice and blindness in every combatant nation. What chance was there of peace between nations when there was constant friction between creeds and classes? "We possess," she lamented, "what is called a civilisation. To some—the minority—it is sweet. To the great majority it is bitter."

She was grieved that her pacifist stand put a barrier between her and her brother, Sir John French, and she did not doubt the sincerity of his views or those of her sister, Catherine Harley. Mrs. Harley, a colonel's widow, and former member of the executive committee of the NUWSS, was Administrator of a Scottish Women's Hospital in France. Later, she served with the French Expeditionary Force at Salonika (where she was decorated with the Croix de Guerre by General Sarrail) and was killed by shrapnel in March, 1917, while running an ambulance unit for refugee Serbs.

Mrs. Despard did not waste energy in recriminations or dogmatic pacifist controversy, as Sylvia Pankhurst was apt to do, but concentrated on expanding the network of social services that, for some twenty-five years, she had been patiently constructing. The WFL's Women's Suffrage National Aid Corps worked, like Sylvia's Federation, to protect working-class families from the full, cruel impact of war. But having more money, more helpers, and wider experience, it was able to accomplish more. Cheap restaurants—in the provinces as well as in London—served vegetarian meals for as little as $\frac{1}{2}d$. Cheap children's clothing, made in the Corps' own workrooms, was distributed in London, Edinburgh, and Glasgow, a small toy factory was opened in the East End of London, and parcels were sent to British prisoners of war in Germany.

When a Freedom Leaguer converted her house in Bromley, near London, into a fifty-bed hospital for women and children (many of whom were turned out of ordinary hospitals to make way for sick or wounded troops), Mrs. Despard raised the money to run it. Her League opened milk depots, mother-and-child clinics, and—a new departure this—a Children's Guest House, which took in up to twenty-five children for as long as three months while their mothers were recovering from childbirth or suffering from illness or exhaustion.

Another new wartime venture was the opening of the Despard Arms, on Hampstead Road (where Mrs. Pankhurst had lived when she came to London with her family in her presuffragette days). The Despard Arms was open from ten in the morning to ten at night, serving food and nonalcoholic drinks to men and women and providing entertainment, clubrooms, some residential accommodations, and bathrooms for public use. Mrs. Despard hoped that it might be the first of many such centers, and it did succeed remarkably in being what she had wanted it to be—"a public house which shall take away the reproach of the name."

The WFL continued to press for the vote. It was, said Mrs. Despard, more than ever necessary for women to stand together and insist on their rights: "So long as materialism—physical force—is the order of the day, so long as the spiritual considerations which women and honest workers of both sexes could bring to the government of the nations are absent, we shall have these epidemics of armed strife, this war hysteria. We must keep our own flag flying and emphasise our demand to have a voice in decisions." Freedom League speakers mounted a suffrage campaign in many of the principal towns in England and Wales, and its members were exhorted in *The Vote* to "Wear your Badge! Never go without it! Our best service for the country is still our demand for citizen rights and duties." When Nina Boyle, former head of the League's Political and Militant Department, left for relief service with Mrs. Harley's unit in Serbia, she reported that on the voyage out, she had "founded a Maritime League for Woman Suffrage," with the captain and first officer as President and Vice-President, respectively. That, commented Mrs. Despard in *The Vote*, was the spirit. One must be a missionary always and everywhere. A WFL meeting at Caxton Hall in October, 1916, passed a resolution demanding that the Government should give immediate attention to the enfranchisement of women on the same terms as men, so that women might be on the voters' register at the next General Election.

The League would not cooperate with the authorities at the expense of its principles. Nina Boyle formed a corps of women police volunteers, but some of its members, following instructions from the League's executive committee, refused to carry out the unpleasant inquisitions demanded by an attempt to renew the "regulated vice" policy of the discredited Contagious Diseases Acts. The rest joined Miss Damer Dawson's women police.

The League organized an especially vigorous protest against the Criminal Law Amendment Bill, which empowered magistrates to send what they called "thoughtless young girls" (considered to be potential prostitutes) to reformatories until they were nineteen and to imprison women suspected of infecting soldiers with venereal disease. At an emergency Freedom League rally, a battery of pre-war suffrage stars fired some telling shots. "If a girl is regarded as guilty of crime," argued Esther Roper, who, as Secretary of the North of England Women's Suffrage Society, had first interested both Christabel and Sylvia Pankhurst in The Cause, "the blame falls on the society in which she lives. Gaiety, joy, harmless fun, have been taken out of her life, she spends her days working long hours in factories: is she to spend her evenings in mean and crowded homes, because the streets are desperately dangerous? The remedy is to make the streets safe. Build clubs and gymnasia for the young-sters, teach them singing, dancing, acting and art if you like, but do not crush the exuberance of life out of them."

Factory girls, to the intense resentment of themselves and their parents, were being followed by the police because they made a noise in the streets, George Lansbury complained at the same meet-ing. The police, he said, should not have such powers given to them even if they were angels—which they were not; and it was objec-tionable that only working-class girls were subjected to such humili-ating surveillance. Maude Royden stated that a girl need not be "heedless and flighty" to come under suspicion. She need only be a girl: "If a girl under eighteen is on the streets anywhere she is at the mercy of any man she meets. He has only to say that she has offended, and to give her in charge to a policeman, and conviction may follow. The policeman need not have witnessed the offence, nor need the accuser appear in court. This could be accurately described as a Bill for the Better Creation of Prostitutes, and it is astonishing to learn that some rescue workers are supporting it. One would have thought that such work as theirs would have convinced them that compulsory salvation was a contradiction in terms."

Week after week *The Vote* spotlighted the absurdities and injus-tices of the bill and, when it was withdrawn, went on to attack Clause 40D of the Defence of the Realm Act, which took its place. Cases were cited of women accused, examined, and found not to be infected; and, as Mrs. Despard pointed out, even if they were in-fected, the disease might well have been passed on by a soldier. She demanded the severest penalty for criminal libel if an accused woman was found to be free of disease, and she stressed that the "vice squads" had little success in deterring habitual prostitutes. At Guildford Police Court, a Miss Emily Blue (the sister of Violet Blue, who had twice been sentenced under Clause 40D) was charged with infecting a Canadian soldier and living an immoral life for two years; she was sentenced to three months' hard labor. "Penal measures," sniped the lady in the black mantilla, "have been singularly ineffective in reforming the Blue family."

Could women be blamed for thinking that "of all the cynical, one-sided laws there have ever been, this is the worst"? How much longer would there be one moral law for men, another for women? Mrs. Despard fastened on the case of Rosa Parnell, a girl clerk who, cold-shouldered by her relatives, frozen out by institutions, and deserted by her soldier seducer, drowned her illegitimate baby in a Birmingham canal after months of agony and rejection—and was sentenced to nine months' hard labor. This, blazed Mrs. Despard, was a monstrous perversion of justice. "Society," she wrote, "told this girl with all the emphasis in its power that it did not want her baby. In ridding it of the encumbrance, she followed its teaching. The crime committed by the girl against society is in no way comparable with society's crime against her. Rosa Parnell has already had three months in prison, and we demand her immediate release."

With Sylvia, she protested against regimentation in wartime industry, with its system of punitive tribunals and imprisonment for "restless workers." Was this the way to get the best results from labor? Forced service such as this could not be called national. It was "the service of slaves." The Government's social policy seemed to her to be one of drift. Why had no proper and equitable system of food rationing been worked out? Were the people supposed to be content with hurried improvisations such as the "meatless days" suggested by Hudson Kearley, Lord Devonport—"the millionaire grocer who," said Mrs. Despard darkly, "by some strange trick of destiny finds himself at the head of the Food Department"? Food for the nation's babies and children must be safeguarded. Local authorities should commandeer what was needed and "stop the wicked profiteering in life values that is perpetually going on."

Government legislation, she complained, was panic-driven and repressive. *The Nation,* a periodical that made similar criticisms, had, by order of the Army Council, been prevented from circulating overseas. The living spirit was gradually being penned in an iron cage of regulations. Britons were in danger of becoming slaves: "If we are to descend into that gulf, what will it matter whether we win the war or not? The indomitable soul, through which alone freedom is made possible, will have gone out from us." One heard much fine talk about the good, constructive things that would be done after the war. But *now* was the time for constructive thought and action —now, before the habit of destruction and postponement hardened beyond hope. Criticism was branded as treachery, yet it was often rooted in a deep love for one's country. "Ours," wrote Mrs. Despard, is the true patriotism. A big Britain—what is that to us? What is it to the myriads whose lives are spent in close factories and sunless courts? Our aim is to keep our country great because free—the home of valiant, clean-souled men and women who are strangers to the vile thing, fear, and who will elect men and women wise enough and strong enough to resist pressure, even if it were with an army behind it."

For her, as for Sylvia Pankhurst, the Russian Revolution, the lifting of the Tsarist incubus, appeared as a new dawn of hope for human progress the world over. In June, 1917, she was one of more than a thousand delegates, representing most shades of Socialist and progressive opinion, who traveled to Leeds to attend what was billed as "The great Labour Socialist and Democratic Convention to hail the Russian Revolution and to organise the British Democracy to follow Russia." The Leeds municipal authorities did their best to prevent the convention by denying the use of a large hall; open-air demonstrations were forbidden, and many hotels and lodging houses refused accommodation to delegates, who were hissed and booed and jostled on their way from the railway station to the Coliseum Picture Palace.

Ramsay MacDonald, in his opening speech, announced, amid thundering cheers, that labor had resumed the initiative it had surrendered to the governing classes on the outbreak of war, that the Russian Revolution had hastened the return of sanity. A Mr. Fred Shaw of Huddersfield exulted: "Let us go cheerfully forward. If we laugh at State coercion the collapse of the capitalist State will follow." Ernest Bevin (who twenty-eight years later became Brit-

ain's Foreign Secretary), representing the dockers of Bristol, said
that he too was in favor of ending the war, but thought it naïve to
assume that Germany was. The leader of the Seaman's Union—
which a few weeks later prevented MacDonald from boarding the
ship that took Mrs. Pankhurst on the first stage of her journey to
Petrograd—wanted to know who would indemnify the widows and
children of men drowned when their ships were sunk by German U-
boats. He was told that profiteering British shipowners should look
after them. Emmanuel Shinwell, Labour War Minister after 1945,
but in 1917 chairman of the Glasgow Trades Council and one of the
fieriest sparks on "Red Clydeside," said that British shipowners, not
German sailors, were the worst enemies of British seamen, and the
sentiment was well received.

Politically a fire of straw, the convention provided a notable
rallying point for the established Socialist stars of the women's
movement. Sixty-six-year-old Dora Montefiore, the heroine of the
1906 "Siege of Hammersmith," who had marched between Clara
Zetkin and Rosa Luxemburg at the Basle Peace Congress of 1912
and was now Secretary of the Workers' Anti-Militarist Committee
(pledged to defeat "the great military conspiracy for the further en-
slavement of the workers of Great Britain") seconded MacDonald's
resolution hailing the Soviets. Imperialism, she declared, had been
shaken to its base. The people of Britain must now follow suit. They
must "dig their trenches and consolidate themselves in order to abolish wage slavery and bring in the co-operative commonwealth."

Mary Macarthur was on the platform with her husband, Will
Anderson. Ethel Snowden, the wife of Philip Snowden, MP, and a
well-known prewar stalwart of the NUWSS, demanded that women
be represented on the thirteen Workers' and Soldiers' Councils that
the convention, imitating Russia, proposed to set up to make an immediate "people's peace." Sylvia Pankhurst, there with a group of
Jews from the East End of London to protest against an attempt to
impose conscription on aliens in Britain, demanded that there be a
fair proportion of workingwomen on the Councils.

But the convention's most rousing reception was reserved for
Mrs. Despard when, backed by Bertrand Russell and Mrs. Pethick-
Lawrence, she rose—strikingly, even hieratically, somber in her
black clothes against a gathering vivid with red ties, red flags, and

red blouses—to second the third resolution. This called upon the Government to "place itself in accord with the democracy of Russia by proclaiming its adherence to and determination to carry into immediate effect a charter of liberties establishing complete political rights for all men and women, unrestricted freedom of the press, freedom of speech, a general amnesty for all political and religious prisoners, full rights of industrial and political association, and the release of labour from all forms of compulsion and restraint."

As the auditorium exploded with applause, Mrs. Despard, supreme representative of the pacifist wing of suffragism, knew a personal triumph comparable with that enjoyed by Mrs. Pankhurst when, at the end of the great Women's War Service Procession of July, 1915, she stood at the side of Lloyd George reviewing her troops, the officially acknowledged symbol of patriotic British womanhood.

Mrs. Despard was the only woman on the provisional committee elected to put the convention's resolutions into effect. It was unequal to the task. Removed from the eager, wishful warmth of the Coliseum, the Workers' Councils fast dissolved in impotent confusion. But Mrs. Despard was soon in the thick of a new movement that sprang directly from a concern expressed at Leeds. Mrs. Snowden had urged there that at least one suitably oriented woman be sent to Petrograd to "deal with Mrs. Pankhurst's cruelly untrue suggestion that the working women of Britain are in favour of a continuance of the war to a brute force victory."

When this proved impossible and when the impervious Mrs. Pankhurst sailed on her keep-Russia-in-the-war mission, a full-scale Women's Peace Crusade was launched, with Mrs. Despard and Mrs. Snowden on the committee. An explanatory telegram was sent to the provisional government in Petrograd and to Lloyd George in Whitehall. Honorary Secretary and a prime mover in the Peace Crusade was Helen Crawfurd of Glasgow, a former suffragette and left-wing Socialist, who, in a letter to the *Labour Leader*, organ of the Independent Labour Party, agitated: "Does Mrs. Pankhurst speak for us? Has her voice ever been raised since this war started on behalf of the workers of this country against the profiteers or exploiters who have taken advantage of the great crisis to rob and plunder the people? The people of Russia have appealed to the common people of

every country to let their voice be heard demanding peace without
annexations and indemnities. They have called to us to subdue our
imperialists as they have vanquished theirs. Shall we turn a deaf ear
to their appeal and allow Mrs. Pankhurst to go forward breathing
the spirit of hatred and revenge in the name of British women?"

Launched in Glasgow on June 10 and continued right up to the
Armistice, the Crusade, despite a barrage of press vilification and
frequent attempts (sometimes led by clergymen) to break up its
meetings, grew rapidly—in numbers if not in political influence.
Money flowed in from women who had lost husbands and sons in
the war. More than a hundred branches were formed. "Advance
women!" Mrs. Crawfurd encouraged. "Great is your power! Who
knows but perhaps the mice will nibble through the ropes that bind
the lion and set him free!" Thousands of Women's Peace Crusade
buttons, with a design in white and blue representing the Angel of
Peace protecting children, were sold. Tens of thousands of leaflets
were distributed. Children's Peace Processions, carrying banners inscribed with such slogans as "I Want My Daddy," were organized.
From London, peace picketer Sylvia Pankhurst wrote for funds "to
buy new banners to replace those captured by the enemy or destroyed by the rain." Crusaders heckled Mrs. Pankhurst when she
spoke at a war-aims meeting and eagerly preached the gospel of a
negotiated peace.

Mrs. Despard not only wrote the Crusade's best-selling leaflet,
An Appeal to Women, but gave her services as a full-time speaker.
Everywhere she drew enormous audiences, orating in a drenching
drizzle in Glasgow, where Christabel Pankhurst made a keep-the-
wheels-of-industry-turning appeal, and working her way south
through Lancashire, Yorkshire, and the Midlands. Still the war
ground on, still the casualties mounted, still more widows and griev-
ing mothers sent their mites to the Crusade. But Mrs. Despard felt
that if its efforts could shorten the war by even a few hours, it meant
so much death and sorrow the less.

At least there were visible signs of a breakthrough on the
suffrage front. When the first installment of the vote for women
came in February, 1918, Mrs. Despard immediately pressed for
membership of Parliament to be opened to women. The presence of
women MP's would be the best guarantee that the flow of social

legislation would hasten and broaden. "The sooner women are on the floor of the House of Commons to insure that there shall be a single standard of morality," she wrote, "the better it will be for the future of our country and of our race."

Others thought differently. Admiral of the Fleet Sir Hedworth Meux, MP, growled: "I do not think the House a fit and proper place for a respectable woman to sit in. We meet at 3 o'clock, or ought to meet at 3 o'clock, for prayers, and we go on till 11 or 12 at night. Is that a thing for a woman to do? No woman is fit by her physical organisation to strand the strain of Parliament."

Despite such die-hard opposition, the Commons, in October, 1918, voted overwhelmingly (274 votes to 25) to allow women MP's. The prospect was exhilarating. To cap it all, Mrs. Despard was elected President of the London Vegetarian Society—the first woman to be so honored. The omens seemed good for the fight that lay ahead.

2 &

The Stateswomen

However else they differed, Christabel and Sylvia Pankhurst, Emmeline Pankhurst and Charlotte Despard shared a common need for plenty of personal scope. In peace or in war, they had to make their contribution in their own idiosyncratic way. They had to run their own show. Though they were sometimes asked to be on committees, they found the language of committees flavorless, their judicial tempo intolerable. Others found it possible to work in a team. These were the committeewomen, the constitutionalists, the diplomats of the feminist movement. The impeccable Mrs. Fawcett was their fount and model, and their personalities, gentler perhaps but nonetheless strong, flowered better in congregation.

Maude Royden, who became a celebrated Nonconformist minister, was one of these. From the turn of the century, she had lived in a curious *ménage à trois* with the Rev. Hudson Shaw, an Anglican clergyman, and his gifted but mentally unstable wife, Effie. With Hudson Shaw, a tireless university extension lecturer, she shared a crusade to bring higher education to the masses. Because of Effie's illness and extreme shyness, Maude Royden became a kind of hostess-*cum*-honorary curate to Hudson Shaw, whom she deeply but platonically loved. Despite his disapproval, she became a convinced and eloquent feminist and an ardent pacifist (he took pride in being a military chaplain, but their different interpretations of the duties of a Christian in wartime never shook their personal relationship).

In a pamphlet written in 1915 for the Fellowship of Reconciliation, a Christian pacifist group that she founded, this gentle but passionate creature, a cripple from birth but possessed of a mind and a prose style both vigorous and finely proportioned, brilliantly stated the dilemma with which the Great War faced people of goodwill, to whom violence was ugly and repulsive. War, she argued, was evil to be sure, but it *was* a great adventure in which people could find the exhilaration of risking their all. She, like many Christians, was certain that the pursuit of peace, the determination to overcome evil with good, was the greatest adventure. The difficulty was how to get this truth across, like a clarion call, to ordinary people who longed for excitement.

"We peace people," she lamented, "have made of peace a dull, drab, sordid, selfish thing. We have made it that ambiguous, dreary thing—*neutrality*. But peace is the great adventure, the glorious romance. And only when the world conceives it so will the world be drawn after it again." Why were the professional peacemongers so wordy, so ineffective, so *unmobilized?* Why had they not flung themselves, if need be, in front of troop trains? Why had they not—even a few hundred of them—been willing to follow the call of Lucy Thoumaian? War could never create true peace, nor mass murder fellowship. But what sort of appeal had the fellowship of pacifists who risked nothing when their ideals were put to the test?

The war was equally repugnant to Emmeline Pethick-Lawrence, who, with her husband, had shrunk from the wilder phase of WSPU militancy in 1912. A member of a prosperous middle-class family in the West Country, she had been influenced by the Socialist ideals of William Morris and Edward Carpenter. She had longed to bring the young people of the big cities' slums into touch with nature, the soil, and give them a sense of their cultural heritage. She had worked in girls' clubs in London before joining the WSPU and helped in the revival of the Old English Folk Song and Dance Movement launched by Cecil Sharp and her friend Mary Neal. She brought a touch of color and pageantry to the harsh sensationalism of the Pankhursts, did more than anyone to project a romanticized image of the cocksure Christabel as the symbol of female youth resurgent, and even took her and the Kenney sisters to Italy on recuperative, mind-broadening holidays. No wealthy dilettante, she had forced herself, though tormented by claustrophobia, to endure several imprisonments and even to undergo forcible feeding.

When she and her husband parted company with the Pankhursts, it seemed to many a brutal expulsion. As Joint Treasurers (Mrs. Pethick-Lawrence was called "the most persuasive beggar in London"), they had raised more than £100,000 for the WSPU and had provided most of the administrative expertise that had built up the Union to a peak of efficiency. Under their painstaking management, in fact, it grew until it had the largest headquarters of any political organization in London. Frederick Pethick-Lawrence, the wealthy Old Etonian "godfather" of the WSPU, had stood bail for nearly a thousand arrested suffragettes and had given them the benefit of his legal knowledge (he was a qualified barrister) in the conduct of their cases before the magistrates. He had refused to pay the costs of the prosecution in the famous Old Bailey trial of 1913, when he and his wife and Mrs. Pankhurst were convicted of conspiracy, and had been declared bankrupt. He had been imprisoned, forcibly fed—and expelled from his club. Now it seemed that the WSPU had bitten the hand that had cared for it at great personal and financial cost.

The Pethick-Lawrences could not agree with Christabel's policy of intensified guerrilla-type warfare. To them it was a psychological mistake, likely to alienate public sympathy. But the Pankhursts stood firm, and the Pethick-Lawrences agreed to go. There were no public recriminations—the "Panks" and the "Peths" still had a common enemy. Years later, Lord Pethick-Lawrence (as he became) wrote: "Mrs. Pankhurst and Christabel shared with one another and with Sylvia, the younger daughter, an absolute refusal to be deflected by criticism or appeal one hair's breadth from the course which they had determined to pursue. To that extent they were insensitive to ordinary human considerations. Many men and women who have made history have been cast in a similar mould. They seem to be used by destiny for some special purpose. . . . They cannot be judged by ordinary standards . . . and those that run up against them must not complain of the treatment they receive."

In any case, the Great War would have split their alliance, for the Pethick-Lawrences continued to deplore violence as a solution. In August, 1914, Mrs. Pethick-Lawrence joined a committee of the Women's Emergency Corps, of which Lena Ashwell was a chief promoter, but, ill at ease among the proliferating uniforms and facile patriotism, she eagerly responded to a request from Rosika Schwimmer, a leading member of the International Suffrage Alliance, for help in reaching the United States to persuade American women to take a lead in pleading for peace by negotiation.

In October, she spoke at a mass meeting in the Carnegie Hall, New York (where, in the same month, Christabel spoke with such a different emphasis). The meeting inaugurated a new and highly successful suffrage drive throughout America. Mrs. Pethick-Lawrence spoke of the need for suffragists to work for the idea of a negotiated peace, and she later teamed up with Rosika Schwimmer in Chicago, where she met Jane Addams, a pioneer social worker of awesome integrity and determination, at her famous settlement, Hull House. A pacifist of long standing (and, until America entered the war in 1917, revered as "America's First Lady"), Jane Addams accepted the presidency of the newly formed Women's Peace Party. While the organization was holding a national conference in Washington, Dr. Aletta Jacobs, head of the Dutch Committee of the International Women's Suffrage Alliance, suggested an International Women's Peace Congress at The Hague, to include representatives of belligerent and nonbelligerent countries.

The idea was rapturously welcomed. In February, 1915, a small international committee, including four British women (Chrystal Macmillan, a member of the executive committee of the NUWSS; Theodora Wilson, a keen suffragist, best known as a writer of children's stories; Kathleen Courtney, a former Honorary Secretary of the NUWSS; and Catherine Marshall, formerly Parliamentary Secretary of the NUWSS), met at Amsterdam to draft a series of resolutions for the Congress, which opened at the end of April. Early in April, the SS *Noordam* sailed from New York with some fifty representatives of the American Women's Peace Party, and Rosika Schwimmer and Mrs. Pethick-Lawrence were aboard. During a tumultuous send-off, the mayor of New York presented them with a specially designed flag (PEACE was worked in white letters on a blue background), which the captain hoisted as the ship left harbor.

Britain was less enthusiastic about the Congress, condemned as tantamount to treason by both Mrs. Pankhurst and Mrs. Fawcett, and 180 British representatives were refused transport at the last moment for the conceivably genuine reason that the submarine menace in the North Sea was too great (the *Noordam* was held up for four days off Deal, but finally went on its way). Olive Schreiner, who was among the 180 frustrated women, fired a sonorous telegram: "The time," she said, "has now come for the great step across the narrow boundaries of nation and race to a larger and wider human fellowship." But it was left to Mrs. Pethick-Lawrence and Kathleen Courtney (who had been appointed English interpreter for the Congress) and Chrystal Macmillan (Chairman of the Resolutions Committee and English Secretary) to keep the British flag flying at The Hague.

The expenses of the Congress were shared by British, Dutch, and German women. Fifteen hundred delegates represented Austria, Belgium, Canada, Denmark, Germany, Britain, Hungary, Italy, the Netherlands, Norway, Sweden, and the United States. It was a unique occasion—the first time that the women of the world had met together to protest against the evils of war. Some delegates wanted a stop-the-war resolution, but the majority felt that this was "unrealistic" (one can almost hear Slyvia Pankhurst and Olive Schreiner snorting) and that resolutions about peace must make a serious effort to outline its terms.

Kathleen Courtney moved a resolution urging women to work with all their might for political enfranchisement so that they could make their will effective in the world. Mrs. Pethick-Lawrence, scrupulously pacifist (and watched by her devoted husband, who had traveled to New York to escort her), moved an amendment to the wording of a resolution advocating pressure on any country that resorted to war without referring its case to arbitration. "This," she said, "has already given rise to misunderstanding in the press, and we are challenged that if we advocate pressure we are advocating the use of force. I therefore think that in order to make quite clear our real meaning it would be well to define the pressure we wish as 'moral, social and economic pressure, ruling out the pressure of physical force.'"

More boldly, she moved a resolution demanding that by international agreement, each country should take over as a state monopoly the manufacture and control of arms and munitions—a step toward complete disarmament. Amid approving cheers, she claimed that it had been proved that so-called national armaments firms were controlled by a group of international shareholders and speculators and that these firms "employ agents to go to the various countries to stir up troubles, to create rebellions, to manufacture panics, so that there may be a demand for the weapons which it is their business to supply." Later she supported a resolution that called for the formation of a conference of neutral nations that "shall without delay offer continuous mediation by inviting suggestions from each of the belligerent nations and by submitting to all of them simultaneously reasonable proposals as a basis for peace."

It was difficult for some of the delegates to debate the resolutions intelligently, since they had not been made available in all the languages spoken. Perhaps the effort of overcoming the language barriers, the need for constant interpretation, produced exhaustion, for an atmosphere of soporific platitude began to permeate the Congress. An attempt to interrupt the pious, almost complacent, flow of resolutions was made by a certain Amy Lillingston, a former suffragette now resident at The Hague. Why, she asked, didn't the Congress wake up to the facts? She had been to prison for the vote and was ready to go again if necessary, but she could not stand all this cant about women being by nature more peace-loving than men. The whole gathering was, in any case, hopelessly unrepresentative. "For every hundred women ready to come to this Congress," she maintained, "a thousand are ready to fight. We know that most women are quite as ready to fight as men. Why go on saying old silly things and platitudes which men have seen through a hundred years ago?" Miss Lillingston had to shout to make her voice heard through a storm of hostile hissing, but she did at least produce a sharp and uncalculated reaction.

Even Jane Addams, in her presidential address, though praising the courage of delegates who had risked ostracism by coming, warned that appeals for the peaceful organization of the world had so far been made too exclusively to reason and moral justice. "Reason," she said, in her quiet, earnest way, "is only part of the human endowment. Emotion and deep-set radical impulses must be utilized as well, even the social and gregarious instincts which we share with the animals themselves." The final list of resolutions was praiseworthily thoughtful and bore a striking resemblance to the famous Fourteen Points later evolved by America's President Woodrow Wilson and his advisers. Universal disarmament was urged, so were the development of a League of Nations to outlaw aggression, the scientific study of the conditions of permanent peace, and the inclusion of women in all the relevant committees and conferences.

A band of envoys was appointed to carry this unexceptionable message to the leaders of the nations of Europe and of the United States. Led by Jane Addams and Aletta Jacobs, and including the tactful and efficient Misses Macmillan and Courtney, it was received by Prime Ministers and/or Foreign Ministers in fourteen countries, by the Pope in Rome, and by President Wilson in Washington. But somehow, like all aggregates of people of goodwill, all congregations of peace-lovers, it was more like a funeral procession than a life march. Politicians were courteous and said they were sorry, but not one of them was persuaded to take a gamble on the great adventure of peace.

Mrs. Pethick-Lawrence was not one of the envoys. She had done a great deal of traveling already, and perhaps she was glad to get home for a breather after such a surfeit of internationalism. The Pethick-Lawrences' home in Surrey (Mr. Pethick-Lawrence, who registered as a conscientious objector in 1918 when his age group was called up, did his alternative service as a laborer on a nearby farm) was a haven for the like-minded, for people who strove to prevent sanity and culture from being swamped by the philistine war. In the autumn of 1915, Mrs. Lawrence became Honorary Treasurer of the newly formed Women's International League of Great Britain. This was the first of a number of national branches formed to continue the work of the Congress at The Hague. Its tone was decidedly respectable—Sylvia Pankhurst, who was on the committee, found it downright cowardly—since it was set by ex-leaders of the nonmilitant NUWSS. Though excommunicated by Mrs. Fawcett because of their attendance at the Congress (which she mistakenly took to be a gathering of root-and-branch pacifists), they retained her excessively "statesmanlike" attitude toward public affairs.

Responsibility, for them, meant, above all, restraint. Sylvia Pankhurst has described how she saw Helena Swanwick, the WIL's Chairwomen, with her pince-nez and precise university intellectual's manner, howled down by a soldier audience. She would insist on dealing in generalities, whereas Sylvia got down to brass tacks about pensions and soldiers' families and housing and the class barrier between officers and men. Yet these "constitutionalists" had their own courage, their own grave, if sometimes scarcely perceptible, momentum. Choosing their words carefully, they declared their opposition to conscription, whether military or industrial. Working on the same lines as the Union of Democratic Control (of which Mr. Pethick-Lawrence was Honorary Treasurer), which demanded an end to secret treaties and greater popular control over foreign policy, the WIL collected many signatures for a petition that urged the imperative need for a sincere attempt to negotiate peace.

"The refusal to do so," said the petition, "has led to the war becoming a war of attrition, and such a war is a moral iniquity. . . . We are the more bound to press the Government, because we see liberties for which our brothers went out to fight and die steadily undermined at home: the poor suffering from the exploitation of national need by profiteers, the dependants of soldiers and sailors— soldiers and sailors themselves—suffering hardship from the rise in prices, discontent stifled (though not removed) by the growing militarism of our governing class, and our civil and political liberties destroyed. . . ."

The wording here is comparatively bold, reverberant, it may be, with muffled echoes of the Emmeline Pethick-Lawrence of the pre-1912 era, of publish-and-be-damned Sylvia, of Maude Royden (Vice-Chairman of the WIL) attempting to expiate her sinful reticence. But the League's main emphasis was on careful, solid, basic education about the causes and effects of war and about the place of women in society. Each week a series of small meetings dealt with such topics as "What Has the Investment of Money to Do with War and Peace?" and "Patriotism and the Pocket" and "What Are Women For?" (a title that surely invited ribaldry). The talks stressed the need for perspective and impartiality in the teaching of history and Scripture in schools ("Is it possible," pondered Miss Royden, "to teach a revolutionary ethic such as that of Christ in state schools?").

The WIL continued to press for the vote, passed a resolution in favor of equal pay and family allowances, and campaigned against Clause 40D. That was *not* the way to combat venereal disease: "The true line of advance is to be found in the provision of free facilities for treatment all over the country, the spread of knowledge and the raising of the moral standard." Strong verbal backing was given in 1918 to the French for Women's Suffrage in its protest against an order for the opening of more official brothels (*maisons tolérées*) for the troops.

Perhaps the most zealous and, in her own rather introverted way, most passionate exponent of the WIL's educative drive was its Chairwoman, Helena Swanwick. Born in Bavaria, she was one of the remarkably gifted Sickert family, of whom the painter Walter Richard Sickert was the most famous. The family settled in England in 1868—Herr Oswald Sickert, a musician and artist, did not want his sons to be conscripted into the Prussian Army and become beer-swilling Bavarians—and Helena, always delicate in health, had quite a job breaking away from the sort of girl-in-waitinghood that Florence Nightingale so graphically described. At Girton College, Cambridge, in the 1880's, she was chaperoned to lectures. She got a first-class degree in Moral Sciences, and soon after, she married Frederick Swanwick, a lecturer at Manchester University. An earnest feminist, she at first subscribed to the funds of the WSPU, but soon found herself out of sympathy with the Pankhursts. Especially did she dislike Christabel, who, despite her physical charms and quick wit, was, in Mrs. Swanwick's opinion, essentially frigid and cynical and driven by a ruthless love of domination. "I used," she wrote, "to find many of her speeches silly: heaven was to come down on earth, sweating to be abandoned, venereal diseases to disappear, eternal peace to reign, when women got the vote. Meanwhile, she created the atmosphere of a dog-fight."

Mrs. Pethick-Lawrence seemed to her a little unsound ("a strong vein of poetry and mysticism"). Mrs. Despard was lovable, almost recklessly unselfish, and had the look of a prophetess, but her speeches were "sibylline and mystical rather than logical," and she was "no good at all on a committee." So Mrs. Swanwick settled for Mrs. Fawcett and the NUWSS. She was appalled by the wholesale abdication of the intellect, the *trahison des clercs*, that followed the outbreak of the Great War. Was it possible that choice minds should abandon their principles and wallow in the squalid joys of regimentation, that intelligent people could be stirred to anything but derision by the mawkish sentimentality of Rupert Brooke's welcome to war as more honorable than a world of peace "grown old and cold and weary"? Her intense belief in the sovereignty of reason, in the power of the lecture room, was affronted but not extinguished. What hope of security was there in the world when the rulers of nations continued to treat each other like defaulting bookies?

Mrs. Swanwick was annoyed by what she saw as Lloyd George's hypocrisy or ignorance in treating Mrs. Pankhurst as the Great Women's Leader, when, in fact, she was nothing but the figurehead of a small body of jingo extremists who had thrown their last remaining shreds of dignity and common sense to the winds. Searching for an oasis of integrity, she discovered it in the Union of Democratic Control, founded by E. D. Morel, Norman Angell, Charles Trevelyan, Ramsay MacDonald, and Arthur Ponsonby to stress the need for an "open" diplomacy and to work out the terms of a peace settlement that would not plant the seeds of future wars. Elected to the executive committee of the UDC, she later became the Chairwoman of the Women's International League and worked with touching diligence to extend the frontiers of her oasis. She traveled in England, Scotland, Wales, and Ireland, shivering on cold platforms, boarding infrequent trains, which were usually crammed with troops, often ill, but always keeping her appointments.

Attempts were made to "smear" her as a "German," and WIL and UDC meetings, said to be inspired and even financed by the Kaiser, were broken up by Hun-baiters. Mrs. Swanwick had a special dread of Australian troops, who seemed to find a keen pleasure in this sport. They simply would *not* listen when she tried to explain that the organizations she represented were not *against* the war, but were concerned with protecting the ideals for which it was being *fought*. She found Scotland, where the people still thought sturdily for themselves, the most fruitful soil for her mission. In one small cottage, her host and hostess slept in the kitchen and gave her their bedroom and one of their two blankets. There was a bracing atmosphere of Spartan living and strenuous thinking. In Douglas Water, a small village where of seventeen young men called to the colors, thirteen were "absolutist" conscientious objectors (those who went to prison rather than accept any form of alternative service), she found an austere paradise of nonconformity. "These people," she reflected, "shame us. They read, they think, they repeat poetry and discuss high politics." Yet they lived in hovels and were as poor as church mice.

Sometimes she was tempted to give up the good fight. It was such a strain always being in opposition, always arguing, always trying to demolish ignorance and misunderstanding, when she longed so for a world in which the elementary facts of social justice and international brotherhood and sexual equality could be taken for granted. Occasionally she arranged to snatch a short holiday from her task of Tantalus. During one such interlude, spent at Kynance Cove in West Cornwall, she let herself go in a blessed, recuperative orgy of poetry reading—William Shakespeare's sonnets, the majestic cadences of Matthew Arnold and Algernon Swinburne, the cooling quietism of Robert Bridges and Alice Meynell, the bitter war poems of Siegfried Sassoon, and, best of all, the slow, lingering stroll of William Wordsworth's reflective blank verse—"always, always, *The Prelude* to hang on to," she sighed.

She found it regrettable that so many able women rushed to submerge their abilities in the drudgery of relief work. Admirable, humane as that might be, it was, in a sense, a taking of the line of least resistance. As fiercely as her bête noire, Mrs. Pankhurst, Mrs. Swanwick resented the assumption that women's main function was to clear up the messes men made. But whereas Mrs. Pankhurst and Christabel tried hard to muscle in on the men's mess-making act, Mrs. Swanwick wanted women to set an example of working at a new and long-term job—the creation of a blueprint for a just, a *realistic*, and a lasting peace. "But," she complained, "they drifted naturally into relief, which, except for a few leaders and organisers, requires only jog-trot feminine capacities and has no permanent effect on policy."

So, with an increasing sense of isolation, she forged on through the enveloping gloom, wincing at cheap and ever-cheaper slogans, her letters opened, her phone tapped, her well-meaning philosophy twisted. She took her allies where she found them now, even the still vaguely suspect Pethick-Lawrences—who, in the freezing spring of 1917, at the invitation of some independent Scots, traveled to Aberdeen, where Mr. Lawrence contested a by-election on the issue of peace by negotiation. For five unpleasant weeks, he and his wife braved a storm of hatred as unreasoning and as vulgar as that faced by Sylvia Pankhurst and Charlotte Despard in London's East End. They were pelted with coal, windows were broken, they were hustled from platforms—and, despite the support of a Labour Party now recovering from its 1914 attack of war fever, collected a mere handful of votes.

Neither Mrs. Swanwick nor Mrs. Pethick-Lawrence succeeded in selling peace or pacifism or collective security as the greatest adventure. Neither did Miss Royden (any more than had her Master, Christ Himself). But they tried—oh, how they tried.

3 §❧

The Hun Coddlers

Mrs. Despard and Sylvia Pankhurst were not alone in feeling that one's attitude toward enemy aliens was an acid test of character and convictions. The most sustained effort to plead their cause with the authorities and to shield them from the vindictiveness of an increasingly bitter public was made by the Society of Friends. Soon after war broke out, the Quakers formed an Emergency Committee for the assistance of Germans, Austrians, and Hungarians in distress. Its main object was to help the British-born wives of interned aliens in their lonely struggle for existence. They needed help badly, for the scale of relief approved by local authorities in London allowed only 10s. a week for a wife and 1s. 6d. for each child. In the provinces, the rates were less. After many protests, the scale was raised —but more than money was needed. The Emergency Committee set out to provide a practical and compassionate social service. To do so, it relied on a small army of volunteer women workers who visited and comforted and made detailed assessments and reports.

In the first three months of the war, more than seven hundred applicants—ranging from an elderly, invalid German Baron to a Hungarian dwarf sacked from his job in a music-hall troupe—were assisted. Three Quaker women converted their homes into hostels for destitute German women dismissed from their posts as governesses or domestic servants, others took in one or more as guests. Some aliens were helped to pay their passages to America or, where permits were granted, to return to their homeland. Dr. Henrietta Thomas (an American-born Quaker) escorted more than one hundred German women across Holland into German territory. Another volunteer accompanied bewildered families on the train journey to the docks at Tilbury and obtained food and drink for their fretting children.

Nearly half the male aliens who lost their jobs were waiters. "Ludwig," wrote an Emergency Committee visitor in 1915, "is Austrian and his wife Mary is Irish, and they live in rooms—with their five children—for which they pay 8s. 6d. a week. He was a waiter for 13 years in a well-known restaurant, and his master has told him many times that he would take him back if only the public or the newspapers would let him." Even worse was the plight of the foreign-born wives of enemy aliens. "Mrs. B.," wrote another visitor, "is only 18. Her husband, a tailor here for many years, went over to Hungary and brought her back to England as his wife only a few weeks before the war began. He was interned at once. Their marriage papers had been left in Hungary, and so no Government grant could be obtained. His poor young wife was left alone . . . possessing no money, and with not a single friend to help or care for her. . . . Last time I called, I left Josef (her baby) two warm vests and a pretty little white frock. When I gave them to her she was kneeling by the cradle, and with tears running down her cheeks, I heard her say, in her very broken English: 'They do not all hate us, baby. . . .'"

By 1917, there were twenty-three thousand men interned at Knockaloe Camp, on the Isle of Man, alone. In London, the Emergency Committee's headquarters staff numbered fifty, and 175 visitors reported to the Visitation Department, which had a detailed card index of six thousand "cases." There were seventeen local committees in Britain, and Friends' committees were working along similar lines in Germany, Ireland, and Australia. When antiforeigner riots broke out after the sinking of the *Lusitania* in 1915, seventy aliens whose homes had been wrecked or threatened were sheltered and fed for more than a month in a Friends' Meeting House in North London. Petty spite was rampant. "Mrs. M.," reported one visitor, "was a keen member of the local church, but has been asked to discontinue attendance." A British-born wife wrote to complain: "I went to my dentist thinking I was going to have my teeth out, instead of which he refused to have anything to do with me and upset me very much about the Germans." In July, 1917, a distracted mother wrote: "Could you put my two boys in some place of safety for a couple of weeks? Saturday night the people came and broke all the windows with big stones, enough to kill anyone in the room. I had to put my children under the bed for safety. If the lady could call, I could tell her all. I am going to walk the streets tonight as they say they are coming to finish us. . . ."

Headquarters often received touching tributes to its visitors. "Dear Mrs. S.," said one woman, "is a big ray of sunshine in my life." The visitor had found her with a son of fifteen and a daughter of nine living in one small room with only one small bed and had supplied a secondhand chair and an old bedstead. An elderly woman, reduced to poverty after losing her job as a governess, wrote from a workhouse infirmary: "The eggs have been so good for me . . . and the two pink blossoms the lady brought me kept their exquisite perfume for six days."

During the last two years of the war, nearly two thousand ailing or delicate children were given long, recuperative holidays at improvised centers (often private homes), and mothers breaking down with worry and undernourishment were cared for at a special rest home. There was a maternity service; milk, fuel, food, and clothing were bought and distributed; and an Employment Department found domestic work for some mothers, while others earned up to 5s. a week making clothes.

The work did not end with the Armistice. In February, 1919, a visitor in a rural district reported seeing the British-born wife of a German who had been caught in Germany in August, 1914, and was presumed missing: "The caravan where she lives is in a lonely place. She owns this and a little strip of land on which she herself has erected fowl-houses and a goat-house. In the summer she makes a living selling fowls, eggs, goats (which she rears) and goats' milk. But in the winter none of these ways of earning money are possible, and she has a 17s. weekly Government grant and three children to look after. We saw her two little boys of 9 and 7, both looking very delicate after influenza. . . . We took some buns out of a bag, and their eyes did shine at the sight! I think people have spoken un-kindly of the woman, so she likes to be in this lonely place. . . ." Acting on this report, the Emergency Committee arranged to send clothing, a milk grant, and money to help with the baker's bill.

These anonymous but pioneering caseworkers, heroic in their determination and tact, persisted in the face of police suspicion and (sometimes) interference and the cheap sneers of a patriotic press, which christened them the "Hun Coddlers." As one newspaper put it: "The efforts of the Emergency Committee to soften the heart of the German tiger by offering a lump of sugar to its cubs in this country are not only farcical but indecent. The heart of Germany can only be softened by high explosives."

The Quakers strove against the thundering current of war not only by helping its least popular victims, but—since, for the majority of them, war was morally taboo—by refusing to take a direct or (in some cases) any part in the war effort. In May, 1915, eight months before military conscription was introduced in Britain, a large gathering of men of enlistment age formed the Friends' Service Committee and, after much deliberation, made an official statement of their aims: "Christ," they said, "demands of us that we adhere without swerving to the methods of love, and therefore if any seeming conflict should arise between His service and that of the State, it is to Christ that our supreme loyalty must be given, whatever be the consequences."

When, at the end of January, 1916, conscription became law, the Service Committee announced: "We regard the central conception of the Act as imperilling the liberty of the individual conscience—which is the main hope of human progress—and entrenching more deeply that Militarism from which we all desire the world to be freed." A majority was in favor of refusing to undertake any form of alternative service, since this would contribute to the war effort by releasing more men for the front. "It is not," they said, "by compromise with an evil thing, but by a passion of goodwill, that the war spirit must be met." It was up to individuals to resist, whatever the cost, according to "their inmost convictions, under the guidance of the Spirit of Christ."

There were many Quakers among the "absolutist" conscientious objectors, who, on religious or political grounds, went to prison rather than compromise in any way. Seven members of the Service Committee were imprisoned as "absolutists," and much of their work was taken over by two women—Dr. Henrietta Thomas and Miss Edith Ellis. Dr. Thomas died as a result of overwork—she was very active on the Emergency Committee as well as on the Service Committee. Edith Ellis, daughter of the Rt. Hon. John Ellis, MP, a former Undersecretary of State for India, opened the family home at Wrea Head, near Scarborough, Yorkshire, to "absolutists" recovering from the effects of penal servitude and herself went to prison for her pacifist convictions.

When, at the end of 1917, Clause 27C of the Defence of the Realm Act ordered that all writings about the war or the making of peace be submitted to censorship before publication, the Society of Friends decided not to obey. Two women were arrested for distributing A Challenge to Militarism, a leaflet describing the fate of conscientious objectors in prison. Edith Ellis, as Acting Secretary, testified that the Service Committee, acting on behalf of the whole body of Friends, was responsible for its publication, and its members were prosecuted accordingly at the Guildhall, London. When the judge retired to consider his verdict, a voice was heard bidding

Friends in court to devote themselves to silent prayer. Nevertheless, the defendants were sentenced—Edith Ellis faced a fine of £100 and 50 guineas costs or three months' imprisonment.

The appeal was heard at the Guildhall in July, 1918. Upright and dignified, the embodiment of all that was best in the older generation of Friends, Edith Ellis, in her statement, told the court that the Quaker attitude toward war had been well known for more than two centuries. Many Friends had been imprisoned for their beliefs. "We believe," she said, in a calm, measured voice, "that we are called upon to trust to the power of God alone and not in that of our armies and navies. As a woman I wish to say that I do not desire any lesser protection, and those of us who realise this are grateful to the young men who have remained true to the same ideal. Our Committee has been specially entrusted with the duty of making known the facts about conscientious objectors in prison. We believe this to be our religious duty. . . . We cannot submit the question of publication to any Government official, or accept his decision. Disloyalty to that which to us is the voice of God can never, we are convinced, make for national or international righteousness."

Unlike most people in court, the judge, Sir Arthur Newton, was not impressed. "We have had," he summed up, "a most deplorable exhibition. Educated men and women have given utterance to sentiments of the most utter disloyalty. One can scarcely contain oneself and restrain one's indignation at such proceedings. Our duty here is a simple matter. We have to administer the law, and the law has been deliberately and ruthlessly broken." The appeal was dismissed with costs, and Edith Ellis went to prison. She found this an unpleasant experience, not because of the strain on her own health, but because she was worried by what she saw there. "Dear Friends," she wrote from Wrea Head after her release, "Holloway is suffering from the moral effects of the war as is no other prison. . . . I am concerned at the number of young girls imprisoned for drunkenness and sexual immorality." It was, she felt, the fault of a defective society. "Can nothing," she appealed, "be done to get among them and show them a real, caring religion, a saving grace?" Like those other pioneers, the suffragettes and the conscientious objectors themselves, she was shocked by what she saw and heard into an awareness of the urgent need not only for prison reform but for a new and tre-

mendous grappling with the needs and sufferings of the underprivileged.

The indignities—and plain brutalities—suffered by CO's in military camps, detention barracks, and civil prisons led to the formation of a Quaker Chaplains' Committee, managed by Mrs. Percy
Bigland. Venturing into a wilderness of prejudice and misunderstanding, the Quaker chaplains (who often acted as prisoners'
"friends" at courts-martial) found that their ministrations were
welcomed by many non-Quakers—including Socialists—who detested the attitude of the official clergy. One Anglican chaplain, for
instance, told the CO's in the prison where he worked that they
"ought to be drowned." Asked by a father to tell his CO son the
news of the death of his favorite cousin in France, he seized the opportunity to abuse the young man as a cowardly shirker who was
sheltering behind the self-sacrifice of brave soldiers.

The emotional strain of trying to enter sympathetically into the
lives and problems of up to twenty prisoners (six minutes was allowed for each, usually with a guard listening at the door of the
cell) was considerable. But it was considered a privilege to minister
to men who, Christian or not, had dared to think and act for themselves and were taking the consequences with commendable fortitude. The "progressive" Christian's attitude toward the war had
been expressed by Dr. Alfred Salter in an article in the *Labour
Leader* in September, 1914, of which about one and a half million
copies were distributed in pamphlet form. "Look!" it said. "Christ in
Khaki, out in France thrusting His bayonet into the body of a German worker. See! The Son of God with a machine gun. . . . Hark!
The Man of Sorrows in a cavalry charge, cutting, hacking, crushing,
cheering. No! No! That picture is an impossible one, and we all
know it." Such, in simple, graphic form, was the view of the pacifist
Quaker chaplains.

Among them were two women—Mabel Thompson and Joan Fry.
So greatly did the CO's, many of them frustrated militants who
would not have hesitated to fight in an anticapitalist war, value their
friendship that they would threaten to strike against prison rules if
an attempt was made to limit their chaplains' liberty. This highly
charged, crackling atmosphere was very different from the cool ra-
tionalism in which Joan Fry, the third child in a large family of

eighth-generation Quaker Frys, had been brought up. When she was four, she lost an eye in a nursery accident. After a heavily chaperoned girlhood and young womanhood of good works and busy charities, she served as a Poor Law Guardian. In 1909, she moved to Guildford to look after the children of her brother—Roger Fry, the painter and art critic—after his wife's death.

She welcomed the questionings that were beginning to challenge the rigidity of traditional Quakerism and helped to restate the old Quaker doctrine of the "inner light." For her, religion was not primarily an attachment to certain extraordinary events in the past, but a realization that one's deepest inner life was connected with God and nourished by communion with Him. Christianity was essentially a reasonable faith, Christ incarnated as much of God as could be manifest in a human life, the New Testament did not contain the final sum of spiritual revelation.

In August, 1914, Joan Fry was past fifty, prominent in local government in Guildford, and recognized as the Quakers' most effective woman speaker. She had just returned from an international peace congress at Constance in Switzerland, and her firmly held pacifist convictions and wide pastoral experience made her an obvious choice as a prison chaplain. In the next four years, she bicycled hundreds of miles to attend the courts-martial of conscientious objectors, to raise their spirits in prison, to try to pry open the clamped minds of military men and "patriotic" clergymen. At one detention barracks, she found that "no woman, not even a cleaner, was allowed in. One man told me that just to see me there in the distance did him good." Prison wardens became embarrassed and irritated when she demanded to see her clients alone. One referred to the CO's in his charge as "your damned men." She was kept out of a military courtroom by a sentry with a fixed bayonet.

There were many such rebuffs, as well as moments of black depression when she was tempted to give up. Even more discouraging than the hostility she met with in her work for CO's was the decision to allow Guildford schoolchildren to work in local factories making airplane components. When she saw children being encouraged to become part of the war machine, she resigned from the Education Committee in protest, so cutting herself off from a work that was particularly close to her heart.

After the Armistice, she devoted herself—a true and daring "Hun Coddler"—to the relief of suffering in a still-blockaded Germany. As a gesture of fellowship, she insisted on speaking in German, however haltingly. When Lady Angela Malcolm, wife of the head of the British Military Mission in Berlin, arrived in a large, chauffeur-driven, beflagged military car to be taken on a conducted tour of Quaker relief units in the city, Joan Fry refused to use it. The tour took place in an old Ford marked with the Quaker star. She was not going to have her work associated with the Army in the minds of the German population.

"If I fail," she wrote, "as a conscious and free agent to fill the one place which I alone can fill, the harmony of the whole is broken and the design of the universe marred." So believing, she drove herself and her staff harder and harder. There was a frostiness, even a touch of intellectual arrogance, in her manner—she disliked the demonstrative and guarded her inner light with a vestal ferocity. She often quoted a saying of St. John of the Cross—"You will be judged on love"—but, for her, the working out of love meant a close watch on the emotions and a life of intense and unrelenting self-discipline.

She was every inch a soldier of the divine.

4 ॐ

Defenders of Conscience

But the militant soul and core of the resistance to conscription was the No Conscription Fellowship (NCF). In this, too, women played a large and—especially after the male leaders of military age had gone to prison—vitally important part. It owed its origin, in fact, to a woman—Lilla, the wife of Fenner Brockway, today Lord Brockway and a veteran Socialist politician, then the editor of the *Labour Leader,* the organ of the Independent Labour Party. Like many young Socialists, Fenner Brockway saw the war as a betrayal of the principles of international brotherhood and of the true interests of the working class in every combatant nation. At his wife's suggestion, he published a letter in the *Labour Leader* inviting all those who intended to refuse military service to enroll in a Fellowship that would work out a common policy and act as a focus of information and organization. For some months, the Brockways' cottage in Derbyshire was the headquarters of the new movement and Mrs. Brockway acted as its Secretary; but the response was so great that early in 1915, a national headquarters was opened in London.

Though the NCF was never actually suppressed, it was under constant suspicion and police surveillance. All its officials were provided with "shadows" who could take over at a moment's notice, and its organization followed lines already indicated by the underground movements of the suffragettes and Sinn Fein. Its Chairman was Clifford Allen (later Lord Allen of Hurtwood). Then twenty-five, he had originally studied for a career in the church, but had been converted to socialism and agnosticism as an undergraduate at Cambridge. After leaving the university, he had been employed as Secretary and General Manager of *The Daily Citizen*, the short-lived official daily newspaper of the labor movement, and was a persuasive advocate of a carefully argued type of intellectual pacifism. Fenner Brockway (himself the son of a missionary), who became the NCF's Secretary, described Allen as slight in physique but possessing an abundance of almost feminine charm. "Never," he wrote later, "had I met a man with a keener brain. Tall . . . with features clear-cut and classic; his skin delicate, wavy, shining brown hair . . . large brown eyes . . . his voice rich and deep. He dressed like a young barrister, with Gladstone collar and large black tie."

The most active section of the NCF's membership was composed of Socialists and Quakers (some men were both), but included many other shades of political and religious opinion. Stormy and passionate were the arguments as its committee tried to evolve a formula acceptable to all. It was not easy for old-fashioned liberals to come to terms with aggressive Socialists who seemed intent on undermining the foundations of society; nor was it easy for free-thinking Socialists to respect the Bible-punching fundamentalism of such sects as the Plymouth Brethren and the Pillar of Fire. The strain of swimming against the tide was so great that some pacifists found it hard to cooperate with anyone. Yet somehow the NCF did bring and bind these warring elements together in very real fellowship.

The Fellowship did not (as was often said by its opponents) attempt to manufacture conscientious objectors. But it did, in its many branches, give hesitant young men a chance to think and talk out the origins and implications of their pacifism. Support was pledged for the dependents of objectors who might otherwise have feared to have the courage of their convictions. The Fellowship's second convention, held after conscription had become law, was attended by two thousand men who were already, in the official phrase, "deemed to be enlisted." Incited by the jingo press, a hostile mob surrounded Devonshire House, the Quaker headquarters in Bishopsgate, where the meeting was held.

Threatening shouts almost drowned the uninflammatory words of Allen's presidential address: "We, representing thousands of men who cannot participate in warfare, and are subject to the terms of the Military Service Act, unite in comradeship with those of our number who are already suffering for conscience's sake in prison or the hands of the military. . . . We appreciate the spirit of sacrifice which actuates those who are suffering on the battlefield, and in that spirit we renew our determination, whatever the penalties, to undertake no service which for us is wrong. We are confident that thus we are advancing the cause of peace and so rendering such service to our fellowmen in all nations as will contribute to the healing of the wounds inflicted by war." To avoid provoking the mob outside to violence, delegates waved their handkerchiefs instead of cheering the speakers. It was an extraordinary, and an extraordinarily moving, occasion—and one that brought a swift reaction from the Secretary of State for War, Lloyd George, in the House of Commons. "I shall," he said ominously, "consider the best means of making the path of that class a very hard one."

The NCF's administrative efficiency owed much to Miss Catherine Marshall. A queenly figure, usually sprucely attired in blue, she joined the NCF in 1915 as a delegate from the Women's International League. Then in her early forties, she had already had wide experience in political campaigning as Parliamentary Secretary of the NUWSS. Since the head office was frequently raided, different committees, nominally independent, carried on the work from as many as six different offices, and records were accordingly duplicated. News traveled rapidly along the NCF grapevine. Prison visitors and prison pickets formed a useful intelligence network. One prison was able to communicate with another. Sympathetic guards provided secret information. CO's in transit threw notes out of train windows. It was surprisingly difficult for army officers, prison wardens, or guards to ill-treat their charges without being called to account. After a year's intensive preparation, the NCF (and its well-briefed members) showed a disconcertingly detailed knowledge of military law, prison regulations, tribunal procedure, and the Military Service Acts.

When "absolutist" CO's came out of prison, they smuggled out detailed lists of grievances and plans for future action, which were submitted to the NCF committee for discussion. Its decision was conveyed by a variety of methods. Once, when it had been decided to advise against a work strike, Catherine Marshall arranged for a white signal (meaning "no") to be hoisted on a tree in a street just outside the prison concerned. A party of children, armed with white kites, was sent out under the supervision of Miss Lydia Smith, a member of the headquarters staff. She saw to it that a number of kites got stuck in the topmost branches of the tree, and the no-strike order was scrupulously obeyed.

Though a convinced pacifist and "absolutist," Catherine Marshall always, as in her suffragist days, used her influence on the side of moderation. Those who wished to defy the authorities by work or hunger strikes were, in her view, misguided—just as, in her view, Mrs. Pankhurst and her suffragettes had been misguided. She worked to restrain them, for fear they would destroy what little public sympathy there might be for her new cause. With other moderates, she argued that since the *raison d'être* of the NCF was resistance to coercion, it was wrong for its members to employ methods that smacked of psychological pressure. To many militant war-resisters, this attitude was little better than sabotage. Sylvia Pankhurst considered it sheer weakness to pull any of the few punches that could be thrown, but she could not make Miss Marshall budge. She did, however, note with approval that Catherine had become happier and less constrained since she began to breathe the invigorating air of the NCF.

There was another reason for the change in Miss Marshall's personality, a more intimate motive for her intense devotion to the work of the NCF. She had fallen in love with its shining glamour boy, Clifford Allen. It was a hopeless passion, but try as she would, she could not eradicate it. Even when Allen's tantalizing presence was removed by imprisonment, the tension was not broken. She visited him regularly at Wormwood Scrubs and spent two weeks at Newhaven as a "court-martial friend" when Allen rejoined the Noncombatant Corps (to which he, like many other "absolutists," had been assigned) there. When, after three courts-martial, he was discharged from prison in December, 1917, ravaged by tuberculosis, and looking paler and more "spiritual" (as even the unimpressionable Beatrice Webb described him) than ever, he stayed first of all with the Ellis family at Wrea Head, then at the Marshall home at Derwentwater in the Lake District.

He talked to Catherine's father about the breakup of the Liberal Party and the growing strength of labor and reveled, perhaps a little unperceptively, in the comfort of Catherine's intellectual companionship. They read aloud to each other from books and magazines and newspapers and earnestly discussed politics and questions of sexual emancipation. Probably he challenged, in his courteous but detailed and relentless way, her belief that the "absolutists" should not "resist" by work strikes. After all, they went to prison in order to try to influence public opinion and official policy, not simply to suffer in noble silence. It was, he thought, important not to stifle the revolutionary spirit of the imprisoned Socialist vanguard—couldn't she see that their very militance would put them in a better position to restrain the spirit of violence with which the Russian Revolution seemed to have infected the Socialist movement?

She loved to hear him develop his themes in his deep, gentle voice, in his logical, forward-looking, statesmanlike manner (had he not influenced guards and wardens to make brotherly concessions by the sweetness of his reason?). But she could not help remembering the sufferings he had undergone, the torture of the perpetual compulsory silence that had forced him, as he had written, to an obsession with "trivial matters of routine. I think of the very knots in the boards each time I scrub them, until I could scratch them out of the floor to rid myself of their arrogant insistence upon themselves." She must have longed to reveal the full depths of her tender concern, but the impervious comradeliness of his manner raised an emotional barrier that, in its turn, tortured her to the verge of breakdown.

By 1916, her own health had already begun to suffer, but not before she had helped to tune the NCF's Records Department to a pitch of remarkable efficiency. In meticulous suffragist style, it contained a complete case history of every CO—some sixteen thousand in all—from his first appearance before a tribunal to his last known prison or camp. So detailed was the picture achieved that the War Office used to apply to the NCF for information in order to reply to questions by sympathetic MP's (themselves primed with ammunition from the same source). Catherine Marshall made full use of her Parliamentary contacts to ensure that the Fellowship was never without a champion—Ramsay MacDonald and Philip Snowden were perhaps the most illustrious—in the House of Commons and the House of Lords.

She even had a brother in an influential job in police headquarters at Scotland Yard. He was useful on occasions—and particularly on one occasion, when a parcel full of vital data had been left by mistake in a hackney cab. Miss Marshall gave her brother to understand that it contained top-secret statements from leading politicians, and it was found and handed over by a squad of specially alerted police. For all her reassuring respectability, she did not hesitate to risk her reputation to help society's outcasts. Nearly two hundred CO's succeeded in evading arrest, and for them, Miss Marshall worked out a scheme whereby they could be employed as window cleaners, cobblers, or odd-jobbers. She once calculated that she was liable for a total of some two thousand years' imprisonment for her many offenses against the regulations that forbade aiding such outlaws.

By persistent diplomatic pressure, she was largely instrumental in ensuring that "absolutist" prisoners were transferred from military to civil prisons. When Fenner Brockway went to prison, she became Acting Honorary Secretary of the NCF, and when, in May, 1916, it was discovered that batches of CO's from various Noncombatant Corps Camps were being sent to France with the intention of shooting them as deserters if (as they all did) they refused to serve, it was she who organized an immediate and effective outcry. Prime

Minister Asquith intervened, and the death sentence was commuted to ten years' penal servitude for the thirty four men involved. Constant vigilance was needed, especially in the first few months after conscription became law, when the Army made a determined attempt to bully men into submission. The uncompromising "absolutists" naturally came in for the worst treatment. About fifteen hundred of them braved repeated courts-martial and reimprisonment (the whole system was reminiscent of the Cat-and-Mouse treatment of the suffragettes) and were not finally released until well on in 1919.

For breaking the silence rule, they were thrust into dark punishment cells and fed on bread and water. If they hunger-struck, they were forcibly fed, sometimes with a tube that was deliberately selected because it was too large. One was forced into a straightjacket too small for him, another was told that he would be certified insane. One man was informed that he would be shot at dawn. He was led out, the order to fire was given—and then he was "reprieved" amid jeering laughter. At Reading Barracks the conscientious objectors' food was brought to them in pails. At some camps, they were pelted with stones. At Dover, those who refused to take part in pack drill were dragged along the floor and beaten about the head. Men were forcibly stripped of their civilian clothes, kicked about, and indecently assaulted. One "recruit" was frog-marched until the blood gushed from his mouth, another had the tip of a walking stick thrust up his nose. A CO suffering from a feverish cold was put into a hut with army convicts suffering from venereal disease, with terrifyingly inadequate precautions against infection. The wife of a man sent to France in 1917 was told that if her husband refused to obey orders, he would be tied to a wagon and "the men allowed to do as they liked with him." From the end of 1917, deaths, including suicides, in prison or after release on medical grounds became common. Seventy-one men died, and the health of many others was permanently wrecked.

Relatives were frequently under the impression that CO's would be shot, and their anxiety was often agonizing. Some died or went mad under the strain, but they got little sympathy from the state. There was no separation allowance for them. If they were destitute, they had to apply to the Poor Law Guardians for relief, which, if it was granted, had to be collected from the police. Violet Tillard, a suffragist who, like Mrs. Despard, had become estranged from a military family, ran the Maintenance Organization, which kept in touch with prisoners' families and supported them in every way possible, and in 1917 she became General Secretary of the NCF.

Early in 1916, the NCF set up a press office on Fleet Street, under the control of Hubert Peet, a well-known free-lance journalist. Now came the first of a steady stream of articles, news items, and letters to the press. Considering the general hostility toward any criticism of the war, these were remarkably well received, and the *Manchester Guardian* even paid the NCF linage for its contributions. When it became obvious that Peet would be arrested, Miss Lydia Smith (a young schoolteacher from a Quaker family who had become Secretary of the Brighton branch of the NCF) was invited to join the staff. In his few remaining weeks of liberty, he taught her all he could of the ways of Fleet Street so that the work could continue without interruption. Later the office was moved to the Adelphi, just off the Strand; and after Bernard Boothroyd, editor of *The Tribunal* (the NCF's weekly newssheet) was arrested, Lydia Smith combined her press work with the editing of *The Tribunal* and the many other publications—including more than a million copies of leaflets—issued.

Lydia found the atmosphere in the NCF offices exhilarating. The Hon. Bertrand Russell, already celebrated as a mathematician and philosopher, was an almost daily visitor to the office. He had been dismissed from his fellowship at Trinity College because of his support for the NCF and his scathing criticism of the stupidity of war. As Chairman of the Fellowship in Allen's absence and chief contributor to *The Tribunal*, he set an almost awe-inspiring example of wit, calm, and lucidity. He regarded the differences among the various types in what he called "the pacifist herd" with a certain detached amusement and was very good at dealing with the religious cranks who dropped in from time to time. One man, inflamed with zeal, leaned over Russell's shoulder as he sat writing at his desk and shouted: "I am Jesus Christ!" "Yes," was the deflating reply, "that's what that other man said." Like Ramsay MacDonald, Russell was determined not to succumb to the delusions of "the minority mind." He disliked the lack of subtlety, the oversimplifications, that war-

time hysteria forced on everyone, not least those who tried to resist
it. "What kept me from war fever," he explained later, "was a desire
for intellectual sobriety, for viewing matters invoking passionate
emotion as if they were elements in a formula of symbolic logic."

The family with whom Lydia Smith stayed were all strong
suffragists, and she made friends with another lodger, a slim, intense
girl called Joan Beauchamp. Joan, the daughter of a farmer at Mid-
somer Norton in Somerset, had broken with family tradition (her father was a Tory and a churchwarden) while studying English literature at Royal Holloway College, where Emily Wilding Davison had
been a student. With two friends—who were bold enough to heckle
Lloyd George on his home ground in Wales and were nearly
lynched for their pains—she became a suffragette and a Socialist.
When Lydia Smith met her, she was still working with Sylvia Pankhurst in the East End, but it was not long before she was persuaded
to put her talent and enthusiasm at the service of the NCF, where
several ex-militants were already employed. Joan worked with
Lydia in the publications department.

The two young women rented a cottage—Chalkpit Cottage—at
Mickleham, near Leatherhead, about twenty miles from London,
and for the next three years were caught up in a whirlwind of ab-
sorbing activity. They interviewed "absolutists" in the brief intervals
between imprisonments and listened to terrible stories from men
who had been through squalid hells of persecution that, but for the
NCF, might never have been publicly exposed. One of the worst
stories came from two members of the Pillar of Fire, a small religious sect that allowed its devotees to serve in the Noncombatant
Corps. With about twenty other CO's, they had been shut up in a
small hut in a Canadian sector in France. They were given vile food,
were periodically beaten up, and the sanitary arrangements consisted of one pail that was seldom emptied. The experience was so
appalling that some men had rubbed excrement in their eyes in the
hope of going blind and so ending the torture.

The NCF, engaged in a running battle of wits with the authorities, was concerned with the implications of the Wheeldon case. On
the basis of information supplied by two Government secret agents,
Alice Wheeldon, a secondhand clothes dealer in Derby, her two
daughters, Harriet Wheeldon and Mrs. Winnie Mason, and her son-

in-law, Alfred Mason (a research chemist), were accused of conspiring to murder Prime Minister Lloyd George and a Labour colleague of his, Arthur Henderson, by firing poisoned darts at them from an air gun. The case was first heard at the Guildhall, Derby, in February, 1917, and seemed likely to develop into a far-reaching attack on the pacifist movement and on Socialist "subversives" in general. Mrs. Wheeldon, a militant suffragette and a left-wing Socialist, did not deny that she would do anything in her power to sabotage an imperialist war, had sheltered a number of CO's and other army deserters (including her own son), and had never concealed her hatred for Lloyd George, the archwarmonger, and for Arthur Henderson, whom she regarded as a Socialist renegade and class traitor. But she maintained that the poison-plot story had been invented by the two *agents provocateurs*, who had wormed their way into her confidence by posing as undercover war-resisters, had asked her to procure poison for the purpose of "eliminating" guard dogs at internment camps, and had then "framed" her.

The case was referred for trial at the Old Bailey, London, in March, 1917, and the Wheeldons and Masons released on bail. Just before the Old Bailey trial, Harriet Wheeldon visited the NCF office and spoke to Lydia Smith, who remembers that, though she was in a state of great agitation and very worried about her mother, she insisted that the attempted-murder charge was completely false. There was great difficulty in getting a defense counsel for the accused—the Wheeldons could not afford a big fee, and barristers were too afraid of damaging their reputation to take the job. Lydia Smith's sister, Emily, who knew the Wheeldons through suffragette work in Derby, finally persuaded a young Indian barrister, Saiyid Haidar Riza, to accept the brief. Despite his efforts, the accused (with the exception of Harriet) were sentenced, after a grossly biased summing up by the judge. Mrs. Wheeldon got ten years' penal servitude; Alfred Mason, seven years; Winnie Mason, five. Neither of the two secret agents went on the witness stand (Attorney General F. E. Smith pleaded security), and Mr. Riza, who described the trial as "a scandalous, a vile, and a vindictive prosecution," faced a bleak future in his profession.

It was a shabby episode, and—perhaps realizing this—the Government did not, as had been feared, make it the excuse for a wider antipacifist campaign. This, at least, was a relief, for already the NCF had been a target for police raids and sporadic Government prosecution. The police were especially interested in the press office. They were, on the whole, civil enough, but the women found their familiar attitude distinctly irritating. It was tiresome for the Misses Marshall, Tillard, Smith, and Beauchamp to be called by their Christian names—with a manner and a grin that implied that the police firmly believed that they were mere decorative obstacles behind whose skirts men were hiding. There were amusing moments, for the police were deeply ignorant as well as mildly impertinent. During one raid, they took away a copy of John Stuart Mill's *On Liberty* and sent back a young constable to ask where "this Mr. Mill" could be contacted. Someone replied that the gentleman was now resident in either heaven or hell.

This became a stock joke on both sides. But the police were, all the same, in deadly earnest, and constant ingenuity was required to keep the work going and *The Tribunal* on sale. When raids on its distributors proved ineffective, attempts were made to stop its publication. In February, 1918, Bertrand Russell and Joan Beauchamp (who, by agreement, appeared as publisher of *The Tribunal*) were prosecuted at Bow Street. In a recent article, Russell had written that "the American garrison, which will soon be occupying England and France, whether or not they will prove efficient against the Germans, will no doubt be capable of intimidating strikers, an occupation to which the American Army is accustomed when at home." It was ruled that this statement, based on an account in an American Government white paper of U.S. troops firing upon miners on strike, would have a "diabolical effect" on Allied morale. Miss Beauchamp was further accused of publishing falsehoods in an article (based on a CO's letter) that described how some soldiers encouraged and even honored the CO's fight. Both the accused were sentenced to a month's imprisonment.

A few days later, an article on "The Moral Aspect of Conscription," impeccably based on extracts from the *Times* and from speeches by the Archbishop of Canterbury and the Bishop of Winchester, reported on the opening of official brothels for British troops in France. The police raided the office, seized all the copies they could find (the British Museum later complained that it had not received its copy, and Lydia Smith referred the librarian to Scotland Yard), and dismantled the National Labor Press, which printed *The Tribunal*. Despite this, another printer was found, only to have his machinery smashed two months later.

The Scotland Yard men who did this remarked that there would be no more trouble from *The Tribunal,* as no other printer would dare to touch it. Yet on publication day of that same week, it appeared—a single sheet, immaculately printed, with the banner headline HERE WE ARE AGAIN!

This magic had been made possible by the NCF committee's action after the first dismantling. Lydia Smith was empowered to buy a handpress, type, and a stock of paper and to hide them in the most suitable place she could find, with the proviso that no one else in the office must know where they were. The press was duly hidden in the house of a sympathetic printer, and on it *The Tribunal* was printed every week until the spring of 1919, when, the danger over, a Kentish printer took it on as a routine job. On one occasion, the "underground" printer heard that the noise of the press was being commented on by neighbors, and moved to another district, with the press (cleverly disguised as a piano) on a handcart.

Another supporter, who worked as a compositor on a national daily newspaper, agreed to do the composing. Neither he nor the printer ever visited the NCF offices; but each week, an old lady (the compositor's grandmother) came along, leading a young child and carrying a knitting bag, and descended to the basement. She had been briefed to say, if questioned, that she was going to visit the caretaker; but her visit was always carefully timed to take place when the caretaker, who knew nothing of the arrangement, was out. When the old lady left, the copy for the next issue of *The Tribunal* was in her bag. Scotland Yard detectives, posted in the house opposite to keep watch until long after the end of the war (the newssheet did not cease publication until January, 1920), never suspected her.

Lydia Smith, who with Joan Beauchamp and Violet Tillard organized this highly efficient operation, was never suspected of being the editor of *The Tribunal*—the police were convinced that the editor was a man. But she and Violet Tillard were prosecuted for refusing to give information about the newssheet's production and stood together in the dock at Bow Street. Miss Smith, who looked much younger than her years, was astonished to hear the magistrate dismiss her under the Probation of Offenders Act, remarking that she was clearly a mere subordinate. The more mature Miss Tillard got two months.

Long-drawn-out proceedings were begun against Joan Beauchamp. In August, 1918, the Government tried to prosecute her on the ground that the imprint on *The Tribunal*, which gave her name as its printer, was untrue. But since she owned the handpress and directly employed and paid the printers, she successfully maintained that she was, in fact, the master printer, and this charge was abandoned. Since the Government contended that she had not printed anything and was shielding the true culprits, it found itself at an impasse. The case dragged comically from Quarter Sessions to the King's Bench and back again to Quarter Sessions before, at the beginning of 1920, Miss Beauchamp, whom everyone knew to be innocent, was sentenced by a baffled prosecutor to three weeks' imprisonment—but was released after eight days.

Meantime, Lydia Smith continued on her busy, and unprosecuted, way. After a visit to Dartmoor Prison, which in 1917 had been converted by the Home Office into a settlement to provide non-"absolutist" CO's with alternative work of "national importance," she wrote a scathing letter that appeared in the *Manchester Guardian*. "There are at the Settlement," she reported, "between 800 and 900 men of all shades of religious and political opinion . . . the one common belief being that the war is wrong. Has the Government, which calls so insistently for efficiency, made any attempt to use the talents of these men in a way which will be most helpful to the community? The answer is unfortunately in the negative." The work provided was purely penal and hopelessly uneconomic. Sixteen prisoners, mostly professional men—one of whom had been engaged on important scientific research before his arrest—were employed at turning an antiquated treadmill that produced six bags of crushed oats a day. Though horses were available, coke was transported from the dumps to the gasworks and furnaces by teams of ten men harnessed to a cart. In one field, she saw a gang of eight men harnessed to a roller—"work that one man and a horse could have performed in a third of the time." Dozens of men had spent three weeks digging a field that could have been plowed in three days. Yet while doing this heavy, futile, and degrading labor, CO's worked longer hours and were given less food than ordinary convicts.

While the women of the NCF were busy helping to create and protect and publicize a large, coherent, and comprehensive pacifist movement, other women were making brave but isolated attempts to rouse public opinion against the juggernaut of war. The ambitious peace crusade of Lucy Thoumaian and Dorothea Hollins never got beyond the stage of wishful thinking, but other crusades, though touchingly tiny, were at least launched. Rosa Hobhouse, the wife of Stephen Hobhouse (Chairman of the Friends' Emergency Committee for the Assistance of Aliens until he went to prison as an "absolutist"), wrote a leaflet and circulated it to all the bishops of the Church of England and to many prominent Free Church ministers. "In these days," it began, "the Spirit saith unto the Churches: 'Your hands are full of blood. When will ye come out of your ways, and arm yourself with the Mind of Christ?'" Since this appeal fell on stony ground, she set out from London in the summer of 1916 with a friend, Mrs. Herbert Cole, on a "peace pilgrimage." The two women walked through Bedfordshire and Northamptonshire distributing hundreds of antiwar leaflets and speaking, to anyone who would listen, in support of a negotiated peace. After five days, they were arrested, charged with conduct prejudicial to recruiting, and shut up for nearly three months in Northampton Prison.

Eva Selena Gore-Booth, elder daughter of Sir Henry Gore-Booth, a big landowner in the West of Ireland, and her friend Esther Roper also embarked on a peace crusade. Both had been prominent in suffrage and women's trade-union work in Manchester before the war. They had, in fact, been the first people to interest Christabel Pankhurst in these questions, had urged her to study law, and had even taken her on a holiday to Venice. Both were keen educationists (Eva Gore-Booth—tall, pale, and nearsighted, a minor poet of some distinction—read aloud from Shakespeare, Shelley, Plato, and Emerson to members of her women's trade-union council at Sunday morning meetings), both were horrified by the moronic cruelty of war. Together they traveled Britain as speakers for the Women's Peace Crusade. They worked, too, for the Friends' Emergency Committee and for the NCF, visiting conscientious objectors

—and Eva's fire-eating Irish nationalist sister, Constance Markievicz —in prison, attending tribunals and courts-martial as "watchers" and "prisoners' friends."

Always ailing—she suffered from tuberculosis—agitated by suffering in any form, Eva Gore-Booth found the work particularly painful and depressing. To her, CO tribunals were places of horror, "strewn with wreckage and haunted with memories of vain appeals and helpless protest." She watched, quivering, while the boards were polite to pub owners claiming exemption because of the "importance" of their trade and insolent to genuine objectors. "One man," she reported, "who looked refined and rather delicate and said he was studying architecture, was asked in the good old hearty English fashion 'how often he had a bath' and if he lay in bed all Sunday and advised to 'get up early and go to bed early and his conscience wouldn't trouble him . . .' on the assumption that the possession of a conscience indicated the presence of an unhealthy mind in an unhealthy body."

One young man in particular impressed her. He claimed exemption from military service because "the Spirit of God in the hearts of men has no power to hurt or kill anyone." Questioned by the inevitable clergyman, he explained that "this Spirit is your own soul, only you do not know it. When you have found your own soul you will understand my words." He was there, he said, to show others the Reality he had found in himself. Brushing this aside, the clergyman asked him what he would do if his mother was attacked by a German with a bayonet.

The young man replied with another question: "Do you believe in God?"

"Look here, young man," snapped the clergyman, "impertinence won't do you any good. You must know I am a clergyman."

"Then you do believe in God," said the young man. "Do you not think, then, that my mother's life would be much safer in His hands than in mine, stained with my brother's blood?"

"Do you ever read your Bible?"

"Not often."

"I thought so. Then you probably don't remember that Christ told us to render unto Caesar the things that are Caesar's."

"Yes, but so few things *are* Caesar's. Some metal coins, the house he has built, the land he has seized, but never my soul or yours. They belong to God alone."

"Do you really claim to be a Christian in any true sense of the word?"

"You may call me what you will," said the young man, "I am one who lives the truth he has found in his soul."

The tribunal refused him any exemption. As he turned to leave the room, he looked up toward the gallery. A woman who had been busy taking notes leaned over the railing to stare at him. Eva Gore-Booth, startled by "something in his face," asked the woman who the young man was, for it seemed to her that she recognized him and his way of speaking. "Oh," was the reply, "it is Someone I have been hoping all my life to meet. People said He would come again, but I never thought to find Him here."

For Eva Gore-Booth, this haunting incident, this haunting reply, crystallized all that she felt about a war that, in the name of orthodoxy and with the meanest of jeers, crucified Christ afresh wherever it found Him.

The Countess

The Countess

Beside the purposeful charity of the "Hun Coddlers" and the highly organized derring-do of the NCF women, the frenzied personal crusade of Constance Markievicz has the doomed and tattered look of a lost cause. Like way-out, free-lance militants such as Emily Wilding Davison, Mary Leigh, and Mary Richardson (who slashed the Rokeby *Venus* in the National Gallery), she could not burn with an even light of steady endeavor, but flared out in a series of explosions. Her passionate attempt to lose her upper-class identity and merge with "the people" never quite succeeded. She found it hard to check her temper, the quick temper of one who, having smashed the certainties of her childhood, never quite knew where she stood. Only those who lived out on a limb could appreciate her position and forgive her truculence. Sylvia Pankhurst loved and admired her. The Countess Markievicz was a woman after her own heart.

Her father, Sir Henry Gore-Booth, was one of the most powerful and most enlightened landowners in the West of Ireland. She (born Constance Gore-Booth in 1868) and her younger sister, Eva, were brought up in the strange, split-minded routine of Anglo-Irish society, Protestants in a sea of Roman Catholicism, dividing their time between the big house at Lissadell, County Sligo, and the "season" in London, never quite sure where their hearts or their loyalties lay.

While Eva soon managed to harness her social discontent to a life's work, Constance tried scattering her doubts and her energies in the accepted unconventionalities of the bored, beleaguered Anglo-

Irish. She was a legendarily ferocious rider to hounds, a great and glorious and attractive tomboy. But she also showed some talent for painting and carving and occasionally wrote poems, and it was, perhaps, in the hope of encouraging this softer, more lyrical, more manageable and marriageable side that her always sympathetic parents sent her to study at the Slade School of Art in London. To the discomfiture of the relatives with whom she stayed, Constance showed an impulsive interest in the outcasts of the big city, bringing home beggars and derelicts of both sexes for a meal, a warm-up, some clothes. Then, in her late twenties, still unattached and unsettled, still eager to mine life's dreamy, seamy side, she was allowed to go to Paris, to continue her art studies in Julien's fashionable studio.

Handsome, ardent, and wealthy, she had a rollicking time and was dashingly wooed and wedded by the archbohemian of her dilettante set—Polish Count Casimir Markievicz. Six years younger than she was, but far more worldly-wise, he had one son by his first wife, who had died. When they went to live in Dublin, they became bored with each other and with the circumscriptions of local high society, on the fringes of which they rather precariously moved. The Count wrote plays (the Countess even acted in some of them, despite the handicap of a monotonously high-pitched voice), painted portraits, and turned rapidly into a professional boon companion. She sent her daughter, Maeve, to live with her mother, Lady Gore-Booth, and began a lonely but obstinate search for a "mission." At forty, she started to take an interest in Irish nationalism and became a suffragette. On a visit to Eva in Manchester in 1908, she joined the WSPU in discomfiting Winston Churchill at the by-election, driving a four-in-hand plastered with slogans about the barmaid's right to her job (it was widely maintained that bartending was a man's job).

In July, 1913, when Asquith, trying to push a Home Rule Bill through Parliament in the teeth of Tory opposition, visited Dublin, the Countess shouted suffragette slogans at him through a megaphone. Later, confetti labeled "Votes for Women" was showered on Asquith and John Redmond, the Irish Parliamentary leader, as they drove through the streets, and the Countess was knocked down and hurt when a protest meeting was violently broken up by antifeminist thugs of the Ancient Order of Hibernians.

In 1909, she had formed a troop of "boy scouts"—the Fianna

Eireann. This was no nursery for upstanding, Robert Baden-Powell-type do-gooders, but a paramilitary organization designed to fit youngsters to fight for their country's honor and independence. As Chief Scout, the Countess, herself a crack shot, taught her lads to use rifles and revolvers in the grounds of her cottage near Dublin, and careless of what her "own sort of people" thought, she blossomed into an out-and-out Home Ruler. Her heroes were James Connolly and James Larkin, the Irish trade-union leaders. She looked forward to a workers' republic in Ireland, an end to the tyranny and privilege of the landlord caste.

In 1913, employers, angered by the success of Larkin's Transport and General Workers' Union in raising the standard of living of the Dublin workers (which was perhaps the lowest in Europe), combined in an attempt to smash trade unionism. A demand that workers should sign a document disavowing their union membership was backed by a mass lockout that involved virtually the entire working population of Dublin. In a city grim with barely suppressed hatred and violence, Madame—as she was often called—identified with the workers. For several months, she helped to run a food kitchen and milk depot for the men's families in the basement of Liberty Hall, the union's headquarters. She raised funds, cooked and served food, visited workers in their homes, and collected a band of welfare workers of all classes.

She became involved, too, with the ubiquitous Dora Montefiore. Fresh from suffragist-Socialist agitation in the United States, Australia, and South Africa, Mrs. Montefiore focused her attention on Dublin. With the backing of the Daily Herald League and labor organizations throughout England and Scotland, she developed a plan for taking the starving children and wives of Dublin workers into English working-class homes until the lockout had ended. More than 350 homes were offered, many of them by Irish Roman Catholics, and care was taken to arrange that the "refugees" would go to Catholic schools wherever possible. Exulting at the prospect of such a shining example of working-class solidarity, Mrs. Montefiore set out for Dublin with two helpers and was given a temporary office in Liberty Hall by Delia Larkin. There was a tremendous rush of applicants, and the first fifty children snatched from the terrible slums —and from the necessity of rummaging for food in the dustbins of the wealthy—were registered, reclothed, and sent to a public bath for cleansing before their journey across St. George's Channel.

This attempt to "deport" (as the Dublin press put it) Irish children to English (and possibly Protestant) homes, to thrust English charity down Irish throats, aroused the full fury of a brute nationalism, urged on by the Roman Catholic clergy, led by the Archbishop of Dublin. Ugly scrimmages took place at the railway station and at the docks. Only eighteen children got through to Liverpool and the temporary comfort of homes in Lancashire. Mrs. Montefiore and one of her helpers were arrested on a charge of kidnapping—they were even accused of being agents of the white-slave traffic—and the Countess hastened to bail them out of Bridewell Prison. After further unavailing struggles against what she called "the sinister forces of capitalism and clericalism," Mrs. Montefiore had to abandon the homes-for-Dublin-kiddies scheme. The funds raised were used to provide free meals and clothes through the agency of Liberty Hall —and the Countess.

It was, some said, largely due to her that the children of thousands of strikers did not starve. Others thought this a myth. To Sean O'Casey, a genuine man of the people (he was still working as a builder's laborer when, years later, his play *Juno and the Paycock* was produced at the Abbey Theater, Dublin), she was a suspect slummer, a chronic high-born dabbler. He could never, he wrote in his autobiography, remember the Countess "doing anything one could call a spot of work. . . . But whenever a reporter from an English or an Irish paper strayed into Liberty Hall and cocked an eye over the scene, there was the Countess in spotless bib and tucker, standing in the steam, a gigantic ladle in her hand . . . so that a picture of the Lady of the Ladle might brighten the papers of the morrow."

When, under threat of civil war from Sir Edward Carson and the Ulster Unionists, Asquith dropped his Home Rule Bill, Madame joined the left-wing Irish Citizen Army. This had evolved from a system of militant pickets established during the bitter, brawling days of the Strike. "We have," proclaimed a March, 1914, manifesto from Liberty Hall (perhaps in part drafted by O'Casey), "the Ulster Volunteers preparing for eventualities in the North, and the National Volunteers actively organising themselves in various parts of Ireland, while all the time the Labour Hercules leans foolishly and lazily on his club. . . . Would it not be a shame if the forces of Labour alone were content to believe all things, endure all things, to starve rather than take, to be stricken and not to strike back?"

With Sean O'Casey, Jim Larkin, Michael Mallin (Secretary of the Silk Weavers' Union), and other rebels, she toured the Dublin area on a recruiting drive, urging the overthrow of the "feudal capitalist state," demanding the nationalization of canals and railways and the abolition of private banks. The ownership of Ireland, both moral and material, she insisted, was vested by right in the people of Ireland. They must fight for their rights, for the time for resolutions was past ("the Boers," Connolly had grumbled as long before as 1900, "are invulnerable on their kopjes, the Boxers are death on missionaries, but we are irresistible on resolutions"). She and the Count saw little of each other, and her daughter was safe at Lissadell. She was free to plunge into the fearfully agitated pool of Irish politics. "A.E." (George Russell), the gentle literary prophet of Irish nationalism, described her as "a fine breathless character, straight as a lance, truthful, and as devoid of fear as any human being I have ever met—but in too much of a hurry, like a child who dibbles down flowers without a root. She should have been born in America. . . ."

Soon there came an open clash between her and Sean O'Casey, Honorary Treasurer and Honorary Secretary, respectively, at a special meeting of the Council of the Irish Citizen Army. O'Casey was against putting the worker-warriors into uniform; the Countess, charmed by the trappings of militancy, was all for it. But there was a deeper difference. O'Casey vehemently denounced her for her connection with the bourgeois National Volunteers. His resolution—"that it could not be expected that Madame could retain the confidence of the Council, and that she should be now asked to sever her connection with either the Volunteers or the Irish Citizen Army"—was defeated, and he resigned from office.

O'Casey saw her as an unwelcome outsider, whose passionate speeches "always appeared strained, rarely had any sense in them, and always threatened to soar into a still-born scream." She had no notion of order, despised anyone who had, and "whirled into a meeting and whirled out again, a sputtering Catherine Wheel of irresponsibility." In his opinion, "no part of her ever melted into the

cause of Ireland, nor did she ever set foot on the threshold of Socialism. She looked at the names over the doors and thought she was
one of the family. The movements to her were no more than the
hedges over which her horses jumped. . . . She bounded into the
Volunteers one night and into the Citizen Army the next. Then she
pounced on Connolly and dazzled him with her flashy enthusiasm.
She found it almost impossible to reason out a question and smoth-
ered the reasonable answer of another with a squeal."

Exasperated, he watched her, with a cockade of feathers flutter-
ing in the brim of her wide-awake hat, walk with waddling, bow-
legged Connolly as, clad in their dark-green uniforms, they inspected the meager ranks of the Citizen Army outside Liberty Hall.
His own romantic sensibilities were shocked when, while others
crowded around to admire the Army's flag, the Plow and the Stars
("the most beautiful flag among the flags of the world's nations"),
Madame sat apart, ostentatiously unimpressed, cleaning her automatic pistol, which, she said, had a more important republican message to deliver than any flag.

Chain-smoking, impulsive, quite indifferent now to her personal
appearance (keen, in fact, to tread mere elegance underfoot), she
dismissed anyone who was not willing to die for the cause as a
traitor. To her, the two hundred thousand Irishmen who answered
John Redmond's call to fight for the Allies were deluded fools. She
agreed with Connolly, who in October, 1914, became Acting General Secretary of the Irish Transport and General Workers' Union
while Jim Larkin was away fund-raising in the United States. Soon
after war was declared, he wrote in *The Irish Worker:* "Should a
German Army land in Ireland to-morrow we should be perfectly justified in joining it if by so doing we could rid this country once for
all from its connection with the Brigand Empire that drags us unwillingly into this war. . . . Let us not shrink from the consequences. Ireland may yet set the torch to a European conflagration
that will not burn out until the last throne and the last capitalist
bond and debenture will be shrivelled on the funeral pyre of the last
war lord."

She threw in her lot with the extremists, with Major John Mc-
Bride, who had fought with the Boers, and Sir Roger Casement,
once the pride of the British Foreign Office, who (as Sir Edward

Carson was rumored to have done in 1913) went to Germany to seek military support. Surrey House, her home in Dublin (where Connolly sometimes stayed), became a haunt of rebels, and its secret press worked overtime churning out antiwar posters, antirecruiting leaflets, pro-German manifestos, Sinn Fein propaganda—all furtively distributed and stuck up after dark. Changing aliases and disguises (the police, who kept her under close watch, referred to her as "the woman who is generally known as the Countess Markievicz"), she took part with relish in secret night maneuvers of the Citizen Army, waiting for the day when the full-scale expeditionary force that Germany had promised would pierce the protective ring of U-boats and join the rebels in a crushing attack on the British garrisons.

Her excitement rose as Connolly's editorials in *The Workers' Republic* grew more and more truculent. At the end of Feburary, 1916, he thundered at British recruiters who were alleged to have said that Irishmen might as well enlist since the Dublin slums were more lethal than the Flanders trenches. "This," he sneered, "is the English idea of wit. . . . But you can die honourably in Dublin slum. . . . Such death is an honourable death, a hundred times more honourable than if you won a V.C. committing murder at the bidding of your country's enemies. Who are the recruiters? They are the men who set the police upon unarmed people in O'Connell Street, who filled the jails with young working class girls, who batoned and imprisoned hundreds of Dublin workers. . . . The trenches safer than the Dublin slums! We may yet see the day that the trenches are safer for these gentry than any part of Dublin."

The rebellion was fixed for Easter Sunday, April 23, 1916. A few days before, the Countess, toying significantly with her beloved automatic, had helped to repel a police raid on Liberty Hall. Proudly, she helped Connolly to prepare the orders for mobilization. The bustle at headquarters was such that some visitors assumed that it must be connected with the usual Sunday night concert at Liberty Hall.

"Rehearsing, I suppose?" they asked.

"Yes," Madame replied.

"Is it for children?"

"No," said Madame, reveling in the ambiguity, "it's for grown-ups."

But the Grand German Plan did not materialize. Only one arms ship was sent, and that, together with Sir Roger Casement, was captured. In the chaos of orders and counterorders that followed, the Countess stuck with those who believed in the value of a heroic gesture, however doomed. She went to stay the night in a friend's house. It was late when she went to bed, but she could not resist giving her automatic a final check, knowing that the Citizen Army and an uncertain number of Volunteers would go into action the next day, whatever the odds against success. Ireland, she believed, must write, in letters of blood, for all—even the crassest—to see, its determination to possess its own soul. Her attention must have drifted, for suddenly her pistol went off and a bullet zipped through the door, narrowly missing several fellow conspirators who were still talking in the next room.

Fortunately, the police did not hear the commotion. Early on Monday morning, she left for Liberty Hall, where some Volunteers and the Citizen Army were loading ammunition and grenades into trucks. At noon, Connolly said: "We are going out to be slaughtered." In Abbey Street, republican troops broke a shop window and dragged out bicycles and motor bicycles to form a barricade. The uprising had begun.

Four battalions—about one thousand in all, under the command of James Connolly—pitted themselves against a force twenty times that size and infinitely better armed. At the foot of Nelson's Pillar, the Irish Republic had been proclaimed in the words of a joint manifesto: "Irishmen and Irishwomen, in the name of God and the dead generations from which she receives her old traditions of nationhood, Ireland, through us, summons her children to the flag and strikes for her freedom. . . ."

The city was ominously quiet (the rebels had no general sympathy) when Madame and a hundred soldiers of the Citizen Army took up positions on Stephen's Green, a small public garden from which it was hoped to cover the southern approach to the city's center. Second-in-command to Michael Mallin, with the rank of lieutenant, she was one of a dozen women with the rebel forces.

Trenches were dug and desultory sniping began. By Tuesday, there were twenty thousand troops in Dublin. Martial law was enforced, and Stephen's Green was raked by machine-gun and rifle fire from surrounding houses. Madame, armed with a hatchet, helped to smash in windows and placed her troops behind barricades of furniture and sandbags. Headquarters was set up in the College of Surgeons at the corner of the Green. Here she nursed the wounded and potted at enemy snipers, and from here she dashed out under fire to help raise barricades of cars, horse cabs, drags, trams, and park seats around the Green. When a civilian—a well-known Sinn Feiner, as it happened—tried to claim back his truck and was shot dead, Madame threatened to court-martial the man who killed him.

But there was little time for courts-martial. By Tuesday, five Volunteers lay dead on the Green in the drizzling rain, and the British heavy artillery had begun to demolish the IRA's strongholds. In the College of Surgeons, the citizen-soldiers slept rolled in cut-up carpets, and chairs were broken up to make fires for cooking. Enemy action was concentrated on the post office and other public buildings held by the scattered rebels, and, penned in the College, Madame had to watch the searchlights fingering the rooftops and listen to the crash of falling masonry as the earth trembled under the heavy guns. To relieve her feelings, she tore down and smashed a large portrait that was hanging in the boardroom—a portrait of Queen Victoria, whose hand, in her regretted, far-off debutante days, Madame had kissed when she was presented at court.

On Saturday, at the end of Easter Week, the noise of firing died down. But on Sunday the tricolor republican flag still flew over the College of Surgeons, and the snipers crawled to their usual gutter posts, among them the Countess. Then, just before two o'clock, she noticed a car approaching. In it were two Volunteers and two British soldiers. A small white flag fluttered from the windshield. The four men got out and brought the news of surrender.

The rebels lined up in the hall, and their commander, Michael Mallin, and the Countess led them into the street. With the other leaders of the rebellion—Thomas Clarke, Sean MacDiarmada, Padraic Pearse, Thomas MacDonagh, Eamon Ceantt, Joseph Plunkett, and James Connolly himself, badly wounded—the Countess was taken to Kilmainham Jail. From her cell she heard the firing-squad volleys that slew her comrades in the yard below. All week she listened to the executions, and then, on May 4, she was brought out for her own summary trial. She was sentenced to death (which she expected and welcomed), but mercy was recommended "solely and simply on account of her sex." The death sentence was commuted to penal servitude for life.

On May 9, James Connolly, hastily patched up to face the firing squad, was taken from Dublin Castle Hospital and strapped into a chair to be shot. A copy of the statement he had made at his court-martial had been smuggled out by his daughter Nora, who had visited him in the hospital: "We went out to break the connection between this country and the British Empire and to establish an Irish Republic. We believed that the call we then issued to the people of Ireland was a nobler call in a holier cause than any issued to them during this war. . . . We succeeded in proving that Irishmen are ready to die endeavouring to win those national rights which the British Government has been asking them to die to win for Belgium. . . . Believing that the British Government has no right in Ireland, never had any right in Ireland, and never can have any right in Ireland, the presence, in any one generation of Irishmen, of even a respectable minority ready to die to affirm that truth makes that Government for ever a usurpation and a crime against human progress. . . . I personally thank God that I have lived to see the day when thousands of Irish men and boys and hundreds of Irish women and girls were ready to affirm that truth and to attest it with their lives if need be. . . ."

These magnificently dignified and unranting words began to strike fire from the dampest republican tinder, and they may have reached the Countess and cheered her exile. She was transferred to Aylesbury Prison in England, a common convict with a common convict's dreary routine and unsanitary conditions, forced to endure the at first entertaining but ultimately tedious conversation of professional prostitutes, thieves, and blackmailers. Here she met Mrs. Wheeldon, convicted of planning an attempt to assassinate Lloyd George, and May Sharpe, popularly known as Chicago May. Born in the Dublin slums, May emigrated to the United States when she was thirteen, married a Nebraskan cattle rustler when she was fourteen and became a widow at fifteen when her husband was shot dead during a raid. After that, she drifted into a life of international crime. In Chicago, she learned the art of picking pockets and blackmailing gullible lovers. In Paris, in 1899, she was imprisoned for her part in a robbery at the American Express offices. In London, in 1907, she got involved in robbery with violence, was sentenced to fifteen years' imprisonment, and was sent to Aylesbury.

Chicago May was the Countess's best friend in prison. The time passed somehow, sewing mailbags, scraping potatoes, scrubbing the cold stone floors. Her pacifist sister, Eva, visited her; so, with some embarrassment, did two exalted official visitors, Lady Constance Battersea and Adeline, Duchess of Bedford. In the world outside, poems were written about her. Her sister was reassuring:

> The peaceful night that round me flows
> Breaks through your iron prison doors,
> Free through the world your spirit goes,
> Forbidden hands are clasping yours. . . .

"A.E." wrote:

> You, brave in such a hope forlorn,
> Who smiled through crack of shot and shell,
> Though the world look on you with scorn,
> Here's to you, Constance, in your cell.

W. B. Yeats, who knew the Gore-Booths well, was less complimentary. He had never approved of her staining her beauty with politics and slumming. In one poem—"On a Political Prisoner"—Yeats imagined her feeding a bird through the bars of her cell:

> She that but little patience knew
> From childhood on, had now so much. . . .
> Did she, in touching that lone wing,
> Recall the years before her mind
> Became a bitter, abstract thing,
> Her thought some popular enmity,
> Blind and leader of the blind,
> Drinking the foul ditch where they lie?

She herself, encouraged by Eva, tried her hand at writing poems and sent them shyly to her sister ("Of course I know they're only jingles").

> High walls hang round on every side,
> A cage of cruel red,
> The sickly grass is bleached and dried,
> As brick the flower bed. . . .

She was not a troublesome prisoner, though her wardresses complained that she was inclined to be slatternly. But she had a few defiant tricks up her sleeve. To the delight of Chicago May (who thought her the grandest women she had ever met), she refused to go into chapel and pray for an Allied victory. As punishment, the two women were made to carry huge, heavy cans of gruel up and down the stairs and around the cells, and the Countess, looking at the dimly lit immensity (blackout sheets of old sacking were nailed across the windows), recited long passages, in Italian, from Dante's *Inferno*.

When Chicago May left (she was deported to America after serving ten years of her sentence), such sparkle as there was in Madame's life vanished. It was at Aylesbury that she began to receive instruction from a priest, and when, during a Government attempt at reconciliation, she and other political prisoners were released in June, 1917, she joined the Roman Catholic Church. It seemed to her wrong to be a Protestant, to be associated with the religion of Ireland's oppressors. So she took the religion of the people.

Standing in an open car, she was given a tumultuous, conquering heroine's welcome back to Dublin and presented with the freedom of the borough of Sligo, in her native county. She felt what she, as a rogue aristocrat, had always longed to feel—that she was loved by the people—and she threw herself into the job of reorganizing the Volunteers for a new liberation drive. At a Sinn Fein convention, she violently accused two eminent representatives of treachery and cowardice during the Easter uprising. She herself came fifth in the ballot for leaders. Then, early in 1918, Britain, with the Germans threatening to break through on the Western Front, tried to fasten conscription (for men between eighteen and fifty) on Ireland. Already shocked by the executions of spring, 1916, the nation closed ranks with Sinn Fein on this issue. Suddenly, Madame and her like were no longer in a tiny minority, and the Volunteers numbered one hundred thousand. Resistance this time was massive and broadly based, and Madame raced about fanning the blaze with speeches hurled like grenades. One of her less receptive listeners, curiously enough, was a member of the WSPU, which, all through the war, ran a campaign urging the Irish to unite to beat the Germans and sent back intelligence reports to headquarters in London.

In May, the Government, at the height of the anticonscription agitation, arrested the Sinn Fein leaders. With the widows of Major John McBride and Tom Clarke, Madame was sent to Holloway. There she tried blowing on the embers of her artistic training, filling a prison notebook with sketches to illustrate some of Eva's poetry—wild, windy, Celtic twilight stuff.

While she was in Holloway, the General Election of 1918 took place. The old "constitutional" Irish Parliamentary Party was smashed, and Sinn Fein triumphed. The Countess—stitching, sewing, and sketching in her cell—was returned as Member for the St. Patrick's Division of Dublin, and so, while others, including Christabel Pankhurst, strove for the honor, she became (technically, at least) Britain's first woman MP. Like the other Sinn Feiners, she would have refused to go to Westminster even if she had been free to do so. But, with that strange miscalculation of Ireland that it had shown for so long, Britain made ready to welcome her. She got a letter from Prime Minister Lloyd George urging her to be present in the House of Commons on the opening day of the Parliamentary session, and a clothes peg with her name beneath it mutely awaited her arrival.

She was released in March, 1919, and soon afterward attended the Dail Eireann at which Eamon de Valera nominated his first Cabinet. Madame was appointed Secretary for Labour—a great compliment and a great joy to her, sworn as she was radically to improve the lot of the lowly, with whose miseries her enlightened parents had been able to do no more than tinker. Very briefly, she was reunited with her husband, who, after fighting with the Russian Army (he was decorated for gallantry and badly wounded), had survived to take up the frayed threads of his old life, first as a teacher in his brother's art school in Kiev, then, after the Russian Revolution, as stage manager in a theater in Warsaw. But the Dublin he had known was dead. The New Dublin was earnest and brooding and political, and his wife was busy with a career in which he had no part. He soon returned to Poland, and she, to whom the Armistice of November 11, 1918, was a merely peripheral event, took up her old campaign, waging it with her old fury in a whirlwind of speeches, for one of which she was arrested, after only two months' freedom, and reimprisoned, this time in Cork. At least it was an Irish prison, at least she was allowed to look after the Governor's garden and get some fresh air, and at least she knew that, outside, the tide continued to turn in favor of Sinn Fein. Dail Eireann had new prestige, and Irish-Americans were promising financial aid.

When she came out in the autumn, she emerged into an atmosphere of terror, a land of raids and ambushes and Black and Tans, in which she, like her fellow nationalists, lived a nerve-racking life on the run, evading curfews and the probing searchlights of armored cars rumbling arrogantly through shuttered, hating streets. She lived (not without a certain reckless enjoyment, even though she was over fifty) in disguise, wearing an ancient cape and a cherry-crowned bonnet. Somehow, by desperate contrivance and bubbling ingenuity, she managed never to miss a meeting of her beloved Fianna or of the hunted Cabinet, in which, prickly as she was with extremist loyalties, her views were sometimes treated with scant respect by the new men of the movement. She even managed, a Shadow Minister of Labour materializing from some dingy hideout, to coerce a few astonished employers into treating their workers more fairly. But in September, 1920, she was arrested again, tried by court-martial for treasonable practices, and sentenced to two years' hard labor in Mountjoy Prison, Dublin, where she spent her third Christmas as a convict.

The worst of the terrorism was over when she was released in July, 1921, but the recriminations about the truce were in full swing. Those who had negotiated with the British Government—and especially Michael Collins—were, in her embittered view, despicable dupes of Lloyd George's trickery. Fiercely, she abhorred the shifts of practical politics. To her, the proposed upper chamber in the Dail was nothing but a device to perpetuate the influence of the land-owning class from which she had torn herself. "I stand," she cried, "for James Connolly's ideal of a Workers' Republic, a co-operative commonwealth! These men are to be set up to uphold English interests in Ireland, to block every ideal that the nation may wish to formulate!" Like Christabel Pankhurst, she dreaded the end of the campaign, the rise of committeedom, the bloodless tact of politicians, the un-Celtic calculations of the economists. "I believe," she said in her grief, as she felt herself and her ideals recede into the embattled past, "that Ireland held by the Black and Tans did more for Ireland than Ireland held by Parliamentarianism! While Ireland is not free, I remain a rebel, unconverted and unconvertible." She would settle for nothing less than a treaty between a free Ireland and a free England. "I have seen the stars," she concluded with touching nobility, "and I am not going to follow a flickering will-o'-the-wisp."

In 1922, for four months, she toured the United States, speaking to raise funds and enthusiasm for the true Republic. A figure of awesome if almost murderous integrity, she was treated like a Queen. "The world," said one San Francisco newspaper, "always bows before something precious. The high places in the history of the human spirit are the places where uncompromising idealists held sway." Yet even this rarefied atmosphere of approval and near sanctification was disturbed by the intrusion of a queer fragment from her unrespectable past. At an influential occasion in the Academy of Music in Philadelphia, she met Chicago May. There, before the assembled swells, the unrepentant revolutionary and the unrepentant thief and prostitute embraced and laughed and remembered old times in Aylesbury Prison.

The Countess returned to Ireland at the end of June to take part in the elections, which resulted in a win for pro-treaty candidates and her own defeat. Deprived of official standing and official inhibitions (if she ever had any), she threw in her lot with the IRA, the irregulars who were still willing to fight for the ideals that she held so dear with as much gallantry and as little hope of success as did the Volunteers of 1916. She took out her old rifle and for five days and nights sniped away at her former colleagues. In the civil war that followed, the provisional government interned thousands of republicans. For once, the Countess was not jailed, but admitted to a hospital in a state of mental and physical collapse.

When she got better, she went to Glasgow, where she helped to edit *Eire,* a scratch weekly newssheet that was smuggled into Ireland and distributed by, among others, her own loyal Fianna boys. A meeting she addressed in the English Midlands was raided by the police, but she was smuggled out the back door. In August, 1923, she was reelected as Member for South Dublin and returned to that city after a year's restless exile. Thousands of republicans still interned staged a mass hunger strike, and Madame, undaunted, openly supported their action. Breathing fire and brimstone, compassion and implacable hatred, she spoke from a truck and was herself arrested and went on a sympathy hunger strike.

As de Valera and other former intransigents gradually, inevitably, came to heel and began to work with the Establishment, Madame, though she continued to represent South Dublin, lost interest in politics. The heckling of renegade politicians, with the help of a loud-howling dog, was no substitute for the heroics of earlier days. Living in chaotic rooms and wearing chaotic clothes, her hair cropped close and her means cropped closer (her family had always provided her with an allowance, which she felt obliged to give away), she found her real pleasure in putting herself at the service of the swarming poor of Dublin's back streets. She carried bags of coal up tenement steps, nursed the sick, or did the cooking for whole families when the mother was ill. Sometimes she would drive out into the countryside in an ancient, rattling Ford, taking a few of her scouts, with her sketchbook and paint box. She worked hard as a local councilor and looked happier than she had ever looked. Then, in June, 1927, she fell ill and was taken to a hospital. She refused to have a private room and lay in a public ward. She died there on July 15. Count Casimir was with her, as well as her seldom-seen daughter, Maeve. Outside, in the rain, a large, silent crowd waited, hour after hour, praying for her recovery.

For two days and nights, she lay in state in the Rotunda Cinema (the Government refused to have her corpse in the Mansion House), guarded by a troop of Fianna boys, while the poor of Dublin filed past her coffin. When she was buried in Glasnevin Cemetery, soldiers with machine guns stood by to prevent a volley of honor being fired over her grave. But in the tremendous cortege there were contingents from nationalist organizations great and small and eight carloads of wreaths. Sir Josslyn and Lady Gore-Booth mingled with Jim Larkin and his band of militant trade unionists. The Fianna sounded the last post (equivalent to taps), and de Valera spoke the last words. "Madame," he said, "is gone. Madame the friend of the toiler, the lover of the poor. Ease and station she put aside and took the hard way of service with the weak and the downtrodden. . . . We knew the kindliness, the great woman's heart of her, the great Irish soul of her. . . ."

Tears flowed and the panoplied priests intoned their prayers. It was an impressive and a moving occasion. But there was something missing, something buried under the fumbling, tumbling tributes and the sentimental newspaper articles and the easy finality of it all. For the Countess had never known any finality except the arbitrary finality of death. Her own best epitaph was contained in a letter to her sister, Eva, written four years before when she was recovering from the effects of her hunger strike. She had been brooding over the way great ideals are meanly tarnished.

"And yet," she puzzled, "I don't know how this can be avoided, for without organisation Christ would be quite forgotten, and all organisation seems in the end to go the same road: and if it does not go in for graft and power it just fizzles out. That is what is wrong with all public bodies and governments, and what the world has got to think out is some scheme by which power can be evenly distributed over every person in the world, and by which the foolish and uneducated can no longer be grouped in unthinking battalions, dependent on the few pushers, self-seekers and crooks, and made slaves of and exploited."

A pity, perhaps, that de Valera could not have read these words out under the machine guns in the Republican Plot at Glasnevin, where Madame was set apart, even in death, among those who loved a losing fight and preferred to sleep the long sleep rather than abandon their impossible dreams.

Even Sean O'Casey admitted that she was "clothed with physical courage as with a garment." One could not, he conceded, blame her for her restlessness, her inability to persevere, her impatience with solid argument: "She was born that way, and her upbringing, in which she received the ready 'Ay, ay, madame, you're right' of the Sligo peasants, stiffened her belief that things just touched were well done. So she whirled about . . . striking her cardboard lath of thought against things to make them change, verily believing that they did, never waiting to see whether they did or not. Well, well, may she rest in peace at last."

Spoils of War

The Candidates

Some suffragists received the first installment of the vote with quali-fied enthusiasm. To Sylvia Pankhurst, who had consistently agitated for universal suffrage, it was little better than an insult to confine the vote to women over thirty who were householders or the wives of householders and to women university graduates over thirty-five. But there was a new development. For the first time, women were to take part in an election not only as voters but as candidates. A bill enabling them to become Members of Parliament had been rushed through late in November, 1918, only three weeks before polling was due to begin. The Government preferred the remote possibility of a few women MP's, even the presence of a Pankhurst or two, to the certainty of creating a predominantly female electorate by the grant of universal suffrage.

Party leaders wooed the new electors with carefully worded messages. Lloyd George was sure that they could bring into public life "a point of view and spirit which will be of incalculable value to the progress of democracy in these islands." Asquith talked of "a privilege which carries with it a great responsibility." Balfour re-minded them that he had always supported women's suffrage and rejoiced to think that its final passage into law was "mainly due to universal recognition of the magnificent work performed by the women of Britain in the country's cause."

Sylvia Pankhurst, disgusted by the unrevolutionary timidity of the Labour Party, refused an invitation to stand as Labour candidate in the Hallam Division of Sheffield. But Christabel, who had excellent high-level contacts and had already been campaigning for some months as the leader of the Women's Party, eagerly prepared for the fray. At a Queen's Hall rally, Mrs. Pankhurst stressed her daughter's qualifications: "She is the woman of the hour and our best representative. I am her most ardent disciple, because I shall ever be grateful to her for what she has achieved. She was the strategist who drew up the plan of campaign which took the question of the citizenship of women out of the region of fads into practical politics. Had her war policy prevailed in the early years, many thousands of lives would have been saved." She revealed that a prominent American politician had assured her that if Miss Pankhurst had been in the British Government, most of the mistakes made by the Allies would have been avoided.

Flora Drummond pointed out that many of the war measures demanded by Christabel in *Britannia*—especially unity of the Allied command—had finally been adopted. "It is absolutely necessary," she boomed, "that Miss Pankhurst should be in the House of Commons. She has taken her degree in international law and done all she could for the rights of small nations. Her pamphlet on Industrial Salvation contains all the ingredients for success." The Rev. Prebendary Gough, a patriotic clergyman, spoke of Miss Pankhurst's foresight in regard to the dangers of Bolshevism. "We remember," he said, "that whatever she did, she did because with all her heart she believed in the right of what she was doing. It is the same true, fearless heart that is working within her now to the glory of England and the blessing of England for all time."

Such sentiments were gratifying, but Mrs. Pankhurst looked for more solid encouragement. Lloyd George was calling for a nonparty vote for the Coalition ticket, and he issued a letter of sponsorship (the "coupon" of this so-called Coupon Election) to all candidates whom he regarded as reliable supporters. If anyone had earned such a mark of favor, Christabel surely had. Mrs. Pankhurst put in several pleas in person, and Christabel herself visited Lloyd George. On November 21 he wrote to Bonar Law, the Conservative leader, asking him to see Miss Pankhurst. He pointed out that under her leadership the WSPU had been "extraordinarily useful to the Government, especially in the industrial districts where there has been so much trouble these last two very trying years. They have fought the Bolshevist and Pacifist element with great skill, and I know that especially in Glasgow and South Wales their intervention produced remarkable results."

Soon afterward, it was announced that Christabel would run as the Women's Party candidate in the industrial constituency of Smethwick, near Birmingham. Since this was a new constituency, she explained, she could not be accused of trying to oust anyone who might be thought to have a right to it. A few days later, Major S. N. Thompson, the Unionist and Coalition candidate, withdrew from the contest, and Christabel got the coupon. Her Labour opponent, J. E. Davison—an experienced trade-union official who was National Organizer of the Ironfounders' Society—denounced this as a diabolical attempt by the Establishment to grab the women's vote. And, indeed, Lloyd George, in his letter to Bonar Law, had observed: "I am not sure that we have any women candidates, and think it highly desirable that we should."

Stung by Christabel's claim that the Labour Party was "corrupted by Bolshevists and led by Bolshevists," Mr. Davison counterattacked by pointing out that it in fact stood for social reform along constitutional lines, "without breaking a single window, firing a single pillar-box, or burning down a single church." Christabel he characterized as "a political flibbertigibbet," who had been "all things by turn and nothing long." He stressed the fact that she had encouraged her suffragettes to deeds of violence from the safety of a haven in Paris, and referred contemptuously to her and her supporters as "Christabelligerents."

Lord Northcliffe, now a great admirer of the Pankhursts, gave Christabel's campaign special coverage in his newspapers, and Mrs. Pankhurst worked feverishly to ensure the victory that now seemed so near. She spoke on many a bleak and grimy street corner in bitter weather, and the *Daily Mail* reported how she "climbed on a table in front of a public house and spoke words of mingled patriotism and zeal for reform to small groups of working men, soldiers and boys who came out of the mists to gather round her."

Christabel, who persisted in characterizing all Socialists (and particularly Mary Macarthur, the Labour candidate in the neighbouring constituency of Stourbridge) as Bolsheviks, counted on the votes of servicemen and ex-servicemen. Her main slogans were

"Make Germany Pay" and "Union Jack versus Red Flag." For the workers, she promised, if elected, to try to "democratise prosperity," to agitate for better housing and shorter working hours. But after six years of absolute but remote control of the WSPU, Christabel, whose thinking had always been curiously abstract, had lost whatever common touch she had had. She was stiff, shy, and aloof and found it hard to establish the easy, homely human contacts that often clinch votes. Even her clothes were wrong—formal and somber and fur-fringed. They gave the amazing lassie from Lancashire, now thirty-eight and still comely, the look of a condescending *grande dame* or a glorified governess.

This impression was deepened by her platform manner. *Britannia* gave the following as an example of Christabel's agility in repartee. "Have you," asked one heckler, "worked in a factory?" "No," was the reply, "but neither have your friends Ramsay MacDonald and Philip Snowden." "Two blacks," said the heckler, "don't make a white." To which Christabel flashed back: "I'm glad to hear that you think Mr. MacDonald and his friends are black." Such sallies could hardly have endeared her to the proletarian heart, and she may, in moments of depression, have reread Lloyd George's message and hoped it was worth more than the paper it was written on. "Dear Miss Pankhurst," it rather stiltedly ran, "Best wishes for your success. Your association has done splendid work during the war in endeavouring to supply the deficiency of labour. I shall always remember the readiness with which you came to the assistance of the Ministry of Munitions when the need for women munition workers arose. I think your presence in Parliament would be of the greatest assistance in the tasks which confront us."

Mary Macarthur made flying and highly effective sorties to Smethwick to speak for Christabel's opponent and traveled north to speak for her husband, Will Anderson, in his Sheffield constituency. Women workers all over Britain contributed their pennies to her expenses, and the *Daily Express* admitted that "if 'Our Mary' could be printed on the voting paper, Miss Macarthur's return by a large majority could be regarded as a certainty." But she was not even allowed to appear on the ballot as Mary Macarthur. The Returning Officer ruled that she must go before the electors as Mrs. Anderson —and many voters failed to recognize her under that name. Her opponents were John William Wilson, a Liberal supporter of the Coalition ticket, and Victor Fisher, a die-hard reactionary of the so-called National Democratic Party, who had been nursing the constituency for a year and was therefore given the "coupon." Systematically and violently he smeared Miss Macarthur as a Bolshevik, a pacifist, and a defeatist, a woman who had tried to hold up the supply of munitions by her trade-unionist activities and now advocated kindness to the defeated Hun.

Throughout a very dirty and tiring campaign, Mary Macarthur refused to dilute her principles. She put special stress on the need for a just and unrevengeful peace. "I would rather," she said, "lose a thousand seats than be party to a settlement containing the seeds of future war." In her opinion, adults should strive to build for their children a world free from hatred and injustice. Her own three-year-old daughter, Nancy, figured in the campaign. There was a "message from wee Nancy," with a photograph of the little girl and a reminder that the Labour candidate stood for "an equal chance for *every* child."

As she drove doggedly, often in the dark, over the large and scattered constituency, she was greeted by touching demonstrations of personal loyalty. Elderly, work-haggard women lifted their hands and testified, with religious fervor, to what she had done for sweated laborers. Once, when she was speaking during a lunch hour near a factory, a procession of workmen straight from the forge, their hands and faces black, surrounded her. "Suddenly," she wrote in *The Woman Worker*, "they began to sing 'Kind, kind and gentle is she, Kind is Our Mary.' When they had finished, they lifted their caps and marched silently away, leaving Mary smiling and weeping. These rough men had discovered a most delicate and chivalrous way to answer the vile campaign of innuendo carried on by Mr. Lloyd George's coupon candidate." By December 14, when polling began, she was exhausted but full of hope.

The Women's Freedom League had three candidates in the field, all in London. Mrs. Despard was the Labour candidate in Battersea, among whose people she had worked for thirty years. Mrs. How Martyn ran in Hendon, and Emily Phipps, a schoolteacher, in Chelsea. Their platform demanded that women have the vote on equal terms with men; that all trades and professions be opened to women on equal terms and for equal pay; that women serve on all juries; and that no one be convicted on police evidence alone. Mrs. Despard dwelt on the need for better health and welfare services, better and longer education, improved housing, rigorous inspection of factory conditions, and a strong League of Nations.

Mrs. Pethick-Lawrence accepted the Labour Party's invitation to contest the Rusholme Division of Manchester solely in order to profess her Women's International League principles. The one hope, she maintained, of averting a second world war was to make a thoughtful and magnanimous peace, and she advocated independence for Ireland and India. It was a hard message to preach to a nation crazy—and greedy—with war fever. Politicians and the press were busy fostering the notion that Germany should pay for the whole cost of the war *and* contribute toward a higher standard of living for the victor masses. Mrs. Pethick-Lawrence had no difficulty in getting crowds to listen to her—a woman candidate was a novelty —but she noticed that she made little impression on women voters. "This election," she summarized, "was their chance of 'doing their bit,' and they were all for 'going over the top' to avenge their husbands and sons." Her keenest supporters were servicemen and ex-servicemen, some of whom spoke and canvassed for her or, if they were still serving abroad, sent letters of sympathy to be read out at meetings.

The results of the election were not declared until December 28, by which time the men who were not yet demobilized had had time to register their votes. Not one of the women candidates had been successful. The result at Smethwick, however, was so close that Christabel demanded—and got—a recount. But J. E. Davison was still the winner, by a mere 775 votes. Mary Macarthur, too, was only narrowly defeated. Then came the postmortems. Time had been too short for a thorough campaign, and, as Miss Phipps complained, it had been a strain trying to cope almost single-handed with endless callers and a heavy correspondence, which ranged from demands to make Germany pay to the promise of a vote if the candidate would arrange for the prophetical writings of Joanna Southcott to be opened forthwith in the presence of the assembled bishops of the Church of England. Plans for family allowances were misconstrued. When Miss Phipps suggested that an allowance would enable working-class mothers to hire domestic help for an hour or so a day and thereby get a rest, she heard one listener comment: "Vote for her? Not likely! A *dreadful* woman she is. Wants to turn me out of the house for a couple of hours a day and put a strange woman in with my old man!"

Mrs. Despard took her defeat philosophically. "The result may create a feeling of despondency," she told readers of The Vote. "But be hopeful. After all, in 1911 would any of us have imagined that in 1918 no less than 16 women would be able to present themselves to the electors?"

2 §ॐ

Nancy Astor's Cannon

When, on October 12, 1915, fifty-year-old Nurse Edith Cavell was shot by the Germans for helping wounded Allied soldiers to escape over the Belgian frontier into neutral Holland, she achieved, overnight, a fame and a recognition that perhaps nothing but the brutal, dynamic waywardness of war could have brought. Her thin, distinguished, ascetic face, her record of conscientious professional zeal, even the fact that she was a clergyman's daughter, made her the perfect propaganda martyr. Her last message—which included what was possibly the war's most famous phrase: "Patriotism is not enough"—was, for most people, a call, not to search their own souls, but to vilify the brutes who were capable of crushing so fine a flower of British virtue. Yet for eight years, as matron of Belgium's first training school for nurses, this duty-ridden, puritanical woman had labored, unnoticed by her countrymen, to revolutionize hospital conditions that were little better than those that faced Florence Nightingale in the England of the 1860's.

Her dramatic death struck the scales from the eyes of British journalists and British politicians. She was, they suddenly discovered, not only a remarkable person, but the very symbol of the new, the patriotic (and therefore the acceptable), militancy of British womanhood. Apparently forgetting the hectic days when suffragettes had cornered him in church, heckled him at political meetings, interrupted his after-dinner speeches, and ambushed him on golf courses, Prime Minister Asquith publicly, if naïvely, admitted: "There are thousands of such women, but a year ago we did not know it."

The exigencies of war brought other belated revelations. The Government's view of Mrs. Pankhurst was utterly transformed. In May, 1914, she had been carried, grimacing with pain, from the battlefield as, with a commando of young WSPU recruits, she tried to penetrate a massive police cordon and deliver a votes-for-women petition to the King at Buckingham Palace. Fourteen months later, she stood on the reviewing platform with Lloyd George and Winston Churchill at the end of a Women's War Service Procession that the WSPU had organized at the request of the Government and with the help of a Government subsidy.

Time and again, and in increasing numbers, women proved the absurdity of conventional estimates of their capabilities, estimates that were themselves the product of men's fear and wishful thinking. Mrs. Stobart commanded an army medical column through one of the most grueling retreats of the war. Flora Sandes fought her way through a series of savage Balkan campaigns. Women in hundreds of thousands proved adequate substitutes for enlisted men in the full range of an industry mechanized to meet the demands of scientific warfare. They not only filled millions of shells, but lifted those weighing up to forty-eight pounds without mechanical help and with no ill effects. Mrs. Pankhurst and Christabel were given full scope to demonstrate their genius for aggressive organization in a black-and-white cause—and one is tempted to think that the war effort would not have suffered if they had substituted for, say, Lloyd George and Winston Churchill. In the fight against war as well as in the struggle to wage it efficiently, women played an important part. Sylvia Pankhurst was almost a Socialist army in herself and created her own miniature welfare state to shame the authorities. The No Conscription Fellowship owed its success to the effectiveness of the women who took over the jobs of the male officials who went to prison as conscientious objectors.

The fierce determination to demonstrate women's self-sufficiency could lead to extremes. Mrs. Stobart was magnanimous enough to include a sprinkling of men (in subordinate roles) when she took her hospital unit to Serbia, and she even allowed her well-trained husband to accompany her. But Dr. Elsie Inglis fought like a fury the suggestion that the arctic conditions of the Rumanian front in winter were too much for her transport drivers, that this was really a man's job. The WSPU's industrial campaign, planned by Christabel Pankhurst, was based on the assumption that women workers, more practical and less easily blown about on winds of Socialist and pacifist theory, must set an example to backsliding men. The same assumption lay behind the Women's Peace Crusade of 1917–1918 and inspired the Women's Conference at The Hague in 1915 and the Women's International League that sprang from it.

The Government was willing to tolerate, even encourage, such zeal. The First World War was the first really total war and demanded a total mobilization of national resources. It was easier, as well as imperative, to give way to such impersonal pressure than to be, as Winston Churchill had put it, henpecked into giving the vote. The war saved the Government's face as well as forced its hand. Faced with the fact that only the mass participation of women made efficient war-making possible, seeing Queen Mary herself cooperating with Mary Macarthur (a trade unionist, a radical Socialist, and a bitter critic of the war), not even Asquith could pretend that the women's movement was an undemocratic aberration of upper-class hooligans. Government speakers now went to great lengths to urge women to a proper sense of duty. "There are still," said a former antisuffragist recruiting for the Land Army, "villages to be found where the women have become imbued with the idea that their place is in the home. That idea must be met and combated."

With this governmental about-face, the Monstrous Regiment of Suffragists was able to settle its internecine differences and close its ranks. Mrs. Pankhurst and Mrs. Fawcett vied with each other in the patriotic fervor with which they urged their followers to various forms of national service. Mrs. Pankhurst, with her cavalier temperament and driving ambition for Christabel, found new and powerful reasons for a close alliance with the aristocratic exponents of the principle of *noblesse oblige,* for whom the war offered fresh outlets to an ingrained tradition of public service. She was more drawn to the autocratic, eccentric Lady Muriel Paget (whom she had met in Petrograd) than to Mary Macarthur, to her old comrade Mrs. Despard, or to her younger daughter Sylvia, whose views and activities she publicly denounced and disowned. As the queen of patriotism and the apostle of total war, she abhorred the disloyal carpings of critics, especially those who belittled the women's movement by treating it as a mere component part of the wider struggle for social and economic justice, the all-engulfing class war. Even the ruins of the prewar Establishment seemed to her (now a romantic Tory in the Churchillian mold) preferable to socialism, which foreshadowed an antiheroic age which she loathed with every vehement fiber of her being.

The sad and bitter split in the Pankhurst family reflected a similar division in the women's movement as a whole. On the one side were those who felt that victory in the war must obliterate all other considerations (furthermore, it would provide magnificent opportunities for doughty feminists); on the other, those who had a different interpretation of their duty as patriots and human beings and refused to take part in what they saw as the abdication of the intellect, the painful *trahison des clercs*. Just as Mrs. Pankhurst denounced Sylvia and other ex-WSPU delinquents, so Mrs. Fawcett excommunicated Mrs. Swanwick, Crystal Macmillan, and Kathleen Courtney, all prominent figures in the NUWSS, for attending the Women's Peace Conference at The Hague. Yet it was the outsiders —the Socialists, the pacifists, the internationally minded progressives—who plotted the future shape and objectives of feminism. While the war faction of the WSPU went out to do battle with restless workers, the Women's International League and the Women's Peace Crusade braved the heckling and the missiles of the patriotic mob, and Sylvia Pankhurst dreamed of a Communist millennium in which every tear (except those of profiteering capitalists and their lackey politicians) would be dried.

In *The Making of Women*, a symposium edited by Victor Gollancz, three powerful writers—Maude Royden, Eleanor Rathbone (who in 1919 succeeded Mrs. Fawcett as President of the NUWSS), and Elinor Burns—outlined the priorities of an enlightened feminism. Possession of the vote, though valuable, would not in itself reconcile the interests of men and women any more than it had reconciled the interests of capital and labor. It would not, for instance, help to define and promote a healthy sexual relationship. It was necessary, wrote Gollancz, to strike a balance between "the puritanism of Miss Christabel Pankhurst, who regarded every man as a monster, and the even more futile attitude of people who arrogated to themselves the absurdly misleading name of Freewomen."

Maude Royden warned of the feminist fallacy that every woman hankered, or should hanker, for a career outside the home. Marriage, childbirth, and child rearing always had been and always would be the natural and the most creative sequence for a woman. But men had done their best to make it a mark of slavery: "Having limited her to marriage both for a living and a career, to heap ridicule upon her if she tries to secure a husband and contempt if she fails—this has been the example in sweet reasonableness which men have set to women." The great prerequisite for a balanced marriage, she believed, was for men to abandon once and for all the belief that the desire for mastery was "essentially noble or virile, that it is an invasion of their own life not to be allowed to invade the lives of others. The old idea that women like to be mastered will die. The demand for imperfect development in women, and abandonment of self-control in the intoxicating sense of being mastered, belong alike to the pathological side of sex." Unless the idea of sexual partnership grew stronger, she forecast, there would be a disastrous increase in abortion, contraception, and sexual neurosis.

It was essential, Miss Royden maintained, to get rid of the notion that motherhood, woman's noblest function, was a "handicap" in an industrial society. The sentimental adulation of the wartime man-woman was superficial and dangerous. "A woman who bears children, runs a household and brings up a family is still only an 'arrested man' and a perpetual minor; but a woman who can clip tickets on a tramcar is recognised at once as a Superwoman—in other words, a man," she wrote. To Maude Royden and Eleanor Rathbone, as to many other thoughtful feminists, the endowment of motherhood (through family allowances) was more important than the ambiguous aim of equal pay for equal work. During the war, wrote Miss Rathbone, many women had experienced for the first time the sense of security and dignity that came from the enjoyment of a settled income, proportioned to the size of their families and paid directly to themselves. "It is not pleasant," she commented, "to reflect how many prototypes there are of the two women in *Punch* who 'did not think the war would last long—it was too good to last.'" Certainly the whole question of women's pay bristled with anomalies. Despite the obvious fact that widows with families were an increasingly important factor in the labor market and that an employment report showed that about half of the women working for wages were helping to support others than themselves, an official survey of subsistence wages estimated that a man's normal requirement was from one and a half to three times that of a woman. But if the state launched an adequate system of family allowances, this would do away with the main reason (family responsibilities) for wage differentiation. Then, and only then, "competition that was at once free and fair would be possible, and the services of women— not only in industry but in the home—would be remunerated on their merits."

Elinor Burns had some radical views on education. Class and sex discrimination should be abolished. Boys and girls of all classes should be educated in state schools up to the age of sixteen. All universities should be residential and should admit women on equal terms with men. But since girls matured earlier than boys, the age of university entrance should be lower for women—sixteen or seventeen rather than nineteen or twenty. In this way, she thought, "the most disastrous phases of life at a boarding school would be avoided and two or three years of professional life added." To prevent the waste of human material revealed during the war, when all but a handful of women were unable to tackle anything except low-grade jobs, women must have full and early opportunities for industrial and professional training.

Mary Macarthur had burned out her life in an attempt to ensure justice for women in commerce and industry. Susan Lawrence, one of her young lieutenants in the Women's Trade Union League, served, with Sir William Beveridge and Sir John Simon, on a Ministry of Reconstruction committee set up in August, 1916, to "advise, in the light of experience gained during the war, upon the opportunities for the employment of women, and the conditions of such employment, after the war." Trade-union insistence that the mass employment of women in industry was a temporary measure and that women should be classed as youths or boys for purposes of payment, employers' constant efforts to pay women as little as possible, and the Government's almost complete failure to fulfill its pledge of equal pay for equal work had combined to create a situation of muddle and complicated resentment. Women provided a cheap labor supply of some four and a half million workers employed alongside the "normal" wage earners. There was a double standard of wages, of industrial training, of industrial combination, and of life.

It was largely due to the efforts of Miss Lawrence (well supplied with ammunition by Mary Macarthur) that when the report of the committee came out in 1919, it advocated a minimum time rate for all workers, plus piece rates, to avoid injustice to slow, infirm, or otherwise handicapped employees. Women, the report insisted, must have an adequate and suitably paid period of training; the hundreds of thousands of women still working in sweated trades should have the protection of a minimum wage and a watchful Trade Board; there should be a forty-four-hour work week and two weeks' vacation a year; women should be represented on workshop committees; and the provision of an efficient welfare service was as necessary for men as for women. There was no ground for the idea that employers were justified in "making welfare a charge upon wages in the case of women, and in paying them, for that reason, less than men similarly employed."

Even more important than the Ministry of Reconstruction's report was that of the War Cabinet Committee on Women in Industry. This group was appointed in September, 1918, as a direct result of a strike, supported by male as well as female transport workers in the London area, against the witholding of a 12½ per cent war bonus from the women. The committee recommended equal pay for equal work, in the sense that "pay should be in proportion to efficient output." Floundering deep in the terminological mire of this Passchendaele of the sex war, it advised that "every job on which women are employed doing the same work as men for less wages should be considered a man's job for the purpose of fixing women's wages" and thought that "in order to maintain the principle of equal pay for equal work in cases where it is necessary to employ men and women of the same grade, capacity and training, but where equal pay will not attract the same grade of man as of woman, it may be necessary to counteract the difference of attractiveness by the payment to married men of children's allowances." No woman should be employed for less than a reasonable subsistence wage; this should be sufficient to provide a single woman over eighteen years of age with "an adequate dietary, with lodging, to include fuel and light, in a respectable home not more than half an hour's journey, including tram or train, from their place of work, with clothing sufficient for warmth, cleanliness and decent appearance, with money for fares, insurance and Trade Union subscriptions, and with a reasonable sum for holidays, amusements, etc."

This was a clear advance over the old theory that women worked for pocket money and had little or no separate personal life, but the tendency of the report to treat women as a class apart, which might with difficulty and tolerance be fitted into the working population, aroused the wrath of the committee's only woman member, Beatrice (Mrs. Sidney) Webb. A prewar opponent of votes for women (like Florence Nightingale, like Mrs. Pankhurst in some respects, she distrusted the mass of her own sex even while fighting for its emancipation), she was a formidable opponent of muddled, unscientific thinking in men or women. In a long and masterly minority report, she tartly complained that "to concentrate upon the employment of women and upon their physiological and social needs, without any corresponding survey of the employment of men and of their physiological and social needs, is to assume, perhaps inadvertently, that industry is a normal function of the male and that women, like nonadults, are only to be permitted to work for wages at special hours, for special rates of wages, under special supervision and subject to special restrictions. I cannot accept this assumption."

In her view, the basic need was for "a closer general approximation, in all classes of society, of incomes to efforts and sacrifices." This called for a Royal Commission of Inquiry into "the sharing of the national product among classes, industries and individuals, in order that not only the maximum productivity of industry in the future, but also the maximum personal development of the citizens, and the improvement of the race, may be better secured than at present." The equal-pay-for-equal-work formula was, she thought, far too vague. The essential principle for all systems of remuneration should be that of "clearly defined occupational or standard rates for all persons of like industrial grade, enforced, but as minima only, on the whole grade or vocation. There is no more need for such rates being made to differ according to sex than according to race, creed, height or weight."

Legal minimum conditions of employment and unemployment should be the same for men and women, and there should be a single code of welfare, with no sex discrimination. To ensure social justice for all employees and to secure national efficiency at all levels and in all types of employment, state intervention not only should be regarded as permanent, but should be greatly extended. "There seems to be no alternative," wrote Mrs. Webb, "assuming that the nation wants children, to some form of State provision, entirely apart from wages, of which the present maternity benefit, free schooling and income tax allowance constitute only the germ." The alternative, to make wages genuinely proportionate to family obligations, would be much more revolutionary and quite fatal to the nation. It would, for example, lead to "a disastrous discrimination against the married man or woman, and still more against parentage."

While Beatrice Webb and Susan Lawrence battled to lay the foundations of a scientifically humane welfare state, other women worked for the internationalist ideal. Mary Macarthur, though her strength was sapped by overwork and grief at the death of her husband in the influenza epidemic of 1919, worked on, through the trade unions and the newly formed International Labor Organization, for social justice and widening cooperation. Mrs. Swanwick, who became editor of *Foreign Affairs* (the journal of the Union of Democratic Control), was a delegate to the assemblies of the League of Nations in Geneva, and ultimately achieved the high respectability of a Companionship of Honor, found that her views were still unpopular in time of peace. When, in 1922, she accompanied Norman Angell to Cambridge to speak on the economic situation in Europe, both were surrounded and jostled by a crowd of Bolshevik-baiting undergraduates, and the police did little to intervene. "It is wonderful," she observed, "how complacent our police are obliged to be to well-dressed mobs."

In April, 1919, triumphantly escorted by a squad of soldiers,

Mrs. Pethick-Lawrence marched once more, as in her suffragette days, from Trafalgar Square to Downing Street, this time with a resolution calling for an end to the hunger blockade on Germany. At the Second International Congress of Women at Zurich, she renewed acquaintance with the pioneers who had gathered at The Hague, and she counted it the most moving experience of her life. When Jeanne Melin of France and Lida Gustava Heymann of Germany embraced on the platform, Mrs Pethick-Lawrence, like many other delegates, wept over this touching symbol of a unity, so soon to be menaced by the boundary-makers of Versailles and the boundary-breakers of Nazism.

Such poignant moments of renewed faith in the power of women to move mountains of stupidity and prejudice were infrequent. In Britain, suffragists re-formed their ranks to combat an antifeminist reaction, mirrored and perpetuated by the press. Instead of being continually amazed at what women could do, newspapers now insisted that they leave the factories and the fields and return to the home, their true sphere, as paid or unpaid domestic servants. No longer saviors and heroines, Britain's "surplus women" were pictured as parasites, scabs, a menace to returning, jobless heroes.

The Women's Freedom League, still led by Mrs. Despard, and the NUWSS—rechristened the National Union of Societies for Equal Citizenship—took a new lease on life. The Six Point Group, led by Lady Rhondda, former suffragette, and backed by all active suffragists, pressed for widows' pensions, equal rights of guardianship for both parents, equal pay for women teachers, and equal opportunities for women in the Civil Service. The statute books soon showed signs that politicians were taking careful notice of this campaign, and the Six Point Group prodded them by issuing Pankhurst-like blacklists of reactionary MP's (as well as white lists of cooperative ones). There were no riots, no broken windows or bones, no one went to prison or was forcibly fed, but the atmosphere, for all that, was aggressive and exhilarating.

It was an atmosphere that might have been expected to appeal to Mrs. Pankhurst and Christabel. But they were out of touch with the new women's movement, absorbed in the last throes of their industrial campaign, preoccupied with their determination to save Britain from the creeping paralysis of socialism. Their Women's

Party, the final expression of a homosexual separatism of which Christabel had been the prime instigator and presiding goddess, made slight headway against the freer comradeship of the sexes which the war had hastened and at which poor Miss Douglas-Pennant had shuddered. Times had changed. In 1908 Mrs. Pethick-Lawrence had presented Christabel as the charming embodiment of young womanhood in revolt, and thousands had worshiped her as such, treasuring pinup postcards of her and other WSPU leaders. Now the ideal was different: not Christabel—with her soft, abundant hair, her plump, rosy, milkmaid cheeks, her full, rather sulky lips, her long dresses and picture hats—but Rebecca West—beautiful, certainly, but in a brisk, streamlined, crop-haired manner, a professional writer and tough radical journalist who had been outspokenly critical of Christabel's puritanical attitude toward the sex war, in which woman was always purer and nobler than man and, as such, would do well to avoid his company, let alone his embraces.

This attitude now found few supporters. Lady Bryon, the idiosyncratic philanthropist who had provided consignments of matches for matchless Tommies, was one. "Don't vote for any party," she exhorted women voters, "but have a party of your own. We want nothing to do with men's party politics. Men think that most women are fools, but women *know* that most men are. A Women's Party of Perfection, whose aims are nothing less, led by a woman of courage and independence, is the crying need of the hour."

The Pankhursts were out of date, figures even of slightly blimpish fun to a new generation of emancipators. Now that the war was over, the door of No. 10 Downing Street was no longer open to them. They were no longer asked to report on the state of the nation or of other nations. They were shuffled from the center of the stage. Defeat in the election was, for them, final. The Women's Party, with its impossible program and its impossible expense, was dissolved. Tower Cressy, the London house that had been so lavishly equipped as a Montessori day school, was bequeathed to a trust headed by Princess Alice and turned into a War Memorial Adoption Home. Christabel vanished from public life and did not try—though the Sex Disqualification Removal Act of 1919 made it possible—to make a career as a lawyer. "Old soldiers," she told her friends, "never die. They simply fade away." She proceeded to do just that. She and her mother had little money. They had never counted costs or taken much thought for the morrow. In England they seemed unemployable. Used to absolute power, they would have made explosive subordinates.

Mrs. Pankhurst and Christabel went to Paris to say good-bye to the aristocratic friends—the Princesse de Polignac and the Baronne de Brimont—who had watched over Christabel in her exile and used their influence with the French Government to prevent her extradition. They also met a number of Allied statesmen, including M. Briand, the former French Foreign minister. When M. Briand jocularly mentioned that it might be a good idea for Frenchwomen to organize a suffragette campaign for the vote, Mrs. Pankhurst was not amused. "I trust," she icily replied, "that the French Government will take steps to make that unnecessary." (The French Government did not take her advice. Seventeen years later, at Longchamp, suffragettes were still to be seen parading on the racecourse with billboards inscribed LA FRANÇAISE DOIT VOTER.)

This was Mrs. Pankhurst's parting shot in Europe. In September, 1919, a displaced person, a casualty of the Great War, she sailed the Atlantic to deliver yet another series of anti-Bolshevist, pro-Empire lectures. Her ambition now was to make enough money to buy a little house in Surrey and settle down with her adopted children. Christabel soon joined her in Canada. She had found a new cause, a new certainty. With all her former verve and urgency, she now spoke and wrote about the vanity of earthly hopes, the imminence of the Second Coming of Christ, which and who alone could end the evils of this ineradicably sinful dispensation. "The shallow optimism of yesterday has vanished," she proclaimed. "Some of us used to imagine that the world must and would get better and better under the treatment of its many reformers. That illusion perished during the war."

The winning of the vote had altered nothing, for women were just as tainted with original sin as men. "Those days of the suffrage campaign," Christabel reflected, "were the days of political childhood. Now is the time to put away childish things. Who would exchange the grandest of our old illusions concerning what the votes of women could do for the assurance of what the Lord Jesus Christ will do in time and eternity?" Economic solutions of mankind's problems were doomed to failure, for material satisfaction bred boredom and spiritual disease. No Labour Government could regenerate human nature or repress satanic activity: "The one thing that counts in this universal crisis is whether an individual or a nation is for or against the Lord Jesus Christ and His supremacy. Statesmen have no right to that name if they do not avail themselves of the information given by biblical prophecy."

The rest of the family continued to tinker with temporal solutions. Mrs. Pankhurst stood by the Empire and urged women to use their influence to preserve what was best in the old order of things. Sylvia went to Moscow to argue fiercely with Lenin about the tactics of the newly formed Communist Party of Great Britain. But Christabel swore allegiance to the one being from whom she was able, perhaps, to take orders—the Son of God Himself. An extraordinary character, who more than anyone else had inspired a whole generation of young women to wade through Miss Nightingale's breakers, Christabel turned her still shapely back on the promised land. A herald now of Armageddon, she looked beyond the intervening futilities to the war that really would end all wars.

Not all the WSPU stars faded away like Christabel. "General" Flora Drummond, the tiny, stout, pug-nosed battler from the Isle of Arran (who had first met the Pankhursts when she was head of a typists' pool in Manchester), formed the Women's Guild of Empire to carry on where the Women's Party and the WSPU's wartime industrial campaign had left off. While fighting for equality of wages and opportunity for women, the Guild appealed to them to save the menfolk from the insidious effects of Socialist propaganda, with its doctrine of class war. As Controller-in-Chief, Mrs. Drummond traveled the country warning of the danger of industrial unrest. The word "Empire," she said, was given a prominent place in the Guild's title because of the growing and regrettable tendency to minimize the virtues of patriotism. "It used to be said," she thundered, "that a Britisher's word was his bond. This is no longer so, when the foreign buyer has to go to other countries because our manufacturers cannot keep to their delivery dates. This lies at the root of the unemployment difficulty."

While the various factions of the feminist movement reorganized themselves for new campaigns, while the Pankhursts—those two terrible flying buttresses of the wartime Establishment—fell away from its peacetime structure, the honor of being the first woman Member of Parliament—an honor so fiercely coveted for Christabel by her mother—went to an unlikely person. In 1919, Nancy, Viscountess Astor took the place of her husband (who, on succeeding to the family title, had to leave the House of Commons) as Conservative MP for Plymouth. This development was received with astonishment, even dismay, by the embattled women who had suffered and sacrificed so much to make it possible. To many of them, Lady Astor, born in Virginia, appeared to be a fortune-hunting Southern belle, a frivolous society hostess, a wholly unsuitable representative of The Cause, one for which they had been prepared to die and which she, who was not even British by birth, had never seriously supported. Yet her wealth and position gave her the chance, brilliantly taken, to bridge the gap between Parliament and the women's organizations, and she revealed herself as a keen and effective feminist in her own right.

As the only woman MP, she was one of the most publicized, most vulnerable people in the country, a position she occupied with a relish, a wit, and a resilience that the humorless and deeply shy Christabel could not have matched. She had to contend with male superciliousness and hostility in the House of Commons, where prejudice was always likely to crack the veneer of politeness ("I canna abide women and Jews," growled a Scottish MP). She successfully withstood the rumbling onslaughts of Winston Churchill himself. When he told her that her intrusion into the Commons was as embarrassing as if she had burst into his bathroom when he had nothing to defend himself with but a sponge, she administered just the right *coup de grace*. "You are not," she snapped, "handsome enough to have worries of that kind." She was, she said, a novel principle and had to be endured. "Don't make too much fun of women in politics," she warned her tormentors. "I know it's a tremendous temptation. We are funny, but so are you." With such quips, she flung open the tight-shut windows of old, claustrophobic controversies and let in such gales of fresh, irreverent air that, man or woman, if you tried to strike an attitude, you were liable to be blown ludicrously off your feet.

"When I got into Parliament," she admitted, "I felt like a bullet out of a cannon. The Women's Movement was the Cannon. I have been exploding ever since." Nancy Astor's Cannon had been fashioned and dragged into position not only by the suffragist Old Guard, but by thousands of volunteer nurses, tens of thousands of servicewomen, and hundreds of thousands of industrial workers; not only by the earnest agony of Dr. Elsie Inglis, but by the curiously, if temporarily, united hands of Mary Regina and Mary Macarthur, the tomboy fling of Flora Sandes, the erratic saga of Lady Muriel Paget, and the gay defiance of "The Two" of Pervyse; not only by the patriotic thunders of Emmeline and Christabel and the high-toned nonconformism of Mrs. Despard and Sylvia Pankhurst and Constance Markievicz, but by the sheer brawn of women welders and brewery workers and railways porters and the quiet, offbeat bravery of the "Hun Coddlers." True, the threat to resume militancy after the war was there, but the war itself turned the women's movement into an irresistible, undeniable force. No Government could afford to trifle with the "other half" of the nation in full, official mobilization. No one could pretend that the Cannon had not been cast and primed. Lloyd George's "mewing cats" were out of the bag. The feminist genie was uncorked, and no one could hope to cram it back into the tiny bottle of the old dispensation.

If the First World War was a clear-cut victory for anything, it was a clear-cut victory for women's emancipation. As Olive Schreiner had demanded in 1911, women were thrown in at the deep end, and they survived. So, as Arnold Bennett and Sir Hall Caine had seen for themselves in the munitions factories, did their femininity. Emancipation did not, as diehards had predicted, unsex women. Miss Schreiner was right again. "When we consider," she had written, "that the most fierce ascetic religious enthusiasms, the flagellations and starvations in nunneries and monasteries, have been unable to exterminate or seriously weaken for a moment the master dominance of this emotion; that, whether in the brutal guffaw of sex laughter which rings across the drinking bars of our modern cities and rises from the comfortable armchairs in fashionable clubs, or in the poet's dreams and the noblest conjugal affections of men and women, it plays still the part it played when hoary monsters ploughed through Silurian slime . . . it is ridiculous to suppose that the attraction of sex for sex should ever be exterminable or in any way modifiable by the comparatively superficial performance of this or that form of labour, or the little more or less of knowledge in one direction or another."

Index

Addams, Jane, 315, 318
Addison, Dr. Christopher, as Minister of Munitions, 261
"A. E." (George Russell), 353, 359
All Russian Women's Union, 67
Allen, Clifford, as Chairman of NCF, 332, 333, 335
Allen, Mary Sophia, as member of WPV, 214–15, 216
Allenby, Field Marshal Lord Edmund, 107–108, 110–11
Allied intervention in Russia, 78, 296, 297
Ampthil, Lord Oliver Arthur Villiers, on Miss Douglas-Pennant's dismissal, 236
Anderson, Dr. Elizabeth Garrett, 6; as Chief Surgeon of Women's Hospital Corps in Paris, 187; at Endell St. Hospital in London, 192–96
Anderson, Will, Labour politician, 252, 372
Andrew, Katharine, Assistant Commandant of WRAF, 231, 233, 234, 237, 242
Angell, Norman, 55, 321, 383
Anglo-Russian Hospital in Russia, 92–94
Antifeminist reaction after the war, 384
Antiforeigner riots, 325
Antisuffrage propaganda in films, 21
Antwerp, fall of, 114, 124
Appeal to Women, An (Despard), 311
Ashwell, Lena, war work of, 203, 204, 315
Asquith, Herbert Henry, and the suffragettes, 17, 23, 24, 33, 53, 57, 60, 62, 63, 273, 288, 350, 376, 377
Association of Women Clerks and Secretaries, 230
Astor, Nancy: patriotic house parties of, during war, 88–89; financial support of welfare work, 280, 292; as first woman MP, 388
Athlone, Earl of, 136, 138
Atrocity tales of the war, 42–45, 114–15
Attlee, Mrs. Clement, 276
Auxiliary services, number of women in, between 1917 and 1919, 221

Back of the Front (Campbell), 43
Bacon, Mrs. Raymond, of N.Y. State Woman Suffrage Association, 51
Bagnold, Enid, as VAD nurse, 199–200
Baines, Jennie, and Socialist Women's League, 295
Baird, Major John, of Air Ministry, 234

Balfour, A. J., Conservative leader, 13, 89
Barker, Lilian, Lady Superintendent at Woolwich Arsenal, 249–52
Bartels, Olive: WSPU organizer, 51; Unit Administrator of Central Records Office of AEF at Tours, 228
"Battle Hymn of the Women" (Wilcox), 21–22
Beale, Alice, suffragette, 49
Beatty, Rose, Assistant Commandant of WRAF, 231, 233, 237, 242
Beauchamp, Joan, work of, with NCF, 339, 341–43
Beerbohm, Max, 17, 53
"Behaviour to Husbands" (Mrs. Ellis), 4
Belgian refugees, 86, 214, 230
Belgian Soldiers' Fund of Manchester, 136
Beneš, Dr. Eduard, 56, 62
Bennett, Arnold, description of women munitions workers, 249, 389
Bentinck, Lord Henry Cavendish, in defense of Miss Douglas-Pennant, 236, 237
Bersey, Lt. Col. William, of RAF, 231, 232, 234, 237, 239, 242
Besant, Mrs. Annie, militant feminist activity of, 10
Bidwell, Miss Mary, work of, with war refugees, 87
Bigland, Mrs. Percy, of Quaker Chaplains' Committee, 329
Billington, Teresa, London Secretary of WSPU, 19, 24
Bipp, treatment of wounds with, 193
Birdwood, Gen. William, 111
Blackwell, Dr. Elizabeth, 5
Blücher, Countess Evelyn: prewar life of, 112–13; wartime experiences of, as Englishwoman in Berlin, 113–19; work in Red Cross office, 115–16; and the Reprisal Question, 116
Bolshevism, 68, 70, 71, 74, 77, 96, 295, 296, 371
Bondfield, Margaret, as trade-union organizer, 10, 77, 79, 261
Booth, Mrs. Bramwell, on smoking by women, 267
Boothroyd, Bernard, editor of NCF's The Tribunal, 338
Boyle, Nina, activity of, as Freedom Leaguer, 27, 305

Bradford, Lady May, as letter writer for soldiers in hospitals, 204–7

Brancker, Gen. Sefton, Master General of Personnel, 235, 236, 237

Britannia, organ of WSPU, 57–58, 60, 62–63, 77, 370, 372

British Army of Occupation on the Rhine, Women's Auxiliary Service with, 221

British-born wives of interned aliens, Quakers' aid for, 324, 326

British Club for Belgian Soldiers, 87

Brittain, Vera, as VAD nurse, 197

Brockway, Fenner, work of, with NCF, 331–32, 336

Brockway, Lilla, work of, with NCF, 331–332

Bryce, Lord James, as antisuffragist, 42, 63

Buchanan, Lady Georgina, and Anglo-Russian Hospital, 92–93

Budapest Women's Suffrage Congress, 303

Burns, Elinor, on enlightened feminism, 378, 380

Bus girls' strike for equal pay, 297

Butler, Josephine, fights Contagious Diseases Acts, 8–9

Butt, Dame Clara, at rally for recruiting women for war factory work, 59

Byron, Lady Fanny, war activity of, 85–86, 385

Caine, Hall, description of women munitions workers, 248, 389

Campbell, Phyllis, report of German atrocities, 43–45

Capitalism, fight against, 282, 284, 286, 293, 295

Carson, Sir Edward, 57, 352

Casement, Sir Roger, 116–17, 354–55, 356

"Cassandra," (Nightingale), 3

Cat-and-Mouse Act of 1913, 31, 187, 273, 285

Cavell, Nurse Edith, 375–76

Cecil, Sir Robert, 57, 62

Cellar House of Pervyse, The ("The Two"), 136

Central Committee for Women's Training and Employment, 256, 278

Challenge to Militarism, A, Quaker pamphlet, 327

Chicago May (May Sharpe), 358–60, 363

Children's Guest House, 304

Children's Peace Processions, 311

Chisholm, Mairi, war work of, in Belgium, 128–39

Christian Socialism, 5

Churchill, Winston: and the suffragettes, 17, 19, 23, 30–31, 72, 237, 350, 377; as

Munitions Minister, 263, 266; and Nancy Astor, 388

Clarion, The, Socialist organ, 29, 264

Clinics for mothers and babies, 279, 304

Clyde Workers' Committee, 40, 41

Codrington, Lady, and the women's patrols, 211

Cole, Mrs. Herbert, peace crusading of, 344

Committee of Enquiry into German atrocities, 42

Committee mania, criticism of, 71

Common Cause, The, newspaper of NUWSS, 13, 20

Connolly, James, Irish trade-union leader, 351, 354, 355–58

Conscientious objectors, 73, 266, 290, 291, 293, 297, 318, 327–30; "absolutists," 322, 327, 328, 334–35, 336–37, 343; and the NCF, 333–46

Conscript shot for desertion, 288

Conscription, 34, 283, 284, 286, 289–90, 319, 326–27; in Ireland, 296, 360; of aliens in Britain, 309; alternative service, 327

Conservative Party, women's branch of, 12

"Constitutional" suffragists of NUWSS, 13

Contagious Diseases Acts, 8, 305

Courtney, Kathleen, at Peace Congress at The Hague, 315, 316

Crawfurd, Helen, of the Peace Crusade, 310

Creighton, Mrs. Mandell: declares against women's suffrage, 12; advocates use of women's patrols, 211, 221

Crewe, Lady Margaret, as chairman of Queen Mary's Work for Women Fund, 256–57

Criminal Law Amendment, 214, 305–6

Crowdy, Dame Rachel, Commandant of VAD in France and Belgium, 228

Crowe, Sir Eyre, attacks on, in *Britannia*, 57–58, 60

Crusade for decency, 28

Curtis-Bennett, Sir Henry, ambushed by suffragettes, 27

Curzon, Lord George: as antisuffragist, 63; and the Douglas-Pennant case, 242

Daily Chronicle, 78

Daily Express, 372

Daily Graphic, 266

Daily Herald, Socialist paper, 28, 272–73

Daily Mail, 63, 371

Daily Mirror, 267

Daily Telegraph, 74, 236

Davison, Emily Wilding, militant suffragette, 5, 58, 349

Dawson, Margaret Damer, founder of WPV, 213–14, 215
Day nurseries, 280
Defence of the Realm Act, 50, 260, 286, 297, 327
Demobilization of civilian workers in war industries, 266–68
Despard Arms, 304–5
Despard, Charlotte: as chairman of WFL, 21–22; in fight against war mentality, 34; early history, and appearance of, 301–2; as editor of *The Vote*, 303; activity of, in social services, 304; at Leeds Conference, 309–10; as Labour candidate for Parliament, 373–74
De Valera, Eamon, 361, 364
Dilution Bulletin, 258, 261
Douglas-Pennant, Hon. Violet: early history of, 229–30; as Commandant of WRAF, 230–36; dismissed as Commandant under strange circumstances, 235–237; trial of dismissal case before Committee of House of Lords, 238–42; aftermath of the case of, 242
Dreadnought, The, see *Woman's Dreadnought, The*
Dreamer, Mabel, war work of, in Serbia, 160–65
Drogheda, Lady Kathleen, relief work of, 134
Drug traffic, WPS service in, 217
Drummond, "General" Flora: as militant suffragette, 27; on industrial campaign among women, 73; post-war activities of, 387
Duval, Victor, of Men's Political Union for Women's Enfranchisement, 49

Easter Rebellion in Ireland, 116, 355–58
Edinburgh University, and women medical students, 6
Eire, 363
Elliott, Maxine, relief work of, 134, 136
Ellis, Edith, work of, with "absolutists" conscientious objectors, 327, 328
Emergency Committee of Quakers, 323–26, 344
Emerson, Zelie, American suffragette in London, 272, 279
Endell Street Hospital in London, 192–96
Enemy aliens, 266, 285–86, 303, 323–26, 344
Entertainment of troops, 193, 203–4
Evening Standard, 138, 240
Exhibition of Sweated Trades, 254–55, 257
Exhibition of Sweated Wartime Labor, 283

Fawcett, Henry, Liberal Cabinet Minister, 13
Fawcett, Mrs. Henry, as leader of NUWSS, 13, 33, 319
Fellowship of Reconciliation, 313
Feminism, enlightened, priorities of, 378–79
Fianna Eireann, 351, 362, 363
Fielding, Lady Dorothie, work of, with Munro Corps in Belgium, 126, 136
Fitzgerald, Admiral Penrose, launches White Feather Movement, 39
Forcible feeding of suffragettes in prisons, 30
Foreign Affairs, journal of Union of Democratic Control, 383
Foreign Office, attacks on, in *Britannia*, 57
Foucault, Marquise de, as wartime chatelaine, 107
Freedom League, see Women's Freedom League
French, Commander John Tracy William, RN, 301
French Expeditionary Force at Salonika, 304
French, Field Marshal Sir John, C-in-C of British Expeditionary Force, 34, 144, 301, 304
Friends, Society of, see Quakers
Fry, Joan, as Quaker chaplain to CO's, 329–31
Furse, Dame Katharine, Director of WRNS, 228, 231, 233, 235, 236, 237

Gallacher, William, chairman of Clyde Workers' Committee, 40
Geddes, Gen. Auckland, Director of Recruitment at War Office, 222, 234, 235, 237
George, Lloyd: at Liberal Party rally (1908), 3; and the suffragettes, 5, 11, 17, 23, 50; becomes ally of the Pankhursts, 53, 56, 57, 58, 60, 64, 73; promotes employing of women in munitions factories, 59–60, 257, 258; becomes Prime Minister, 62; and WRAF squabble, 236; and Health Insurance Act, 255–256; as Minister of Munitions, 257, 259, 260, 262; on women Parliamentary candidates, 371
German aid to Irish rebels, fiasco of, 355, 356
German atrocities, Committee of Enquiry into, 42
Gladstone, William Ewart, P.M., against women's suffrage, 12, 20
Gleason, Mrs. Helen, work of, with Munro Corps in Belgium, 126

Gollancz, Victor, 378–79
Gore-Booth, Eva, peace crusading of, 344–346
Grange, Baroness Ernest de la, as "The Mother of the British Army," 107–12
Great Scourge, The (Christabel Pankhurst), 56
Grenfell, Hon. Monica, as VAD nurse, 198–199
Grey, Sir Edward, and the suffragettes, 16, 53, 57, 58, 61, 62
Gwynne-Vaughan, Dame Helen: as Chief Controller (Overseas) of women's auxiliary corps, 222–29; as Commandant of WRAF, 235

Halahan, Commander Henry, 137
Haldane, Richard Burdon, and the suffragettes, 53, 57
Hands Off Russia protest meetings, 297
Hardie, Keir: and the suffragettes, 13; founder of International Labour Party, 272; first Labour MP, 281, 282
Harley, Mrs. Catherine, war activities of, 304
Haverfield, Hon. Evelina: as militant suffragette, 18; war work of, 88, 183
Hawke, J. A., KC, counsel for Miss Douglas-Pennant, 238
Hayward, W. G., clerk with National Health Insurance Commission, 233, 234
Health Insurance Act, 255–56
Health of Munition Workers' Committee, 263–64, 265
Henderson, Arthur, Pankhursts electioneer against, 76
Henry, Sir Edward, Chief Commissioner of Police, 214
"Heroines of Pervyse, The," 133
Higher education for women in nineteenth century, 7–8
Hobhouse, Rosa, peace crusading of, 344
Hollins, Dorothea, peace crusading of, 344
Holloway prison, 3, 5, 17, 32, 34, 328, 361
Home Rule Bill, 350, 352
"Hun Coddlers," Quakers branded as, 326
Hunger strikes of suffragettes, 30–32

Illegitimate babies, adoption of, 56–57
Independent Labour Party, 12, 13, 33, 310, 331
Independent WSPU, 50
India, self-government for, 296
"Inferno of Halloway, The" (Christabel Pankhurst), 47
Inglis, Dr. Elsie: early history of, 177–78; Serbian war work of, 178–86, 377
International Labor Organization, 383

International Labour Party, 272
International Socialist Conference in Stockholm, 74, 295
International Suffrage Alliance, 13, 315
International Women's Peace Congress at The Hague (1915), 54, 283, 286, 315–318, 377, 378
Internment camp on Isle of Man, 325
Irish Citizen Army, 352–54, 355
Irish Worker, The, 354
Italian Relief Fund, 86

Jacobs, Dr. Aletta, head of Dutch Committee of International Women's Suffrage Alliance, 315, 318
Jessie, Tennyson, inspection of WAAC's in France by, 224–25, 227
Jex-Blake, Sophia, 6, 7
Joynson-Hicks, MP, on smoking by women, 267

Kaiser, counts support of English suffragettes, 35
"Keep the Home Fires Burning," 203
Keller, Helen, 29
Kenney, Annie: WSPU activities of, 15, 16, 18, 19, 23, 49; on lecture tour in U.S., 50–51; as aide to Mrs. Pankhurst, 56, 58; on industrial campaigns among women, 73
Kenney, Jessie: as aide to the Pankhursts, 46, 61–62, 65–66; in Russia with Mrs. Pankhurst, 65–70, 96
Kerenski, Aleksandr, 65, 68, 69, 70, 78
King Albert of Belgium, 133, 138
Kingsley, Charles, 5
Kipling, Rudyard, as die-hard antisuffragist, 63
Kitchener, Horatio, attacks on, by Lord Northcliffe, 63
Kitchener war poster, 40–41
Knocker, Mrs. Elsie, with Munro Corps in Belgium, 126, 128, 130–33, 136
Knox, Lady Sybil, as voluntary worker for WSPU, 71

Labor internationalism, 74
Labor Supply Committee, 259–60
Labour Leader, of Independent Labour Party, 310, 329, 331–32
Labour Party, 256, 295, 369, 371
Ladies' Discussion Society, first women's suffrage group (1865), 11–12
La Motte au Bois, Chatelaine of, 108, 111
Lancet, The, 7
Lansbury, George: 13, 32, 306; launches *Daily Herald,* 28, 272; anti-war activities of, 276, 284

Lansdowne, Lord, letter of, on peace with Germany, 74
Larkin, James, Irish trade-union leader, 273, 351, 353, 354
Law, Bonar, 371
Lawrence, Dorothy, sapper, 139–49
Lawrence, Susan: as editor of *The Woman Worker*, 263, 276; on Ministry of Reconstruction committee, 380–81
Lawson, Gen. Sir Henry, proposes uniformed women's corps, 222
Leach, Mrs. Burleigh, Chief Controller of WAAC, 231, 233
League of Rights for Soldiers' and Sailors' Wives and Relatives, 287, 303
Leaving Certificate System, 259, 262
Lectures to Ladies on Practical Subjects (Kingsley), 5
Leeds Conference of Labor, Socialist, and democratic organizations, 295, 308
Leigh, Mary, militant suffragette, 27, 349
Leila, Lady Paget: early history of, 99; with hospital unit in Serbia, 99–107
Lenin, Nikolai, returns to Russia from exile, 69, 95
Letter writing for soldiers in hospitals, 204–7
Liberal Party: rally (1908), 3; women's branch of, 12
Liebknecht, Karl, Socialist leader, 118
Livingston, Major Gen. Guy, of RAF, 231, 237, 242
London Suffrage Society, 179
Londonderry, Lady Edith, Women's legion of, 222
Lowther, Lady, work of, for Belgian prisoners in Germany, 87–88
Lugard, Lady Flora, work of, with Belgian refugees, 86–87
Lusitania, sinking of, 116, 164, 325
Lyttelton, Hon. Mrs. Alfred, work of, with war refugees, 87

Macarthur, Mary: develops work of unions, 10; as trade-union organizer, 77, 83, 252–56, 380; war work of, 256–68, 377; Sylvia Pankhurst's criticisms of, 278; at Leeds Conference, 309; as Labour candidate for Parliament, 371, 372–73
MacDonald, Margaret, develops work of union, 10
MacDonald, Ramsay: and the suffragettes, 13, 72, 73, 76; antagonism of Mrs. Pankhurst to, 13, 55, 66; pacifism of, 55, 66; at Leeds Conference, 308; and Union of Democratic Control, 321; as supporter of NCF, 336

Macmillan, Chrystal, and Peace Congress at The Hague, 315, 316, 318
Macmillan, Mrs. Peggy, as voluntary worker for WSPU, 71
Macnaughton, Sarah: war work of, in Belgium, 40, 123–24, 128; industrial recruiting by, 40–42
Macready, Sir Nevil, Chief Commissioner, 220, 223
Maintenance Organization for families of CO's, 338
Making of Women, The (ed. Gollancz), 378–79
Mallin, Michael, Irish trade-union leader, 352, 356, 357
Manchester Guardian, 90, 338, 343
Manners, Lady Constance, and convalescent home for New Zealand officers, 90
Maritime League for Woman Suffrage, 305
Markievicz, Constance, Irish extremist, militant crusading of, 345, 349–65
Marsh, Charlotte "Charlie," militant suffragette, 50
Marshall, Catherine: gives aid to pacifists in resisting conscription, 34; and Peace Congress at The Hague, 315; work of, with NCF, 333–36
Martin-Nicholson, Sister Joan, and stories of German atrocities, 42–43
Masaryk, Dr. Alice, and Czechoslovakian relief, 97–98
Masaryk, Prof. Tomáš, exiled Czech patriot, 56, 66, 70
Maurice, Rev. Frederick, founder of Christian Socialism, 5
McBride, Major John, Irish extremist, 354, 361
McKenna, Reginald, Chancellor of the Exchequer, 284–85, 303
Medical profession, attitude toward women in medicine, 5–7
Medical school, first in Britain for women, 7
Men's Political Union for Women's Enfranchisement, 49
Metropolitan Women Police Patrols, 221
Meux, Admiral Sir Hedworth, MP, 312
Military Service Act, 333
Milk depots, 304
Mill, John Stuart, 5, 12
Milling the Militants, 26
Ministry of Reconstruction's Women's Employment Committee, 268, 380–81
Monarchy, suffragists' demonstrations against, 27, 293
Monstrous Regiment of Suffragists, closing the ranks of, 377–78

Montefiore, Dora, as campaigner for women's rights, 18–19, 309, 351–52
Montenegrin Relief Fund, 86
Moore, Eva, takes up cause of "The Two," 136, 138, 139
"Moral Aspect of Conscription, The" (*Tribunal*), 341
Moral-welfare patrolling of WPS, 218–19
Morel, E. D., and Union of Democratic Control, 321
Morning Post, 237
Munitions Act, 73, 259, 262
Munitions areas, WPS work in, 218
Munitions women workers, 247–56, 376, 389
Munro Corps in Belgium, 125–39
Munro, Dr. Hector, socialist nudist, 125–128, 129, 135
Murray, Dr. Flora: reports on suffragettes in Holloway prison, 32; as Administrator of Women's Hospitals Corps in Paris, 187; at Endell St. Hospital in London, 192–96

Nation, The, 308
National Council Against Conscription, 290
National Distress Funds, 276
National Health Insurance Commission, 233, 236
National Labor Press, 342
National Union of Societies for Equal Citizenship, 384
National Union of Women's Suffrage Societies (NUWSS), 13, 15, 33, 378
Nationalization of industry, 296–97
New Statesman, left-wing publication, 272
New York State Woman Suffrage Association, 51
New York Tribune on Christabel Pankhurst, 51
Nightingale, Florence, 3, 4–5, 8, 90, 387
Noncombatant Corps, 335, 336–37, 339
No Conscription Fellowship (NCF), 331–346, 376
Northcliffe, Lord Alfred, 53, 57, 63, 97, 257, 292, 371
Novello, Ivor, and "Keep the Home Fires Burning," 203
Nurses supplied by VAD's, 197

O'Casey, Sean, 352–53, 365
Old-age pensioners, 288
Orczy, Baroness, founds Women of England's Active Service League, 39–40
Orderlies supplied by VAD's, 197

Pacifism, 55, 66, 275, 281–95, 301, 303, 313, 315, 316; WSPU campaign

against, 74; and Fellowship of Reconciliation, 313; and the NCF, 333–46
Pacifist wing of suffragism, 310
Paget, Lady Muriel: early conditioning of, 90–91; war work of, 92; in Russia with Anglo-Russian Hospital, 93–96; in Odessa, 96–97; in Washington, 97; relief work of, 97–99
Paine, Gen. Sir Godfrey, RAF's Master General of Personnel, 230, 231–32, 234, 235, 239
Pankhurst, Adela, Socialism of, 295
Pankhurst, Christabel: background and early activity of, 15–17; nicknamed "Parnell in Petticoats," 16; transformation of public image of The Cause by, 18; in crusade for decency in *The Suffragette*, 28; support by, of her mother's suffragette drives, 46; support of the war by, 48–49; tour of U.S., 51–53; platform commentary on current affairs, 72; draws up twelve-point program of Women's Party, 75–76; as Women's Party candidate for House of Commons, 80, 370–72; post-war activities of, 384–87
Pankhurst, Mrs. Emmeline: switches support to Labour Party, 12; organizes Women's Social and Political Union, 14; characteristics and background of, 14–15; activity and violence of, 17; oratorical skill of, 20–21; monomaniac intensity of, 24–25; on men's sexual irresponsibility, 27–28; at Old Bailey Trial in 1913, 30; leads deputation to Buckingham Palace, 32; attitude at start of W W I, 45; private life of, 46; as recruiter for the war, 54–56; on effects of war on soldiers' morals, 56; and striking Welsh miners, 58; as an elder stateswoman, 65; in Russia on special government mission, 65–70, 96, 310; on "special mission" to the U.S., 78; as recruiter of women war workers, 257; Government's change of view on, 376; post-war activities of, 384–87
Pankhurst leadership, revolt against, 49–50
Pankhurst, Dr. Richard M., political program of, 14, 15
Pankhurst, Sylvia: as WSPU orator, 19; hunger-and-thirst strikes of, 31–32; suffragist activity of, in London's East End, 32; early history of, 271; as outspoken Socialist, 272, 273, 294, 295; alienated from mother and sister, 272, 273; agitation for universal suffrage, 272, 273–74, 292; active opposition to the war, 275, 281–95; agitation for reforms, 275–76, 284, 293; as the Terror of the Ministries,

278; welfare services of, 279–81, 285, 376; post-war activities of, 387
Parliament: and the suffrage movement, 12; "Black Friday" march of suffragettes on, 31; granting of membership in, to women, 80, 311–12, 361, 369; first women candidates for, 369–75
"Parliament As We See It" (Sylvia Pankhurst), 293–94
Parnell, Charles, Irish national leader, 16
Paterson, Emma, founds first women's trade union, 9
Peace Conference at The Hague (1915), 54, 283, 286, 315–18, 377, 378
Peace negotiation petition of WIL, 319–20
Peet, Hubert, work of, with NCF, 338
Pensions and separation allowances, 278, 287–88
Pethick-Lawrence, Emmeline: and Christabel Pankhurst, 17–18, 314; activity of, in WSPU, 19, 314; breaks with the Pankhursts and WSPU, 24, 314; and Women's International League, 292; at Leeds Conference, 309; in America on peace movement drive, 315; at Peace Congress at The Hague, 316–17; as Labour candidate for Parliament, 374; post-war activities of, 384
Pethick-Lawrence, Frederick: support of, for WSPU, 19, 314; breaks with the Pankhursts and WSPU, 24, 314
Piccadilly Flat case, 28–29
Pine, Sister C. E., in charge of home for Mrs. Pankhursts war babies, 65
Pole-Carew, Lady Beatrice, war work of, 88
Police force strike in London, 297
Polish Relief Fund, 86
Political prisoners, 297
Ponsonby, Arthur, and Union of Democratic Control, 321
Poor Laws, and Poor Law Guardians, 276, 277, 301, 330, 337
Pratt, Edith, Deputy Commandant of WRAF, 231, 233
Prisoner-of-war camps in Germany, 290
Prisoners-of-war in England, 290–91
Prometheus Unbound (Shelley), description of the New Woman, 21
Prostitution, government regulation of, 285, 293, 306–7
Pulteney, Gen. William, 110
Punch, and antisuffragist journalism, 12
Purity campaign, 29

Quakers: aid for enemy aliens, 323–26, 344; activity against conscription, 326–327; work of, for conscientious objectors,

327–30; Chaplain's Committee, 329; as members of NCF, 332, 333
Queen Amelie of Portugal, war work of, 88
Queen Eleonora of Bulgaria, 152
Queen Elizabeth of Belgium, 138
Queen Mary, in W W I, 83–85, 377
Queen Mary's Army Auxiliary Corps (QMAAC), 227
Queen Mary's Work for Women Fund, 256
Queen Mary's Workshops, 84, 257, 278, 285

Rajah's Heir, The (Despard), 301
Rathbone, Eleanor, on enlightened feminism, 378, 379–80
Rawlinson, Gen. Henry, 137
Rebel's Social and Political Union, 279
Red Cross and Ambulance News, 152
Red Cross Society, 123, 127
Redmond, John, Irish Parliamentary leader, 134, 350, 354
Regimentation in wartime industry, 307
Registration for men and women, 283, 284, 303
Reprisal Question, 116
Rest home for nurses on leave, 86
Rhondda, Lady Margaret: as Director of Women's Dept. of Ministry of National Service, 234; as leader of the Six Point Group, 384
Richardson, Mary, militant suffragette, 349
Rinehart, Mary Roberts, reporting on Belgium front, 133–35
Robertson, Sir William, Britannia's attack on policies of, 62, 77
Roe, Grace: militant suffragette, 34–35, 228; WSPU activities of, 46, 48, 49; activity of, on Britannia, 60
Rokeby Venus by Velázquez, slashing of, by suffragettes, 26, 349
Roper, Esther: as Secretary of North of England Women's Suffrage Society, 306; peace crusading of, 344–45
Royal Army Medical Corps (RAMC), 190
Royden, Maude: works against unfairness of women's wages, 10–11; on prostitute problems, 306; and the Hudson Shaws, 313; on enlightened feminism, 378–80
Ruskin, John, 5
Russell, Bertrand: on brutalizing effect of war, 55; calls Serbia a barbarous backwater, 56; at Leeds Conference, 309; works with NCF, 338, 341
Russell, Gen. Sir Andrew Hamilton, 110
Russia: March, 1917, Revolution, 65, 184, 295, 308; provisional government of, 65, 68, 69, 70; Anglo-Russian Hospital in, 92–94; Bolshevik Revolutions, 96

Runciman, Walter, President of Board of Trade, 277–78

St. John, Lady Isabella, as a determined mother, 145–49
Salter, Dr. Alfred, as pacifist Quaker chaplain, 329
Salvation Army, and equal recognition of men and women, 14
Sandes, Flora, in Balkan campaigns, 165–173, 376
Sassoon, Lt. Siegfried, criticism by, of the military mind, 294
Save-the-Balkans campaign in England, 51
School children, plight of, in the war, 289
Schreiner, Olive: demands of, for women's rights, 22, 389; on women as effective soldiers, 33
Schwimmer, Rosika, of International Suffrage Alliance, 315, 316
Scott, Lady Sophie, war work of, 88
Scottish Women's Hospital Units, 88, 130, 154, 178, 230, 304
Self-rule of small nations, 296
Separation allowances and pensions, 278, 287, 288
Serbia: Mrs. Pankhurst's activity in behalf of, 56, 58, 61; Britons backing of cause of, 150
Serbian Relief Fund, 86, 88, 154, 155, 159
Sex discrimination in education, 7
Sex Disqualification Removal Act (1919), 385
Shaw, Bernard, 79, 281
Shinwell, Emmanuel, Labour War Minister, 309
Sickerts, gifted family of, 13, 320
"Siege of Hammersmith," 19, 309
Sinclair, May: with Munro Corps in Belgium, 125–27; poem to the Corps, 129
Sinn Fein, 355, 357, 360, 361, 362
Six Point Group, 384
Smith, Lesley, as VAD nurse, 200–203
Smith, Lydia, on staff of NCF's The Tribunal, 338, 339, 342–43
Smyth, Dame Ethel: on crimes against young children, 28; friend of Mrs. Pankhurst, 32, 45, 65
Smyth, Norah, friend and benefactor of Sylvia Pankhurst, 273, 280, 292
Snowden, Ethel: service with NUWSS, 13; at Leeds Conference, 309
Snowden, Philip, Labour MP, 13, 76; as supporter of NCF, 336
Socialism, 67, 79, 272, 273, 294, 295, 301
Socialist Conference in Stockholm (1917), 74, 295

Socialist Women's League of Australia, 295
Socialists: of "Red Clydeside," 40, 73–74, 309; as members of NCF, 332
Society of Apothecaries, 6
Society for Training Serbian Women in England, 150
Soldiers' and Sailors' Families Association (SSFA), 276
Soliloquies of a Subaltern, 39
Soup kitchens in Flanders, 124–25
South Wales Belgian Refugee Committee, 230
Soviet Russia, Dreadnought survey of, 297
Spy ring, WPS work in breaking up, 217
Stead, W. T., journalist, 9, 29
Stobart, Mrs. St. Clair: hospital work in Belgium, 123, 153–54; early history of, 150–52; in Balkan War, 152–53; hospital work in Serbia, 154–60, 377
Suffrage drive in America, inauguration of, 315
Suffrage groups, adjustment to W W I, 33
Suffrage propaganda in films, 26
Suffragette, The, organ of WSPU, 28, 29, 33, 47, 54, 57; renamed Britannia, 57
Suffragettes: violent activities of, 20, 24, 26; mass manufacture of martyrs, 30; hunger strikes by, 30–32; in prison, 34–35; in WPV, 215
Swanick, Helena: as editor of The Common Cause, 13, 19; fights against war mentality, 34; as Chairwoman of WIL, 319, 321–23; appraisal of fellow feminists, 320–21; post-war activities of, 383
Sweatshops, House of Commons inquiry into, 254–55
Synge, Dr. Ella, report of, on prisoner-of-war camps in Germany, 290

Taylor, Mrs. Mona, letter to Churchill on suffragettes, 19
Tchaykovsky, Dr. Barbara, clinic work of, 279, 280–81
Ten Hour Act, 9
"The Two," in Belgian relief work, 131, 133, 134; awards to, 138
Thomas, Dr. Henrietta, work of, with enemy aliens, 324, 327
Thompson, Mabel, as Quaker chaplain to CO's, 329
Thoumaian, Lucy, Swiss Suffragist, 283, 313, 344
"Tickets of leave" for released suffragettes, 31
Tillard, Violet, work of, with NCF, 338, 342
Times History of the War, The, 88, 212

Times of London, 25, 63, 236, 257, 341
Tobacco Fund, 86
"Tommy's Little Mothers," 204–7
Trade unions: first for women, 9; opposition of, to women in factory war work, 58; attitude toward women's wages, 380–381
Trades Union Congress, 9–10, 256
Trevelyan, Charles, and Union of Democratic Control, 321
Tribunal, The, newsheet of NCF, 338, 341–343
Trotsky, Leon, release of, from prison by Kerenski, 69
Tsar, abdication of, 65, 95

Under the Searchlight, 242
Union of Democratic Control, 55, 319, 321, 383
Unmarried mothers, 28, 219, 282, 293

Venereal diseases, 56, 131, 285, 320
Voluntary Aid Detachments (VAD), 196–203
Voska, M., work of, for Czechoslovak independence, 62
Vote, The, magazine of the Freedom League, 303, 305, 306, 375
Votes for women: Government drafts bill for first installment of (1917), 64; first installment of, passed (1918), 76, 311, 369
Votes for Woman, WSPU's journal, 18

Wages for women, 10, 59, 258, 259, 260, 261–62, 265–66, 275, 380, 381
Walker, Melvina, in peace campaign, 294
Wallas, Graham, warnings against Socialism of, 79
War babies, 56–57, 61, 65, 282, 285
War Cabinet Committee on Women in Industry, 268, 381–82
War Refugees' Committee, Allocation Department, 87
Ward, Mrs. Humphrey, declares against women's suffrage, 12
Watson, Mrs. Chalmers, appointed Chief Controller (Home) of women's auxiliary corps, 222, 235
Watson, Prof. Seton, *Times* correspondent, 56
Webb, Sidney, and Socialism, 79, 295
Webb, Beatrice: declares against women's suffrage, 12; on War Cabinet Committee on Women in Industry, 382–83
Weir, Lord, Air Minister, 233, 234, 236, 237

Welfare system in industry, 264–65
Welsh miners on strike, 58, 286
West, Rebecca, journalist on *The Clarion,* 29, 264
What 88 Million Women Want, 26
Wheeldon case, 64, 339–40
White Cross League, 279
White Feather Movement, 39
Wilcox, Ella Wheeler, 21
Wilson, Theodora, suffragist, 315
Woman and Labour (Schreiner), 22
Woman Worker, The, 253, 258, 262, 263, 265, 373
Woman's Dreadnought, The, 274, 275, 276–77, 282, 288, 294, 297
Woman's Story of the War, The (Anon.), 227
Women, economic situation of, in nineteenth century, 9–11
Women of England's Active Service League, 39–40
Women given right to be MPs, 80, 311–312, 361, 369
"Women of Pervyse, The," 133, 138
Women Police Service, work of, 216–21, 305
Women Police Volunteers (WPV), 213, 215
Women in war industries, 33–34, 58–60, 90; *see also* Munitions women workers
Women Uitlanders (Montefiore), 18
Women's Army Auxiliary Corps (WAAC), 222–29; military status of, 233; quartering of, 224; uniforms of, 224–25; rumors of immorality in, 225–26, 227
Women's Battalions of Russia, 68, 78
Women's branches of Liberal and Conservative Parties, 12
Women's Convoy Corps, 152, 153
Women's demonstrations of capabilities, 376–77
Women's emancipation, W W I as clearcut victory for, 389
Women's Emergency Corps, 88, 315
Women's Freedom League, 21, 22, 24, 302, 303, 304, 305, 373, 384
Women's Guild of Empire, 387
Women's Hospital Corps, 187–91, 192–196
Women's International League (WIL), 286, 292, 318–20, 378
Women's International Peace Conference at The Hague (1915), 54, 283, 286, 315–18, 377, 378
Women's Legion Motor Transport Section, 222
Women's Movement: divisions in, 378; as Nancy Astor's Cannon, 389

Women's National Service League, 153
Women's Party: twelve-point program of, 75–76; alienation of women "progressives" by, 78; launched in Canada, 79; Christabel Pankhurst as Parliamentary candidate of, 370–72
Women's patrols, kinds of situations dealt with, 212–13
Women's Peace Crusade, 310–11, 344, 377, 378
Women's Peace Party, 315, 316
Women's Protective and Provident League (1875), 9
Women's Reserve Ambulance Corps, 88
Women's Revolution, 32, 33, 211
Women's role in war, traditional appraisal of, 39
Women's Royal Air Force (WRAF), 221, 230–36
Women's Royal Naval Service (WRNS), 221
Women's Social and Political Union (WSPU): 14, 15, 24, 378; attacks of, on war policies of government, 57–58;

open-air Patriotic Meetings of, 61; industrial campaigns among women, 71–72, 73, 377; becomes the Women's Party, 75
Women's suffrage group, first meeting of (1865), 11–12
Women's Suffrage National Aid Corps of WFL, 304
Women's Trade Union League, 10, 252, 380
Women's Volunteer Reserve, 88
Women's War Service Procession, 310, 376
Woolwich Arsenal, women at work in, 248
Work of women, movement to curtail, 10–11
Workers' Anti-Militarist Committee, 309
Workers' Educational Association, 230
Workers' Suffrage Federation, 289, 292
Wright, Sir Almoth, as antisuffragist, 25–26, 63

Yeats, W. B., 359
YMCA entertainment at the fronts, 203